Environmental Imaginaries
of the Middle East and North Africa

Ohio University Press Series in Ecology and History
James L. A. Webb, Jr., Series Editor

Conrad Totman
The Green Archipelago: Forestry in Preindustrial Japan

Timo Myllyntaus and Mikko Saikku, eds.
Encountering the Past in Nature: Essays in Environmental History

James L. A. Webb, Jr.
Tropical Pioneers: Human Agency and Ecological Change in the Highlands of Sri Lanka, 1800–1900

Stephen Dovers, Ruth Edgecombe, and Bill Guest, eds.
South Africa's Environmental History: Cases and Comparisons

David M. Anderson
Eroding the Commons: The Politics of Ecology in Baringo, Kenya, 1890s–1963

William Beinart and JoAnn McGregor, eds.
Social History and African Environments

Michael L. Lewis
Inventing Global Ecology: Tracking the Biodiversity Ideal in India, 1947–1997

Christopher A. Conte
Highland Sanctuary: Environmental History in Tanzania's Usambara Mountains

Kate B. Showers
Imperial Gullies: Soil Erosion and Conservation in Lesotho

Franz-Josef Brüggemeier, Mark Cioc, and Thomas Zeller, eds.
How Green Were the Nazis? Nature, Environment, and Nation in the Third Reich

Peter Thorsheim
Inventing Pollution: Coal, Smoke, and Culture in Britain since 1800

Joseph Morgan Hodge
Triumph of the Expert: Agrarian Doctrines of Development and the Legacies of British Colonialism

Diana K. Davis
Resurrecting the Granary of Rome: Environmental History and French Colonial Expansion in North Africa

Thaddeus Sunseri
Wielding the Ax: State Forestry and Social Conflict in Tanzania, 1820–2000

Mark Cioc
The Game of Conservation: International Treaties to Protect the World's Migratory Animals

Karen Brown and Daniel Gilfoyle, eds.
Healing the Herds: Disease, Livestock Economies, and the Globalization of Veterinary Medicine

Marco Armiero and Marcus Hall, eds.
Nature and History in Modern Italy

Karen Brown
Mad Dogs and Meerkats: A History of Resurgent Rabies in Southern Africa

Diana K. Davis and Edmund Burke III, eds.
Environmental Imaginaries of the Middle East and North Africa

Environmental Imaginaries of the Middle East and North Africa

Edited by Diana K. Davis
and Edmund Burke III

With an Afterword by Timothy Mitchell

OHIO UNIVERSITY PRESS
ATHENS

Ohio University Press, Athens, Ohio 45701
ohioswallow.com
© 2011 by Ohio University Press
All rights reserved

To obtain permission to quote, reprint, or otherwise reproduce or distribute material from Ohio University Press publications, please contact our rights and permissions department at (740) 593-1154 or (740) 593-4536 (fax).

Printed in the United States of America
Ohio University Press books are printed on acid-free paper ∞ ™

First paperback printing in 2012
ISBN 978-8214-2040-9

HARDCOVER 20 19 18 17 16 15 14 13 12 11   5 4 3 2 1
PAPERBACK 21 20 19 18 17 16 15 14 13 12   5 4 3 2 1

Library of Congress Cataloging-in-Publication Data
Environmental imaginaries of the Middle East and North Africa / edited by Diana K. Davis and Edmund Burke III ; with an afterword by Timothy Mitchell.
   p. cm. — (Ohio University Press series in ecology and history)
 Includes bibliographical references and index.
 ISBN 978-0-8214-1974-8 (hardcover : alk. paper)
 1. Human ecology—Middle East—History. 2. Human ecology—Africa, North—History. 3. Middle East—Environmental conditions. 4. Africa, North—Environmental conditions. 5. Middle East—Environmental conditions—Historiography. 6. Africa, North—Environmental conditions—Historiography. 7. Middle East—Foreign public opinion, British. 8. Middle East—Foreign public opinion, French. 9. Great Britain—Colonies—History. 10. France—Colonies—History. I. Davis, Diana K. II. Burke, Edmund, 1940–
 GF670.E58 2011
 304.20956—dc23
             2011031113

Contents

List of Illustrations   vii
Preface by Edmund Burke III   ix
Acknowledgments   xiii

Introduction. Imperialism, Orientalism, and the Environment in the Middle East
History, Policy, Power, and Practice
DIANA K. DAVIS   1

Chapter 1. "A Rebellion of Technology"
Development, Policing, and the British Arabian Imaginary
PRIYA SATIA   23

Chapter 2. Restoring Roman Nature
French Identity and North African Environmental History
DIANA K. DAVIS   60

Chapter 3. Body of Work
Water and Reimagining the Sahara in the Era of Decolonization
GEORGE R. TRUMBULL IV   87

Chapter 4. From the Bottom Up
The Nile, Silt, and Humans in Ottoman Egypt
ALAN MIKHAIL   113

Chapter 5. Drafting a Map of Colonial Egypt
The 1902 Aswan Dam, Historical Imagination, and the Production of Agricultural Geography
JENNIFER L. DERR   136

Chapter 6.	Remapping the Nation, Critiquing the State *Environmental Narratives and Desert Land Reclamation in Egypt* JEANNIE SOWERS	158
Chapter 7.	Salts, Soils, and (Un)Sustainabilities? *Analyzing Narratives of Environmental Change in Southeastern Turkey* LEILA M. HARRIS	192
Chapter 8.	Hydro-Imaginaries and the Construction of the Political Geography of the Jordan River *The Johnston Mission, 1953–56* SAMER ALATOUT	218
Chapter 9.	Environmentalism Deferred *Nationalisms and Israeli/Palestinian Imaginaries* SHAUL COHEN	246
	Afterword TIMOTHY MITCHELL	265
	Contributors	275
	Index	279

Illustrations

Figures

0.1	Camels in sand dunes	2
0.2	Ski Dubai	15
1.1	*Flying Over the Desert at Sunset, Mesopotamia*, by Carline	37
2.1	Roman ruins at Timgad, Algeria	67
3.1	*Le Pays de la soif*, by Fromentin	92
4.1	Nile between al-Rauḍa and Mainland Cairo, Egypt	124
5.1	View of the Aswan Dam, Egypt	137
5.2	The island of Philae, Egypt	143
6.1	The Sheikh Zayed (Toshka) Canal, Egypt	169
7.1	Cotton bales, Turkey	196
7.2	Lake from rising groundwater, Turkey	197
9.1	*Olive Columns*, by Morin, Jerusalem	257

Maps

0.1	The Middle East and North Africa	5
2.1	The Maghreb	64
6.1	Land reclamation in Egypt	163
7.1	Recent irrigation projects in the Harran Plain, Turkey	195
8.1	The Johnston plan watershed	224

Tables

8.1	Water distribution from each plan	229
8.2	Water duty according to the Johnston and the Israeli plans	233
8.3	Comparing different plans' land distribution	234

Preface

Edmund Burke III

The modernist fables that underlie the developmentalist states of the Middle East and North Africa (MENA) have only recently begun to attract the attention of scholars in their own right. As French and British colonial fantasies of recovering the supposed agricultural productivity of Roman North Africa have given way to the similarly delusional dreams of experts who have sought to modernize postcolonial states in the region, the subject of their underlying environmental imaginaries has come to the fore.[1] It is the considerable merit of the studies in this volume to document the continuities in the environmental imaginaries that have shaped the modernization projects of both colonial and postcolonial states over the past two centuries.

Colonial writers believed that the Middle Eastern environment suffered irreversible degradation after classical antiquity. Different authors ascribed the alleged decline to different causes, including the goat, the Bedouin, and Islam. The real culprit, according to Theodore Wertime, may well have been ancient metallurgy, which was enormously inefficient.[2] Archeological evidence from around the Mediterranean tends to support this finding. According to a major European Union–funded study, the principal wave of deforestation in the Mediterranean coincided with the onset of the Bronze Age.[3] The same study finds that the Mediterranean environment was essentially stable (with oscillations) from the Roman period until the nineteenth century.

Colonial understandings of the environmental history of the MENA region were distorted by orientalist assumptions. It is the aim of the essays in this book to explore just how and why they mattered. Having said this, it is important to recognize that human-induced environmental change was not the monopoly of modern actors. The Middle Eastern environment itself was shaped and reshaped by long-term historical processes. Neither the huge canal systems in the Tigris/Euphrates valley nor the artificial oases in the deserts and plateaus were necessary for human survival. Rulers made choices. The environmental costs, as always, were borne by later generations. Thus the question: Are modern engineers and technocrats the heirs of the pharaohs? Or is there something that distinguishes them from ancient technologists?[4]

Here we need to see the imperial dreams of Cromer and Lyautey (proconsuls of empire in Egypt and Morocco respectively) and those of postcolonial experts as the products of their world historical context: the age of fossil fuels (1800 CE–present).[5] The age of fossil fuels reflected the enormous multiplication of the quantity of energy available to humans with the coming of steam power and electricity. In this respect the material realities that shaped modern dreams of power differed fundamentally from those that shaped the world of the engineers and statebuilders of classical antiquity and the Islamic empires that followed them.

Premodern people operated under the constraints of the solar energy regime (to 1800 CE) in which human and animal power constituted the principal sources of energy, along with wood energy. (Water and wind power in this period generated a small percentage of the total energy then available.) In an effort to dramatize the huge difference between the energy available in classical antiquity and that available in modern times, consider this thought experiment. According to Vaclav Smil, the total energy expended by the tens of thousands of slaves who constructed the Great Pyramid is roughly equivalent to energy expended by a single moderate-sized bulldozer.[6] This is not to belittle the achievements of classical engineers in any respect. It is simply to point out the energetic limits of the world in which they existed. The rerouting of rivers in ancient Mesopotamia and the construction of the pyramids still command our awe.

The environmental orientalism of the planners and engineers of the colonial and postcolonial era thus reflects the fundamentally different energetic context of modern times (even if the energetic equations of the colonial and postcolonial eras were themselves significantly different). The colonial period largely coincided with the age of coal (1750–1950), whereas the postcolonial period (1950–present) was shaped by petroleum and natural gas. However, colonial engineers and experts were still somewhat constrained by the energy dynamics of the solar energy age. Whereas the Suez Canal (1869) and the first Aswan dam (1902) were constructed by corvée labor, the Nasser High Dam was constructed by modern earthmoving equipment. Dreams of empire were enabled by the changing energetic contexts.

If energy regimes shaped what engineers and experts could accomplish, they also distanced them from understanding the consequences of their interventions. In the rain-fed agricultural systems of the solar energy regime (most of human history), the consequences of faulty engineering were soon exposed. The fact that deforestation of the hills soon led to floods in the plains was soon understood. Most complex societies devised hedges against the Malthusian scissors of drought, famine, and disease. Ambitious projects like the Grand Canal had huge energy price tags, and were therefore rare, and well scouted in advance.

In the fossil fuel era, the illusion of omnipotence pertained. Forests could be felled, river courses diverted, giant dams constructed, and the energetic costs were seen as manageable. Petroleum and natural gas, along with greed and orientalist visions, made it all possible. The inevitable externalities (unprecedented flooding, landscape degradation, and pollution) were rarely foreseen. Here's the bottom line: what made environmental orientalism and the "rule of experts" possible were the new energetic conditions of modern times.[7] The production of environmental imaginaries (capitalism and the modern state as well) grew out of this epochal transformation in human energy regimes.

Imperial dreams such as the Aswan High Dam, hubristic though they are, were not solely the manifestation of human vanity and greed. Nor were they in any simple way the result of seeing the world through orientalist glasses, though both were certainly involved. They also stemmed from the dramatic transformation in human demography of modern times. In the face of ever-rising populations, engineers and technocrats, both indigenous and expatriate, sought solutions for societies otherwise hard-pressed by the huge increase in numbers. Without the Aswan High Dam, Egypt would have experienced the devastating 1980s Sahel famine.[8]

Notes

1. Diana K. Davis, *Resurrecting the Granary of Rome: Environmental History and French Colonial Expansion in North Africa* (Athens: Ohio University Press, 2007).

2. Theodore A. Wertime, "The Furnace versus the Goat? Pyrotechnological Industries and Mediterranean Deforestation," *Journal of Field Archaeology* 10, no. 4 (1983): 445–52.

3. A. T. Grove and Oliver Rackham, *The Nature of Mediterranean Europe: An Ecological History* (New Haven: Yale University Press, 2003). See also John Perlin, *A Forest Journey: The Role of Wood in the Development of Civilization* (New York: Norton, 1989).

4. See my "The Transformation of the Middle Eastern Environment, 3000 B.C.E.–2000 C.E.," in *The Environment and World History, 1500–2000*, ed. Edmund Burke III and Kenneth L. Pomeranz (Berkeley: University of California Press, 2009), 81–117.

5. On the foregoing, see my "The Big Story: Human History, Energy Regimes and the Environment," in *The Environment and World History, 1500–2000*, ed. Edmund Burke III and Kenneth L. Pomeranz (Berkeley: University of California Press, 2009), 33–53.

6. Vaclav Smil, *Energy in World History* (Boulder, Colo.: Westview Press, 1994).

7. Timothy Mitchell, *Rule of Experts: Egypt, Techno-politics, Modernity* (Berkeley: University of California Press, 2002).

8. Mike Davis, *Late Victorian Holocausts: El Nino Famines and the Making of the Third World* (New York: Verso, 2001).

Acknowledgments

Many debts are incurred during a collaborative project such as this. First and foremost, we would like to thank the contributors to the volume and Timothy Mitchell for writing the afterword. They are all exceedingly insightful, innovative, and accomplished scholars with whom it has been a genuine pleasure to work. Their grace and good humor at meeting deadlines, discussing their work, and making revisions made it easy and fun to work on this project. We also warmly thank the editorial director at Ohio University Press, Gillian Berchowitz, and James L. A. Webb, Jr., editor of Ohio's Series in Ecology and History, for their enthusiasm and support of this project. It has been a delight to work with them and their expert production team, including Nancy Basmajian, Jean Cunningham, and Beth Pratt. We are furthermore indebted to the anonymous reviewers of the volume for their insightful comments and helpful suggestions for revision.

In addition, Diana Davis would like to thank Terry Burke, a mentor and friend from whom she has learned so much over the years, for his collaboration on this project. For their help with various aspects of her work in this volume, she is also very grateful to Abbas Amanat, Mark Cioc, Julia Clancy-Smith, Paul Claval, Steven Greenhalgh, Roger Louis, Ian Manners, James McCann, Pernilla Ouis, Susan Slyomovics, Jeannie Sowers, and Michael Watts. At the University of California at Davis, she would like to thank, for their help and support, Dean George R. Mangun and Assistant Dean Steven Roth, as well as all of her new colleagues in the Department of History, especially Louis Warren, Ari Kelman, and Omnia El Shakry. Dan Goldstein and Jason Newborn, her colleagues at the UC Davis Shields Library, also deserve her special thanks for all their help. Her research would not have been possible without the many who helped her, and to whom she is indebted, in France at the Bibliothèque Nationale de France, Paris; the Centre des Archives Diplomatiques de Nantes; and the Centre des Archives d'Outre-Mer, Aix-en-Provence. For the pure joy and love they bring into her life, and the patience with which they bear the work necessary for a project such as this, she is eternally grateful to James, Max, and Corbin. For their many years of guidance and friendship, she dedicates this book to Ian R. Manners and W. Roger Louis.

Introduction

Imperialism, Orientalism, and the Environment in the Middle East

History, Policy, Power, and Practice

Diana K. Davis

REPRESENTATIONS OF the Middle East nearly inevitably include desolate scenes of empty and parched deserts, punctuated, perhaps, with a lonely string of camels, a verdant but isolated oasis, or a beach with large dunes of golden sand, sometimes with a pyramid, an oil derrick, or a minaret in the background. We see and read about such imagery, around the world, in tourist advertisements, in films, in the news media, and even in scholarly writing about the region. The environment figures very large in the majority of these visual and written representations. Inherent in this imagery is the fact that much of the Middle East and North Africa, a largely desert region, has been considered ecologically marginal since at least the late nineteenth century. More often than not, these lands have been defined as degraded by human action over many centuries.

Recent research, however, has shown instead that these regions are not desertified disasters despite their frequent portrayal as such.[1] In fact, the peoples of the Middle East and North Africa have lived and thrived for millennia, successfully coping with the common environmental conditions of

Figure 0.1. "A Lookout into the Desert." This undated postcard illustrates typical scenes of the Middle East from the late nineteenth and early twentieth centuries. Original postcard: "EGYPT—A Lookout into the Desert," by photographers Lehnert and Landrock. *From the collection of Dr. Paula Sanders, Rice University. Reproduced by permission.*

high temperatures and low rainfall of their arid and semiarid environments. The environment in many parts of the Middle East and North Africa has been carefully and painstakingly transformed to improve human life for much of the last five to seven thousand years and longer. The sophisticated irrigation and water-control systems developed in the region provide just one example of such environmental management.²

With the rise of Anglo-European imperial power in the region, though, in the nineteenth and early twentieth centuries, an environmental imaginary began to be constructed that frequently portrayed the Middle East and North Africa as being on the edge of ecological viability or as a degraded landscape facing imminent disaster.³ Because the local inhabitants were most often blamed for the environmental degradation, by deforestation, overgrazing, or overirrigation, for example, this environmental imaginary allowed the telling of stories, or narratives, that facilitated imperial goals in the name of "improvement" and, later, of environmental "protection."

I have detailed elsewhere how this Western environmental imaginary spawned an environmental narrative of presumed degradation constructed by the French to engender dramatic economic, social, political, and environmental changes in North Africa that successfully promoted their colonial project during the nineteenth and early twentieth centuries.⁴ Closely related environmental imaginaries of the Middle East and North Africa, as Shaul Cohen has demonstrated, allowed the development of a narrative of deforestation in the Levant that has facilitated the appropriation of rural land by Jewish settlers to Palestine, in the name of reforestation, since the late nineteenth century.⁵ Deforestation narratives have been particularly strong in the Levant region since the nineteenth century, where some of the most emotional accounts of forest destruction have hinged on the presumed widespread destruction of the Lebanese cedar forests illustrated in the cover image by Louis-François Cassas.[6] Similar narratives of overgrazing and desertification were used during the British Mandate in Palestine to justify forestry policies as well as laws aimed at controlling nomads, such as the 1942 Bedouin control ordinance, in the name of curbing overgrazing.[7] Such environmental imaginaries, once constructed, can be extremely tenacious and have surprisingly widespread effects.

By "environmental imaginary," I mean the constellation of ideas that groups of humans develop about a given landscape, usually local or regional, that commonly includes assessments about that environment as well as how it came to be in its current state. This use of imaginary draws more on the conceptualization of the "social imaginary" than on other uses of the term in psychological or philosophical studies.[8] Social groups may develop an environmental imaginary, for instance, by living and working in a common place. Because environmental imaginaries nearly always contain ideas about how the environment reached its current state, though, narratives of environmental change, environmental histories, are intimately linked with environmental imaginaries.[9] Therefore, such stories, or narratives, about environmental change, both inform environmental imaginaries and develop as a result of environmental imaginaries. Neither the imaginary nor the narrative(s) concerning the environment is static. Underlying each is a congeries of power relations that may shift and change to varying degrees depending on the time and place. Who tells the story of environmental change and what it means for the present and future can determine who wins and who loses when that imaginary is operationalized in the form of, for example, agricultural policies, "reforestation" projects, or environmental and economic development plans.[10]

This becomes particularly important in imperial and colonial settings. "While environmental imaginaries stem from material and social practices in [particular] natural settings,"[11] when they are developed about "faraway" places, they necessarily are informed by environmental representations constructed by others. Those constructing the knowledge that informed the environmental imaginary "back home" during the colonial period were, most of the time, new to the region being described and catalogued.[12] It is not too surprising then, that much of what was written and visually rendered about foreign environments, information that informed Anglo-European environmental imaginaries, represented the environment most often as alien, exotic, fantastic, or "abnormal," and frequently as degraded in some way.[13]

Much of the early Western representation of the Middle East and North Africa environment, in fact, might be interpreted as a form of environmental orientalism in that the environment was narrated by those who became the imperial powers, primarily Britain and France, as a "strange and defective" environment compared to Europe's "normal and productive" environment.[14] The consequent need to "improve," "restore," "normalize," or "repair" the environment provided powerful justifications for innumerable imperial projects, from building irrigation systems to reforestation activities to the bombing of "unruly" tribes to the sedentarization of nomads as a measure to prevent "overgrazing." The perceived extreme aridity and the constraints that this was seen to place on "normal" agricultural production fueled an intense interest in hydraulic management by the British and the French. Determined to boost production of economically profitable crops such as cotton, a great deal of energy and resources was spent on dams, canals, and other technologies to improve and spread irrigation infrastructures in most of the Middle East and North Africa.[15] This has left a legacy for hydraulic management perhaps greater than any other form of environmental management (such as forestry or range management) in the region that is reflected in the majority of chapters in this volume that treat water in some way. Many of these imperial environmental narratives, especially of deforestation and overgrazing, informed the discipline of ecology as it was developing in the late nineteenth and early twentieth centuries, and thus several of the narratives became institutionalized in ecological science despite their questionable accuracy.[16] It is perhaps because of this cloak of technological and scientific authority that environmental orientalism in the Middle East and North Africa has never been, to the best of my knowledge, interrogated by postcolonial scholars and others in a systematic way for the hidden relations of power rooted in its very specific forms of knowledge production.

Since the publication in 1978 of Edward Said's influential book *Orientalism*, scholars have demonstrated, in varied and sometimes contested ways, how the "orient" of the Middle East and North Africa has been represented and what the results of such representations have been.[17] Many different kinds of representations of the Middle East and North Africa have been critically analyzed, including texts written by poets, novelists, and travel writers, and many different kinds of visual renditions of the region and its peoples, especially photography and painting, and contemporary multimedia. Startlingly few of these analyses, however, have explored the Middle East and North African environment itself, and how it has been represented, from a critical perspective. One notable exception is Timothy

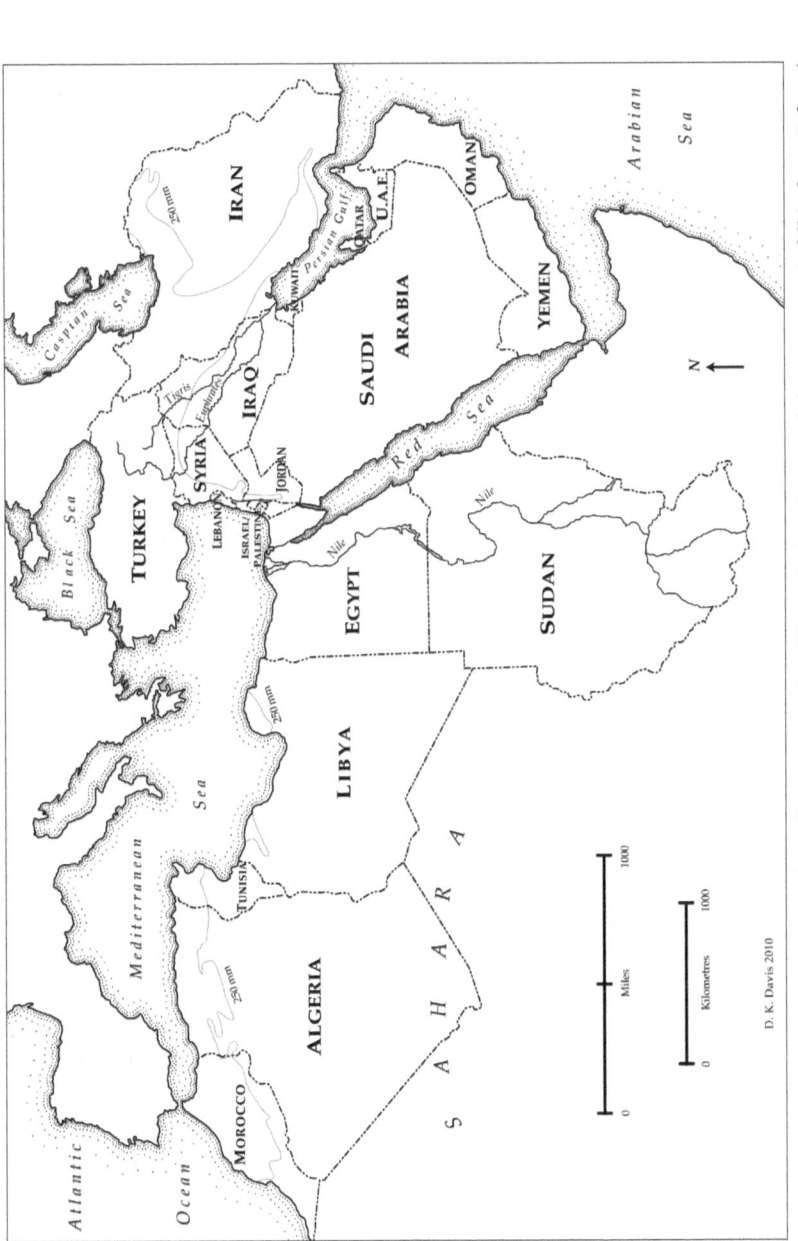

Map 0.1. The Middle East and North Africa, illustrating political boundaries, rivers, and the 250 mm rainfall isohyet. Below (to the south of) the 250 mm rainfall isohyet, rain-fed agriculture is nearly impossible. Agriculture without irrigation is reliable only in areas that receive above 400 mm of rainfall each year. Between 250 and 400 mm annual rainfall, agriculture without irrigation is extremely tenuous and often fails. Modified after Gerald Blake, John Dewdney, and Jonathan Mitchell, *The Cambridge Atlas of the Middle East and North Africa* (Cambridge: Cambridge University Press, 1987). Created by Diana K. Davis, 2010.

Mitchell's research on Egypt and particularly his analysis of the country as an "object of development."[18] Several parts of his book analyze how the Egyptian environment has been represented, for what reasons, and for whose benefit. Mitchell's is one of the only critical analyses of a Middle East and North African environment that takes seriously the important and far-reaching effects of environmental representation and narrative on policy, power, and practice both in the past and today.[19]

The authors in this book thus make a significant contribution by considering many of the social, political, technological, economic, and ecological implications of environmental imaginaries of the Middle East and North Africa over the long durée as well as in more recent, postcolonial settings. Together, they cover the last three centuries in a wide array of Middle East and North African countries and regions, today called Egypt, Iraq, Israel, the Maghreb (Algeria, Morocco, Tunisia), Palestine, and Turkey. Although not the focus of any single chapter, Lebanon, Libya, and Syria are also discussed by several of the authors.

Mitchell's work on Egypt has shown how international development actors such as USAID (United States Agency for International Development) and many in the Egyptian government bureaucracy in the last half of the twentieth century drew on the long-standing Western imaginary of Egypt as a marginal environment with limited resources, dependent on the Nile. The evocatively "narrow ribbon" of fertile land along the Nile, he argues, is nearly always juxtaposed with an apparent crisis of overpopulation. Such an imaginary is used to justify plans for immediate action in the sectors of agricultural and economic reform even as it naturalizes and depoliticizes serious problems of social inequality and poverty that may then be more easily and profitably ignored. Mitchell termed this framing of Egypt's economic development "a problem of geography versus demography."[20]

At the turn of the century, during the period of the British protectorate, a similar framing took place based on the Anglo-European environmental imaginary of Egypt. Jennifer Derr shows in her chapter that the British came to Egypt with certain conceptions of the environment and the powers of technology in the form of irrigation infrastructures that guided their actions and, ultimately, the very shape of the environment along the Nile. Whereas "overpopulation" was not a strong motivation for their development of irrigation works in colonial Egypt, the production of cotton was. Derr argues, though, that the drive to increase cotton production was not the only motivation for the building of the Aswan dam in 1902. She demonstrates that the British held a "technocratic imagining" of the Egyptian environment that was deeply influenced by their belief that this desiccated, marginal environment had been astoundingly more productive during the biblical period, "the time of Joseph."

British efforts to try to regain this historical glory, assuming that more advanced irrigation and agricultural systems existed during biblical times, and eliding waterworks undertaken during the Ottoman period, underlay much of the rationale to build the dam and develop perennial irrigation in Egypt. In his chapter, though, Alan Mikhail shows that the Ottoman period was actually quite important in Egypt's development. He suggests that Egyptian peasants and the Ottoman state were deeply and personally engaged in a "responsible management" of the Nile and associated irrigation structures based on a commonly held cooperative vision of the environment in the eighteenth century. His work argues that the "microlevel" negotiations over and communal efforts to dredge irrigation canals were largely successful in maintaining a productive agricultural system. By contrast, the negative effects that the operationalization of the British colonial imaginary had on the environment, in the form of waterlogged soils and rising salinity, and on the Egyptian farmers, many of whom suffered loss of property and the transformation effectively into sharecroppers, were largely unanticipated.[21] Nonetheless, Derr concludes in her chapter, this British environmental imaginary underlay the transformation of the very geography of Egypt's land, water, economy, and social relations in long-lasting ways.

Land reclamation, making uncultivable land cultivable, in Egypt is perhaps as old as irrigation technology itself. Reclamation of land during the British colonial period was part and parcel of the expansion of irrigation. In her chapter, Jeannie Sowers focuses on Egyptian land reclamation to show how dominant state narratives of the environment developed in the second half of the twentieth century only to be increasingly challenged recently by disparate groups including those in agribusiness, civil society, and the environmental sciences. She dates the now ubiquitous neo-Malthusian narrative of overpopulation in the narrow Nile valley to the interwar period and charts the reconstructions of environmental imaginaries under postwar Egyptian regimes. During the Nasser period, the British environmental imaginary, which focused on irrigation and land reclamation for the entire Nile river basin, was partly reconfigured into a project of national sovereignty and state populism. In doing this, the Nasser regime promoted an intensification of land reclamation, as populist rhetoric abounded that called for a new contract with the spatially constrained peasantry.

Originally focused on the outskirts of the Nile Valley, land reclamation visions under Nasser, Sowers shows, spread to Egypt's southwestern desert, designated the "New Valley," also known as Toshka. Drawing on colonial tropes of how spreading irrigation technologies would create a clean and productive citizenry, early land reclamation plans were put into practice during Nasser's rule on a small scale with irrigation water pumped from underground aquifers. Land reclamation was seized with renewed energy under Mubarak, who aimed not only to raise modern organic produce in the "pristine desert environment" of the Toshka valley, but also to develop the new, clean model Egyptian citizen while enticing private agribusiness to Egypt's agricultural sector. Sowers illustrates that state environmental narratives in the postcolonial period recombined elements of Anglo-European environmental imaginaries with the ideologies of nationalism and populism. Equally important, she demonstrates that the environmental imaginaries and narratives of less powerful, nonstate, groups can successfully challenge these hegemonic discourses in unexpected ways. She sketches how agribusiness managers have developed new narratives of land reclamation, motivated by Egypt's changing political economy, that critique the regime's uncertain land tenure policies and unpredictable policy interventions. Moreover, she explains how narratives of environmental decline, coupled with criticisms of arbitrary decision-making, have allowed environmentalists, journalists, and some public intellectuals to claim that the Toshka project represented not the successes, but rather the shortcomings, of Mubarak's authoritarian regime.

British environmental imaginaries and their transformations also form the subject of Priya Satia's chapter on Iraq during and after the First World War. Satia details how the British environmental imaginary of "Arabia," as the region was called then, changed over time facilitating a new technological vision of development and new colonial policies.[22] The imaginary was informed by established orientalist notions and biblical interpretations but also, importantly, by British misgivings resulting from their trials in the South African War and their experiences during World War I. Satia argues that the British Arabian imaginary was transformed from an early one of the region as a utopia to a more sober view that it was a barren, fallen Eden to the later interpretation that it was in need of restoration with British imperial knowledge—so that Arabia would once again become the productive cradle of civilization, a resurrected Babylonia. Such changes in how the environment was conceived allowed the fusion of development and surveillance in the form of aerial policing and shelling to bring "peace and prosperity" in ways that have been previously unrecognized.

For the British arriving in Arabia, Satia illustrates that the environment appeared "extraterrestrial" in its strangeness, "infinitely mysterious," more like the face of the moon than the earth, and, it seemed to them, unknowable. At first seen mostly as a desert paradise free from the defects of British industrial urban life, within a short time this environment was being condemned as a chaotic wasteland, ruined by the Ottomans, that needed to be reclaimed with the aid of British technology and expertise. This technical vision of Iraq included irrigation improvements derived from the British experience in India, but, more important to Satia's argument, it included the development and refinement of aerial surveillance. Romantic associations between the fighting tactics of Arab nomads and the airplane's quick abilities provided an interpretation of the airplane as the perfect tool to survey the "unmappable nomad terrain" of Mesopotamia. The British used this new tool after the war as they took mandatary control of the region to subdue the "unruly tribes" with bombardment in order to allow the "development" of Iraq to proceed. Deeply ingrained views shaped by environmental determinism, though, led to portrayals of the tribes as tough inhabitants of a harsh environment that could tolerate random acts of violence in ways that others could not. Thus, Satia, concludes, was brutality justified in the name of technocratic development that had to overcome, in the British Arabian imaginary, a difficult and unknowable desert environment and people, a socioecological state of exception that haunts our world today.[23]

Nearly a century earlier, in North Africa, the French similarly justified many colonial policies for dealing with the local populations based in large part on their environmental imaginary of the Maghreb. The widespread Anglo-European perception of the North African environment in the early nineteenth century was one of great fertility that had lapsed under negligent Ottoman administration. Soon after the French conquered Algeria in 1830, though, they developed a new colonial environmental narrative that blamed the local inhabitants, particularly the nomads, for apparently deforesting and desertifying the region over the last several hundred years since the "Arab invasions." This colonial narrative, Diana Davis argues in her chapter, was based on the erroneous belief that during the Roman period North Africa had been more fertile and much more heavily forested than when the French arrived in Algeria. She shows that most French settlers in Algeria, and later in Tunisia and Morocco, developed an identity that claimed Roman heritage. Moreover, many of these settlers vehemently believed that they had to restore the environment to its former Roman glory with reforestation projects and agricultural improvements in order to prove themselves the heirs of Rome. That is, their identity hinged in important ways on restoring the environment, which they saw as an environment of "self," to its rightful state. This contrasts with the exotic and "abnormal" environmental imaginaries most other imperial/colonial powers constructed of their overseas territories. Davis suggests, furthermore, that the perceived need to restore the environment to its mythical former fertility also informed certain notions of French imperial and, to a certain degree, national identity, especially in the early twentieth century in ways not previously considered. Their colonial environmental history of North Africa allowed many of the French to identify themselves as heroes who had restored the ruined environment and proved themselves the true heirs of Rome.

In his chapter, George Trumbull charts what he terms the reimagining of the Sahara by the French in the era of decolonization, a crucial but overlooked component of the economic history of the great desert. Related, in part, to the environmental narratives described by Davis, Trumbull explains that the French vision of the Sahara as a sea of sand, as a place danger, of intractable thirst and frequently death, dominated in the nineteenth century. Although there was interest in trying to increase both water supplies and economic activities in the desert during that time, little was achieved. By the mid-twentieth century, though, the French imaginary of the Sahara was transformed, according to Trumbull, and reconceived as a utilitarian space, as they sought to economically develop the desert through mining and petroleum extraction during a period of national crisis. By this time, large amounts of subterranean water had been discovered, and this newfound resource generated dreams of populating the Sahara with workers and managers complete with cottages and gardens growing roses. He calls this a transformation of the environmental representation of the great desert one that is essentially a "passage from menace to management." In this way, the Sahara, in the French mind, was reconfigured for mastery that could prove the grandeur of France even as it was losing the battle to control the rest of Algeria. Some even dreamed of eliminating the desert altogether, believing that enough irrigation and planting could change the climate itself, revealing the widespread underlying belief that deserts are "unnatural" aberrations. As Trumbull notes, the local peoples who had lived successfully in the Sahara for generations were ignored, as was their knowledge of water supplies and environmental management. The Algerians, however, had their own imaginary of their environment, including the desert. This is implied in the words of the famous nineteenth-century Algerian freedom fighter, 'Abd al-Qâdir, as quoted by Trumbull, "If you knew the secrets of the desert, you [the French] would think like me; but you are ignorant of them."

The chapters discussed up to this point all focus primarily on Western, Anglo-European environmental imaginaries of the Middle East and North

Africa, how and why they were formed and transformed, and how they affected a wide array of subjectivities, policies, and practices. As the example from contemporary Egypt shows, successive Egyptian regimes have invoked various elements of colonial environmental imaginaries in order to further state power and private profit in a variety of sectors including agriculture. The chapter by Sowers and that by Trumbull, though, provide glimpses of the different environmental imaginaries of more local, non-Western groups in the Middle East and North Africa in the nineteenth and twentieth centuries. Do these visions constitute an alternative to what has been suggested here as "environmental orientalism"? If they do, what are the implications and are they significant? By examining the narratives of farmers, government officials, extension agents, and political groups, in several Middle Eastern and North African countries, the remaining chapters in the volume provide examples with which we might begin to try to explore these questions further.[24]

Leila Harris analyzes multiple local narratives of environmental change in contemporary southeastern Turkey in order to compare the stories of scientists, local, small-scale farmers, and agricultural extension agents. She argues that both divergent and convergent narratives, or "story lines," are able to reveal underlying environmental imaginaries. Significantly, Harris shows how important it is to consider such narratives in the context of detailed histories of sociopolitical and economic change affecting the region at the local, national, and international levels. We find a common faith in technoscience shared by all the actors in this example that is widely believed to be able to increase the productivity of already good land, rather than as a "fix" for previously ruined land. This might be surprising in the light of the common Anglo-European imaginary of a degraded Middle Eastern and North African environment. As Harris explains, though, it is not surprising when one understands the long-standing treatment of the Kurds in the region, who aspire to attain "development" on a level with the rest of Turkey, or when one understands the desire of the Turkish state to be perceived as "modern" by the West to facilitate goals such as entry into the European Union. These indigenous voices, marshaling their own environmental visions and understandings, offer a "stark contrast to general crisis narratives" of resource degradation with foundations in the Anglo-European environmental imaginary. For environmental plans to succeed, for "sustainable" development to be possible, Harris concludes, these voices must be heard and heeded.

Competing "hydro-imaginaries" of the Jordan River basin form the subject of Samer Alatout's chapter on the construction of the political geography of the river and its lands in the 1950s, just after the creation of the state of Israel. Alatout shows very clearly how three different environmental imaginaries of the river basin—American, Arab, and Israeli—fostered three different narratives of hydrological reality with related prescriptive policies that in turn legitimized three very different political geographies of the region. The Americans employed a naturalizing and depoliticizing watershed perspective of the river and its basin that generated a cooperative planning approach in order to create a strong coalition of states able to rebuff anticipated Soviet incursions in the region, thus privileging U.S. foreign policy early in the cold war era. The plan of the Arab states drew on Arab nationalism and a kind of moral economy of water that gave importance to the sources of the Jordan waters, which, in turn, justified a pan-Arab politico-environmental approach excluding Israel. In its effort to define the Jordan River as a national resource for its development, the Israeli state employed an imaginary that was built on a highly efficient technonature in which the highest agricultural profit using the best technology justified who received water and, important since they were eager to pump river water to the Negev desert, where it was delivered. The details of the three different narratives analyzed by Alatout provide striking examples of how and why different and competing environmental imaginaries, hegemonic and local, can be extremely important in national and international politics, economics, development, and foreign relations.

The Palestinian environmental imaginary, as Alatout noted, was neglected in the 1950s water negotiations. This "indigenous" imaginary forms a primary subject of analysis, however, for Shaul Cohen in his chapter comparing the environmental imaginaries of Palestinians and Israelis in the context of nationalism(s) and environmentalism. He shares with Davis an interest in how visions of the environment, and how they have changed over time, inflect notions of social identity, national and otherwise. Cohen concludes that, for the moment, environmentalism is taking a backseat to other much more pressing issues for both the Israelis and Palestinians, such as security and national development. He provides, however, revealing details on the formulation and deployment of these two competing environmental imaginaries. As Cohen details, the Israelis have appropriated much of the Anglo-European environmental imaginary of a ruined landscape in need of restoration. In this case, the Arabs living under Ottoman administration, the Palestinians, are held responsible for degrading the environment, and therefore, it is argued, the Israelis are justified in owning the land so as to restore its "lost and rightful fertility." For the Palestinians, in contrast, the vision of the environment hinges more on how their former "Palestinian

Eden" has been lost and degraded by the creation of Israel, while claiming that they are better stewards of the land than are the Israelis. Both sides thus wear the "mantle of the victim," and both form notions of identity with claims of superior environmental knowledge and care. They share, then, what amount to "nationalist narratives of the environment" and the goal of environmental protection. Indeed, as Cohen explains, it was hoped that environmental protection would help forge Israeli/Palestinian cooperation in the optimistic time following the Oslo accords of 1993 that might help lead to peace. Instead, resources and energy on both sides have gone into other, more urgent, sectors, namely security, while environmental protection has been mostly deferred.

As these three chapters illustrate, alternative, often nationalist, environmental imaginaries of the Middle East and North Africa have indeed adapted and reconfigured, to a greater or lesser degree, the Anglo-European preconceptions of "environmental orientalism." Their development, like their deployment, is dependent on specific historical contexts that must be considered when analyzing them and their implications. It must also be taken into account, though, that a great deal of "scientific research" on the environment in the Middle East and North Africa has been conducted by Anglo-Europeans and others steeped in the Western environmental imaginary of a ruined landscape. The inaccurate narrative of degradation, alongside a valorization of technological fixes, has been incorporated into the educational and research systems of the postcolonial Middle East and North Africa to a significant degree, just as it has in the global North. As some of the chapters in this book show, many people born and raised in the region do subscribe to Anglo-European environmental imaginaries to varying degrees. What we can't yet answer, but hopefully future research will, is how many people in the region have internalized such environmental imaginaries, to what degree, and with what results.

The example of the United Arab Emirates (UAE) provides an interesting opportunity to think about some of the potential implications of these questions. If many people in the Middle East and North Africa held some sort of common identity as the inhabitants of a degraded or desertified environment, what would be the social, political, and economic ramifications? The UAE, a federation of seven sheikhdoms on the Gulf coast of the Saudi Arabian peninsula, formerly called the Trucial States, gained its independence in 1971 after 120 years of British protection. Since independence, primarily under the leadership of its first president, Sheikh Zayed bin Sultan Al Nayhan (1918–2004), the UAE has maintained an official campaign to "roll back the desert," which constitutes 80 percent of its territory. It has, for example, planted more than one hundred million trees and created many parks and "green spaces."[25] In Abu Dhabi, the largest state, the rate of afforestation since 1980 is an astounding 26 percent annually.[26] In addition, UAE agriculture has been greatly expanded, and the sectors of agriculture, afforestation, and parks creation account for at least 80 percent of all water consumption.[27] This intensive effort to green the Emirates, however, has created problems of pollution from fertilizers and the overuse of groundwater—over 80 percent of total groundwater has already been withdrawn, much of it nonrenewable fossil aquifer water.[28] Desalinization is increasingly being relied on, a technology that is hugely energy-intensive and that emits large amounts of CO_2 and hot water detrimental to marine life. As of 2008, desalinated water provided most of the municipal (nonagricultural) water supplies, and treated sewage is increasingly being used to irrigate landscaping.[29]

In other sectors, such as real estate development, nature has also been "improved," as in the case of the human-generated archipelago of three hundred islands called "the world," which contains individual islands with expensive private villas, or the manipulations of the creek Khor Dubai to create a wildlife-filled lagoon with seven artificial islands in the middle of the planned "Business Bay" financial center.[30] The Palazzo Versace Hotel in Dubai has apparently built (or is planning to build) what is claimed to be the world's first refrigerated beach to complement their "chilled public lagoon pool."[31] In Dubai developers have also built the "largest indoor snow park in the world" with five ski runs and conifers apparently growing in the winter wonderland.[32] The resort has been open since December 2005, and in November 2009 they developed the technology to make it snow indoors during the day when people are actually skiing, thus bringing "a unique sight and environment to people who haven't been to the mountains of Europe."[33] The long-term outcome, though, may include the collapse of such mega-projects in Dubai and the rest of the UAE that appear unsustainable if current energy and water consumption trends continue.

Scholars who have studied these phenomena in the UAE tend to attribute the desire to "green" the emirates partly to the idea that within Islamic culture paradise is conceived as a green garden, partly to efforts to legitimize state power and boost nation-building, partly to elite desires to appear to be a "modern" state, and partly to government and commercial interests in attracting Western business and tourism.[34] What is less well accounted for, however, is the effect of Anglo-European environmental imaginaries of a degraded or marginal environment that can be made "better" and more "normal" with more vegetation, more water, and "cooling" of

Figure 0.2. Inside Ski Dubai, where it is kept cold enough to produce snow while outside temperatures soar above 100 degrees Fahrenheit. *Photo by Keirn OConnor, posted to Wikimedia Commons: http://commons.wikimedia.org/wiki/File:Ski_Dubai_Chair.jpg. Licensed for sharing, copying, and distributing.*

the torrid desert sands. The Anglo-European environment in conjunction with Western models of consumption and leisure are implicitly and explicitly held up as the ideal to attain. This was expressed well by one Emerati woman at Ski Dubai not long after it had opened. At the end of a ski run, with a big smile on her face, she proclaimed proudly, "Now it is Europe here too."[35] In this case, though, unlike many others, blame has not been attributed, in any of the official narratives, to a particular human group for ruining the environment. President Zayed said, for instance, that "a man without resources cannot change a country and so is not to be blamed for it. This was the case when our ancestors could not do anything."[36] In other parts of the Middle East and North Africa, however, as the chapters in this volume attest, this same imaginary has produced repressive policies, including forced sedentarization and relocation for groups deemed to be environmentally destructive, such as nomads. Critically interrogating the environmental imaginaries of the Middle East and North Africa, as this volume has begun to do, holds promise for future research that may be able to inform more environmentally sustainable and socially equitable development in the region.

Notes

1. See UNEP, *Global Deserts Outlook* (Nairobi, Kenya: United Nations Environment Programme, 2006), available at http://www.unep.org/geo/GDOutlook, last accessed 25 February 2010. The primary environmental problems in the Middle East are those of pollution and overusing limited water supplies, not of massive deforestation, overgrazing, and desertification. For more details, see Diana K. Davis, "The Middle East," in *Encyclopedia of World Environmental History,* ed. Shepard Krech, John R. McNeill, and Carolyn Merchant (New York: Routledge, 2003), 840–44; Mark A. Blumler, "Biogeography of Land-Use Impacts in the Near East," in *Nature's Geography: New Lessons for Conservation in Developing Countries,* ed. Karl Zimmerer and Kenneth Young (Madison: University of Wisconsin Press, 1998), 215–36; Avi Perevolotsky and No'am Seligman, "Role of Grazing in Mediterranean Rangeland Ecosystems," *BioScience* 48, no. 12 (1998): 1007–17; Linda Olsvig-Whittaker, Eliezer Frankenberg, Avi Perevolotsky, et al., "Grazing, Overgrazing and Conservation: Changing Concepts and Practices in the Negev Rangelands," *Sécheresse* 17, nos. 1 and 2 (2006): 195–99; Sharon E. Nicholson, "Desertification," in *Encyclopedia of World Environmental History,* ed. Shepard Krech, John R. McNeill, and Carolyn Merchant (New York: Routledge, 2003), 297–303; James F. Reynolds and D. Mark Stafford Smith, eds., *Global Desertification: Do Humans Cause Deserts?* (Berlin: Dahlem University Press, 2002); William M. Adams, *Green Development: Environment and Sustainability in a Developing World,* 3rd ed. (London: Routledge, 2009), chap. 8; Bruno Messerli and Matthias Winiger, "Climate, Environmental Change, and Resources of the African Mountains from the Mediterranean to the Equator," *Mountain Research and Development* 12, no. 4 (1992): 315–36; Diana K. Davis, "Scorched Earth: The Problematic Environmental History that Defines the Middle East," in *Is There a Middle East?,* ed. Michael E. Bonine, Abbas Amanat, and Michael Ezekiel Gasper (Stanford, Calif.: Stanford University Press, in press); and Diana K. Davis, *Resurrecting the Granary of Rome: Environmental History and French Colonial Expansion in North Africa* (Athens: Ohio University Press, 2007), 177–86.

2. In some cases, such irrigation systems also illustrate the follies of several states' efforts to gain power and prestige with environmentally inappropriate water-control projects throughout history. Providing adequate drainage, for example, has been a problem for thousands of years. See Edmund Burke III, "The Transformation of the Middle Eastern Environment, 1500 BCE–2000 CE," in *The Environment in World History,* ed. Edmund Burke III and Kenneth Pomeranz (Berkeley: University of California Press, 2009), 81–117.

3. Although the primary imperial powers in the Middle East and North Africa in the late nineteenth and early twentieth centuries were the British and the French, I use the term "Anglo-European" here to denote the broad array of Western countries with interests in the region and whose scholars, artists, and travelers made significant contributions to its representation. These countries

include, but are not limited to, France, Britain, the United States of America, Germany, and Italy.

4. Davis, *Resurrecting*.

5. Shaul E. Cohen, *The Politics of Planting: Jewish-Palestinian Competition for Control of Land in the Jerusalem Periphery* (Chicago: University of Chicago Press, 1993).

6. Louis-François Cassas (1756–1827) traveled widely in southern Europe and the Near East for his work as a draftsman, engraver, and archaeologist. From 1784 to 1787 he lived in the Ottoman empire and traveled to places we now know as Turkey, Syria, Egypt, Israel/Palestine, and Cyprus. See Joshua Drapkin, "Cassas, Louis-François," Grove Art Online: http://www.oxfordartonline.com, last accessed 20 December 2010. The ink and watercolor rendering of the *View of the Cedar Forests of Lebanon seen from the Tripoli Road* (1800–1801) seen on the cover of this book illustrates well the romantic view of the forests of the Middle East common among Europeans at that time. Despite the popularity of this romantic view, later in the nineteenth century, the deforestation narrative became dominant and remains so today. Contemporary research, however, has undermined this deforestation narrative and shown deforestation history in the region to be more complicated than previously thought, with some deforestation in some areas but not others. See discussion of the paleoecological data in Davis, "Scorched Earth," and also more recent research including Lara Hajar et al., "Environmental Changes in Lebanon during the Holocene: Man vs. Climate Impacts," *Journal of Arid Environments* 74, no. 7 (2010): 746–55, and F. H. Neumann et al., "Vegetation History and Climate Fluctuations on a Transect along the Dead Sea West Shore and Their Impact on Past Societies over the Last 3500 Years," *Journal of Arid Environments* 74, no. 4 (2010): 756–64. The cedars of Lebanon, in fact, may well be relics from the last ice age rather than a species wholly destroyed by human improvidence as so often claimed. See Lara Hajar et al., "*Cedrus libani* (A. Rich) Distribution in Lebanon: Past, Present and Future," *Comptes Rendus Biologies* 333, no. 18 (2010): 622–30, esp. 626.

7. Davis, "Scorched Earth."

8. For example, the work of Jean-Paul Sartre and Jacques Lacan has not greatly influenced my use here of the term "imaginary." I draw more on the work of human geographers, particularly political ecologists, who have attempted to delineate how such social-environmental imaginaries are constructed and how they are used in a variety of settings. For more details, see Richard Peet and Michael Watts, eds., *Liberation Ecologies: Environment, Development, Social Movements* (New York: Routledge, 1996), 37, 267–69. For a case study, see J. Todd Nesbitt and Daniel Weiner, "Conflicting Environmental Imaginaries and the Politics of Nature in Central Appalachia," *Geoforum* 32, no. 3 (2001): 333–49.

9. What we understand as environmental history is most often the single environmental narrative (usually among several competing narratives) that has for one reason or another become dominant, or the most widely accepted

narrative, in a given social group. In certain cases, environmental imaginaries and the narratives and policies for development that accompany them become hegemonic. In such cases, the imaginaries and associated policies may be carried to other environments where their application is inappropriate and often harmful to the environment and the people living in it. See Peet and Watts, *Liberation*, 268. See also Kate B. Showers, *Imperial Gullies: Soil Erosion and Conservation in Lesotho* (Athens: Ohio University Press, 2005), for an excellent discussion of hegemonic narratives of soil erosion developed in the west and the problems created when they are transferred to a very different environment in southern Africa.

10. For an excellent discussion, see Jeremy Swift, "Desertification: Narratives, Winners and Losers," in *The Lie of the Land: Challenging Received Wisdom on the African Environment*, ed. Melissa Leach and Robin Mearns (London: International African Institute, 1996), 73–90. For a more sophisticated, theoretical discussion of these ideas, see Paul Robbins, *Political Ecology* (Oxford: Blackwell, 2004), esp. 107–26.

11. Peet and Watts, *Liberation*, 267.

12. Of course, later in the colonial period in places like India and Algeria many people of European heritage had been born in the "colony," but by that time the dominant environmental imaginary had been constructed and did not often change significantly.

13. For excellent discussions of representations of "foreign nature" and "tropicality," see David Arnold, *The Problem of Nature: Environment, Culture and European Expansion* (Oxford: Blackwell, 1996); Derek Gregory, "(Post)Colonialism and the Production of Nature," in *Social Nature: Theory, Practice, and Politics*, ed. Noel Castree and Bruce Braun (Malden, Mass.: Blackwell, 2001), 84–111; and Nancy Leys Stepan, *Picturing Tropical Nature* (Ithaca, N.Y.: Cornell University Press, 2001). See also Davis this volume.

14. The only other scholarly work to use the term "environmental orientalism" and to try to grapple with its implications is Suzana Sawyer and Arun Agrawal, "Environmental Orientalisms," *Cultural Critique* 45, no. 1 (2000): 71–108. This article does not, though, treat the Middle East or North Africa; it focuses on the Americas.

15. For details, see Burke, "Transformation."

16. For a detailed example from colonial North Africa related to Mediterranean basin "natural vegetation" maps, see Davis, *Resurrecting*, 131–64.

17. For a few recent examples, see Zachary Lockman, *Contending Visions of the Middle East: The History and Politics of Orientalism*, 2nd ed. (Cambridge: Cambridge University Press, 2009); Edmund Burke III and David Prochaska, eds. *Genealogies of Orientalism: History, Theory, Politics* (Lincoln: University of Nebraska Press, 2008); Derek Gregory, *The Colonial Present: Afghanistan, Palestine, Iraq* (Oxford: Blackwell, 2004); Alexander Macfie, *Orientalism* (London: Longman, 2002); and Thierry Hentsch, *Imagining the Middle East*, trans. Fred

Reed (Montreal: Black Rose Books, 1992). See also Edward Said, *Orientalism* (New York: Vintage Books, 1978).

18. See Timothy Mitchell, *Rule of Experts: Egypt, Techno-Politics, Modernity* (Berkeley: University of California Press, 2002).

19. Davis, *Resurrecting,* is another, more recent, book that does this.

20. Mitchell, *Rule,* 209. See "The Object of Development," 209–43, for details. The very real problems of the provision of social services to the large Egyptian population and the feelings of being "squeezed" by average Egyptians should not be ignored or downplayed. Mitchell's analysis, rather, shows that the priorities of the state, and its spending, tend to go elsewhere, using the crisis narrative for legitimation.

21. It should be noted that there were people with long experience in Egypt (and India) who tried to warn about the likely problems of perennial irrigation, like the engineer William Willcocks, but all too often their advice was not heeded.

22. Iraq and the surrounding region were variously referred to as Arabia, Mesopotamia, and sometimes the Holy Land during the early part of the twentieth century.

23. Unfortunately, such crude environmental determinism and associated racist worldviews are still with us and are of particular geopolitical importance in the Middle East. See Diana K. Davis, "Power, Knowledge and Environmental History in the Middle East," *International Journal of Middle East Studies* 42, no. 4 (2010): 657–59. For an interrogation of the state (space) of exception in the region today, see Gregory, *Colonial Present.*

24. It is worth noting that "indigenous" is not synonymous with "local," "vernacular," "peasant," or "subaltern." The term is used here in opposition to "Western" or "Anglo-European" to highlight potential differences in environmental imaginaries and narratives of those of Middle East and North African origin.

25. Chris Ryan and Morag Stewart, "Eco-Tourism and Luxury—The Case of Al Maha, Dubai," *Journal of Sustainable Tourism* 17, no. 3 (2009): 292.

26. Pernilla Ouis, "Engineering the Emirates: The Evolution of a New Environment," in *Engineering Earth: The Impacts of Megaengineering Projects,* ed. Stanley Brunn (Boston: Kluwer, 2011), 1409–23.

27. Pernilla Ouis, "'Greening the Emirates': The Modern Construction of Nature in the United Arab Emirates," *Cultural Geographies* 9, no. 3 (2002): 337.

28. Ouis, "Engineering."

29. See the UNFAO's AQUASTAT database for the UAE at http://www.fao.org/nr/water/aquastat/countries/untd_arab_em/index.stm, last accessed 10 September 2010. It is worth noting that water for agriculture is provided free of charge and that municipal supplies are subsidized by the state. Ibid.

30. Ouis, "Engineering." For a scathing commentary on development in Dubai and the "indentured Asian labour force that sustains them," see Mike Davis, "Fear and Money in Dubai," *New Left Review* 41 (September–October 2006): 47–68.

31. See the Palazzo Versace Gold Coast and Dubai Fact Sheet: http://www.tdireconsultancy.com/images/propertyimg/Palazzo%20Fact%20Sheet.pdf, last accessed 11 September 2010. See also Jonathan Leake, "Chill Out, You Beautiful People, the Versace Beach Is Refrigerated," *Sunday Times*, 14 December 2008, online at http://www.timesonline.co.uk/tol/news/environment/article5338099.ece, last accessed 4 November 2010.

32. For information, photos, and virtual tours, see http://www.skidubai.com/ski-dubai/resort, last accessed 2 March 2010. It is not clear whether the trees are real or ornamental.

33. See anonymous article "Let It Snow at Ski Dubai," Ski Dubai website, http://www.skidxb.com/news/news-2.aspx, last accessed 2 March 2010.

34. For examples, see Ryan and Stewart, "Eco-Tourism," and Ouis, "Greening."

35. Quote from a story on the BBC World News television broadcast, 16 February 2006.

36. Quote from the introductory material of the Zayed Bin Sultan Al Nahayan Charitable and Humanitarian Foundation, http://www.zayedfoundation.com/home.aspx, last accessed 26 February 2010.

Bibliography

Adams, William M. *Green Development: Environment and Sustainability in a Developing World*. 3rd ed. London: Routledge, 2009.

Arnold, David. *The Problem of Nature: Environment, Culture and European Expansion*. Oxford: Blackwell, 1996.

Blumler, Mark A. "Biogeography of Land-Use Impacts in the Near East." In *Nature's Geography: New Lessons for Conservation in Developing Countries*, edited by Karl Zimmerer and Kenneth Young, 215–36. Madison: University of Wisconsin Press, 1998.

Burke, Edmund, III. "The Transformation of the Middle Eastern Environment, 1500 BCE–2000 CE." In *The Environment in World History*, edited by Edmund Burke III and Kenneth Pomeranz, 81–117. Berkeley: University of California Press, 2009.

Burke, Edmund, III, and David Prochaska, eds. *Genealogies of Orientalism: History, Theory, Politics*. Lincoln: University of Nebraska Press, 2008.

Cohen, Shaul E. *The Politics of Planting: Jewish-Palestinian Competition for Control of Land in the Jerusalem Periphery*. Chicago: University of Chicago Press, 1993.

Davis, Diana K. "The Middle East." In *Encyclopedia of World Environmental History*, edited by Shepard Krech, John R. McNeill, and Carolyn Merchant, 840–44. New York: Routledge, 2003.

———. "Power, Knowledge and Environmental History in the Middle East." *International Journal of Middle East Studies* 42, no. 4 (2010): 657–59.

———. *Resurrecting the Granary of Rome: Environmental History and French Colonial Expansion in North Africa*. Athens: Ohio University Press, 2007.

———. "Scorched Earth: The Problematic Environmental History that Defines the Middle East." In *Is There a Middle East*, edited by Abbas Amanat, Michael Bonine, and Michael Gasper. Stanford: Stanford University Press, in press.
Davis, Mike. "Fear and Money in Dubai." *New Left Review* 41, no. Sept.–Oct. (2006): 47–68.
Gregory, Derek. *The Colonial Present: Afghanistan, Palestine, Iraq.* Oxford: Blackwell, 2004.
———. "(Post)Colonialism and the Production of Nature." In *Social Nature: Theory, Practice, and Politics*, edited by Noel Castree and Bruce Braun, 84–111. Malden, MA: Blackwell, 2001.
Hajar, Lara, Louis François, Ihab Jomaa, Michel Déqué, and Rachid Cheddadi. "*Cedrus libani* (A. Rich) Distribution in Lebanon: Past, Present and Future." *Comptes Rendus Biologies* 333, no. 18 (2010): 622–30.
Hajar, Lara, M. Haidar-Boustani, C. Khater, and Rachid Cheddadi. "Environmental Changes in Lebanon during the Holocene: Man vs. Climate Impacts." *Journal of Arid Environments* 74, no. 7 (2010): 746–55.
Hentsch, Thierry. *Imagining the Middle East.* Translated by Fred Reed. Montréal: Black Rose Books, 1992.
Leake, Jonathan. "Chill Out, You Beautiful People, the Versace Beach is Refrigerated." *Sunday Times*, 14 December 2008, Online: http://www.timesonline.co.uk/tol/news/environment/article5338099.ece.
Lockman, Zachary. *Contending Visions of the Middle East: The History and Politics of Orientalism.* 2nd ed. Cambridge: Cambridge University Press, 2009.
Macfie, Alexander. *Orientalism.* London: Longman, 2002.
Messerli, Bruno, and Matthias Winiger. "Climate, Environmental Change, and Resources of the African Mountains from the Mediterranean to the Equator." *Mountain Research and Development* 12, no. 4 (1992): 315–36.
Mitchell, Timothy. *Rule of Experts: Egypt, Techno-Politics, Modernity.* Berkeley: University of California Press, 2002.
Neumann, F. H., E. J. Kagan, S. A. G. Leroy, and U. Baruch. "Vegetation History and Climate Fluctuations on a Transect along the Dead Sea West Shore and their Impact on Past Societies over the Last 3500 Years." *Journal of Arid Environments* 74, no. 4 (2010): 756–64.
Nesbitt, J. Todd, and Daniel Weiner. "Conflicting Environmental Imaginaries and the Politics of Nature in Central Appalachia." *Geoforum* 32, no. 3 (2001): 333–49.
Nicholson, Sharon E. "Desertification." in *Encyclopedia of World Environmental History*, edited by Shepard Krech, John R. McNeill, and Carolyn Merchant, 297–303. New York: Routledge, 2003.
Ouis, Pernilla. "Engineering the Emirates: The Evolution of a New Environment." In *Engineering Earth: The Impacts of Megaengineering Projects*, edited by Stanley Brunn, 1409–23. Boston: Kluwer, 2011.
———. "'Greening the Emirates': The Modern Construction of Nature in the United Arab Emirates." *Cultural Geographies* 9, no. 3 (2002): 334–47.

Peet, Richard, and Michael Watts, eds. *Liberation Ecologies: Environment, Development, Social Movements.* New York: Routledge, 1996.

Perevolotsky, Avi, and No'am Seligman. "Role of Grazing in Mediterranean Rangeland Ecosystems." *BioScience* 48, no. 12 (1998): 1007–17.

Reynolds, James F., and D. Mark Stafford Smith, eds. *Global Desertification: Do Humans Cause Deserts?* Berlin: Dahlem University Press, 2002.

Robbins, Paul. *Political Ecology.* Oxford: Blackwell Publishing, 2004.

Ryan, Chris, and Morag Stewart. "Eco-Tourism and Luxury—The case of Al Maha, Dubai." *Journal of Sustainable Tourism* 17, no. 3 (2009): 287–301.

Said, Edward. *Orientalism.* New York: Vintage Books, 1978.

Sawyer, Suzana, and Arun Agrawal. "Environmental Orientalisms." *Cultural Critique* 45, no. (2000): 71–108.

Showers, Kate B. *Imperial Gullies: Soil Erosion and Conservation in Lesotho.* Athens: Ohio University Press, 2005.

Stepan, Nancy Leys. *Picturing Tropical Nature.* Ithaca, N.Y.: Cornell University Press, 2001.

Swift, Jeremy. "Desertification: Narratives, Winners & Losers." In *The Lie of the Land: Challenging Received Wisdom on the African Environment,* edited by Melissa Leach and Robin Mearns, 73–90. London: International African Institute, 1996.

UNEP. *Global Deserts Outlook.* Nairobi, Kenya: United Nations Environment Programme, 2006.

Chapter 1

"A Rebellion of Technology"

Development, Policing, and the British Arabian Imaginary

Priya Satia

WE HAVE inherited two contrasting images of Iraq. It is, on the one hand, the fertile crescent, the everlastingly prolific river valley, the very cradle of civilization; and, on the other, the archetypal wasteland, a barren desert of glaring sun and bleak horizons testifying at once to man's and nature's cruelty, a forbidding carapace concealing a curselike bounty of fossil fuel. Iraq is the quintessential environmental imaginary, its river-snaked deserts a symbol of the intimacy of human creativity and destruction. It is the consummate stage for history as morality play.

This dual image, in the minds of policymakers both local and distant, has crucially shaped Iraq's history, not least the fate of those rivers and deserts, up to the devastation wrought by the unholy alliance of today's unending war and drought. In this chapter, I want to explore just how Iraq became the site of such dramatic environmental imagining and how, in the early twentieth century, British fascination with nature's strange countenance there ironically produced a colonial state with a narrowly technical vision. After examining early British imaginings of "Arabia"[1] as a desert utopia free from the ugliness of industrial life, I will show how the pressures of the Great War cast that imaginary in a more forbidding light—the barren Iraq. As technology's tarnished aura began to dazzle once again, British personnel in Iraq began to dream of a restored cradle of civilization—the prolific Iraq. When British rule officially began in 1919, these images of a desert utopia and regenerated Babylonia together inspired a new application of technology, also understood in a developmental vein: aerial control. In this twist of colonial fate, we find the "rebellion of technology" that Walter Benjamin saw as the essence of "imperialistic war": "Instead of draining rivers, society directs a human stream into a bed of trenches; instead of dropping seeds from airplanes, it drops incendiary bombs over cities."[2] In Iraq, a toxic brew of environmental imaginaries fueled technology's rebellion.

Behind those imaginaries were historically specific British cultural needs. It was not merely orientalism that shaped prewar British imaginings of a desert utopia but the particular cultural anxieties of the early twentieth century, when the trials of the South African War convinced many Britons that their bourgeois nation had strayed from the path of true glory. Edwardian Britons saw in Arabia a kind of extraterrestrial utopia happily impervious to modern technology and government. In the crucible of the next war, however, British cultural anxieties shifted radically and the indulgent prewar view morphed into a Faustian determination to remake the region, to reconnect this dreamland with the real world and make it a new kind of utopia, a resurrected Babylonia. The British empire strove to prove to the world that it could overrule the verdict of the Western front, that it could show that technology and empire were still constructive forces, benign and effective instruments of global improvement.

In their determination to retrieve this desert imaginary from the barbarous illegibility to which the Ottomans had supposedly condemned it, the British eventually took to the sky. Particularly after the Iraqi rebellion of 1920, the airplane became the linchpin of British efforts to at once develop and police Iraq—indeed, to collapse those two objectives into a single vision. The airplane seemed to them capable of subjecting what they conceived of as a flat, featureless terrain to panoptic surveillance, while at once restoring its ancient position as the commercial crossroads of the world. It was in Iraq that the bomber was first packaged as the vehicle of peace;[3] there, that political language took permanent refuge in euphemism, so that, as George Orwell noted, "Defenseless villages are bombarded from the air, the inhabitants driven out into the countryside, the cattle machine-gunned, the huts set on fire with incendiary bullets: this is called *pacification*."[4]

In short, this story reveals the intimate connection between the history of the modern discourse and practices of development and surveillance, between the welfare state and the warfare state.⁵ Security—economic, social, military, political—was the new coin of the imperial realm after World War I; and it was in the British mandate of Iraq that it was minted. The critical point here is that the technologies of development and security share common military-industrial and cultural roots. The modern notion of development did not begin, as is usually assumed, as a primarily post–World War II phenomenon in Africa, but earlier, in World War I–era Iraq where it underwrote fresh imperial conquest.⁶ Staking out the land of two rivers as a material object was as much a development effort as a military one, emerging out of a joint effort to create a particular kind of battlefield and to rebuild an ancient granary that might redeem the technological undoing of civilization during that war. It was only in a fallen Eden that the British could articulate a vision of development that did not threaten the preservationist ethos that emerged from the wartime critique of technology as essentially destructive—even when that vision of "development" took the form of aerial policing. The collection of environmental imaginaries of Iraq meant that, there, development could be framed *as* preservation, as a restoration of the country's lost greatness.

Good Desert, Bad Technology

The story starts at the turn of the twentieth century, when Mosul, Basra, and Baghdad, three humble provinces of the Ottoman Empire, began to engage the attention of British imperial planners with a new intensity. Their traditional ally astride the land route to India, the Ottoman Empire, had begun to rumble from within as provincial movements for autonomy gathered strength. Even more troubling, Germany had begun to rival British influence inside the empire, particularly in the stretch from Baghdad to the Gulf. In this context, the British government began to plan for the possible demise of their long sick friend at the edge of Europe. And this meant knowing something about the vast stretch of Asia that they knew quaintly as "Arabia," and which acquired the new name "Middle East" in the course of the scholarly and diplomatic conversation they launched.

Long enchantment with the universally adored childhood tales from the *Arabian Nights* and the Bible radically shaped British efforts to increase knowledge about Middle Eastern politics. To the agents, officers, and scholars assigned with the task, Arabia inspired imaginative pleasure above all else; once they gained entry to the notoriously forbidden region, they could scarcely perceive a real place in real time.⁷ As an environmental imaginary, it was positively extraterrestrial, simply "uncanny," in the words of the naturalist and agent of the Directorate of Military Operations, Douglas Carruthers. He felt "suddenly transplanted to the . . . moon."[8] Just when occultists were making astral journeys to barren planets with winged guides, British travelers in Arabia found themselves beyond the pale of the planet they called home.[9] It was, to the great relief of those nostalgic for the days of pioneer-style Victorian exploration, "Still Unknown."[10] And, most important, essentially unknowable: its apparent featurelessness and natural phenomena such as mirage, dust storms, and shifting riverbeds and sand dunes made it so protean and deceptive to the British eye that Britons deemed it a cartographic impossibility.[11] Whatever its actual topographical reality, it remained for them something of a desert idyll, "very much the same everywhere."[12] The journalist Meredith Townsend recognized early on that most Englishmen, "filled . . . with the 'idea' of Arabia," tended to exaggerate the region's aridity.[13] As Peter Brent puts it, Arabia had become "neither more nor less than the desert. . . . The landscape had become everything."[14] British observers often thought of this separate desert universe as a space out of time as much as off the map, a place where they could "step straight from this modern age of bustle and chicanery into an era of elemental conditions . . . back into the pages of history to mediaeval times."[15]

On the whole, then, as an environment, Arabia was not, to British observers, empirically knowable or fully real. It was beyond "the longest arm of the law,"[16] a place so "infinitely mysterious . . . misty and unreal, incomprehensible . . . unfathomable," it could not yield facts but might restore faith.[17] If travel to this otherworldly place numbed the senses, it did allow one to "see, hear, feel, *outside the senses.*"[18] Indeed, this was its very attraction to the sort of officer and traveler who ventured there, finding in intelligence suitably patriotic cover for an escape from Western science, which had begun to produce an unsettling sense of human insignificance and inexorable cosmic entropy.[19] Arabia was a biblical land, a place for miraculous conviction, visionary prophets, and extremes of experience.[20] It was not, to them, the kind of place you could *discipline* in the way that European environments were increasingly being disciplined. And this was a good thing in the eyes of many Edwardians anxious about European decadence. Mark Sykes, then an honorary attaché at the embassy in Constantinople, praised the poetic Arabs for having no place in "civilised community"—defined contemptuously as "a community living in towns and in houses, suffering from infectious and contagious diseases, travelling in railway trains, able to read and write, possessing drinking shops, reading newspapers, surrounded by a hundred unnecessary luxuries, possessing rich and poor, slums and palaces, and convinced that their state is the most edifying in the world."[21] It was a place that had escaped the affective and aesthetic sacrifices demanded by "progress": Townsend's influential *Asia and Europe* (1901) mused,

> Imagine a clan which prefers sand to mould, poverty to labour, solitary reflection to the busy hubbub of the mart, which will not earn enough to clothe itself, never invented so much as a lucifer match, and would consider newspaper-reading a disgraceful waste of time. Is it not horrible, that such a race should be? more horrible, that it should survive all others? most horrible of all, that it should produce, among other trifles, the Psalms and the Gospels, the Koran and the epic of Antar?[22]

Arabia was a place that not only did not need development but proved the bankruptcy of the very concept. Such notions, so dramatically shaped by the cultural anxieties of the Edwardian moment in which the British began to think intently about the region of modern-day Iraq, were quickly put to the test when Britain went to war against the Ottoman Empire in 1914.

Bad Desert, Good Technology

The Mesopotamia campaign began as a small, Government-of-India operation for the defense of Indian frontiers and British interests in the Persian Gulf.[23] However, once at the Gulf, Indian Army Force D began to rapidly advance north along the Tigris and Euphrates rivers in a characteristic effort to shore up what it already held. Baghdad quickly became its object, not least because its fabled past ensured that everyone at home had heard of it: "It was the Arabian nights."[24] For Britons, the campaign might have remained a picturesque subplot of the war's grand narrative but for a monumental failure in the midst of its surge upriver: A reverse at Ctesiphon forced the troops under General Charles Townshend to retreat to Kut, where they were besieged through the winter of 1915–16. After more than twenty thousand troops were lost in botched rescue attempts, nine thousand soldiers and thousands of noncombatants surrendered to the Turks in April 1916—"the British Army's greatest humiliation in the First World War."[25] The London War Office took control of the campaign, and Parliament launched an inquiry. In its report of June 1917, the Mesopotamia Commission censured the Indian army and government for their rash and ill-advised decision to advance on Baghdad and their inadequate provisioning of the force, particularly with respect to transport and medical facilities.²⁶ Meanwhile the force, supplied by a reformed Indian government and led by a new commander, captured Baghdad in October 1917, an event hailed as "the most triumphant piece of strategy . . . since war started."²⁷ The troops continued north until they routed the Turks near Mosul in October 1918.

The Indian government's central role in this drama was the product of yet another environmental imaginary: the official perception of the land of two rivers as a geographical and political extension of the vast barren and tribal world of the North West Frontier.²⁸ Hence the Indian government's initially dilatory attitude toward transport and other provisions; frontier wars were by definition exercises in resourcefulness and economy. The notion was powerful enough to structure observation on the ground: the popular war correspondent Edmund Candler insisted, "The physical features of the country are familiar to our Indian troops," adding, "The villages resemble those of the Punjab or the North-West Frontier."²⁹ The Mesopotamia Commission's report belatedly enlightened the Indian authorities that the "climatic and military" conditions of the frontier and Mesopotamia were in fact "very different."³⁰

To be sure, Mesopotamia's ties with India were also real: Administratively, the London and Indian governments overlapped in Mesopotamia.³¹ The Persian Gulf was the "maritime frontier of the Indian Empire on the west," in Curzon's formulation.³² Trade, Shia pilgrimage, and the Oudh Bequest (which channeled millions of rupees from India to the holy cities through British mediation) also ensured close ties between India and Iraq.³³ Moreover, during the war, the Raj reached into all aspects of military life in Mesopotamia, extending the fiction of Mesopotamian contiguity.³⁴ Summary incorporation of Mesopotamia into the Indian geographical imaginary did not require much of a conceptual leap.

This frontier vision strengthened the British view of Mesopotamia as a storybook land, an essentially unreal place. As the tragedy of the Western front unfolded, the Mesopotamian campaign promised the adventure and heroism of old-fashioned imperial adventure. "In exile from the world," they could fight "war as we used to imagine it"; Mesopotamia proved that "in the right place war even to-day can be a romance."³⁵ References to the Arabian Nights were on everyone's lips.³⁶ Mesopotamia promised "release" from the killing fields of France into fabled locales,³⁷ the "land of Holy Writ."³⁸ In letters and memoirs, soldiers described being "immensely moved by the close contact" with the Garden of Eden, Ezra's tomb, the Tower of Babel, Ur of the Chaldees, and other Old Testament sites.³⁹ They felt transported to a divine land where miraculous natural phenomena were daily occurrences. There, a war correspondent wrote, "you live the story of the Bible, and you do not wonder in the least if it is true; you know it is."[40]

But the narrative of imperial adventure also triggered a subtle shifting of the image of an Arabian escape from technology. In the script of imperial conquest, Mesopotamia was cast in the role of a colonial heart of darkness: a "treeless waste of swamp and desert," "bleak emptiness to conquer," in Candler's unminced words.[41] A soldier put it pertly: "Adam and Eve might well have been excused in such a country." "Mesopotamia welcomes no man," he concluded.[42] Its freedom from the technological burdens of modern life, which had made it a refuge for Edwardians, now made it a no-man's-land in its very essence. Its mirages, sandstorms, and limitless horizons seemed to overwhelm technology's meager purchase on the country: Camels resembled "huge dissipated compasses" and floating ships, infantry became sheep, a motor car became a "few filmy lines," and wagons merely black dots.[43] Visual signaling was almost useless in "a fairyland that danced and glimmered."[44] Soldiers struggled to observe their fire and discern its results.[45] The country remained unmapped for much of the war, largely because British surveyors found it impossible to map. Official intelligence summaries and private reports described rivers that shifted course daily, unnavigable marshes, and homes and villages whose locations were fleeting at best. Overnight, the ground could change from a land to a naval battlefield.[46] Mesopotamia was fundamentally remote, "far away from home, civilization, and comfort," in the rueful words of one naval captain.[47] Technology could only improve a land so far from England, so close to God, especially after the disaster at Kut, when "the conditions of France were repeated in Mesopotamia."[48] As the campaign went badly wrong, the more treacherous aspects of its biblical ecology gained ground in British representations. "We were in a country of excess, where the elements are never moderate or in humour," wrote Candler, "and there was something almost Biblical in the way the deities of this ancient land conspired to punish us ... malice in the sky and soil ... heat and drought; hunger and thirst and flies; damp and cold, fever and ague, flood, hurricane and rain." At the actual site of the Great Flood, these punishments seemed like a "Biblical visitation."[49]

"No-man's-land," the war's most evocative spatial symbol, represented technology's desolation of nature into the heart of darkness in France.[50] But technology maintained a positive image in Mesopotamia, which was depicted as a vast, autarkic wasteland, a fallen Eden disconnected from the world and its economy that the British had come to rescue from Ottoman tyranny. This environmental imaginary excused the military failures. The difficulty of using modern boats on the narrow and tortuous rivers north of Al Qurnah was put down to the "idiosyncrasies of the Tigris" rather than design errors.[51] The Mesopotamia Commission Report echoed that while "a river is generally regarded as an admirable line of communication," the Tigris was in a class all its own. It was, in the memorable words of the commander-in-chief, "a very fickle lady who never sleeps two nights running in the same bed."[52] Basra, unlike Indian and Egyptian ports, was "only an anchorage . . . and beyond—a swamp." Basra Intelligence catalogued these "Physical and Climatic Difficulties of the Mesopotamian Theatre of War," explaining that, "in Iraq all military problems . . . are affected by climate and physical conditions to an extent rarely met with in any theatre of war." The Mesopotamia Commission's report likewise opened with a section on the challenges posed by the country's "Physical and Climatic Peculiarities."[53] The "bad desert" imaginary utterly dominated the postmortem on the military difficulties.

Military failure in Mesopotamia was considered the fault of Mesopotamia, not of British military prowess or modern equipment. Rather than lament that technology had paralyzed military activity, those involved in the Mesopotamian campaign lamented that military technology was either in too short supply or too sophisticated for their backward theater.[54] The Indian government had failed to provide wire-cutters, water-carts, rockets, mosquito nets, periscopes—the stuff of "war carried on under modern conditions."[55] In France, Candler noted, the wounded were whisked away in "smooth motor ambulance wagons" and provided "every saving device that Science can lend," while in Mesopotamia, "all was chaos." The campaign's mobility was a mark of backwardness, frustrating both efficient medical service as well as "the business of range-finding and registering, so easy in the stationary conditions on the Western front," however fruitless the ability in those conditions.[56] Modern warfare had come to mean the *mobile* supply of an army *immobilized* in a clearly demarcated battlefield. With hindsight, Mesopotamia's early mobility appeared a travesty of modern warfare rather than an escape from it; the country, and consequently the campaign, was simply not developed enough.

The force's successes after Kut strengthened faith in technology as enabling rather than paralyzing. The trench warfare following the siege was the campaign's rite of passage to a modernity no longer diminished by its colonial quality; after the War Office takeover and the Indian government's technological transfers, "bloody, remorseless trench fighting . . . was a thing of the past." Armed with all the paraphernalia of modern warfare, they now waged "war as it should be waged, with the spirit of movement in it, the new scenes a background to the drama of battle."[57] At Ctesiphon, a naval officer mused on the great armies and historic figures that "had passed this way before the coming of men in khaki, with their aeroplanes and wireless."[58] Defying the wisdom from France, that "modern warfare" had rendered long advances impossible without "a certain calculated sacrifice which is generally prohibitive," here the British were modern and yet highly mobile.[59] The ad hoc solutions to the practical problems posed by Mesopotamian topography marked the campaign as uniquely inventive, similarly heralding a warfare of the future: "All the five arms of the Force—the Navy, Cavalry, Infantry, Artillery, and Flying Corps—were working together in a way that was new in war," enthused Candler.[60] The campaign suggested that trench warfare was not the last stop of modern warfare, that stalemate could end, and that war might still be a productive enterprise. If technology's dark side was exposed in France, a new aspect of it was unveiled in Iraq: in the hands of "experts," it could resurrect a military campaign and, at once, a devastated civilization. Thus, during the war, British imaginings about Mesopotamia as a romantic, otherworldly, autarkic land underwrote a positive image of technology at a moment when technology's image was cracking elsewhere. Those imaginings staked out Mesopotamia as the consummate site of modern technological development.

Reclaiming the Cradle of Civilization

And so, India sent iron, steel, and timber for the construction of river embankments, wharves, docks, bridges; also dredgers for canal construction; railroad and electrical plant; telegraphic and telephonic equipment; engines; vehicles; boats; machinery; labor; and experts. Basra became a "a hive of industry."[61] In August 1917, days before his famous declaration that the British government was in favor of responsible government in India, Edwin Montagu described to Parliament how Indian resources "were gradually changing the appearance of the country and eradicating the blight of Turkish misrule."[62]

With the constructive vision of technology erected in the environmental imaginary of a wasteland, the campaign soon claimed redemption of the cradle of civilization as its true calling. The abject failure at Kut had raised the stakes of the campaign. Mesopotamia was represented less as a miserable backwater, a mere "side-show," and more as the place where war could find meaning, less an escape from industrialism than the proving ground for industry and empire. By "reclaim[ing] a wilderness" and "rebuild[ing] a civilization after many years of anarchy and desolation" for "a new country and a new people, "the force determined to give meaning to the sacrifices of British soldiers, explained one officer. Theirs was the blessed task of revitalizing not just any civilization but one of "mysterious and divine" origins. Gertrude Bell, then a powerful force in the British civil administration, confessed feeling "rather like the Creator."[63] In a terrain hallowed by its past and by the sacrifice of British lives, Britons constructed a new imperial identity that could even explain away the, retrospectively charming, missteps that had landed them in such a Great War in the first place. A sailor wrote in 1917:

> We Britons spend our lives in making blunders, and give our lives to retrieve them. But . . . the dawn has come, and with it the confident assurance that in this new burden of Empire—the task of restoring Mesopotamia to her former prosperity—the generations to come will gain inspiration from the long chronicle of heroic deeds which make up the story of her deliverance. The lives of Britain's sons have not been sacrificed in vain.

The British were the bearers of a new "dawn" for Iraqis—and for Britons.[64]

Whereas the Indian government saw the region as an indivisible part of its domain, many in Britain saw it as a fallen frontier of the West; indeed many Arabists, who had long romanticized Arabs as a naturally free and democratic people akin to the "freeborn Englishman," fought bitterly against the Indianization of the nascent colony.[65] Rather than "unchanging," wartime representations stressed that this bit of the East had metamorphosed from a locus of secular power and worldly riches tightly bound to Hellenistic-Christian culture to a "sordid relic." "When European Christendom looks to-day at the desolation of these lands," wrote the historian Edwyn Bevan, "it is looking at a lost piece of itself." Technology promised to precipitously reconnect Mesopotamia with the rest of the world after Kut revealed how dangerous its utopic autarky was. Restoring Mesopotamia's position along the great artery of commercial traffic was a development goal born of military failure. The object of the campaign was nothing less than a "regenerated Babylonia, in which the ancient streams reflect once more mighty structures of men and gardens like Paradise, and in the streets of whose cities traffickers from all the earth once more meet." Man would once again be "master of the great waters," prophesied Bevan, and the wanton destruction wrought by feckless and savage imperial tyrants since the Mongol invasion brought to an end. The British would resurrect an older imperial tradition of *improvement*, the tradition of the Persians, Seleucids, Parthians, Sassanides, and the Saracen caliphs.[66] British personnel dreamt of Mesopotamia's restored position as a supplier of cotton and wheat.⁶⁷ The conviction that they could not possibly worsen such a derelict land made the steady grind of imperial administration especially reassuring.⁶⁸ These were by no means idiosyncratic or private views; in Parliament, Robert Cecil, assistant secretary of state for foreign affairs, earnestly praised the "very satisfactory progress . . . being made . . . in redeeming [Mesopotamia] from the state of ruin into which it had fallen under the Turks."⁶⁹

In short, developing Mesopotamia was hailed as an act of restoration, not transformation, a refitting of the ancient land with modern technology that would enable it to resume its traditional role in a modern world. And so we witness the birth of yet another environmental imaginary, a vision of a restored cradle of civilization. Technologies such as dams, aircraft, and roads would not only produce battlefields from Mesopotamia's disordered landscape but also produce Mesopotamia itself as a geographical and political object. They would both improve the fabulous and terrible country and bring it within the realm of the knowable, within the pale of the economy that development sought to make.

The project of reclaiming Mesopotamia and rejoining it to a prosperous West seemed to some to invest the entire war with meaning. In an essay much circulated among the troops, Bell described how, once again, the ancient markets of Iraq would thrive and would "add immeasurably to the wealth of a universe wasted by war," besides providing new fields for European industry.⁷⁰ "Nowhere, in the war-shattered universe," she held, "can we begin more speedily to make good the immense losses sustained by humanity." Candler too found it "comforting to think that the war which had let loose destruction in Europe was bringing new life to Mesopotamia."⁷¹ And in this global salvation lay the salvation of the British Empire. An officer confided to a fellow combatant,

> All this show of ours out here is . . . a beginning of something that will materialise a hundred or two hundred or a thousand years hence. We are the great irrigating nation and that's why we're here now. . . . We'll fix this land up . . . and move the wheels of a new humanity. Pray God, yes—a new humanity! One that doesn't stuff itself silly with whisky and beef and beer and die of apoplexy and high explosives.⁷²

Mesopotamia proved that the British could still *civilize*, if they had lost civilization itself. General A. G. Wauchope saw in the advance on Baghdad the apotheosis of the British imperial dream:

> Watching these columns of Englishmen and Highlanders, of Hindus, Gurkhas and bearded Sikhs advancing [within sight of the Median Wall], one felt the conviction that this struggle was being fought for the sake of principles more lofty, for ends more permanent, for aims less fugitive, for issues of higher service to the cause of humanity, than those that had animated the innumerable and bloody conflicts of the past.[73]

The cultural resonances of the cradle of civilization and the land of the Bible infused his imperial ideal with even greater moral fire. The fall of Baghdad in 1917 inspired wonder and hope: it was no ordinary city, but, many pointed out, a place "famous for the men and armies that had crossed it."[74] By crossing it, the British too had achieved epoch-making imperial greatness; far from bankrupt, the empire had finally arrived.

To Britons in Mesopotamia, their efforts provided a fitting rebuke to the growing number of anti-imperialists at home and abroad. "British seed" would make the desert "bloom as the rose," an officer announced to those "fluent decriers of their own country" who called empire "a thing of pitiless blood and iron."[75] As in Egypt and Punjab, explained Mark Sykes in an official note, here too the British imperial ideal was "not . . . conquest but . . . redemption."[76] The imaginary of a developed Mesopotamia offered proof of the strangely selfless and attractive nature of British imperialism: "Truly we are a remarkable people," Bell mused. "We save from destruction remnants of oppressed nations, laboriously and expensively giving them sanitary accommodation, teaching their children, respecting their faiths," yet remain cursed by subjects, who, nevertheless, "when left to themselves . . . flock to our standards. . . . It's the sort of thing that happens under the British flag—don't ask us why." British occupation was thus exempt from the sins ordinarily associated with such a regime. Montagu pointedly remarked in Parliament, "It was interesting to compare British occupation in Mesopotamia with German occupation in Belgium. (Hear, hear.)" Surveying "the sound and colour of the reviving world," Bell felt she was "really part of Mesopotamia and not part of an army of occupation."[77] Moreover, the prodigious Indian effort for Mesopotamia proved, according to an exultant parliamentary paper, that even Indians knew Britain ruled them for their good, and not for exploitation.[78]

This mix of heady rhetoric and mundane technocratic activity was typical of a moment in the formation of British imperial identity when, as Robert Colls has put it, "The traditions of an ancient realm were held aloft to signify Englishness to the world, while behind all that it was understood that modern men ran the business."⁷⁹ The return of a king to the Baghdad of Haroun was one thing, "but," one sentimental American noted a decade after the war,

> in the shadows beside the dais stand men in green-brown uniforms—blue-eyed men of a tribe that [earlier] had no standing in Arabia.... Angles they call these men, and they are not like the other conquerors who flowed into Iraq with sword and torch in the days whose record may be read in the ash piles along the Tigris. They are children—fussy children—eternally worried over the removal of rubbish, the "improvement" of roads and bridges that for hundreds of years served our ancestors... the disciplining of the police force and what not.

Efficient as these imperial professionals were, they were not Orwell's famously lamented dull "clerks" of the 1920s, the "well-meaning, over-civilized men, in dark suits," prefiguring his nightmare vision of bureaucracy. The sentimental American concluded, "The flying carpet of the Cairo air-mail has come to rest in the landing field beyond Hinaidi and a sergeant is inspecting its hot motors.... Who can say that romance is dead in a spot such as this...?"⁸⁰ These new joiners were rather "young men of spirit," looking for adventure in the postwar world, inspired by the recuperative vision of technology in the Middle East. So warmly did the light of hope glow in Mesopotamia in the dimly lit postwar world that soldiers at a loose end sought transfer there to find an assuredly constructive role. James Mann, an aspiring political officer (who would be killed in the rebellion later that year), reasoned with his mother, "If one takes the Civil Service, or the Bar, or Literature, or Politics, or even the Labour movement, what can one do that is constructive? Here on the other hand I am constructing the whole time."⁸¹

Thus, British officials, journalists, and politicians claimed a special status for the new colony—it was *the* site for imperial expiation through technocratic development. Of course, there were early enthusiasts of development in other parts of the empire as well, but Iraq's special relevance as a site for articulation of this vision of empire was guaranteed by representations of it as the fallen cradle of civilization where development would hail a new age of miracles. In India, by contrast, signs of wartime modernization were most often viewed as a violation of the colony's romantic aura, betokening social, cultural, and political chaos.⁸² The idea of developing Iraq did not raise the preservationist fears of rapid economic change upsetting indigenous social and political order that otherwise tended to undermine the fulfillment of visionary wartime plans for colonial development.[83] Although in practice development focused on activities, such as the settlement of tribes and provision of transportation, that would make Iraq a supplier of raw materials for industrial Britain rather than an industrial nation in its own right, there even this limited notion of colonial development implied something grander. There, the ability to produce primary goods was not the mark of backwardness but of the country's resurgence as a glorious imperial entrepôt. Proponents of Iraq's development claimed more exalted goals than Joseph Chamberlain had at the turn of the century when as colonial secretary he had unsuccessfully pushed investment of state funds for colonial development.

Certainly, the very existence of British-Indian technical expertise in transforming nature was predicated on past exercises in imperial development, such as the river projects in India and Egypt.[84] Indeed, like Egypt, Mesopotamia was constituted as a geographical and political entity centered on the basic developmental "problem" of an ancient river system ringed by desert and a backward population.[85] But the wartime development of Iraq differed from these antecedents—and from, say, state management of poverty in Britain—in the totality of its ambition, in its positing of an entire proto-nation-state as its object.[86] It was in wartime Mesopotamia that the "technoscience" Timothy Mitchell has described first evolved on a national scale to "improve the defects of nature, to transform peasant agriculture, to repair the ills of society, and to fix the economy."[87]

Much of the early hope was ultimately disappointed after the war. In 1919, Britain demanded that the new League of Nations award them the mandate to rule Iraq as compensation for British sacrifices for the country's development,[88] reconfiguring a war of conquest as an international development effort. (The geographical sleight-of-hand that blurred Mesopotamia into India helped justify [even disguise] this imperial addition as yet another frontier annexation shoring up the territory already held.) The Iraqis, of course, never bought the mandate scheme; to them, it was a flimsy semantic disguise for colonial rule, and from 1920 to 1932 when they finally joined the League as a nominally independent nation, they continually forced the British to rename and reframe their relationship. Meanwhile, many of the developmental projects the British undertook (mainly, after all, to serve the needs of the army) were quickly abandoned, partly because of financial stringency and partly because, after the Iraqi rebellion of 1920, air control more or less hijacked the development discourse—anticolonial rebellion triggering the "rebellion of technology."[89]

Watching the Cradle Rock

The airplane ultimately emerged as the joint focus of developmental and disciplinary discourses about Iraq in this period. Aircraft were ubiquitous in Mesopotamia after Kut. As a new technology with their own otherworldly mystique, they became intimately associated with the Mesopotamian site of exception. As a 1921 cabinet paper put it, "Great as was the development of air power in the war on the western front, it was mainly concerned with aerial action against enemy aircraft and co-operation with other arms. . . . In more distant theatres, however, such as Palestine, Mesopotamia and East Africa the war has proved that the air has capabilities of its own."[90] Why did this most quintessentially modern technology strike British officials as so peculiarly suited to the romantic wasteland of Mesopotamia?

British Arabists were fervent proponents of airpower. To them, it, like the innovative deceptions and irregular warfare it supported, were particularly suited to a Middle Eastern environment. Attracted to Arabia as a medieval utopia, they saw in the airplane a means of restoring chivalry and vitality to modern warfare.[91] Airpower also seemed to offer a means of overcoming the information problems posed by an unmapped desert; a bird's-eye view promised vision beyond the mirages, sandstorms, and horizonlessness that bedeviled two-dimensional observation. Picturing Mesopotamia as a uniformly featureless terrain, a sort of giant aerial field,

Figure 1.1. *Flying Over the Desert at Sunset, Mesopotamia.* 1919. By Sydney W. Carline. The romance of desert flight as envisioned by a popular artist just after World War I. *Reproduced with the permission of the Imperial War Museum, London, UK.*

political officers pined, "Oh for some aeroplanes. If there was a country in the whole world eminently suited to these machines this one is: Flat flat as your hand."[92] Since "in Mesopotamian battles, little can be trusted that is seen," explained General Wauchope, "commanders are bound to rely on reports by aeroplane, messengers, and telephones."[93] Aerial photography reached its highest development in Mesopotamia, as did air signalling.[94]

Underlying this burgeoning new military science was a sense that aircraft were existentially suited to this region. Over the austere terrain of the biblical deserts flight seemed to reach new heights of sublimity and even divinity.[95] British Arabists perceived a basic congruence between the liberty of action of the aircraft and the desert warrior, both operating in empty, unmapped, magical spaces. T. E. Lawrence, who had searched in Bedouin warfare for an alternative to the anonymous mass slaughter of the Western front, prophesied, "What the Arabs did yesterday the Air Forces may do to-morrow. And in the same way—yet more swiftly." Both could move beyond mere concentration of force and replace it with "an intangibly ubiquitous distribution of force—pressing everywhere yet assailable nowhere."[96] He joined the Royal Air Force in 1922, seeing in it the same sort of literary potential as the desert sublime.[97] His views were echoed by other Arabists and in the RAF.[98] "There appears to be a sort of natural fellow-feeling between these nomad Arabs and the Air Force," remarked Robert Brooke-Popham, the RAF's director of research. "Perhaps both feel that they are at times in conflict with the vast elemental forces of nature."[99] The "desert with all its mysterious fascination" had "an unreal atmospheric quality comparable with the sky. Perhaps," pondered a wing-commander, "this is why people call it 'The Blue.'"[100]

Within this discourse about aircraft as a nomad technology ideally suited to rendering a nomad terrain legible lurked an awareness of their uses in controlling that terrain.[101] By annihilating the distances that otherwise kept nomadic tribes beyond the reach of any state's scrutiny, aircraft seemed to possess "enormous political possibilities": When the Mesopotamian tribes the British liberated "[got] out of hand and require[d] a lesson," officials found that "an aerial raid with bombs and machine guns often has an overwhelming and sometimes an instantaneous effect in inducing submission."[102] Such experiments revealed to the Cabinet aircraft's uses in the "attack and dispersal of considerable bodies of ground troops."[103]

Those lessons were put to use immediately after the war in 1919 when aircraft and bombs were employed against unrest all over the Eastern empire. But notions of Iraq's peculiar suitability made it the only colony where airpower became a permanent instrument of imperial administration and policing.[104] The RAF officially took over in October 1922, although it had become the dominant military force from the rebellion. It commanded eight squadrons of fighters and light bombers, four armored-car units, and several thousand Iraq Levies. Army garrisons were gradually reduced to protect only the nine RAF bases equipped with wireless telegraphy. The short range of most available aircraft made advanced landing grounds and emergency fuel and bomb dumps crucial to the system. The RAF patrolled the country from a network of bases, bombarding villages and tribes as needed to put down unrest and subversive activities. Air action was used against Turkish and Najdi raiders into Iraq (at a time when frontiers were a work in progress) as well as Kurdish and Arab rebellions within Iraq proper.[105] It was in Iraq that the British first practiced, if never perfected, the technology of bombardment; there that they first attempted to fully theorize the value of airpower as an independent arm of the military. Reasons of cost and topography mattered, of course, but it was cultural imaginings about the place of airpower in the cradle of civilization that made Iraq, rather than any other place, the first site of "air control."[106]

British Arabists, unsurprisingly, were enthusiastic supporters of the scheme. Lawrence dated his conviction that "aircraft could rule the desert" to the war.[107] He, Arnold Wilson (the civil commissioner in Iraq), and other Arabist officials were important influences on Winston Churchill, postwar secretary of war and air. In 1921, as colonial secretary, Churchill inducted Lawrence and his colleagues from the Middle Eastern wars, Reader Bullard, Hubert Young, and Richard Meinertzhagen, into a new Middle East Department, where they deemed Mesopotamia peculiarly suitable for air operations, better than Europe, for aesthetic as much as topographical reasons—the power of the environmental imaginary: Mesopotamia's presumed flatness promised many landing grounds, little cover to insurgents, and the possibility of "radiating" British power throughout the country from a handful of fittingly spartan bases, while the reality of its varied and protean topography, when acknowledged, was held to offer ideal training for the RAF, exposing it to every sort of terrain—mountains in Kurdistan, marshes in the south, riverain territory in between, and so forth. Air action was deemed *in*appropriate for police action in the densely populated urban environments of Britain, Ireland, and even Palestine.[108] Lawrence insisted, "The system is *not* capable of universal application."[109]

But the imaginary was, after all, imaginary: Despite the promise of omniscience, the regime was plagued by reports of pilot disorientation, visibility problems, and instances "of quite inexplicable failures to identify such objects as columns of Armoured cars . . . and even whole sections of bedouin tribes on the move."[110] Aircraft often bombed the wrong targets.[111] Insurgents found cover in watercourses, hillocks, and other features of the allegedly "featureless" landscape.[112] Even assessing the effect of bombing operations was "largely a matter of guesswork."[113]

However, in an infamously deceptive land, all this inaccuracy, indeed information itself, was deemed of little consequence: Arnold Wilson explained that complaints about RAF observation failures were necessarily exaggerated, as was all information in the country, not least because the mirage prevented anyone from judging the accuracy of a pilot on high. Second, in the end, the accuracy issue was moot, since aircraft were meant to be everywhere at once, "conveying a silent warning." This *"moral effect"* of patrolling aircraft "which can drop Bombs whenever necessary would effectually check disturbances."[114] Even destruction of "property" did not matter as it might in an advanced civilization, given the austerity of tribal existence, a condition imagined to extend to all Iraqis.[115] Richard Meinertzhagen, wartime intelligence chief now at the Colonial Office, assured his colleagues in Iraq, "Bombs dropped on men in the open seldom have much effect beyond fright," and advised dropping the matter of results as aerial observation of casualties was "always misleading."[116]

Moreover, the experts assured, desert inhabitants in a biblical land expected harsh existence; they could tolerate random acts of violence in a way that others could not.[117] In 1932, at the disarmament conference in Geneva, the British High Commissioner in Iraq assured his colleagues that unlike the outrages inevitably committed by ground troops, "bombing from the air is regarded almost as an act of God."[118] Lawrence likewise strove to explain the "impersonally fateful" nature of air bombing from an Arab's point of view: "It is not punishment, but a misfortune from heaven striking the community."[119] The perception of environmental excesses that had inspired an effort to join this biblical land to the modern world in the name of civilization simultaneously underwrote the notion that it could tolerate a level of brutality no other place could, also in the name of civilization.

This cavalier attitude rendered casualties entirely, well, casual: "If the Civil Commissioner is going on to Mosul," read a General Headquarters telegram to Wilson, "will he be so kind as to drop a bomb on Batas"—the sort of kindness he apparently never objected to.[120] So, despite innumerable reported errors, the air control experiment was pronounced entirely successful in "this kind of turbulent country."[121] From Iraq, air control spread to Palestine, Transjordan, and elsewhere, albeit in modified version.[122] In its Iraqi cocoon, the RAF was safe from criticism of its accuracy, protected by the British imaginary of a place so otherworldly it was beyond empirical verification. Current historiography has remained captive to this imaginary, claiming air control actually *worked* in desert regions as opposed to India, East Africa, and so on, because deserts have "clearly defined, completely visible targets and little possibility of cover."[123]

The misperception proved horrifically costly in Iraqi lives. "Recalcitrant" tribes, which included not only those attacking British communications and personnel but also those refusing to pay taxes, were bombed into submission. Entire villages were bombed for "general recalcitrance" (refusal to submit to government), harboring wanted rebel leaders, and evading the high rates of British taxation.[124] In Iraq, the RAF found validation as a service and experience that it applied more notoriously in World War II. In short, the environmental imaginary of land so barren that bombardment could not possibly worsen it was crucial to the history of bombardment as a military strategy. The vindication of air control grew out of racism but also long-circulating imaginings of a land miraculously exempt from the this-worldliness that constrained human activity in other parts of the world. Arabia's legendary otherworldliness made it fit to bear the unearthly destruction wreaked by bombers. The environmental imaginary of Iraq was the foundation of Britons' understanding of the moral world of Arabia as radically distinct from their own. The "most extraordinary and romantic" world of the RAF in Iraq compounded the sense of being in a place apart, only tenuously linked to "civilisation." The regime's miraculous wireless infrastructure and rumors of Lawrence's presence only fed the Arabian mystique.[125] Thus, Arabia offered the air staff a means of selling the new warfare to the public by exhibiting it in a fabulous land, a world apart, where the destruction wrought by bombardment was submerged in the desert sublime.[126] British officials may have found Arabia extraterrestrial, but it was their technological innovations that ultimately produced the surreal world of random bombardment in which Iraqis were condemned to live, literally removing Iraq beyond the reach of secular and humanitarian law.

Crucially, this policing regime was understood in the same developmental vein as the wartime infrastructure projects. Air control, its defenders argued, facilitated greater understanding between administrators and Iraqis by enabling British personnel to roam without fear (and, incidentally, gather the intelligence that would guide future bombardments).[127] Moreover, airpower's supreme role in the country had made Baghdad the "Clapham Junction of the air," at last fulfilling that noble dream of remaking an ancient cosmopolitan crossroads.[128] Far from disruptive, aircraft were a fitting gesture to the agelessness of the Orient, enthused the *Times*, recalling the sorcerers who, once upon a time, had made Sindbad the Sailor turn airman on the back of a great bird. Motorcars too were like "snorting land monsters which rush across the deserts." "Naturally, the inhabitants take these things as a matter of course," assured the paper, for "the age of miracles has happily returned, and we may see strange Arabian nights in the coming years."[129] Clio would return as Baghdad's lingering aura of mystery was "violated by the whirring wheels . . . of trains, of cars, of aeroplanes."[130] Aircraft also exercised a more traditional civilizing effect by demonstrating the advanced state of British civilization. The famous furrow ploughed across the desert to guide pilots to Baghdad was lauded as a feat of British ingenuity. The "romance" of desert flight derived from the "demonstration of the power of modern inventions which are able to conquer vast open spaces of the world, as yet little known to civilised man"—technology remained the handmaiden of progress.[131] The air afforded a lofty view from which to observe the effects of the new loftier imperialism, to witness, in the words of the *Illustrated London News*, "adoring Asia kindle and hugely bloom."[132] (It also fittingly revealed the otherwise invisible traces left by their ancient imperial forebears.) Aerial surveillance and disciplining fit neatly into this vision of liberal empire in the sky. Flying over the desert, Hubert Young of the Foreign Office, "felt that a new era had dawned, and that with the goodwill of His Majesty's Government and the powerful help of the Royal Air Force the Arabs of Iraq would undoubtedly win their independence at last."[133]

If these arguments did not convince, others claimed a dose of repression would pave the way to gentler improvements. A wing commander argued irresistibly, "The cheaper the form of control the more money for roads and development and the sooner it will be no longer necessary to use armed forces to do with explosives what should be done by policemen and sticks."[134] Although some, like George Buchanan, wartime head of river conservation, considered the abandonment of wartime projects "a tragedy of heroism, suffering, wasted lives, and wasted effort,"[135] others saw in air control the salvation of the wartime hopes for a global payoff from the Mesopotamian adventure. The development of the geographical center of the world's most ancient and most modern traffic routes would "safeguard humanity from famines, wars, and social revolution," insisted postwar stalwarts.[136] The press and politicians continued to urge development of Iraqi resources on the premise that "a country once so rich may surely be made rich again by modern methods," stubbornly anticipating "some recompense for the great sacrifices we made in the Great War."[137]

Thus, the Middle East, "the Land of the RAF," became as essential to British preeminence in airpower as airpower was to Britain's ability to control the Middle East. After the so-called independence of Iraq in 1932, the RAF kept key elements of Iraqi defense—aircraft, wireless, armored cars, intelligence sources—out of the hands of the nascent Iraqi army.[138] For them, Iraq's independence was decidedly "more apparent than real."[139] Squadrons were reduced gradually, but the country was reoccupied during the Second World War, and the RAF departed only in 1958.

IN BRITAIN, the early-twentieth-century imaginary of Mesopotamia inspired an understanding of colonialism as a vehicle for technocratic developmentalism. But encompassed within that concept were modern tactics of violent surveillance. Benjamin might have diagnosed a rebellion of technology, but this story suggests development and policing are two sides of the same technocratic coin, the joint ends of the modern welfare/warfare state, sharing common military-industrial roots. Frantz Fanon noted this more sinister face of development long ago: "Raftways across the bush, the draining of swamps and a native population which is non-existent politically and economically are in fact one and the same thing."[140] This is not, of course, to suggest that development offers no desirable end but to highlight its more sinister political uses in the hands, particularly, of autocratic states and global institutions. Environmental imaginaries have been critical to the creation of what Edmund Burke called "geographical morality," the notion that the peculiarities of place license departure from universalist principles of law and humanity for exceptional technologies and rules. The environmental imaginary is what has made Iraq an apparently permanent state of exception in official minds.

In the British episode lie the roots of the Iraqi state's long fetishizing of technological solutions to political and social problems, including Saddam Hussein's simultaneously developmentalist and punitive obsessions with draining the southern marshes. Restoration of those wetlands has remained a low priority for the post-2003 occupying governments of Iraq, who, like the British earlier, have diverted technocratic expertise to a truly Orwellian pacification effort, unleashing an environmental emergency with dire consequences for human and wildlife in the region. There is, on the one hand, the detritus of war—unexploded mines and shells, many laced with carcinogenic radioactive chemicals—and, on the other, the sewage, oil, and other hazardous waste released into the air, soil, and water by bombed-out infrastructure and industrial plants. Hanging over the whole disaster is a desperate lack of water.[141]

As Timothy Mitchell has noted, the supposed abject aridity, mineral wealth, and lack of natural national cohesion of the entire region of the Middle East pose the canonical developmental problem.[142] Certainly, our environmental imaginary of Iraq in particular has evolved. We have, for instance, broken the old habit of blurring it into India—although President Bush nearly resurrected it with his certainty that Afghanistan's Al Qaeda was in Iraq—and oil figures more prominently than grain in images of Iraq's share of global wealth. But the image of an autarkic, hermetic desert that forbids modern ideas and goods continues to tempt those dreaming of a regenerated Babylonia, and the years of sanctions and occupation in pursuit of that imperial folly have helped make the image of autarky something of a reality. With drones overhead, Iraq is once again the site of a first in the history of aerial technology. Like the British army decades ago, today's American occupiers speak a development language that constitutes itself as a neutral form of knowledge standing apart from its object, Iraq, despite their own role in producing its current devastation.

Notes

1. British experts stressed the impossibility of ever defining the borders of "Arabia" precisely but used the term generally to refer to the desert and Arab-speaking areas of the Ottoman Empire.

2. Walter Benjamin, "The Work of Art in the Age of Mechanical Reproduction" (1937), repr. in *Illuminations,* ed. Hannah Arendt, trans. Harry Zohn (New York: Schocken Books, 1968), 242.

3. See David Edgerton, *Warfare State: 1920–1970* (Cambridge: Cambridge University Press, 2006), 284, 312, 317.

4. George Orwell, "Politics and the English Language," 1946, http://www.george-orwell.org/Politics_and_the_English_Language/0.html (accessed 15 September 2010).

5. By "development," I mean a statist effort to use public investment for the avowed purpose of raising a colony into a modern nation-state (as opposed to the more general Victorian notion of empire as a means of upliftment).

6. See Frederick Cooper, "Modernizing Bureaucrats, Backward Africans, and the Development Concept," in *International Development and the Social Sciences: Essays on the History and Politics of Knowledge,* edited by Frederick Cooper and Randall Packard (Berkeley: University of California Press, 1997), 70; Frederick Cooper and Randall Packard, Introduction to *International Development and the Social Sciences,* 7; Stephen Constantine, *The Making of British Colonial Development Policy, 1914–1940* (London: F. Cass, 1984), 303–4; Paul B. Rich, *Race and Empire in British Politics* (Cambridge: Cambridge University Press, 1986), 145; Timothy Mitchell, *Rule of Experts: Egypt, Techno-Politics, Modernity* (Berkeley: University of California Press, 2002), 82–83.

7. See for instance Francis R. Maunsell, "The Hejaz Railway," *Geographical Journal* 32, no. 6 (1908): 570. For more on this and later citations in this paragraph, see my book, *Spies in Arabia: The Great War and the Cultural Foundations of Britain's Covert Empire in the Middle East* (New York: Oxford University Press, 2008), chaps. 2, 3.

8. Douglas Carruthers, *Arabian Adventure: To the Great Nafud in Quest of the Oryx* (London: H. F. and G. Witherby, 1935), 68.

9. Alex Owen, *The Place of Enchantment: British Occultism and the Culture of the Modern* (Chicago: University of Chicago Press, 2004), esp. 159.

10. David G. Hogarth, "Problems in Exploration I. Western Asia," *Geographical Journal* 32, no. 6 (1908): 549–50.

11. See, for instance, John G. Lorimer, ed., *Gazetteer of the Persian Gulf, Oman, and Central Arabia*, vol. 2, *Geographical and Statistical* (Calcutta: Government Press, 1908), 199, 759n, 767, IOR: L/PS/20/C91/4, British Library (BL); Gertrude Bell, *Amurath to Amurath* (New York: Dutton, 1911), 167, 201; Mark Sykes, *The Caliph's Last Heritage* (London: Macmillan, 1915), 436; Carruthers, *Arabian Adventure*, 120.

12. David Hogarth, comment on lecture by Capt. S. S. Butler, "Baghdad to Damascus via El Jauf, Northern Arabia," 22 February 1909, *Geographical Journal* 33, no. 5 (1909): 533.

13. Meredith Townsend, *Asia and Europe: Studies Presenting the Conclusions Formed by the Author in a Long Life Devoted to the Subject of the Relations between Asia and Europe*, 2nd ed. (New York: G. P. Putnam's, 1904), 161.

14. Peter Brent, *Far Arabia: Explorers of the Myth* (London: Weidenfeld and Nicolson, 1977), 145.

15. G. Wyman Bury [Abdullah Mansur, pseud.], *The Land of Uz* (London: Macmillan, 1911), xxi. The Romantics had also looked to Eastern philosophy and culture for alternatives to Occidental materialism, but Edwardians were more interested in escape than imitation and combined escape with intelligence work. Nor did they recoil from the "real" Orient as the Romantics had. See, for instance, David Fraser, *The Short Cut to India: The Record of a Journey along the Route of the Baghdad Railway* (Edinburgh: W. Blackwood, 1909), 234. On the Romantics, see Edward Said, *Orientalism* (1978; New York: Vintage, 1979), 100–115.

16. Carruthers, *Arabian Adventure*, 42.

17. Bell, 1928, quoted in *Gertrude Bell: The Arabian Diaries, 1913–1914*, ed. Rosemary O'Brien (Syracuse, N.Y.: Syracuse University Press, 2000), 9–10.

18. Louisa Jebb, *By Desert Ways to Baghdad* (Boston: Dana, Estes, 1909), 264–65. Emphasis added.

19. See, for instance, Bell, *Amurath to Amurath*, 193. On Edwardian anxieties about science, see Samuel Hynes, *The Edwardian Turn of Mind* (Princeton: Princeton University Press, 1968), 134–38; Stephen Kern, *The Culture of Time and Space: 1880–1918* (Cambridge, Mass.: Harvard University Press, 1983), 38; Owen, *Place of Enchantment*.

20. See, for instance, Sykes, *Caliph's Last Heritage*, 57. See also Satia, *Spies in Arabia*, chaps. 2, 3.

21. Mark Sykes, *Dar-ul-Islam: A Record of a Journey through Ten of the Asiatic Provinces of Turkey* (London: Bickers and Son, 1904), 12n.

22. Townsend, *Asia and Europe*, 307.

23. See John S. Galbraith, "No Man's Child: The Campaign in Mesopotamia, 1914–1916," *International History Review* 6, no. 3 (1984): 358–85; Stuart A. Cohen, "The Genesis of the British Campaign in Mesopotamia, 1914," *Middle Eastern Studies* 12, no. 2 (1976): 119–32; Paul K. Davis, *Ends and Means: The British Mesopotamian Campaign and Commission* (London: Associated University Presses, 1994); Briton Cooper Busch, *Britain, India, and the Arabs, 1914–1921* (Berkeley: University of California Press, 1977), chap. 1.

24. Lieutenant Colonel L. A. Lynden-Bell, interview with Peter Liddle, TS, October 1977, GS 0993 (Lynden-Bell Papers), Liddle Collection, Leeds University Library, Leeds (hereafter Liddle). For further discussion, see Satia, *Spies in Arabia*, chap. 5.

25. Richard Popplewell, "British Intelligence in Mesopotamia: 1914–1916," *Intelligence and National Security* 5, no. 2 (1990): 139.

26. Davis, *Ends and Means*.

27. J. T. Parfit, *Serbia to Kût: An Account of the War in the Bible Lands* (London: Hunter and Longhurst, 1917), 45.

28. On this, see my "Developing Iraq: Britain, India and the Redemption of Empire and Technology in the First World War," *Past and Present* 197, no. 1 (2007): 244–45.

29. Edmund Candler, *The Long Road to Baghdad*, 2 vols. (New York: Houghton Mifflin, 1919), 1:34.

30. Beauchamp Duff, quoted in *Mesopotamia Commission Report (MCR)*, Parliamentary Papers, 1917–18 (Cd. 8610), xvi, 37; *MCR*, 13, 105.

31. See Satia, *Spies in Arabia*, chap. 1.

32. Quoted in V. H. Rothwell, "Mesopotamia in British War Aims, 1914–1918," *Historical Journal* 13, no. 2 (1970): 277.

33. Sugata Bose, *A Hundred Horizons: The Indian Ocean in the Age of Global Empire* (Cambridge, Mass.: Harvard University Press, 2006); Juan Cole, *Roots of North Indian Shī'ism in Iran and Iraq: Religion and State in Awadh, 1722–1859* (Berkeley: University of California Press, 1988); Meir Litvak, "Money, Religion, and Politics: The Oudh Bequest in Najaf and Karbala, 1850–1903," *International Journal of Middle Eastern Studies* 32, no. 1 (2001): 1–21 and "A Failed Manipulation: The British, the Oudh Bequest and the Shi'i Ulamaof Najaf and Karbala," *British Journal of Middle Eastern Studies* 27, no. 1 (2000): 69–89.

34. See Satia, "Developing Iraq," 246–47. This article explains how the geographical imaginary played into a real expectation that Iraq would be ruled from India and describes the impact of the Indian administrative heritage.

35. Arthur Tillotson Clark, *To Bagdad with the British* (New York: D. Appleton, 1918), 2, 47–49.

36. See, for instance, Martin Swayne, *In Mesopotamia* (London: Hodder and Stoughton, 1917), 102; Wilfrid Nunn, *Tigris Gunboats: A Narrative of the Royal Navy's Co-operation with the Military Forces in Mesopotamia from the Beginning of the War to the Capture of Baghdad (1914–17)* (London: A. Melrose, 1932), 153.

37. See, for instance, F. S. G. Barnett to his mother, 10 March 1917, GS 0089 (Barnett Papers), file 2, Liddle; Army YMCA of India, "The Land of Two Rivers," found in various editions among the papers of many soldiers in Mesopotamia in the Liddle archive (30,000 copies had been printed in the first edition alone).

38. Candler, *Long Road*, 2:198.

39. Edward Kinch, autobiographical notes covering early life in England and career in Iraq, 1896–1959, MS, n.d., 27, Kinch Papers, file 1/2, Middle East Centre Archive, St Antony's College, Oxford (hereafter MEC). For the countless other examples, see Satia, "Developing Iraq," 218n23.

40. Eleanor Franklin Egan, *The War in the Cradle of the World: Mesopotamia* (New York: Harper, 1918), 76.

41. Candler, *Long Road*, 1:33, 176.

42. Swayne, *In Mesopotamia*, 17, 51.

43. Candler, *Long Road*, 1:47, 111–20. For other examples, see Satia, "Developing Iraq," 220n30.

44. Wilkinson D. Bird, *A Chapter of Misfortunes: The Battles of Ctesiphon and of the Dujailah in Mesopotamia, with a Summary of the Events Which Preceded Them* (London: Forster Groom, 1923), 58.

45. See, among numerous examples, Eric V. R. Bellers to his mother, 14 August 1917, MES 007 (Bellers Papers), Liddle.

46. See Satia, *Spies in Arabia*, chap. 3.

47. Nunn, *Tigris Gunboats*, 10.

48. Candler, *Long Road*, 1:164.

49. Ibid., 1:72; Edmund Candler, "A Truce in the Desert," *Times*, 22 March 1916, 7.

50. See Paul Fussell, *The Great War and Modern Memory* (London: Oxford University Press, 1975); Eric J. Leed, *No Man's Land: Combat and Identity in World War I* (Cambridge: Cambridge University Press, 1979).

51. Lake, quoted in *MCR*, 47, 53. See also Davis, *Ends and Means*, 189–94; *MCR*, 52–54.

52. Vincent-Bingley Report, *MCR*, Appendix 1, 145; Charles Munro, qtd. in George Buchanan, *The Tragedy of Mesopotamia* (London: W. Blackwood, 1938), 129.

53. Buchanan, *Tragedy of Mesopotamia*, 45; "The Physical and Climatic Difficulties of the Mesopotamian Theatre of War," 14 August 1916, Leith-Ross Papers, National Army Museum; *MCR*, 9.

54. On the view on the Western front that technology was paralyzing, see Leed, *No Man's Land*, 122–23.

55. *MCR*, 37–38.

56. Candler, *Long Road*, 1:47, 56.

57. Ibid., 2:223–24.

58. Nunn, *Tigris Gunboats*, 168.

59. Candler, *Long Road*, 1:51, 132.

60. Ibid., 2:80.

61. Geoffrey Collins, second in command at Basra, October 1917, quoted in Davis, *Ends and Means*, 230.

62. Montagu, House of Commons debate, 6 August 1918, reported in *Times*, 7 August 1918, 8.

63. Henry Birch Reynardson, *Mesopotamia, 1914–15: Extracts from a Regimental Officer's Diary* (London: Andrew Melrose, 1919), 272; Bell to her family, 5 December 1918, quoted in Elizabeth Burgoyne, *Gertrude Bell: From Her Personal Papers*, 2 vols. (London: E. Benn, 1958–61), 2:101.

64. Conrad Cato, *The Navy in Mesopotamia: 1914 to 1917* (London: Constable, 1917), 106, 117.

65. See Satia, *Spies in Arabia*, chap. 2.

66. Edwyn Bevan, *The Land of the Two Rivers* (London: E. Arnold, 1918), 10–11, 112, 124–26. For further examples, see Satia, "Developing Iraq," 226n51.

67. See, for instance, Reynardson, *Mesopotamia*, 50.

68. [Gertrude Bell], *The Arab of Mesopotamia* (Basra: Government Press, 1917), 117; Candler, *Long Road*, 2:185, 188.

69. Robert Cecil, House of Commons debate, 23 July 1918, quoted in Arnold T. Wilson, *Mesopotamia, 1917–1920: A Clash of Loyalties* (London: Oxford University Press, 1931), 99.

70. [Gertrude Bell], "Turkish Provinces: The Anatolian Coast," in *Arab of Mesopotamia*, 201–2.

71. Bell to Florence Bell, 15 November 1917, in *The Letters of Gertrude Bell*, ed. Lady Bell, 2 vols. (London: E. Benn, 1927), ii, 431–32; Candler, *Long Road*, 2:183. See also "A New Mesopotamia," *Guardian*, 13 December 1919, 2; Clark, *To Bagdad with the British*, 244.

72. Quoted in Swayne, *In Mesopotamia*, 166.

73. Candler, *Long Road*, 2:i, 176; A. G. Wauchope, "The Battle That Won Samarrah," chap. 8 of *With a Highland Regiment in Mesopotamia, 1916–1917, by One of Its Officers* (Bombay: Times Press, 1918), 85.

74. Clark, *To Bagdad with the British*, 239.

75. Reynardson, *Mesopotamia*, 172.

76. "Political Note on our Advance in Irak," 17 September 1917, Sykes Papers, box 2, file 7, document 78, MEC.

77. Bell to Hugh Bell, 10 November 1922, in *Letters of Gertrude Bell*, 2:657; Montagu, speech in House of Commons debate on Indian reform, 6 August

1918, reported in *Times*, 7 August 1918, 8; Bell to Hugh and Florence Bell, 31 January 1918, in *Letters of Gertrude Bell*, 2:441–44.

78. *East India (Military)*, P.P., 1914–16 (Cd. 7624), 49:15.

79. Robert Colls, "The Constitution of the English," *History Workshop Journal* 46 (1998): 105.

80. Robert J. Casey, *Baghdad and Points East* (London: Hutchinson, 1928), vii–viii; George Orwell, "The Lion and the Unicorn: Socialism and the English Genius" (1941), pt. 1, http://www.k-1.com/Orwell/index.cgi/work/essays/lionunicorn.html; Casey, *Baghdad and Points*, 98.

81. Mann to his mother, 25 January 1920, in *An Administrator in the Making: James Saumarez Mann, 1893–1920*, ed. by his father [James Saumarez Mann Sr.] (London: Vintage, 1921), 206. See also John Glubb, *The Story of the Arab Legion* (London: Hodder and Stoughton, 1948), 19.

82. Meeta Sinha, "'Where Electricity Dispels the Illusion [of the *Arabian Nights*]': The British and the Modern in Interwar India," paper presented at the Pacific Coast Conference of British Studies, Irvine, 2006.

83. See Constantine, *Making of British Colonial Development Policy*, 2, 11, 16–25, 31, 47, 52, 54, 56, 287, 294, 299; Cooper, "Modernizing Bureaucrats," 65, 67, 70.

84. On the imperial reach of Indian engineering, see David Gilmartin, "Imperial Rivers: Irrigation and British Visions of Empire," in *Decentring Empire: Britain, India and the Transcolonial World*, ed. Durba Ghosh and Dane Kennedy (New Delhi: Orient Longman, 2006), 76–103.

85. Mitchell, *Rule of Experts*, 210.

86. On the nineteenth-century roots of development, see Michael Cowen and Robert Shenton, "The Invention of Development," in *Power of Development*, ed. Jonathan Crush (London: Routledge, 1995), 29, and Michael Watts, "'A New Deal in Emotions': Theory and Practice and the Crisis of Development," in *Power of Development*, ed. Jonathan Crush (London: Routledge, 1995), 48, 51. On the centrality of colonialism to development, see Mitchell, *Rule of Experts*, esp. 4–6, 82–83; Christopher Hamlin, *Public Health and Social Justice in the Age of Chadwick: Britain, 1800–1854* (Cambridge: Cambridge University Press, 1998), 264–66.

87. Mitchell, *Rule of Experts*, 15.

88. See Busch, *Britain, India, and the Arabs*, 158, 190, 275.

89. For a contemporary account of the rebellion, see Aylmer Haldane, *The Insurrection in Mesopotamia* (London: W. Blackwood, 1922). This fairly large conventional war lasted several months and involved much of the country, including Kurdistan. Roughly a thousand British and Indian troops were killed, and another thousand were wounded. Roughly ten thousand Iraqis were killed.

90. Air Staff, "On the Power of the Air Force and the Application of that Power to Hold and Police Mesopotamia," March 1920, AIR 1/426/15/260/3, The National Archives (TNA).

91. For further details on this point and others in this section, see Satia, *Spies in Arabia*, chaps. 4, 5, 7.

92. Dickson to Gwenlian Greene, 7 February 1915, 1st booklet, Papers of Harold R. P. Dickson, MEC.

93. *With a Highland Regiment in Mesopotamia,* 70–71 (in chap. 7, whose author is identified as Andrew G. Wauchope) (repr. from *Blackwood's Magazine,* 1917).

94. Satia, *Spies in Arabia,* chap. 4.

95. See, for instance, Young to Shuckburgh, 23 October 1921, CO 730/16, TNA.

96. Quoted in Basil Henry Liddell Hart, *T. E. Lawrence: In Arabia and After* (London: Jonathan Cape, 1934), 438.

97. See, for instance, Lawrence to Trenchard, 5 January 1922, quoted in Philip Knightley and Colin Simpson, *The Secret Lives of Lawrence of Arabia* (London: Nelson, 1969), 166.

98. See for instance Philby, chap. 7, in *Mesopotage,* MS, [1930s], Papers of H. St. John B. Philby, MEC; Bell, quoted in John Laffin, *Swifter Than Eagles: The Biography of Marshal of the Royal Air Force Sir John Maitland Salmond* (Edinburgh: W. Blackwood, 1964), 176.

99. Robert Brooke-Popham, "Aeroplanes in Tropical Countries," lecture, in proceedings of meeting of the Royal Aeronautical Society on 6 October 1921, *Aeronautical Journal* 25 (1 March 1922), Brooke-Popham Papers, Liddell Hart Center for Military Archives, King's College, London (LHCMA). He reiterated this thought after serving as air officer commanding Iraq from 1928 to 1930 and as high commissioner and commander-in-chief in 1929. See notes for a lecture at Downside on 7 February 1932, Brooke-Popham Papers, file 2/3. LHCMA.

100. Wing-Commander R. M. Hill, lecture at Royal Aeronautical Society, quoted in *The Royal Air Force,* by F. V. Monk and H. T. Winter (London: Blackie and Son, 1938), 47.

101. On state projects to render "nomad" terrain legible, see also Mitchell, *Rule of Experts,* 78, 230; James C. Scott, *Seeing Like a State: How Certain Schemes to Improve the Human Condition Have Failed* (New Haven, Conn.: Yale University Press, 1998); Jonathan Crush, Introduction to *Power of Development,* ed. Jonathan Crush (London: Routledge, 1995), 2, 15.

102. Salmond, RFC, HQ, Egypt, to CGS, GHQ EEF, 12 November 1916, WO 158/626, PRO; Capt. William Leith-Ross, "The Tactical Side of I(a)," n.d., 8–9, ARC 1983-12-69-10, Leith-Ross Papers, National Army Museum, London.

103. Air Staff, "On the Power of the Air Force," AIR 1/426/15/260/3, PRO.

104. On uses of airpower in 1919, see David Omissi, *Air Power and Colonial Control: The Royal Air Force, 1919–1939* (Manchester: Manchester University Press, 1990), 11; Sven Lindqvist, *A History of Bombing,* trans. Linda Haverty Rugg (2000; trans., New York: W. W. Norton, 2001), 42–43.

105. In a single two-day operation, a squadron might drop several dozen tons of bombs and thousands of incendiaries and fire thousands of rounds of

small arms ammunition. The last British battalion left in 1927; the last Indian, in 1928. Also see Jafna Cox, "A Splendid Training Ground: The Importance to the Royal Air Force of Its Role in Iraq, 1919–32," *Journal of Imperial and Commonwealth History* 13, no. 2 (1985): 157–84.

106. On other arguments for air control, see Satia, *Spies in Arabia*, 10, 240. For more detail on points made throughout this section, see *Spies in Arabia*, chap. 7.

107. Lawrence to Herbert Baker, quoted in John Mack, *A Prince of Our Disorder: The Life of T. E. Lawrence* (Boston: Little, Brown, 1976), 320; Lawrence to Liddell Hart, 1933, in *The Letters of T. E. Lawrence*, ed. David Garnett (London: Jonathan Cape, 1938), 323. See also C. S. Jarvis, *Arab Command: The Biography of Lieutenant-Colonel F. G. Peake Pasha* (London: Hutchinson, 1946), 83.

108. See, for instance, memorandum on the scheme for the employment of the forces of the crown in Mesopotamia, n.d., AIR 20/526, TNA; CAS, Scheme for the Control of Mesopotamia by the Royal Air Force, 12 March[?] 1921, AIR 5/476, TNA; Wilson, *Mesopotamia, 1917–1920*, 238–39; Air Staff, "On the Power of the Air Force," AIR 1/426/15/260/3, TNA; "Notes on the Value of the Air Route between Cairo and Baghdad for Strategic and Other Purposes," n.d., AIR 9/14, TNA; Churchill, memo, May 1, 1920, quoted in Martin Gilbert, *Winston S. Churchill*, vol. 4: *1916–1922, The Stricken World* (Boston: Heinemann, 1975), 481; Winston Churchill, "Policy and Finance in Mesopotamia, 1922–23," 4 August 1921, in *Winston S. Churchill, Companion, Part 3: Documents April 1921–November 1922*, ed. Martin Gilbert (London: Heinemann, 1977), 1576–81.

109. Lawrence to Liddell Hart, 1933, in *Letters of T. E. Lawrence*, 323.

110. Major General T. Fraser to WO, 3 August 1922, AIR 5/202, TNA. See also John Glubb, *The Changing Scenes of Life: An Autobiography* (London: Quartet, 1983), 60; John Glubb, *Arabian Adventures: Ten Years of Joyful Service* (London: Cassell, 1978), 135; Report regarding the value of aeroplanes as main weapon of an Administration in the maintenance of law and order . . . , n.d., AIR 23/800, TNA; SSO Basrah, Memo on operations against outlaws of Albu Khalifah, to GHQ, 19 July 1921, CO 730/4, TNA.

111. See, for instance, 18th Division, Intelligence report, 15 June 1921, AIR 1/432/15/260/23 (A-B), TNA.

112. See, for instance, A. Haldane, report to WO, 25 November 1920, Cabinet Paper, February 1921, AIR 5/1253, TNA, and Air Staff comments parallel to Haldane's report, January 1921.

113. E. A. S., minute, 30 March 1922, on a phone conversation with Wilson, CO 730/20, TNA.

114. Arnold T. Wilson, note on use of Air Force in Mesopotamia, February 26, 1921, AIR 5/476, TNA; Office of no. 30 Squadron, Baghdad, Report on RAF operations in South Persia, to GOC, 8 April 1919, AIR 20/521, TNA.

115. See Air Vice-Marshal Arthur Gould Lee, *Fly Past: Highlights from a Flyer's Life* (London: Jarrolds, 1974), 53; Laffin, *Swifter Than Eagles*, 181.

116. Meinertzhagen, minute, 29 March 1922, on Cox to S/S CO, 25 March 1922, CO 730/20, TNA.

117. See, for instance, Glubb, note on the Southern Desert Force, [c. 1930s], Glubb Papers, box I, file: Iraq S. Desert (1), 1927–1928, MEC.

118. F. H. Humphreys to Sir John Simon, 15 December 1932, AIR 8/94, TNA.

119. [Lawrence, June 1930], quoted in Basil Henry Liddell Hart, *The British Way in Warfare* (New York: Macmillan, 1933), 159.

120. Reported in Bell to her father, December 12, 1920, quoted in Burgoyne, *Gertrude Bell*, 2:190.

121. Salmond, Air Ministry, Iraq Command Report for Oct.October 1922—Apr.April 1924, Nov.November 1924, AIR 5/1253, TNA.

122. See Churchill to Shuckburgh, 11 January 1922, in *Churchill*, 4/3:1723; Omissi, *Air Power*, 28–29, 39–59, 44–45; Charles Townshend, *Britain's Civil Wars: Counterinsurgency in the Twentieth Century* (Boston: Faber and Faber, 1986), 99–113; David Killingray, "'A Swift Agent of Government': Air Power in British Colonial Africa, 1916–1939," *Journal of African History* 25, no. 4 (1984): 429–44.

123. Lindqvist, *History of Bombing*, 68; Malcolm Smith, *British Air Strategy between the Wars* (Oxford: Clarendon, 1984), 29.

124. See commanding officer of 17th Division, report, 26 June 1921, AIR 1/432/15/260/23 (A-B), TNA; Thomas, memorandum, to PO Muntafik, 13 July 1920, E11758/2719/44/1920, FO 371/5230, TNA; [Hall?], minute, 11 August 1921, on Cox to CO, 30 June 1921, 39645, CO 730/2, TNA; Cox to Churchill, 6 October 1921, on operations at Batas and elsewhere, CO 730/7, TNA; Omissi, *Air Power*, 174. See also Charles Townshend, "Civilization and 'Frightfulness': Air Control in the Middle East between the Wars," in *Warfare, Diplomacy and Politics: Essays in Honour of A. J. P. Taylor*, ed. Chris Wrigley (London: Hamish Hamilton, 1986), 153. For an exemplary episode, see Peter Sluglett, *The British in Iraq: 1914–1932* (London: Ithaca, 1976), 262–70. It is difficult to say how many Iraqis were killed in these operations, from the bombs themselves as well as through starvation and the burning and machine-gunning of villages, but a hundred or more casualties was certainly not unusual in a single operation.

125. Brooke-Popham, "Aeroplanes in Tropical Countries"; Claude H. Keith, 3 December 1927, in *Flying Years*, Aviation Book Club ed. (London: J. Hamilton, 1937), 137–38; Young to Shuckburgh, 23 October 1921, CO 730/16, TNA; Herbert Baker chap. in *T. E. Lawrence, by His Friends*, ed. Arnold W. Lawrence (London: J. Cape, 1937), 206.

126. Air Staff, 1921, quoted in Townshend, "Civilization and 'Frightfulness,'" 159.

127. Bullard and Meinertzhagen, minutes, September 1921, on Cox, telegram, 24 September 1921, 48218, CO 730/5, TNA; CAS to Sir R. Maconachie, British Legation, Kabul, 10 January 1933, AIR 9/12, TNA.

128. See, for instance, "Britain and Mesopotamia," *Daily Telegraph*, 10 May 1921; Richard Coke, *The Arab's Place in the Sun* (London: Thornton Butterworth, 1929), 11–12.

129. "A Traveller in Mesopotamia," review of *By Tigris and Euphrates*, by E. S. Stevens, *Times*, 14 December 1923, 8.

130. "Four Centuries of History," review of *Four Centuries of Modern Iraq*, by Stephen Hembley Longrigg, *Times*, 22 January 1926, 17.

131. Ilay Ferrier, "The Trans-Desert Route—Baghdad—Jerusalem," 1926, Papers by Ilay Ferrier, IOR, Eur Mss C874, India Office Records, British Library, London.

132. *Illustrated London News*, 1 February 1919, 149 (the quotation alludes to Stephen Phillips's poem *Marpessa*, first published in 1897).

133. Hubert Young, *The Independent Arab* (London: J. Murray, 1933), 338.

134. R. H. Peck, "Aircraft in Small Wars," *Journal of the Royal United Services Institute* 73, no. 491 (1928): 541.

135. Buchanan, *Tragedy of Mesopotamia*, 182, 261, 276–78, 284–85.

136. Captain R. J. Wilkinson, "The Geographical Importance of Iraq," *Journal of the Royal United Services Institute* 61, no. 468 (1922): 665.

137. "Progress in Mesopotamia," editorial, *Times*, 17 March 1923, 11; Amery at the Leeds Luncheon Club, quoted in "The Middle East," *Times*, 9 February 1926, 11.

138. See Satia, *Spies in Arabia*, chaps. 7, 8.

139. Air Policy with Regard to Iraq, n.d. [October–November 1929], AIR 2/830, TNA.

140. Frantz Fanon, *The Wretched of the Earth*, trans. Constance Farrington (New York: Grove, 1963), 250.

141. See, for instance, George Black, "Is Environmental Destruction a War Crime?" *OnEarth* (Winter 2005), http://www.nrdc.org/onearth/05win/briefings.asp (accessed 15 September 2010); Souad N. Al-Azzawi, "Depleted Uranium Radioactive Contamination in Iraq: An Overview," *Global Research*, 31 August 2006, http://www.globalresearch.ca/index.php?context=viewArticle&code=AL-20060831&articleId=3116 (accessed 15 September 2010); Jeffrey St. Clair and Joshua Frank, "Ecological Warfare: Iraq's Environmental Crisis," *CounterPunch*, 25 October 2007, http://www.counterpunch.org/stclair10252007.html (accessed 15 September 2010); Steven D. Hanks, "Left in the Desert: The Environmental Fallout of the Iraq War," emagazine.com, http://www.emagazine.com/view/?4285 (accessed 15 September 2010).

142. Mitchell, *Rule of Experts*, 44, 210–11, 223.

Bibliography

Archives

India Office Records, British Library, London
Papers by Ilay Ferrier (Eur Mss C874).

Liddell Hart Center for Military Archives, King's College, London
Brooke-Popham Papers

Liddle Collection, Leeds University Library, Leeds
GS 0993 (Lynden-Bell Papers), GS 0089 (Barnett Papers), MES 007 (Bellers Papers).

Middle East Centre Archive, St Antony's College, Oxford
Papers of Kinch, Sykes, Harold R. P. Dickson, Philby, Glubb

National Archives, London
AIR 1, 2, 5, 8, 9, 20, 23
CO 730
FO 371
WO 158

National Army Museum, London
Leith-Ross Papers (ARC 1983–12–69–10)

Parliamentary Papers

Newspapers

Daily Telegraph
Guardian
Illustrated London News
Times

Books and Articles

Al-Azzawi, Souad N. "Depleted Uranium Radioactive Contamination in Iraq: An Overview." *Global Research*, 31 August 2006. Available at http://www.globalresearch.ca/index.php?context=viewArticle&code=AL-20060831&articleId=3116. Accessed 15 September 2010.

Bell, Gertrude. *Amurath to Amurath*. New York: Dutton, 1911.

[———.] *The Arab of Mesopotamia*. Basra: Government Press, 1917.

———. *Gertrude Bell: The Arabian Diaries, 1913–1914*. Edited by Rosemary O'Brien. Syracuse, N.Y.: Syracuse University Press, 2000.

———. *The Letters of Gertrude Bell*. Edited by Lady Bell. 2 vols. London: E. Benn, 1927.

Benjamin, Walter. "The Work of Art in the Age of Mechanical Reproduction." 1937. In *Illuminations*, edited by Hannah Arendt, translated by Harry Zohn, 217–52. New York: Schocken Books, 1968.

Bevan, Edwyn. *The Land of the Two Rivers*. London: E. Arnold, 1918.

Bird, Wilkinson D. *A Chapter of Misfortunes: The Battles of Ctesiphon and of the Dujailah in Mesopotamia, with a Summary of the Events Which Preceded Them*. London: Forster Groom, 1923.

Black, George. "Is Environmental Destruction a War Crime?" *OnEarth* (Winter 2005). Available at http://www.nrdc.org/onearth/05win/briefings.asp. Accessed 15 September 2010.

Bose, Sugata. *A Hundred Horizons: The Indian Ocean in the Age of Global Empire*. Cambridge, Mass.: Harvard University Press, 2006.
Brent, Peter. *Far Arabia: Explorers of the Myth*. London: Weidenfeld and Nicolson, 1977.
Buchanan, George. *The Tragedy of Mesopotamia*. London: W. Blackwood, 1938.
Burgoyne, Elizabeth. *Gertrude Bell: From Her Personal Papers*. 2 vols. London: E. Benn, 1958–61.
Bury, G. Wyman [Abdullah Mansur, pseud.]. *The Land of Uz*. London: Macmillan, 1911.
Busch, Briton Cooper. *Britain, India, and the Arabs, 1914–1921*. Berkeley: University of California Press, 1977.
Butler, S. S. "Baghdad to Damascus via El Jauf, Northern Arabia." *Geographical Journal* 33, no. 5 (1909): 517–33.
Candler, Edmund. *The Long Road to Baghdad*. 2 vols. New York: Houghton Mifflin, 1919.
Carruthers, Douglas. *Arabian Adventure: To the Great Nafud in Quest of the Oryx*. London: H. F. and G. Witherby, 1935.
Casey, Robert J. *Baghdad and Points East*. London: Hutchinson, 1928.
Cato, Conrad. *The Navy in Mesopotamia: 1914 to 1917*. London: Constable, 1917.
Clark, Arthur Tillotson. *To Bagdad with the British*. New York: D. Appleton, 1918.
Cohen, Stuart A. "The Genesis of the British Campaign in Mesopotamia, 1914." *Middle Eastern Studies* 12, no. 2 (1976): 119–32.
Coke, Richard. *The Arab's Place in the Sun*. London: Thornton Butterworth, 1929.
Cole, Juan. *Roots of North Indian Shī'ism in Iran and Iraq: Religion and State in Awadh, 1722–1859*. Berkeley: University of California Press, 1988.
Colls, Robert. "The Constitution of the English." *History Workshop Journal* 46 (1998): 97–128.
Constantine, Stephen. *The Making of British Colonial Development Policy, 1914–1940*. London: F. Cass, 1984.
Cooper, Frederick. "Modernizing Bureaucrats, Backward Africans, and the Development Concept." In *International Development and the Social Sciences: Essays on the History and Politics of Knowledge*, edited by Frederick Cooper and Randall Packard, 70. Berkeley: University of California Press, 1997.
Cooper, Frederick, and Randall Packard, eds. *International Development and the Social Sciences: Essays on the History and Politics of Knowledge*. Berkeley: University of California Press, 1997.
Cox, Jafna. "A Splendid Training Ground: The Importance to the Royal Air Force of Its Role in Iraq, 1919–32." *Journal of Imperial and Commonwealth History* 13, no. 2 (1985): 157–84.
Crush, Jonathan, ed. *Power of Development*. London: Routledge, 1995.
Davis, Paul K. *Ends and Means: The British Mesopotamian Campaign and Commission*. London: Associated University Presses, 1994.

Edgerton, David. *Warfare State: 1920–1970*. Cambridge: Cambridge University Press, 2006.
Egan, Eleanor Franklin. *The War in the Cradle of the World: Mesopotamia*. New York: Harper, 1918.
Fanon, Frantz. *The Wretched of the Earth*. Translated by Constance Farrington. New York: Grove, 1963.
Fraser, David. *The Short Cut to India: The Record of a Journey along the Route of the Baghdad Railway*. Edinburgh: W. Blackwood, 1909.
Fussell, Paul. *The Great War and Modern Memory*. London: Oxford University Press, 1975.
Galbraith, John S. "No Man's Child: The Campaign in Mesopotamia, 1914–1916." *International History Review* 6, no. 3 (1984): 358–85.
Gilbert, Martin. *Winston S. Churchill. Vol. 4: 1916–1922, The Stricken World*. Boston: Heinemann, 1975.
———, ed. *Winston S. Churchill, Companion, Part 3: Documents April 1921–November 1922*. London: Heinemann, 1977.
Gilmartin, David. "Imperial Rivers: Irrigation and British Visions of Empire." In *Decentring Empire: Britain, India and the Transcolonial World*, edited by Durba Ghosh and Dane Kennedy, 76–103. New Delhi: Orient Longman, 2006.
Glubb, John. *Arabian Adventures: Ten Years of Joyful Service*. London: Cassell, 1978.
———. *The Changing Scenes of Life: An Autobiography*. London: Quartet, 1983.
———. *The Story of the Arab Legion*. London: Hodder and Stoughton, 1948.
Haldane, Aylmer. *The Insurrection in Mesopotamia*. London: W. Blackwood, 1922.
Hamlin, Christopher. *Public Health and Social Justice in the Age of Chadwick: Britain, 1800–1854*. Cambridge: Cambridge University Press, 1998.
Hanks, Steven D. "Left in the Desert: The Environmental Fallout of the Iraq War." emagazine.com. Available at http://www.emagazine.com/view/?4285 Accessed 15 September 2010.
Hart, Basil Henry Liddell. *The British Way in Warfare*. New York: Macmillan, 1933.
———. *T. E. Lawrence: In Arabia and After*. London: Jonathan Cape, 1934.
Hogarth, David G. "Problems in Exploration I. Western Asia." *Geographical Journal* 32, no. 6 (1908): 549–70.
Hynes, Samuel. *The Edwardian Turn of Mind*. Princeton: Princeton University Press, 1968.
Jarvis, C. S. *Arab Command: The Biography of Lieutenant-Colonel F. G. Peake Pasha*. London: Hutchinson, 1946.
Jebb, Louisa. *By Desert Ways to Baghdad*. Boston: Dana, Estes, 1909.
Keith, Claude H. *Flying Years*. Aviation Book Club ed. London: J. Hamilton, 1937.
Kern, Stephen. *The Culture of Time and Space: 1880–1918*. Cambridge, Mass.: Harvard University Press, 1983.
Killingray, David. "'A Swift Agent of Government': Air Power in British Colonial Africa, 1916–1939." *Journal of African History* 25, no. 4 (1984): 429–44.

Knightley, Philip, and Colin Simpson. *The Secret Lives of Lawrence of Arabia.* London: Nelson, 1969.
Laffin, John. *Swifter Than Eagles: The Biography of Marshal of the Royal Air Force Sir John Maitland Salmond.* Edinburgh: W. Blackwood, 1964.
Lawrence, Arnold W., ed. *T. E. Lawrence, by His Friends.* London: J. Cape, 1937.
Lawrence, T. E. *The Letters of T. E. Lawrence.* Edited by David Garnett. London: Jonathan Cape, 1938.
Lee, Arthur Gould. *Fly Past: Highlights from a Flyer's Life.* London: Jarrolds, 1974.
Leed, Eric J. *No Man's Land: Combat and Identity in World War I.* Cambridge: Cambridge University Press, 1979.
Lindqvist, Sven. *A History of Bombing.* 2000. Translated by Linda Haverty Rugg. New York: W. W. Norton, 2001.
Litvak, Meir. "A Failed Manipulation: The British, the Oudh Bequest and the Shi'i Ulama of Najaf and Karbala." *British Journal of Middle Eastern Studies* 27, no. 1 (2000): 69–89.
———. "Money, Religion, and Politics: The Oudh Bequest in Najaf and Karbala, 1850–1903." *International Journal of Middle Eastern Studies* 33, no. 1 (2001): 1–21.
Lorimer, John G., ed. *Gazetteer of the Persian Gulf, Oman, and Central Arabia.* Vol. 2: *Geographical and Statistical.* Calcutta: Government Press, 1908.
Mack, John. *A Prince of Our Disorder: The Life of T. E. Lawrence.* Boston: Little, Brown, 1976.
Mann, James Saumarz. *An Administrator in the Making: James Saumarez Mann, 1893–1920.* Edited by his father [James Saumarez Mann Sr.]. London: Vintage, 1921.
Maunsell, Francis R. "The Hejaz Railway." *Geographical Journal* 32, no. 6 (1908): 570–84.
Mitchell, Timothy. *Rule of Experts: Egypt, Techno-Politics, Modernity.* Berkeley: University of California Press, 2002.
Monk, F. V., and H. T. Winter. *The Royal Air Force.* London: Blackie and Son, 1938.
Nunn, Wilfrid. *Tigris Gunboats: A Narrative of the Royal Navy's Co-operation with the Military Forces in Mesopotamia from the Beginning of the War to the Capture of Baghdad (1914–17).* London: A. Melrose, 1932.
One of Its Officers. *With a Highland Regiment in Mesopotamia, 1916–1917.* Bombay: Times Press, 1918.
Omissi, David. *Air Power and Colonial Control: The Royal Air Force, 1919–1939.* Manchester: Manchester University Press, 1990.
Owen, Alex. *The Place of Enchantment: British Occultism and the Culture of the Modern.* Chicago: University of Chicago Press, 2004.
Orwell, George. "The Lion and the Unicorn: Socialism and the English Genius." 1941. Available at http://www.k-1.com/Orwell/index.cgi/work/essays/lionunicorn.html. Accessed 15 September 2010.

---. "Politics and the English Language." 1946. Available at http://www.george-orwell.org/Politics_and_the_English_Language/0.html. Accessed 15 September 2010.

Parfit, J. T. *Serbia to Kût: An Account of the War in the Bible Lands*. London: Hunter and Longhurst, 1917.

Peck, R. H. "Aircraft in Small Wars." *Journal of the Royal United Services Institute* 73, no. 491 (1928): 535–50.

Popplewell, Richard. "British Intelligence in Mesopotamia: 1914–1916." *Intelligence and National Security* 5, no. 2 (1990): 139–72.

Reynardson, Henry Birch. *Mesopotamia, 1914–15: Extracts from a Regimental Officer's Diary*. London: Andrew Melrose, 1919.

Rich, Paul B. *Race and Empire in British Politics*. Cambridge: Cambridge University Press, 1986.

Rothwell, V. H. "Mesopotamia in British War Aims, 1914–1918." *Historical Journal* 13, no. 2 (1970): 273–94.

Said, Edward. *Orientalism*. 1978. New York: Vintage, 1979.

Satia, Priya. "Developing Iraq: Britain, India and the Redemption of Empire and Technology in the First World War." *Past and Present* 197, no. 1 (2007): 211–55.

---. *Spies in Arabia: The Great War and the Cultural Foundations of Britain's Covert Empire in the Middle East*. New York: Oxford University Press, 2008.

Scott, James C. *Seeing Like a State: How Certain Schemes to Improve the Human Condition Have Failed*. New Haven, Conn.: Yale University Press, 1998.

Sinha, Meeta. "'Where Electricity Dispels the Illusion [of the Arabian Nights]': The British and the Modern in Interwar India." Paper presented at the Pacific Coast Conference of British Studies, Irvine. 2006.

Sluglett, Peter. *The British in Iraq: 1914–1932*. London: Ithaca, 1976.

Smith, Malcolm. *British Air Strategy between the Wars*. Oxford: Clarendon, 1984.

St. Clair, Jeffrey, and Joshua Frank. "Ecological Warfare: Iraq's Environmental Crisis." *CounterPunch*, 25 October 2007. Available at http://www.counterpunch.org/stclair10252007.html. Accessed 15 September 2010.

Swayne, Martin. *In Mesopotamia*. London: Hodder and Stoughton, 1917.

Sykes, Mark. *The Caliph's Last Heritage*. London: Macmillan, 1915.

---. *Dar-ul-Islam: A Record of a Journey through Ten of the Asiatic Provinces of Turkey*. London: Bickers and Son, 1904.

Townsend, Meredith. *Asia and Europe: Studies Presenting the Conclusions Formed by the Author in a Long Life Devoted to the Subject of the Relations between Asia and Europe*. 2nd ed. New York: G. P. Putnam's, 1904.

Townshend, Charles. *Britain's Civil Wars: Counterinsurgency in the Twentieth Century*. Boston: Faber and Faber, 1986.

---. "Civilization and 'Frightfulness': Air Control in the Middle East between the Wars." In *Warfare, Diplomacy and Politics: Essays in Honour of A. J. P. Taylor*, edited by Chris Wrigley, 142–62. London: Hamish Hamilton, 1986.

Wilkinson, R. J. "The Geographical Importance of Iraq." *Journal of the Royal United Services Institute* 61, no. 468 (1922): 660–65.

Wilson, Arnold T. *Mesopotamia, 1917–1920: A Clash of Loyalties*. London: Oxford University Press, 1931.

Young, Hubert. *The Independent Arab*. London: J. Murray, 1933.

CHAPTER 2

Restoring Roman Nature

French Identity and North African Environmental History

Diana K. Davis

FRENCH COLONIAL occupation and expansion across North Africa in the nineteenth and twentieth centuries were closely connected with a widespread belief that the French were the heirs of Rome. Although the importance of the Roman legacy for several French colonial actions has been recognized, for example in the military, the agricultural sector, and identity formation among the French living in North Africa, the significance of its impact for thinking about the relationship between the environment and identity has not been widely explored. This essay suggests that the imperative of restoring what was incorrectly perceived as a deforested and desertified environment to its mythical former fertility under Roman administration became, for certain segments of the French population, an integral part of notions of French imperial and, to a certain degree, national identity.

The belief that the environment, assumed to have been ruined by the "natives," had to be restored was especially widespread among the French colonists in Algeria and later in Tunisia and Morocco, as well as in the colonial lobby in the metropole. For many, the allegedly degraded landscape threatened to defeat the colonial project and to debase European civilization in the Maghreb. The restoration of the environment through massive reforestation and other environmental improvement projects was seen as crucial to the survival of the French and other Europeans in North Africa. It was commonly argued, for instance, that since Roman civilization could not have flourished if North Africa had not had a forest cover of at least 30 percent, the French must reforest the region. Equally important, agriculture must be improved with French methods in order to re-create the granary of Rome. European experiences with nature in other parts of the world, experiences that were generally efforts to tame a wild and threatening "foreign" nature, stand in stark contrast to the French project of restoring the "natural" landscape, a landscape of "self," to its former fertility and glory, and thereby proving themselves the true heirs of Rome.

Ferocious Colonial Nature

Analyses of European experiences with non-European natures around the world agree that the vast majority of these encounters produced descriptions of the landscape that classified the biophysical environment as exotic. That is, compared to European landscapes familiar to the writers (explorers, colonists, missionaries, etc.), newly discovered lands contained plants, animals, and land forms that were unfamiliar and therefore classified as "other" compared to the "normal" European landscape of "self." Such a binary, categorizing European nature as normal, temperate nature and non-European natures as exotic and decidedly "other" or abnormal, helped define Europeans' sense of self at a crucial time. As Derek Gregory has explained, "Writing tropical nature as 'other' thus conveyed 'its discursive differentiation from home and the familiar,' and in doing so helped to establish the 'superiority' of the domestic over the exotic."[1] This categorization also facilitated notions of "improvement" that were used throughout the colonized world to justify European intervention.[2]

In some parts of the world, such as the tropical Pacific islands and certain parts of the Americas and Africa, the exoticness of the landscape was sometimes portrayed as attractive, luxuriant, and fertile, especially early in imperial encounters.[3] In fact, it was frequently the "very 'otherness' of these lands which has made them appear so compelling, especially as a testing ground for imperial energy and imagination."[4] As Europeans gained years of experience in foreign lands, however, those perceptions tended to change, and representations of exotic landscapes became increasingly negative.

The historian Nancy Stepan has called this "the darkening of the sublime tropics," a phenomenon she illustrates with Alexander von Humboldt's and other European's representations of the Americas over time.⁵ She and the historian David Arnold both attribute a large part of this change in European attitudes toward, and representations of, tropical nature to the problems of fighting the endemic diseases of these regions, many of them new to European medical knowledge.⁶ This went hand in hand with fears of moral and physical degeneration and with the debasement of European civilization in these exotic lands.

It is perhaps in the colonial settings of the nineteenth century that the portrayal of exotic nature by Europeans as negative and defective (wild, gigantesque, ferocious, diseased, barren, etc.) became most pronounced. This occurred not only in the "tropical world" as defined by the tropics of Cancer and Capricorn, but also nearly anywhere that the environment was warm and did not resemble Europe, including India, Africa, and much of South America and Asia.⁷

For the British in India, nature was never seen as edenic, for example, but rather as a series of exotic, difficult, and diseased environments that required forceful management. According to British representations, in some areas irrigation canals were required, in others drainage works were needed, in still others the defiled forest needed to be replanted, and nearly everywhere agriculture had to be "improved." The perceived strangeness and inadequacy of the Indian environment and its peoples justified British imperial intervention in countless ways even before the nineteenth century.⁸

Over the course of the nineteenth century, southern Africa was subject to European (primarily British) representations of nature that wove a story that also justified a European colonial presence. This narrative of a previously fertile, indeed somewhat edenic but exotic land, placed blame on the indigenous inhabitants, the Tswana, for deforesting and otherwise ruining the environment. In the eyes of some influential colonial actors such as John Croumbie Brown, the official colonial botanist, the local peoples had been such bad stewards of the land that they were being punished by God with drought.⁹ This narrative, and variations on it, facilitated many important colonial goals in southern Africa during the nineteenth century, from justifying reforestation and other forestry measures to agricultural and soil conservation interventions in the name of stopping erosion.¹⁰

At the other end of the continent, in French North Africa, however, a different story, with a different representation of nature, was crafted early in the nineteenth century. Although it shared with the British narratives a strong tendency to blame the indigenous populations for perceived environmental ruin, it made the unique claim that the landscape was not exotic or "other" but rather that nature in North Africa represented a landscape of

Gallo-Roman "self." This narrative proclaimed that the French, as the heirs of Rome, had the duty and the honor of restoring the ruined North African environment to its former glorious fertility under Roman administration. The environment, however, was not as badly degraded, deforested, or desertified as so widely claimed during the colonial period.[11] Nonetheless, once constructed early in the occupation, this story served a wide variety of purposes promoting the French colonial venture for nearly 150 years.

Nature and Narratives in French North Africa: The Heirs of Rome

When the French conquered Algiers in 1830, their information about North Africa and its environment was limited despite its proximity to France. The French, like most Europeans of the time, believed that North Africa was a region of legendary natural fertility that had flourished in the past and had constituted the granary of Rome. This story, based nearly entirely on readings of classical texts by the Greeks and Romans, included the belief that North Africa was the most fertile region in the world and that it had been heavily forested during Roman times.[12] The new, colonial, addition to this story was that the environment of North Africa had been despoiled since the golden years of Roman imperial administration by the ravening hordes of nomads and their livestock that had deforested, overgrazed, and desertified the land since the eleventh-century Arab "Hillalian invasion."

Within two decades of the French occupation of Algeria, this story of the previously lush and fertile North African landscape being ruined by the indigenous Algerians, especially nomads, had taken shape. In 1847, the year before Algeria was made an official province of France, it was eloquently articulated by a member of the government-sponsored commission for the scientific exploration of Algeria: "This land, once the object of intensive cultivation, was neither deforested nor depopulated as today; it was the abundant granary of Rome."[13] This medical doctor, M. Périer, also spelled out a sentiment that would become increasingly widespread over the course of the French colonial period in North Africa: that the French were the legitimate heirs of Rome in all her imperial glory. He proclaimed that "it is therefore our responsibility to raise Algeria from her fallen state, and to return her to her past [Roman] glory."[14]

This narrative was used widely from the mid-nineteenth century not only to justify but also to motivate the development and implementation of economic, environmental, legal, and social policies in France's southernmost province. The primary results of the utilization of this declensionist environmental narrative were the appropriation of forest, agricultural, and grazing

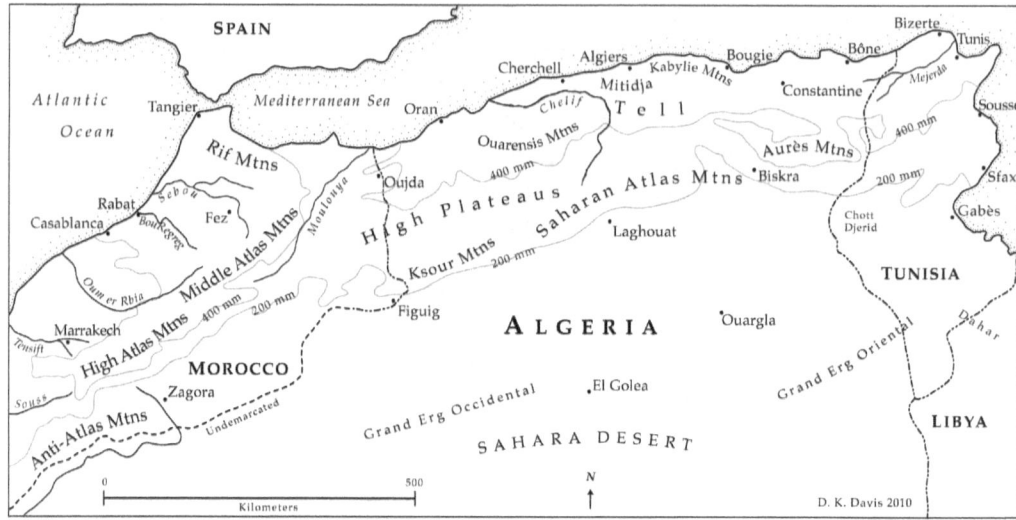

Map 2.1. The Maghreb. Modified after multiple sources. Created by Maria Lane, 2006. Reproduced with permission.

lands for the French state and the colonists, the transformation of subsistence production into capitalist production, and social control of the indigenous North Africans, especially the nomads and forest dwellers, all in the name of environmental protection. The local Algerians lost nearly all their forests and most of the best agricultural and grazing lands as a result. Many were forced into dire levels of poverty, and the social disruption caused was profound.[15]

This story and its related policies were widely applied with minor variations to the protectorates of Tunisia and Morocco when they were conquered in 1881 and 1912 respectively, with similarly negative effects on the local populations. In Morocco, for instance, the young recruits in the indigenous affairs service were taught that "France is the legitimate successor of Rome. . . . The great Roman people of whom we are the heirs conquered this region well before the Arabs."[16] The instructor for this course, Jean Colin, after explaining that the "natives" had ruined the environment, encouraged his recruits by promising, "like Rome, we will again expand the cultivable area, dry out the swampy regions, and transform them into fertile plains," since it was the duty of France to revive the Roman oeuvre.[17] This they did with a fair amount of success.[18]

What is profoundly different about the French colonial environmental history of the Maghreb, compared to most other European environmental histories of their imperial territories, is that the French considered North Africa a landscape of "self" because they believed themselves the heirs of Rome. The Maghreb was not considered a foreign or dangerous landscape in the way that the tropical jungles of South America, central Africa, or southeast Asia frequently were. In describing Algeria in 1847, a French artillery captain, M. de Mont Rond, for example, explained that North Africa was not like the barbaric territories: "There were no lands inhabited by savages among whom a stranger would surely find death; there was no gigantic river similar to the Amazon that crossed south America."[19] Indeed, the landscape of North Africa contained familiar vegetation—quite similar to that of southern France—just not quite enough of it. In the French imaginary, with enough reforestation, enlarged agricultural production, and careful tending in the form of banning fires and curbing grazing, the North African landscape—even the Sahara desert—would once again become the granary of empire, this time France's empire.

Thus one of the ways the French thought they could fulfill their Roman and imperial legacy was to "restore" the North African landscape to its former glory and fertility with large reforestation and other environmental and agricultural improvement projects. Many even believed they could restore a more humid and salubrious climate through reforestation—indeed that they had to in order to preserve French civilization. One influential colonist and adviser to the Algerian government, for example, Dr. Paulin Trolard, exhorting his countrymen to plant trees everywhere, promised that if "we decide to fight until our climate is transformed [by reforestation], it will be wealth, it will be life, it will be Algeria returned to its original [Roman] fertility: it will be Algeria becoming the granary of France!"[20] Failure to undertake such measures of environmental restoration, warned Dr. Trolard, would result in dire consequences. He explained in typically alarmist style that, if nothing were done, "the Sahara, this hearth of evil, stretches its arms towards us every day; it will soon enclose us, suffocate us, annihilate us!"[21]

For the French living in Algeria, it took only a few decades for the vision of restoring the allegedly ruined environment to Roman prosperity and fertility to become a key part of their colonial identity. This is a primary reason the landscape was not portrayed as exotic, but rather as Gallo-Roman "self." France's long history of invoking Roman heritage made this easy.

France and Rome: The Politics of National and Imperial Identity

Long before France developed any sense of "national identity," at least since the reign of Louis XIV (1643–1715), ties had been drawn between France and Rome. Before the mid-seventeenth century the nobility in France generally had claimed descent from the Germans, whereas the peasants were thought to be the descendants of Gallo-Romans.[22] During the last half of the seventeenth century, under the administration of Louis XIV and his court, a program took shape "to make France an empire in the image of ancient Rome."[23] For Louis XIV, adopting Roman symbols of power, from dressing up in period costumes to landscaping the gardens at Versailles to evoke Rome, was a way to increase his own power and, hopefully, to create his own empire.

Fascination with the Roman empire continued into the eighteenth century, and study of their classical texts, along with those of ancient Greece, formed a substantial part of the education of elites in France during the period leading up to the revolution of 1789.[24] During the postrevolutionary period, many republicans, as Mike Heffernan has explained, "saw revolutionary France as the modern re-incarnation of the ancient Roman republic. . . . As such, modern enlightened France had a right and a duty to re-establish the traditions and values of the ancients in their former heartlands."[25] The French expeditions shortly thereafter to Italy, Egypt, and Greece were all inspired, to a certain degree, by the growing belief in France that the French were the heirs of Rome and its former empire. With the 1798 Napoleonic expedition to Egypt, the association between France and Rome as imperial powers in Africa was forged.[26]

By the early to mid-nineteenth century, the period most often identified as that during which "national identities" began to be formed, the notion that France was the heir of the Roman empire was firmly established.[27] Jules Michelet, a revered spokesperson for France, who conceived of the country as a person, held this view. In his widely read and highly influential 1846 book *The People*, Michelet proclaimed that "we are the Romans of Rome, and the Frenchmen of France."[28] It is not surprising, then, that the French began early in their occupation of North Africa to proclaim a Roman legacy there. Claiming a glorious Roman past for North Africa served the goals of many in France and the Maghreb particularly well.

The Roman experience was analyzed for guidance about how to conquer and colonize the region, and, more important, the fact that the Romans had succeeded in colonizing North Africa was held up as a primary justification for French colonization. Only three years after capturing Algiers, the king of France, for example, encouraged the troops in Algeria, in 1833, to "finish the conquest and return to civilization this shore of the Mediterranean surrendered, since the destruction of the Roman empire, to anarchy and barbarism."[29]

The French military deliberately modeled itself in several ways on the Roman experience in North Africa during the early years of conquest and expansion in Algeria. General Bugeaud, for instance, based on his reading of Roman texts, implemented new warfare tactics such as mobile

Figure 2.1. Arch of Trajan and Capitoline temple, Roman Imperial Period, Timgad, Algeria, Gerard Degeorge. *The Bridgeman Art Library International. Reproduced by permission.*

columns.[30] Roman texts also provided advice on how to administer a colony in North Africa, including how to proceed with agricultural development and how to better deal with the "natives."[31] One of the primary rationales for sedentarizing the nomads, for example, was the claim that the Romans had successfully done so and that it had created conditions of security and prosperity that France should emulate.[32] The many Roman ruins that dotted the landscape were not only a testimonial to the successful Roman past and French future in North Africa, but also, in many cases, provided very real material benefits for the French in the form of functioning cisterns, roads, and aqueducts.[33]

Historians have explained that invoking the story that the French were the true heirs of Rome in North Africa also served an important ideological function that further solidified French hegemony. Patricia Lorcin argues that "the substitution of a remote Western [Roman] past for a recent Islamic one and the institutionalization of Algeria as spatially French were important steps in marginalizing the presence and culture of the Arabs and Berbers."[34] Moreover, in the words of Yves Lacoste, "turning the Arabs into invaders was one way of legitimizing the 'French presence,'" and it "provided a historical basis for turning Arabs and Berbers against each other."[35]

Since the French colonial environmental narrative blamed the indigenous Algerians, and especially the nomads, for ruining the North African environment, the local populations were thus condemned on two levels: for being illegitimate invaders of what was portrayed as long-standing French (Roman) territory and for destroying what had been a lush and fertile environment. This narrative construction provided powerful ammunition for the French in Algeria to morally and legally dispossess the Algerians (and later the Tunisians and Moroccans) of their property, to confiscate their forests, to undermine their livelihoods, and to govern and "civilize" them.

Although this story was well developed by the mid-nineteenth century and widely accepted in Algeria and within the pro-colonial lobby in France, it did not gain wider French support until later in the century. The French deputy, Amédée Desjobert, summed up the sentiment of many anticolonialists in France when he stated in 1846 that "we have established that we cannot colonize [in Algeria] as did the Greeks and Romans."[36] Support for colonialism in general had been low in France during the first half of the nineteenth century. It may have reached a nadir in the early 1880s when an anticolonial backlash in France to Prime Minister Jules Ferry's procolonial actions brought down his government.[37]

An important turning point in popular sentiment toward colonialism occurred three years later, however, with the 1889 colonial exposition in Paris, which generated much interest in French overseas adventures. Will Swearingen explains that after the 1889 exposition, "French pride and patriotism, smarting since the 1870–1871 [Franco-Prussian] war, sensed a healthy outlet in colonialism."[38] Within just a few years, many organizations supporting colonization had been formed, including the Committee for French Africa (1890), the "colonial group" in both the French Chamber of Deputies and the French Senate (1892), the French Colonial Union (1893) composed of more than four hundred French companies with colonial interests, and the Colonial League (1907).[39] Many others followed over the next several years. It was not until the interwar years, however, that a slim majority of average French citizens could be said to support French colonialism and to take pride in a "greater France."[40]

Another change has been identified that bears directly on the reception of this colonial narrative in France around the turn of the century. The geographer Vidal de la Blache put forth the idea that a key component of national identity in France derived from the diversity of people being able to "master the environments where they settled."[41] Mastering the French environment and having hard-working people who were members not only of their different provincial towns and regions but also and equally members of the French nation gave France her national identity. This interpretation "seduced public opinion in the late nineteenth and early twentieth centuries" in France and was widely influential.[42]

All these ideas—that France was the heir of imperial Rome, that the North African environment had been deforested and degraded since the end of the Roman empire, that colonial expansion was necessary and "good," and that mastering the environment was an imperative of being French—combined in French North Africa to create a kind of French imperial identity that hinged in part on restoring the environment to its former Roman lushness and fertility through reforestation and agricultural improvements. As Algeria, Tunisia, and Morocco were arguably viewed into the 1950s as France's most successful colonial ventures, many invested a great deal in this vision.[43] It helped feed both French colonial identity in the Maghreb territories and certain notions of imperial and national identity in France.

The height of these sentiments was reached in the 1930s and was expressed in the 1930 celebrations of the centenary of the conquest of Algeria as well as at the 1931 colonial exposition in Paris. Although the French government organized and directed the huge propaganda effort in the 1930 celebrations to garner popular support for Algeria, it was, in part, successful.[44] There were myriad iterations of proud French claims to Roman heritage in North Africa in centenary publications and in the popular press. Various newspapers and magazines proclaimed that, in the Maghreb, "France is the heir of Rome and is superior to her [Rome]."[45]

The six-volume *History of French Colonies and the Expansion of France in the World* began to be published in Paris for a French audience in 1929 with the second volume, on Algeria, appearing in 1930. It shared many similarities with the propaganda of the 1930 Algerian centenary. The author of the volume on Algeria, Augustin Bernard, a widely published expert on North Africa, included many passages describing Algeria as the former granary of Rome whose environment had been ruined by the "natives." He explained, however, that "France had recovered the work of Rome in the same spirit as its predecessor."[46] Moreover, he proudly proclaimed that "France had, more than the Romans themselves, made immense progress with Algerian agriculture, extended the cultivated area, incorporated the best of the existing agricultural plants and introduced new ones."[47] He concluded that "thanks to the diffusion of the French language, vehicle of our ideas, the Algerian people that are being formed are truly ours, they are the young shoot from the old Gallo-Roman trunk."[48] This was vital since, in the words of this respected professor, "our final goal, conforming to our ideal of yesterday and today, to the ideal of Richelieu and of Louis XIV as well as of the French Revolution, is the foundation of a France overseas, where our language and our civilization will be revived."[49] Bernard believed that France had succeeded in attaining these goals in Algeria. He concluded with pride in his 1937 volume on Northwest Africa for Vidal de la Blache's fifteen-part *Universal Geography*, that, indeed, France had succeeded in all three of its North African territories just "as did the Romans."[50]

Restoring Roman Nature: Fulfilling the Vision

This French environmental imaginary of North Africa was not just rhetoric or polemic—it had very real effects on both the physical environment of the territories and on a variety of laws, policies, and development plans across the region. Its acceptance and utilization are visible in many of these laws and policies, and especially in the multiple changes enacted on the North African landscape in the realms of agriculture and forestry.

Prior to the 1880s, the French colonial environmental narrative was used nearly exclusively within colonial Algeria to effect changes sought either by the colonists or the Algerian government. This narrative informed important legal changes, made in the name of environmental protection, during the period, including the land use laws of 1838, 1846, 1863, and 1873, and the forestry law of 1874. All of these laws favored French and European colonists and the colonial state over indigenous Algerians and resulted in the loss of property and use-rights to a wide array of landscapes from forests to fields to pastures previously used for subsistence by rural Algerians.[51] This trend would continue throughout the period of French rule in the Maghreb, and similar results were obtained in Tunisia and Morocco.

During the 1880s, after pro-colonial rule had been firmly established in Algeria, the colonial environmental narrative of North Africa began to become more apparent in France itself. It was at its most obvious, perhaps, in the many fearful discussions and debates of deforestation and the need for reforestation in Algeria. Heavily influenced by the ubiquitous story of the deforestation of the North African environment by the "natives," and the need to restore it to its Roman fertility, fruitfulness, and forestedness, concerned French colonists took their cause to Paris. Influential groups such as the Ligue du Reboisement de l'Algérie (Algerian reforestation league) used the narrative to lobby continuously and persuasively for reforestation in Algeria, an activity that required both money and political willpower. Powerful political figures like parliamentarian (and later minister) Eugène Étienne were sympathetic to their cause.

By 1883, signs that the colonial environmental vision was being taken seriously in France were becoming increasingly apparent. That year, the minister of agriculture in Paris, persuaded in part by the reforestation arguments of Dr. Trolard, president of the Ligue du Reboisement, decreed a new policy that provided tree seedlings to Algerian colonists at no charge.[52] In 1886, the concerns about deforestation and debates over forestry in Algeria captured enough concern in France that an Algerian forestry group was formed in the French senate.[53] Throughout the 1870s, 1880s, and into the early 1890s, the budget for the Algerian forest service was increased as were personnel. The number of fines for forest infractions multiplied precipitously. The power of the forest service grew so great that, in the words of one historian, it became "a veritable state within a state" and ran roughshod over the local Algerians.[54]

The most far-reaching change enacted by the French government in Paris to be based on the French colonial environmental imaginary was the 1903 Algerian Forest Code.[55] Building on decades of vocal concern by foresters and others in Algeria that massive deforestation had occurred since Roman times, this punitive and restrictive new law placed a special emphasis on reforestation. The chief forest inspector, Henri Lefebvre, had lamented only three years before this, in 1900, the destruction of the thick forests of antiquity and proposed that a close examination of geologic maps could provide the vision for "the reconstitution of the forests of Algeria from the Roman period."[56] Two decades before this, forest inspector Reynard had voiced similar concerns, including even the arid south of Alger province. He claimed that this region "was at an earlier time highly populated: many Roman ruins cover the country. . . . The rivers there have gradually diminished with general deforestation. This idea is corroborated by the numerous traces of ancient forests."[57] Like the vast majority of foresters working in or visiting Algeria from France, Reynard believed that the forests must be restored because, since the Roman period, the local Algerians, especially the nomads, had burned and overgrazed and thus had "created the sand dunes where all vegetation has disappeared."[58] The director of forestry in France, Louis Tassy, had expressed similar concerns in his 1872 report on Algerian forests.[59]

In addition to codifying several disparate decrees promulgated earlier in the colonial period dealing with conserving existing forests by criminalizing forest fires, grazing, growing, and gathering on forest land, the 1903 forest law reflected ubiquitous concerns about deforestation and desiccation. It facilitated the expropriation of land nearly anywhere, even sand dunes, for reforestation perimeters in the name of environmental protection for the public good.[60] This was because written into the law was the incorrect belief, drawn from the colonial environmental narrative, that deforestation necessarily caused climatic deterioration and desiccation, and that planting trees would "bring back the rains."

A series of six bylaws were added to the 1903 law in June 1904 that spelled out how the 1903 forest law would be applied. One of the conclusions of the report commissioned to formulate the bylaws was that Algeria should be at least 30 percent forested whereas it was only 10 percent forested and therefore approximately five million hectares urgently needed to be reforested.[61] Within a year of the passing of the Algerian forest law, reforestation perimeters began to be declared. To organize this important work, a special reforestation service was created in 1908.[62] By the 1930s, 408,000 hectares had been placed under nineteen different reforestation perimeters.[63] This was in addition to the nearly 2.5 million hectares of Algerian forest, roughly 75 percent of total forest, owned by the state at this time.[64] By the early 1950s, 7.5 million hectares had been identified as potential reforestation perimeters and more than two million hectares actually had been demarcated reforestation perimeters.[65]

The 1903 forest law and the less comprehensive laws that preceded it, along with the powerful land laws of 1846, 1863 and 1873, significantly transformed the landscape of Algeria. What had been a landscape dominated by indigenous forest use, subsistence agriculture, and vast expanses of pasture land held in common by the Algerian tribes, became a highly regulated, privately and state-owned landscape dominated by European agribusiness. Whereas the colonial state dominated the protection and production of the vast majority of Algeria's forestland, private ventures led the transformation of Algeria's agricultural landscape. Driven by the belief that during the Roman period, large amounts of wheat, vines, and olives had thrived and supported large populations, colonists did their best to emulate the ancient example. Until the 1880s, wheat dominated European agricultural production, in large part because it was not capital intensive. With the phylloxera crisis in France and the drop in international prices of wheat, the 1880s saw a phenomenal growth in viticulture in Algeria and Tunisia. In Algeria, 15,000 hectares of vines in 1878 had increased to 110,000 hectares by 1890.[66]

This spectacular growth was fueled in many cases by the French colonial environmental imaginary. A striking example comes from the young protectorate of Tunisia, annexed by France in 1881. The director of agriculture, Paul Bourde, deeply influenced by the colonial environmental narrative, believed that under Roman administration this region "had long ago a great reputation of fertility," and he blamed the "Arab invasion" for its "sterilization."[67] He wrote in the report justifying a new decree that the

Romans had initiated olive cultivation in Tunisia, creating a huge forest in the region of Sfax, in the first century and "they became very rich."[68] Armed with this imaginary, in 1893 he enacted policies that favored and encouraged the planting of olive and fruit trees on a massive scale by European colonists and capitalists. Over the next half century, thanks to these policies, the landscape, especially around Sfax, was completely transformed by the planting of more than 6 million olive trees and 2.3 million fruit trees.[69]

In Algeria, one of the biggest transformations of the landscape, and probably one of the largest efforts at reforestation, was produced with the planting of eucalyptus trees. An Australian native plant, eucalyptus was introduced to North Africa by Prosper Ramel, and its propagation and spread were avidly encouraged by one settler in particular, François Trottier. Known as the apostle of eucalyptus, he was deeply inspired by the colonial environmental imaginary. Trottier not only planted thousands of the trees himself, he also wrote multiple influential and widely read tracts during the late 1860s and 1870s extolling the virtues of eucalyptus for Algeria. Echoing common sentiments in Algeria at this time, Trottier proclaimed that reforesting with eucalyptus would supply wood for Algeria and France, that it would regularize the rains, improve the climate, purify the country, and thus favor civilization. Such changes he believed were necessary to prevent the moral deterioration commonly encountered when living in Africa.[70] By the late 1870s, approximately four million eucalyptus trees had been planted.[71] Hundreds of thousands more were planted later by various parties, including municipal governments around Algeria, railway and mining companies, and many settlers. By the mid-1870s, so many eucalyptus trees had been planted that one French journalist remarked that "a stranger who was not instructed of its exotic origin would take it for one of the indigenous trees of the region."[72] By the 1890s, eucalyptus trees had been planted in most villages and towns of Algeria. For his successful efforts at reforesting Algeria, Trottier was awarded the prestigious Cross of the Legion of Honor in 1878.[73]

In Morocco, the last territory to be conquered by the French in North Africa, the French colonial environmental imaginary was invoked from the very beginning of French control. The first and most influential of the governors-general of Morocco, Louis H.-G. Lyautey, believed that Morocco had been one of the granaries of Rome, and he acted on that belief.[74] For much of the colonial period in Morocco, agricultural development was driven by the legend of the granary of Rome, especially in the cereals sector. Known as the "wheat policy," the development and expansion of wheat cultivation in Morocco into the early 1930s reshaped significant portions of the protectorate's agricultural land.[75]

In the realm of forestry, a single man, the director of forestry Paul Boudy, developed the 1917 Moroccan forest code (based on Algeria's) and its attendant policies, fundamentally reshaping lands categorized as forest as well as curtailing forest resource use and access. An article he published at the end of his career in 1954, titled "The Resurrection of the Moroccan Forest," provided a triumphant overview of the forest service's work and also summed up many of Boudy's beliefs about forests in Morocco. He estimated that about two-thirds of Morocco's original forests had been destroyed since the "Arab invasions."[76] Like Trolard before him, Boudy believed that North Africa should have a rate of woodedness of 30 percent, and that it did have earlier, during the thriving and productive Roman period.

In the first tome of his four-volume masterpiece, the *North African Forest Economy*, Boudy eloquently articulated the still dominant colonial environmental narrative.[77] He added to his arsenal of documentation the new "natural vegetation" maps drawn up by the ecologist Louis Emberger in the 1930s, which "scientifically proved" the massive deforestation that had until then been deduced primarily from literary sources and questionable botanical theories.[78] These maps, though, were created by using the French colonial environmental narrative and simply put in authoritative map form the story that had been told of deforestation since the early years of the Algerian occupation.

The impact of Emberger's natural (potential) vegetation maps, as well as Boudy's inflated deforestation statistics derived from these maps, on the North African environment has been profound. During the late colonial period the maps and statistics informed countless projects to try to reforest the region, control erosion, and prevent further deforestation. Still considered some of the most authoritative sources on North African ecology and forestry today, Emberger's maps and Boudy's *North African Forest Economy* continue to be cited in support of a variety of local, regional, and international environment and development projects. Many of these projects fail since they are based on spurious ecological information, and, moreover, they are often socially disruptive.[79] Millions of hectares of land and millions of people in North Africa have been touched in some way by this long-lasting French colonial environmental history.

THE LEGACY of the French colonial environmental imaginary, then, is still with us today in the form of a commonly accepted environmental history of North Africa that continues to drive a significant amount of environmental and agricultural policy formulation at national and international scales.[80] Embedded in many of these reports and plans is the idea that indigenous

North Africans don't respect vegetation, especially trees, whereas those in the "civilized world" of Europe and North America revere trees and understand the ecological importance of vegetative cover. This, too, is largely a legacy of the French colonial environmental history of the Maghreb. It was repeated with great frequency during the colonial period that "the natives manifest a veritable hatred for trees."[81] Such claims were usually contrasted with the love the French had of trees and the care with which they protected their forests and other important plants. This was a common sentiment among most Europeans at the time as it was in North America.

The dichotomy of tree lovers versus tree haters played well into the sense of identity that the French developed in colonial North Africa. Building on long-established traditions of seeing themselves as the heirs of Rome in France, as well as in Rome's former imperial territories, the French quickly adopted this trope in the Maghreb. The tree-loving French envisioned themselves bringing civilization to the desert by planting trees and saving the forest from abuse by the local inhabitants, thus re-creating the supposedly thick forests of the Roman era. Looking to Roman examples and claiming Roman heritage also helped guide them in the war of conquest, develop agricultural improvement plans, sedentarize the troublesome nomads, and construct a distinct colonial identity as "Latin Africans."[82]

This chapter has explored the role of the French colonial environmental history of North Africa as a key component of colonial identity among the settlers living in the Maghreb and also how it informed certain notions of French imperial and thus national identity in France. Restoring the allegedly ruined environment to its imperial Roman glory with reforestation and agricultural improvements was something nearly all the French could point to with pride. Especially during the 1930s and 1940s, a sense of "imperial identity" grew stronger in France as a result of multiple factors, including the strong promotion of colonization by the government as well as historical impetuses such as the psychological toll of the Franco-Prussian war.[83]

As many of their other colonial possessions were beginning to fall apart, the Maghreb territories, especially Algeria, became even more important to the French. Held up as models of colonial success, they were in many ways crucial to notions of French imperial identity in large part because the "affirmation of French greatness was central to all definitions of French identity."[84] And as Krishan Kumar has recently argued, "The making of French national identity, just like the making of English national identity, has to be seen at least in part as a product of imperial ambitions and imperial rule."[85] In reality, though, ideas of imperial identity likely remained more an official and elite discourse than a focus of attention for the lay public.[86]

The French colonial environmental imaginary of North Africa thus may be seen as an important component of French settler identity in North Africa and also as an overlooked component of imperial and national identity in France, especially in official circles. As the heirs of Rome in North Africa, many French felt it was their duty and also a matter of honor to restore "their environment" to its ancient productive glory. Since the North African landscape was perceived as a landscape of "Gallo-Roman" self, rather than a foreign, exotic, and threatening landscape, restoring it was seen as a relatively simple affair. Reforestation, agricultural improvements, and outlawing many indigenous uses of the land were deemed to be sufficient to create a "new France" in North Africa.

The belief that the North African environment was a landscape of "self," degraded but relatively easily restored to productivity, sets the French experience with nature there apart from the vast majority of European imperial experiences with nature around the globe. Rather than forging an identity out of the need to "tame" or "control" an exotic, wild, and dangerous landscape as occurred in so many other European colonial encounters, the French in North Africa identified themselves as heroes who had restored the ruined environment and proved themselves the true heirs of Rome.

Notes

I thank Paul Claval for his thoughtful comments on an early draft of this chapter. I am also grateful to Michael Greenhalgh for providing me with a copy of his article cited below.

1. Derek Gregory, "(Post)Colonialism and the Production of Nature," in *Social Nature: Theory, Practice, and Politics*, ed. Noel Castree and Bruce Braun (Malden, Mass.: Blackwell, 2001), 98 cited. Gregory is drawing on Edward Said's influential book *Orientalism* and quoting Nancy Stepan, "Tropical Nature as a Way of Writing," in *Mundializacion de la ciencia y cultural national*, ed. A. Lafluente, A. Elena, and M. L. Ortega (Madrid: Doce Calles, 1991), 495–504. See also Nancy Leys Stepan, *Picturing Tropical Nature* (Ithaca, N.Y.: Cornell University Press, 2001), 17–18.

2. See Richard Drayton, *Nature's Government: Science, Imperial Britain, and the "Improvement" of the World* (New Haven: Yale University Press, 2000), for a good discussion of imperial notions of improvement.

3. Richard H. Grove, *Green Imperialism: Colonial Expansion, Tropical Island Edens and the Origins of Environmentalism, 1600–1860* (Cambridge: Cambridge University Press, 1995).

4. Stephen Daniels, *Fields of Vision: Landscape Imagery and National Identity in England and the United States* (Cambridge: Polity Press, 1993), 5.

5. See Stepan, *Picturing*.

6. David Arnold, *The Problem of Nature: Environment, Culture and European Expansion* (Oxford: Blackwell, 1996), see esp. 141–68. Arnold traces this change favoring more negative representations of tropical nature to approximately the mid-eighteenth century (see 150–53). See also Suzana Sawyer and Arun Agrawal, "Environmental Orientalisms," *Cultural Critique* 45, no. 1 (2000): 71–108.

7. See discussion in Stepan, *Picturing*, 17–18 and Arnold, *Problem*, esp. chap. 8, of various definitions of tropics and tropicality.

8. See Arnold, *Problem*, 169–87. See also David Gilmartin, "Models of the Hydraulic Environment: Colonial Irrigation, State Power and Community in the Indus Basin," in *Nature, Culture, Imperialism: Essays on the Environmental History of South Asia*, ed. David Arnold and Ramachandra Guha (Delhi: Oxford University Press, 1998), 210–36.

9. See Richard H. Grove, *Ecology, Climate and Empire: Colonialism and Global Environmental History, 1400–1940* (Cambridge: White Horse Press, 1997), 86–123.

10. See Kate B. Showers, *Imperial Gullies: Soil Erosion and Conservation in Lesotho* (Athens: Ohio University Press, 2005).

11. What the evidence demonstrates, in contrast to the colonial story, is that Roman overcultivation began to produce land degradation that was "followed [by] a phase of relative soil conservation and vegetative regeneration with the more nomadic land-use system of the Arabs." Bruno Messerli and Matthias Winiger, "Climate, Environmental Change, and Resources of the African Mountains from the Mediterranean to the Equator," *Mountain Research and Development* 12, no. 4 (1992): 332. For details explaining the evidence showing that North Africa has not suffered significant deforestation or environmental degradation over the last two thousand years, see Diana K. Davis, *Resurrecting the Granary of Rome: Environmental History and French Colonial Expansion in North Africa* (Athens: Ohio University Press, 2007), chap. 1.

12. For a full articulation of this French colonial environmental narrative and its consequences, see Davis, *Resurrecting*.

13. J.-A.-N. Périer, *Exploration scientifique de l'Algérie: Sciences médicales: De l'hygiène en Algérie*, 2 vols. (Paris: Imprimerie Royale, 1847), 1:29.

14. Ibid., 30.

15. See Charles-Robert Ageron, *Les Algériens musulmans et la France (1871–1919)* (Paris: Presses Universitaires de France, 1968); M'hammed Boukhobza, *Monde rural: Contraintes et mutations* (Alger: Office des Publications Universitaires, 1992); Jean Brignon, Abdelaziz Amine, Brahim Boutaleb, et al., *Histoire du Maroc* (Paris: Hatier, 1967); Jean Poncet and André Raymond, *La Tunisie* (Paris: Presses Universitaires de France, 1971); and Djilali Sari, *La Dépossession des fellahs* (Alger: Société Nationale d'Édition et de Diffusion, 1978).

16. Jean Colin, *L'Occupation romaine du Maroc, cours préparatoire* (Rabat: Service des Affaires Indigènes, 1925), 3.

17. Ibid., 13.

18. See Will D. Swearingen, *Moroccan Mirages: Agrarian Dreams and Deceptions, 1912–1986* (Princeton: Princeton University Press, 1987) for an excellent discussion of the development of agricultural policies and practices in Morocco.

19. M. de Mont Rond, *Histoire de la conquête de l'Algérie de 1830–1847* (Paris: Imprimerie de E. Marc-Aurel, Éditeur, 1847), 6. He clarified that Algeria, at the northern, European, end of the African continent, does not share anything with the continent of which it is a part. Rather, "the air there is generally healthy and temperate, the plants and the trees more European than tropical, wheat ... appears to be there in its native soil ... and its production is the most abundant and the easiest." Ibid., 7.

20. *Bulletin de la Ligue du Reboisement de l'Algérie,* no. 1, 1882, 2, 6.

21. Ligue du Reboisement, *La Forêt: Conseils aux indigènes* (Alger: Imprimerie de l'Association Ouvrière P. Fontana, 1883), 2. Trolard believed that the Sahara had been created by the nomads' overgrazing and deforesting the environment. Another influential colonist, August Warnier, went so far as to proclaim that "France itself, so prosperous, would soon become a desert if it were in the hands of the Arabs." Auguste Warnier, *L'Algérie devant l'empereur, pour faire suite à L'Algérie devant le sénat, et à L'Algérie devant l'opinion publique* (Paris: Challamel Ainé, 1865), 28.

22. Paul Claval, "From Michelet to Braudel: Personality, Identity and Organization of France," in *Geography and National Identity,* ed. David Hooson (Oxford: Blackwell, 1994), 40.

23. Chandra Mukerji, "The New Rome: Infrastructure and National Identity on the Canal du Midi," *Osiris* 24, no. 1 (2009): 15.

24. See Harold Parker, *The Cult of Antiquity and the French Revolutionaries* (Chicago: University of Chicago Press, 1937).

25. Michael J. Heffernan, "An Imperial Utopia: French Surveys of North Africa in the Early Colonial Period," in *Maps and Africa,* ed. J. Stone (Aberdeen: Aberdeen University African Studies Group, 1994), 82.

26. Patricia M. Lorcin, "Rome and France in Africa: Recovering Colonial Algeria's Latin Past," *French Historical Studies* 25, no. 2 (2002): 295–329.

27. For discussions of national identity, see David Hooson, Introduction to *Geography and National Identity,* ed. David Hooson (Oxford: Blackwell, 1994), 1–12, and Benedict Anderson, *Imagined Communities: Reflections on the Origin and Spread of Nationalism* (London: Verso, 1991).

28. Jules Michelet, *The People,* trans. John P. McKay (Urbana: University of Illinois Press, 1973), 185. Michelet clarified a few pages later that France "is not a mixture of two principles. In her the Celtic element has combined with the Roman, and the two are really one. The Germanic element, which some people are always talking about, is really imperceptible. She proceeds directly from Rome, and she ought to teach Rome—its language, its history and its law"

(193). Michelet is considered one of the key actors who articulated broadly held notions of national identity in France at this time. See Claval, "Michelet to Braudel." As Claval points out, Michelet also saw diversity as one of the defining qualities of France's identity, a notion shared by Vidal de la Blache.

29. Edouard Lapène, *Vingt-six mois à Bougie ou collection de mémoires sur sa conquête, son occupation et son avenir* (Paris: Éditions Bouchene, 2002), 131.

30. For details, see Jacques Frémeaux, "Souvenirs de Rome et présence française au Maghreb: Essai d'investigation," in *Connaissances du Maghreb: Sciences sociales et colonisation,* ed. Jean-Claude Vatin (Paris: CNRS, 1984), 29–46; and Lorcin, "Rome and France."

31. As Heffernan explains, "In a conscious effort to replicate Roman imperial practice, [Governor-General] Clauzel began to experiment with agricultural projects on 'vacant' Algerian land," and by 1835, "the first recognisable settler village was established at Boufarick, south of Algiers." See Heffernan, "Imperial Utopia," 84.

32. See Augustin Bernard and Napoléon Lacroix, *L'Évolution du nomadisme en Algérie* (Alger: Adolphe Jourdan, 1906), 20–22.

33. See Michael Greenhalgh, "The New Centurions: French Reliance on the Roman Past during the Conquest of Algeria," *War and Society* 16, no. 1 (1998): 1–28.

34. Lorcin, "Rome and France," 308. See also Edmund Burke, "The Image of the Moroccan State in French Ethnological Literature: A New Look at the Origin of Lyautey's Berber Policy," in *Arabs and Berbers: From Tribe to Nation in North Africa,* ed. Ernest Gellner and Charles Micaud (Lexington, Mass.: Lexington Books, 1972), 175–99. In his early work the historian Charles-Robert Ageron was the first to explore these ideas. See Charles-Robert Ageron, *Politiques coloniales au Maghreb* (Paris: Presses Universitaires de France, 1972), and Ageron, *Algériens*.

35. Yves Lacoste, *Ibn Khaldun: The Birth of History and the Past of the Third World,* trans. David Macey (London: Verso Editions, 1984), 75–76, 78.

36. Amédée Desjobert, *L'Algérie en 1846* (Paris: Guillaumin, 1846), 5. Indeed, some in the anticolonial lobby portrayed North Africa as a "barren wasteland, filled with savage beasts and wild tribesmen." Heffernan, "Imperial Utopia," 83.

37. Robert Aldrich, *Greater France: A History of French Overseas Expansion* (London: Macmillan, 1996), 97.

38. Swearingen, *Moroccan Mirages,* 6.

39. For more details, see Aldrich, *Greater France,* 89–121.

40. Ibid.

41. Claval, "Michelet to Braudel," 50.

42. Ibid. Notions of French identity have been heavily debated over the years. For a couple of influential texts, see Fernand Braudel, *L'Identité de la France* (Paris: Flammarion, 1986), and Edmond Lipiansky, *L'Identité française: Représentations, mythes, idéologies* (La Garenne-Colombes: Éditions de l'espace européen, 1991).

43. France's North African territories, especially Algeria, were held up as "models of colonial installation" to be emulated in other parts of French Africa. See Auguste Chevalier, *L'Agronomie coloniale et le Muséum National d'Histoire Naturelle: Premieres conférences du cours sur les productions coloniales végétales & l'agronomie tropicale* (Paris: Laboratoire d'Agronomie Coloniale, 1930), 2.

44. See Charles-Robert Ageron, *Histoire de l'Algérie Contemporaine, Tome II: De l'insurrection de 1871 au déclenchement de la guerre de libération (1954)* (Paris: Presses Universitaires de France, 1979), 403–11.

45. Quote from the French newspaper *Le Temps*, quoted ibid., 406.

46. Augustin Bernard, *L'Algérie*, ed. Gabriel Hanotaux and Alfred Martineau, vol. 2 of *Histoire des colonies françaises et de l'expansion de la France dans le monde*, 6 vols. (Paris: Librairie Plon, 1930), 535.

47. Ibid., 523. Similar ideas were expressed in popular publications as well. The 1930 *Michelin Guide to North Africa*, for example, proudly proclaimed that "the tradition of Rome has been renewed, but more humanely, generously, and extensively" because France brought the "benefits of civilization." From the 1930 *Michelin Guide to Morocco, Algeria and Tunisia*, quoted in Ellen Furlough, "Une leçon des choses: Tourism, Empire and the Nation in Interwar France," *French Historical Studies* 25, no. 3 (2002): 455. This article contains an interesting discussion of imperial national identity in 1930s France and the role of tourism to North Africa.

48. Bernard, *L'Algérie*, 532.

49. Ibid., 534. Just a few years later, in the 1937 volume on Northwest Africa for Vidal de la Blache's fifteen-volume *Universal Geography*, Bernard repeated many of his earlier claims. In this volume, though, Bernard explained that Rome had actually had an easier time administering North Africa because "they had not found, as had the French, a country ruined by long centuries of anarchy." Nor had the Romans had to "clash" with Islam. See Augustin Bernard, *Afrique septentrionale et occidentale: Première partie: Généralités—Afrique du nord*, vol. 1 of *Géographie universelle*, ed. Paul Vidal de la Blache, 15 vols. (Paris: Librairie Armand Colin, 1937), 77.

50. Ibid., 276.

51. See Davis, *Resurrecting*, for a detailed overview of how the colonial environmental narrative strongly informed these legal changes and their results.

52. See letter of 29 March 1883 from the Ministère de l'Agriculture, Direction des Forêts, Paris, to M. le Lievre, Senateur de Département d'Alger, reprinted in *Bulletin de la Ligue*, no. 18 (1883), 345–46.

53. *Bulletin de la Ligue*, no. 53 (1886), 1055.

54. Ageron, *Histoire*, 208. The 1892 "Ferry Report" exposed many of the excesses and problems in the Algerian forestry department but little was done to correct them.

55. For the first seventy years of French occupation of Algeria, the French Forest Code had been applied to Algeria with several associated decrees that had been created to deal with forests in Algeria. The 1903 Algerian Forest Code

was also based on the metropolitan French Forest Code, and it likewise privileged industrial production such as timber and cork over subsistence uses such as grazing, which it outlawed.

56. Henri Lefebvre, *Les Forêts de l'Algérie* (Alger-Mustapha: Giralt, 1900), 100.

57. J. Reynard, *Restauration des forêts et des pâturages du sud de l'Algérie (province d'Alger)* (Alger: Typographie Adolphe Jourdan, 1880), 6.

58. Ibid., 15–16. As early as 1851, these ideas were being refuted by specialists such as agronomist Auguste Hardy, who wrote that "the deforestation of Algeria is a natural consequence of its climate: it is caused more by the pernicious influence of the harmful winds and the poor seasonality of the rains than by the pasturing of animals and the fires set by herders, where the cause is so constantly sought." Auguste Hardy, "Note climatologique sur l'Algérie au point de vue agricole," in *Recueil de traités d'agriculture de d'hygiène à l'usage des colons de l'Algérie*, ed. Ministre de la Guerre (Alger: Imprimerie du Gouvernement, 1851), 48. Another scholar who refuted part of the conventional deforestation narrative was the geographer Élisée Reclus, author of the twelve-volume *New Universal Geography* describing the earth and its peoples. Although Reclus believed that the forests in the Maghreb were indeed thicker and more extensive long ago, he apportioned part of the blame for deforestation to the Romans themselves. He is also one of the only writers on North African forests to note the robust regrowth of many forest trees that was and is common in the region. See Élisée Reclus, *L'Afrique septentrionale*, vol. 11 of *Nouvelle géographie universelle: La terre et les hommes*, 12 vols. (1886), 365.

59. Louis-François Victor Tassy, *Service forestier de l'Algérie, rapport adressé à m. le gouverneur de l'Algérie* (Paris: Typographie A. Hennuyer, 1872).

60. See Angel-Paul Carayol, *La Législation forestière de l'Algérie* (Paris: Arthur Rousseau, Éditeur, 1906), 169–71.

61. Gouvernement Général de l'Algérie (GGA), *Commission d'études forestières* (Alger: Imprimerie Typographique et Papeterie J. Torrent, 1904), 101.

62. Paul Boudy, *Économie forestière nord-africaine: Milieu physique et milieu humain* (Paris: Éditions Larose, 1948), 1:479.

63. Ibid.

64. For figures, see ibid., 369 and John Ruedy, *Modern Algeria: The Origins and Development of a Nation* (Bloomington: Indiana University Press, 1992), 95.

65. Boudy, *Économie forestière*, 1:380–82. Probably due to financial constraints, only about 3 percent of this large area declared reforestation perimeters was actually reforested (ibid.).

66. Charles-Robert Ageron, *Modern Algeria: A History from 1830 to the Present*, trans. Michael Brett (London: Hearst, 1991), 60.

67. Paul Bourde, *Rapport sur les cultures fruitières et en particulier sur la culture de l'olivier dans le centre de la Tunisie* (Tunis: Imprimerie Générale [Picard, 1899), 3.

68. Ibid., 25.

69. Jean Poncet, *Paysages et problèmes ruraux en Tunisie* (Paris: Presses Universitaires de France, 1962), 257–58.

70. François Trottier, *Notes sur l'eucalyptus et subsidiairement sur la nécessité du reboisement de l'Algérie* (Alger: Typographie et Lithographie de F. Paysant, 1867), 5–6. The fear of moral and physical deterioration in North Africa was common among settlers in Algeria. Many believed that deforestation had led to an unhealthy desiccation and a torrid climate that threatened European civilization in the Maghreb. This underlying fear motivated many settlers to advocate for reforestation. For more details, see Davis, *Resurrecting*, 72, 102–6, 109–22, and 149–50. See also Caroline Ford, "Reforestation, Landscape Conservation, and the Anxieties of Empire in French Colonial Algeria," *American Historical Review* 113, no. 2 (2008): 341–62. Although it is true, as Ford points out, that these anxieties motivated a great deal of attention to issues of deforestation and reforestation in Algeria, similar anxieties that connected deforestation and other environmental degradation with questions of climate change, race, hygiene, and the (im)possibilities of European colonization were quite common throughout the global south and not unique to Algeria. See Gregory, "(Post)Colonialism"; Grove, *Green Imperialism*; Stepan, *Picturing*; and Arnold, *Problem*, among many other examples.

71. Achilles Filias, *Notice sur les forêts de l'Algérie: Leur étendue; leurs essences; leurs produits* (Alger: Imprimerie Administrative Gojosso, 1878), 20.

72. J. E. Planchon, "L'Eucalyptus globulus au point de vue Botanique, économique et médical," *Revue des Deux Mondes* 7, no. 1 January (1875): 163.

73. Narcisse Faucon, *Le Livre d'or de l'Algérie: Histoire politique, militaire, administrative, événements et faits principaux, biographie des hommes ayant marquée dans l'armée, les sciences, les lettres, etc.* (Paris: Challamel, 1889), 516. A street in Algiers was named Trottier in the 1880s.

74. Louis Lyautey, *Paroles d'action* (Paris: Imprimerie Nationale Éditions, 1995), 444–45.

75. See Swearingen, *Moroccan Mirages*, for details.

76. Paul Boudy, "L'Oeuvre forestière française au Maroc," *Bulletin de la Société Forestière de Franche-Comté et des Provinces de l'Est* 27, no. 1 (1954): 3.

77. Boudy, *Économie forestière*, 223–29.

78. For details, see Davis, *Resurrecting*, 149–57.

79. See ibid., 169–75, for examples.

80. See, for example, Diana K. Davis, "Neoliberalism, Environmentalism and Agricultural Restructuring in Morocco," *Geographical Journal* 172, no. 2 (2006): 88–105.

81. Bernard and Lacroix, *L'Évolution*, 44. See also Paul Boudy, *L'Arbre et les forêts au Maroc: Cours préparatoire au service des affaires indigènes* (Rabat: Résidence Générale de France au Maroc, Direction Générale des Affaires Indigènes, 1927), and Auguste Terrier, *Le Maroc* (Paris: Librairie Larousse, 1931), 187, who claimed that "as everywhere, the Arab has destroyed the tree."

82. See Lorcin, "Rome and France," for a full articulation of these ideas of Roman heritage for identity formation in colonial Algeria.

83. For a discussion of the 1931 colonial exhibition and "imperil identity" in France, see Charles-Robert Ageron, "L'Exposition coloniale de 1931: Mythe républican ou mythe impérial?," in *Les Lieux de mémoire: La République*, ed. Pierre Nora (Paris: Gallimard, 1984), 561–91. He concludes that a sense of imperial identity in France was likely stronger in the 1940s than in the 1950s.

84. Anne Sa'adah quoted in Krishan Kumar, "English and French National Identity: Comparisons and Contrasts," *Nations and Nationalisms* 12, no. 3 (2006): 428 n. 5.

85. Ibid., 417.

86. Paul Claval, personal communication via e-mail, February 2010.

Bibliography

Ageron, Charles-Robert. *Les Algériens musulmans et la France (1871–1919)*. Paris: Presses Universitaires de France, 1968.

———. "L'Exposition coloniale de 1931: Mythe républican ou mythe impérial?" In *Les Lieux de Mémoire: La République*, ed. Pierre Nora, 561–91. Paris: Gallimard, 1984.

———. *Histoire de l'Algérie contemporaine, Tome II: De l'insurrection de 1871 au déclenchement de la guerre de libération (1954)*. Paris: Presses Universitaires de France, 1979.

———. *Modern Algeria: A History from 1830 to the Present*. Translated by Michael Brett. London: Hearst 1991.

———. *Politiques coloniales au Maghreb*. Paris: Presses Universitaires de France, 1972.

Aldrich, Robert. *Greater France: A History of French Overseas Expansion*. London: Macmillan, 1996.

Anderson, Benedict. *Imagined Communities: Reflections on the Origin and Spread of Nationalism*. London: Verso, 1991.

Arnold, David. *The Problem of Nature: Environment, Culture and European Expansion*. Oxford: Blackwell, 1996.

Bernard, Augustin. *Afrique septentrionale et occidentale. Première partie: Généralités—Afrique du nord*. Vol. 1 of *Géographie universelle*, edited by Paul Vidal de la Blache. 15 vols. Paris: Librairie Armand Colin, 1937.

———. *L'Algérie*. Edited by Gabriel Hanotaux and Alfred Martineau. Vol. 2 of *Histoire des colonies françaises et de l'expansion de la France dans le monde*. 6 vols. Paris: Librairie Plon, 1930.

Bernard, Augustin, and Napoléon Lacroix. *L'Évolution du nomadisme en Algérie*. Alger: Adolphe Jourdan, 1906.

Boudy, Paul. *L'Arbre et les forêts au Maroc. Cours préparatoire au service des affaires indigènes*. Rabat: Résidence Générale de France au Maroc, Direction Générale des Affaires Indigènes, 1927.

———. *Économie forestière nord-africaine: Milieu physique et milieu humain*. Vol. 1. Paris: Éditions Larose, 1948.

---. "L'Oeuvre forestière française au Maroc." *Bulletin de la Société Forestière de Franche-Comté et des Provinces de l'Est* 27, no. 1 (1954): 1–10.
Boukhobza, M'hammed. *Monde rural: Contraintes et mutations.* Alger: Office des Publications Universitaires, 1992.
Bourde, Paul. *Rapport sur les cultures fruitières et en particulier sur la culture de l'olivier dans le centre de la Tunisie.* Tunis: Imprimerie Générale (Picard and Cie), 1899.
Braudel, Fernand. *L'Identité de la France.* Paris: Flammarion, 1986.
Brignon, Jean, Abdelaziz Amine, Brahim Boutaleb, Guy Martinet, and Bernard Rosenberger. *Histoire du Maroc.* Paris: Hatier, 1967.
Burke, Edmund. "The Image of the Moroccan State in French Ethnological Literature: A New Look at the Origin of Lyautey's Berber Policy." In *Arabs and Berbers: From Tribe to Nation in North Africa*, edited by Ernest Gellner and Charles Micaud, 175–99. Lexington, Mass.: Lexington Books, 1972.
Carayol, Angel-Paul. *La Législation forestière de l'Algérie.* Paris: Arthur Rousseau, Éditeur, 1906.
Chevalier, Auguste. *L'Agronomie coloniale et le Muséum National d'Histoire Naturelle: Premieres conférences du cours sur les productions coloniales végétales & l'agronomie tropicale.* Paris: Laboratoire d'Agronomie Coloniale, 1930.
Claval, Paul. "From Michelet to Braudel: Personality, Identity and Organization of France." In *Geography and National Identity*, edited by David Hooson, 39–57. Oxford: Blackwell, 1994.
Colin, Jean. *L'Occupation romaine du Maroc, cours préparatoire.* Rabat: Service des Affaires Indigènes, 1925.
Daniels, Stephen. *Fields of Vision: Landscape Imagery and National Identity in England and the United States.* Cambridge: Polity Press, 1993.
Davis, Diana K. "Neoliberalism, Environmentalism and Agricultural Restructuring in Morocco." *Geographical Journal* 172, no. 2 (2006): 88–105.
---. *Resurrecting the Granary of Rome: Environmental History and French Colonial Expansion in North Africa.* Athens: Ohio University Press, 2007.
de Mont Rond, M. *Histoire de la conquête de l'Algérie de 1830–1847.* Paris: Imprimerie de E. Marc-Aurel, Éditeur, 1847.
Desjobert, Amédée. *L'Algérie en 1846.* Paris: Guillaumin, 1846.
Drayton, Richard. *Nature's Government: Science, Imperial Britain, and the "Improvement" of the World.* New Haven: Yale University Press, 2000.
Faucon, Narcisse. *Le Livre d'or de l'Algérie: Histoire politique, militaire, administrative, événements et faits principaux, biographie des hommes ayant marquée dans l'armée, les sciences, les lettres, etc.* Paris: Challamel, 1889.
Filias, Achilles. *Notice sur les forêts de l'Algérie: Leur étendue; leurs essences; leurs produits.* Alger: Imprimerie Administrative Gojosso, 1878.
Ford, Caroline. "Reforestation, Landscape Conservation, and the Anxieties of Empire in French Colonial Algeria." *American Historical Review* 113, no. 2 (2008): 341–62.

Frémeaux, Jacques. "Souvenirs de Rome et présence française au Maghreb: Essai d'investigation." In *Connaissances du Maghreb: Sciences sociales et colonisation*, edited by Jean-Claude Vatin, 29–46. Paris: CNRS, 1984.

Furlough, Ellen. "Une leçon des choses: Tourism, Empire and the Nation in Interwar France." *French Historical Studies* 25, no. 3 (2002): 441–73.

Gilmartin, David. "Models of the Hydraulic Environment: Colonial Irrigation, State Power and Community in the Indus Basin." In *Nature, Culture, Imperialism: Essays on the Environmental History of South Asia*, edited by David Arnold and Ramachandra Guha, 210–36. Delhi: Oxford University Press, 1998.

Gouvernement Général de l'Algérie (GGA). *Commission d'études forestières*. Alger: Imprimerie Typographique et Papeterie J. Torrent, 1904.

Greenhalgh, Michael. "The New Centurions: French Reliance on the Roman Past during the Conquest of Algeria." *War and Society* 16, no. 1 (1998): 1–28.

Gregory, Derek. "(Post)Colonialism and the Production of Nature." In *Social Nature: Theory, Practice, and Politics*, edited by Noel Castree and Bruce Braun, 84–111. Malden, Mass.: Blackwell, 2001.

Grove, Richard H. *Ecology, Climate and Empire: Colonialism and Global Environmental History, 1400–1940*. Cambridge: White Horse Press, 1997.

———. *Green Imperialism: Colonial Expansion, Tropical Island Edens and the Origins of Environmentalism, 1600–1860*. Cambridge: Cambridge University Press, 1995.

Hardy, Auguste. "Note climatologique sur l'Algérie au point de vue agricole." In *Recueil de traités d'agriculture de d'hygiène à l'usage des colons de l'Algérie*, edited by Ministre de la Guerre, 37–62. Alger: Imprimerie du Gouvernement, 1851.

Heffernan, Michael J. "An Imperial Utopia: French Surveys of North Africa in the Early Colonial Period." In *Maps and Africa*, edited by J. Stone, 81–107. Aberdeen: Aberdeen University African Studies Group, 1994.

Hooson, David. Introduction to *Geography and National Identity*, edited by David Hooson, 1–12. Oxford: Blackwell, 1994.

Kumar, Krishan. "English and French National Identity: Comparisons and Contrasts." *Nations and Nationalisms* 12, no. 3 (2006): 413–32.

Lacoste, Yves. *Ibn Khaldun: The Birth of History and the Past of the Third World*. Translated by David Macey. London: Verso Editions, 1984.

Lapène, Edouard. *Vingt-six mois à Bougie ou collection de mémoires sur sa conquête, son occupation et son avenir*. Paris: Éditions Bouchene, 2002.

Lefebvre, Henri. *Les Forêts de l'Algérie*. Alger-Mustapha: Giralt, 1900.

Lipiansky, Edmond. *L'Identité française: Représentations, mythes, idéologies*. La Garenne-Colombes: Éditions de l'espace européen, 1991.

Lorcin, Patricia M. "Rome and France in Africa: Recovering Colonial Algeria's Latin Past." *French Historical Studies* 25, no. 2 (2002): 295–329.

Lyautey, Louis. *Paroles d'action*. Paris: Imprimerie Nationale Éditions, 1995.

Messerli, Bruno, and Matthias Winiger. "Climate, Environmental Change, and Resources of the African Mountains from the Mediterranean to the Equator." *Mountain Research and Development* 12, no. 4 (1992): 315–36.

Michelet, Jules. *The People.* Translated by John P. McKay. Urbana: University of Illinois Press, 1973.

Mukerji, Chandra. "The New Rome: Infrastructure and National Identity on the Canal du Midi." *Osiris* 24, no. 1 (2009): 15–32.

Parker, Harold. *The Cult of Antiquity and the French Revolutionaries.* Chicago: University of Chicago Press, 1937.

Périer, J.-A.-N. *Exploration scientifique de l'Algérie: Sciences médicales: De l'Hygiène en Algérie.* 2 vols. Paris: Imprimerie Royale, 1847.

Planchon, J. E. "L'Eucalyptus globulus au point de vue Botanique, économique et médical." *Revue des Deux Mondes* 7, no. 1 January (1875): 149–74.

Poncet, Jean. *Paysages et problèmes ruraux en Tunisie.* Paris: Presses Universitaires de France, 1962.

Poncet, Jean, and André Raymond. *La Tunisie.* Paris: Presses Universitaires de France, 1971.

Reboisement, Ligue du. *La Forêt: Conseils aux indigènes.* Alger: Imprimerie de l'Association Ouvrière P. Fontana, 1883.

Reclus, Élisée. *L'Afrique septentrionale.* Vol. 11 of *Nouvelle géographie universelle: La terre et les hommes*, edited by Élisée Reclus. 12 vols. 1886.

Reynard, J. *Restauration des forêts et des pâturages du sud de l'Algérie (province d'Alger).* Alger: Typographie Adolphe Jourdan, 1880.

Ruedy, John. *Modern Algeria: The Origins and Development of a Nation.* Bloomington: Indiana University Press, 1992.

Sari, Djilali. *La Dépossession des fellahs.* Alger: Société Nationale d'Édition et de Diffusion, 1978.

Sawyer, Suzana, and Arun Agrawal. "Environmental Orientalisms." *Cultural Critique* 45, no. 1 (2000): 71–108.

Showers, Kate B. *Imperial Gullies: Soil Erosion and Conservation in Lesotho.* Athens: Ohio University Press, 2005.

Stepan, Nancy. "Tropical Nature as a Way of Writing." In *Mundializacion de la ciencia y cultural national*, edited by A. Lafluente, A. Elena, and M. L. Ortega, 495–504. Madrid: Doce Calles, 1991.

Stepan, Nancy Leys. *Picturing Tropical Nature.* Ithaca, N.Y.: Cornell University Press, 2001.

Swearingen, Will D. *Moroccan Mirages: Agrarian Dreams and Deceptions, 1912–1986.* Princeton: Princeton University Press, 1987.

Tassy, Louis-François Victor. *Service forestier de l'Algérie, rapport adressé à m. le gouverneur de l'Algérie.* Paris: Typographie A. Hennuyer, 1872.

Terrier, Auguste. *Le Maroc.* Paris: Librairie Larousse, 1931.

Trottier, François. *Notes sur l'eucalyptus et subsidiairement sur la nécessité du reboisement de l'Algérie.* Alger: Typographie et Lithographie de F. Paysant, 1867.

Warnier, Auguste. *L'Algérie devant l'empereur, pour faire suite à L'Algérie devant le sénat, et à L'Algérie devant l'opinion publique.* Paris: Challamel Ainé, 1865.

CHAPTER 3

Body of Work

Water and Reimagining the Sahara in the Era of Decolonization

George R. Trumbull IV

"IF YOU knew the secrets of the desert, you would think like me; but you are ignorant of them, and ignorance is the mother of evil."[1] This supremely confident boast, attributed apocryphally to the celebrated Algerian intellectual, poet, and resistance leader, the Emir ʿAbd al-Qâdir, illuminates the centrality of environmental representations to the engendering of projects in the Algerian Sahara. Knowledge of the secrets of the desert, and the definition of such secrets, remained a contested field throughout the history of French intervention in Algeria. As French colonial apologists confronted the challenges of empire in the twentieth century, they increasingly mobilized an array of representations aimed at remaking the land and people of the desert, a body of images both congruent with and dissimilar to earlier representations of the land of thirst and fear.

Colonial understandings of the Sahara as a potential site of economic activity depended on the genesis of new kinds of representation of the environment. Rather than functioning as an unmediated flow of speculative capital from metropole to colony, the economic history of French colonialism, at least in the Sahara, necessitated first a variety of representational investments, from the penny press to the avant-garde tableaux. French interest in the Sahara, for much of the history of colonial Algeria, operated as much at the level of the spectral as the speculative. Any potentially profitable use of the Sahara centered on reconfiguring the Sahara as environmentally suitable for mastery, no mean task. Discussions of profit and investment in the Algerian Sahara arose more frequently as representations, depictions, and hypotheses than as lines in a ledger or tallies of profit and loss. Indeed, such tallies prove nearly impossible to reconcile in any systematic way for the Sahara: the French investment in the desert remained more in paper and in canvas than in cash and in specie. Water functions as a metonym, illustrating the genesis of knowledge and ignorance of, and bodily experiences situated in, the desert. The French colonial authors discussed here—government officials, military officers, travelers, scientists, economists, popularizers of empire, and others—defined Saharan communities in particular, however, through their environmental aspects, drawing on both tropes of desert description rooted in the nineteenth century and twentieth-century fascinations with the potential for technological control over the land. Situated in space through reference to specific landscapes, social practices, ecologies, and natural phenomena, these communities emerge, not solely as social groupings defined as urban or rural, nomadic or sedentary, but also as environmentally defined foci for colonial study and action. This chapter argues that geographic and economic representations of desert environments, and in particular water, operated as mutually reinforcing categories of mediated knowledge that ultimately served to open up the Sahara as a reimagined, utilitarian space for new, technological forms of empire.

Historians have demonstrated the degree to which Algerian communities often remained opaque to French colonial administrators.[2] Indeed, colonial officers more often figured as rather easily manipulated figures of limited power than as representatives of an all-encompassing, all-knowing colonial state whose power intruded on every aspect of Algerian life; in Algeria at least, France neither knew all, nor encompassed all, nor permeated all.[3] Hence, the very relationship between empire and community in colonial Algeria was a tenuous one; Algerians often had good incentive to attempt to insulate their communities, whether socially, religiously, or geographically, from colonial officials. If colonial administrators ignored 'Abd al-Qâdir's secrets of the desert, it was perhaps not by accident, but rather due to the will and actions of people like 'Abd al-Qâdir himself.

Analyzing the discontinuities of the history of people in their environments has given rise to multiple methods of historical inquiry. In a 1995 essay, Alfred Crosby memorably dismissed American environmental historians as "more interested in dirt than in perceptions . . . of dirt. . . . They have no doubts about the reality of what they deal with, nor about their ability to come to grips with it. . . . They do not suffer from epistemological malaise." If true, that lack of epistemological malaise seems something of an intellectual luxury, if not a blessing.[4] In contrast, the historian of Germany David Blackbourn posed the question, "What of real geographies?," a question more provocative to historians, I think, than to geographers.[5] People live in tangible worlds, not only in discursive ones, though these various environments exist in superimposition upon one another. Experiences of thirst and experiences of taste both represent means of environmental inquiry. In an essay on conservation history, Frank Uekötter, following on Blackbourn, contends that "nature is not only a cultural construct but also a physical reality. . . . Nature has its own logic, and does not care for human attributes of 'good' or 'bad' results," nor, presumably, for 'Abd al-Qâdir's categories of ignorance and evil. Environmental historians of Africa have largely eschewed reinscribing the false binary of representational and "real" environmental histories. As James McCann has noted, "Environmental and landscape history is also . . . the history of ideas, perceptions and prescriptions about" the land.[6] Although McCann explicitly excludes the Maghreb from his frame of reference,[7] Diana K. Davis has persuasively demonstrated the centrality of environmental narratives to colonial practice in North Africa.[8]

The historiography on deserts in particular remains somewhat thinner than that of environmental history more broadly. Recent interest in the history of the Sahara specifically has focused especially on patterns of political control rather than on discourses and practices of—or claims to—environmental mastery.[9] Even fewer scholars have attempted to conceive of the history of deserts in a comparative framework. Nevertheless, work on other deserts points at fruitful research directions within the history of the Sahara. In particular, Robert Vitalis's argument about the connections between Jim Crow, American capitalism, and the oil industry in Saudi Arabia raises important questions about the nature of discriminatory imperial systems and the peculiar social worlds of desert technological communities.[10]

Wealth of Another Nature

The environmental delineations of desert life dictated, in part, certain definitions of community in colonial Algeria. Early, nineteenth-century discussions of desert environments helped frame, though did not determine, debates about the Sahara throughout French colonialism in Algeria. In 1859, Jules Duval, a magistrate, administrator, journalist, and economist in the then-province of Oran, neatly cleaved his world in two: "The Tell," the hills of littoral Algeria, "reflects . . . the mores, the sciences, the arts of civilization. . . . Everything else is the Sahara. . . . Here wealth is of another nature."[11] Other natures—deserts in place of hills—implied, for Duval, other human natures, other forms of wealth and organization. Geography—physical, spatial difference—marked for this administrator clear disjunctures, despite the movement, migrations, and exchanges that linked desert, plain, and coast. In a later text, he maintained that "through its benefits, the artesian well gives to the Sahara material life and, up to a certain point, moral life."[12] Water coded for a range of moral attributes subsumed under the imperial rubric of "civilization," and its mere presence proved, Duval claimed, transformational in the moral lives of desert Algerians.

This cleavage required particular constructions of desert environments and life. Various writers through the French occupation of Algeria referred to the Sahara as the Ocean of Sand, a label attributed to the Roman stoic and traveler Strabo.[13] Those with actual experience in the desert dismissed the label as misleading, fanciful, a gross misunderstanding of the diverse environments of the Sahara. The explorer Fernand Foureau rather plaintively noted that, in fact, vast rocky expanses and sizable mountains rendered his voyages considerably more difficult than navigating the vast, flat expanse of sand conjured by the phrase.[14] The military commander V. Colomieu contended that, in 1862, an ocean voyage offered significantly fewer dangers than a desert one.

> The poets have often compared the desert to the Ocean. . . . To this just comparison one must add that the Ocean is known, its reefs are marked, its harbors described and illuminated with lighthouses, while the map of the desert does not exist, reefs are more numerous there. . . . A map of the desert would exist, but, whatever care taken in establishing it, it would be insufficient to guide the voyager in an effective manner.[15]

However poetic the ocean of sand as a category, explorers and colonial military officers found it lacking as an effective description of the Sahara itself. Colomieu presented the geographic menaces of the Sahara as, in some sense, unknowable, unmappable, incapable of textual or poetic representation. Paradoxically, the depths of the sea held fewer surprises for him than the expanses of the desert.

Other hazards awaited in the Sahara, as well. Referring to what is now eastern Algeria and western Libya, Eugène Daumas's 1853 *Mœurs et coutumes de l'Algérie* called it "veritable desert, the ocean of sand, of whom the Tuareg have made themselves the pirates."[16] Colomieu, too, singled out pirates as an element that rendered at least some truth to the comparison to the sea.[17] The nomadic Tuareg, many of whom made their living pillaging caravans, found themselves transformed, not inaptly, into pirates of the desert. Ocean narratives, whether of sand or water, do not require pirates, but seem more captivating for readers with their presence. However facile the analogy, for Daumas, environmental conditions defined the Tuareg as a community of pirates.

But the Sahara exists, and not just as a discursive ocean of sand. It is a real place, real in Blackbourn's sense, physically, corporally, environmentally, and historically real. As Colomieu noted, its "pure reality is rather terrible: thirst kills, and sand covers over the cadavers."[18] In Arabic, Algerians refer to one particularly desolate part of the desert as the *bilâd al-'atash wa al-khawf*: the land of thirst and fear. People died in the desert. They died, however, in different parts of the desert, in some parts more than in others. Arabic distinguishes different portions of the desert in different ways. *Fayfâ*', in colloquial *fiafi*, referred, like *sahrâ*', to the desert generally, but also at times specifically to the portions of the Sahara with inhabited oases. *Qifâr* called to mind wastelands, not full desert, but rocky, stony, apparently useless land that nevertheless could spring to life with the infrequent and unpredictable rains. Algerians sometimes referred to this as *khalâ*', the void. The most deadly and empty parts of the Sahara, however, were the *falâ*, the completely sterile lands without water.[19] These terms distinguished, usefully, between different environments, between dry lands with scattered oases, dry lands with the potential for providing good, if temporary, forage, and for dry lands threatening all but the best prepared travelers with death.

Some early explorers attempted to elucidate distinctions similar to those articulated in Arabic by Algerians. James Richardson, in his 1850 *Routes du Sahara*, remarked that "generally, the Great Desert, in many places, is not as arid and as dry a country as is generally depicted."[20] Nevertheless, the repetition of the adverb "generally" indicates something of a struggle with perception, a looming sense that the very definition of the Sahara had ossified into one category of environmental understanding that elided crucial differences among different ecosystems.

Despite the utility of these distinctions, "the land of thirst and fear" as articulated through nineteenth-century texts and images became definitive.

French writers on the Sahara applied it more broadly geographically, and imbuing the phrase with near-talismanic qualities, used it to summarize the ecological and psychological challenges of a desert empire. The menace of the desert was not drowning (except during flash floods), but rather thirst. The *bilâd al-'atash wa al-khawf* marked the Sahara as an environmental community defined through both bodily and emotive experiences. Those stark deaths became fodder for representational, as well as bodily, constructions of desert life. The sands of the Sahara, in particular, have long proved fertile ground, if not for agriculture, then for the germination of Orientalist romance. Not surprisingly, this romance emerged early on in France's imperial project in North Africa. Eugène Fromentin, the traveler, writer, and artist who inducted many in metropolitan France into his cult of Saharan romance, visually situated the Sahara in a clear Orientalist trajectory. His 1859 *La rue Bab-el-Gharbi à Laghouat* depicted, in near-canonical fashion, an Orientalist scene of the so-called Arab street, inscribing colonialist representations of feminine seclusion, masculine public life, and decadence on canvas. Ten years later, however, the jumbled bodies of *Rue* take on a decidedly more sinister tone in 1869's *Le pays de*

Figure 3.1. The Land of Thirst *(Le Pays de la soif)*. 1869. By Eugène Fromentin (1820–76). From Musée d'Orsay, Paris, France/Giraudon. *The Bridgeman Art Library International. Reproduced by permission.*

la soif. Fromentin's palette has little changed, and though his subject matter ostensibly has, the prone colonized body still takes central position in the canvas. Fromentin's "land of thirst" communicated the physical experiences of the desert to a wider audience. Thirst, rooted in specific environmental landscapes, became an artistic still life rooted in a specific geographic and embodied landscape.

Water, Mastery, Miracles

Mastery over the landscape, mastery over thirst and the material conditions of life, served, for many writers, as the marker of colonial domination. Wrote the Oranais bureaucrat Duval,

> Among the works undertaken by France in Algeria, there is one that . . . effects in the material economy, and even in the social constitution of populations, a rapid and marvelous metamorphosis: . . . the artesian well, those gushing fountains, as admired by the learned as by the ignorant, blessed in the deserts even more than in the heart of civilized countries.[21]

The introduction of water, in the guise of artesian wells, into the Sahara would fundamentally remake, according to Duval, the very social composition of desert communities. "It is in the Algerian and French Sahara," he continued, "that are accomplished these marvels, which, in other ages, would have merited their authors the aura of heroes and demi-gods."[22] Duval accorded to the mastery of water, and, importantly, to the people who master it in this "Algerian and French Sahara," the transformational powers of the near-divine. As miraculous as artesian wells may have seemed in the midst of the desert, they were by no means new, or French; Saharans had long used the technology to tap aquifers and underground springs. All of Duval's excitement arose from the prospect of the introduction of a slightly more efficient variety of an existing technology. The transformative act here was not technological, and it involved no magical greening of the desert wastes through the actions of heroes or demigods. It depended, instead, on the *act* of mastery itself, and on the origins of the hand who held the pump. Duval never accorded to Saharan artesian wells the kind of mastery he saw in their French-created replacements.

Artesian wells by no means represented the only form of mastery over the environment that excited nineteenth-century French writers engaged with the Sahara. More famously, proposals to create a gigantic inland sea in the desert likewise relied more on the conceiving of the act of mastering hostile environments than on the utility or advisability of doing so. In 1879, the president of the Commission du Trans-Saharien, Gazeau de Vautibault, took on the question of water directly. He admitted that "the Trans-Saharan will have the disadvantage of requiring the transport of rather expensive quantities of water,"[23] but dismissed this criticism of the project as one rooted in ignorance. He emphasized, not incorrectly, that the Sahara possessed, in fact, sizable reservoirs of water underground. His argument depended, however, on a certain sleight of hand: discussing one region, he noted that "in this part of the Sahara, as in others, there is really more water than the caravans indicate,"[24] setting aside entirely the question of whether "more" water, in fact, sufficed. The project as a whole in fact would utilize three separate sources of water: artesian wells, surface water, and water stored underground in the courses of dry riverbeds, yet Gazeau de Vautibault's discussion divorced the assertion of the existence of water from analysis of its potential for use.

In other proposals, mastery over specific natural spaces and clearly identified aspects of real environments took precedence over clear articulations of the productive outcomes of such plans and proposals. Less spectacular were the 1865 discussions of the potential creation of a thermal spa in Hammam-Meloun, in the then-province of Algiers. M. Ville painstakingly detailed the process for creating a hotel, baths, and infrastructure for transporting the invalid and ailing to distant Hammam-Meloun. The desert climate surrounding the oasis, he claimed, could provide a recuperative site. "The natives," he continued, "would keep their habitual place of encampment and would thus furnish to the patients a new distraction through the spectacle of their original customs during the season of the baths."[25] He "admitt[ed] that the sojourn on the plateau of Hammam-Meloun offers inconveniences of every nature: too small a space, debilitating heat, foul air, monotony of view, and thus, sadness and ennui among the patients."[26] Moreover, he deemed prospects for patronage quite poor: Europeans in Algeria were too few and consisted largely of soldiers unlikely to frequent the spa, and Algerian Muslims bathed separately from Europeans, and usually for free. As the Arabic name indicates, Hammam-Meloun had, in fact, a bath at its thermal waters, one shared by Algerian Muslims and Jews. At any rate, he noted ruefully, they seemed unlikely to patronize the hotel.[27] In short, Ville spent pages outlining in painstaking detail quite possibly the worst spa ever, guaranteed to bore its scant patrons to death, or kill them with hyperthermia, or asphyxiate them with noxious, sulfurous fumes, before ultimately bankrupting its owners. "Our goal," he explained, "is not to engage a businessman to attempt today so costly an enterprise and [one] which is of a nature to present many risks. We have solely sought to demonstrate that it is possible."[28]

To the best of my knowledge, no speculator has constructed the ill-advised thermal baths of Hammam-Meloun. Nevertheless, an engineer made detailed figures and calculations of costs and technical details for the organization and transportation of water at an out-of-the-way thermal site in the arid plains of the Algerian desert. He then published it with the official publisher of the prestigious Corps impériaux des ponts et chaussées et des mines. Ville wrote to demonstrate the possibility of mastering the desert environment. In the land of thirst and fear, Ville offered the measurements and figures to prove the possibility, if not the advisability, of the creation of a thermal bath in the heart of the desert. The environmental fact of hot springs and their potential utility overriding the economic aspects of his plan, Ville generated a body of geographic representations that sketched out imagined desert interventions, however ill advised.

What became of the audacious M. Ville? The vicissitudes of desert development apparently conquered him, and he retreated. Duval notes that, "abandoning to the secrets of the future the mysteries of the Great Desert, industrial science fell back towards the Tell, and for several years, under the direction of M. Ville, chief engineer of mines, the Mitidja has been, in thirty places, attacked by teams of drills."[29] The nineteenth century's representational legacy, like that of Ville, in the desert wedded colonial environmental knowledge to economic possibility. As Benjamin Claude Brower demonstrates, the middle to late nineteenth century witnessed the emergence of concerted efforts to describe the Sahara, "like . . . Napoleon's famed scientific mission to Egypt."[30] The ideology of "peaceful penetration" and the reality of Algerian deaths formed what Brower correctly calls "the multiple logic of violence in colonial Algeria."[31] At the same time, late nineteenth century and early twentieth century explorers, travelers, tourists, missionaries, artists, ethnographers, and others met with greater and lesser degrees of success in their attempts to systematize knowledge about the Sahara as an environmental and cultural space.

In particular, the deaths of explorers in the Sahara largely overshadowed attempts at systematizing knowledge about the ecological conditions of the desert. Most notably, commemoration of the deaths of Paul Flatters and the marquis de Morès revolved around configuring the Sahara as more of a place of political threats than one of the menace of thirst.[32] Environmental, biological, and ecological knowledge of the desert, of course, did not stagnate, yet death became more a question of violence than of thirst. Duval, in a sense, did not err in positing a retreat of "industrial science."

Trellised Roses and Portioned-Out Miracles

Nevertheless, even the future's secrets could not unveil one mystery of the Great Desert, of the land of fear. One "myth with which one does not trifle: thirst; one can die of thirst in the Sahara,"[33] even in 1957, when, as Jean Lartéguy noted in his *Sahara: An I*, "on this ocean of sand, in the guise of caravelles, have been launched all-terrain trucks of the geophysical companies."[34] In the 1950s as in the 1850s, those interested in the Sahara had to come to terms with the meaning of its environmental extent, its physical limitations, the possibility of death. Frequently, they defined, too, their embedding in place through embodied experiences of the environment. The travel writer and playwright Stéphane Désombre titled a chapter, with inestimable directness, "How I Almost Desiccated."[35]

New metrics, however, began to supplement the rather more visceral scales of measurement such as that of Désombre. Increasingly, pluviometrics and hydrology began to define the Sahara scientifically. Most obviously, geologists and publications of the Institut Pasteur mobilized such statistics as part of their disciplinary apparatus,[36] but perhaps more surprisingly, popular works that aimed at familiarizing a general audience with the Sahara, such as Jacques Britsch's *Perspectives sahariennes*, and politicians, such as Albert Sarraut and Pierre Cornet, made recourse to similar numbers.[37] Even general-audience texts marshaled statistics and data, rainfall measurements, and water tables for the creation of environmentally specific representations of expertise. In the mid-twentieth century, precise, numerical definitions came to define the Sahara in terms of centimeters of rainfall and rapidity of evaporation, consolidating knowledge of the desert in tables, charts, and graphs.

Numerical definitions of the desert did not stamp out more descriptive ones. Suzanne Normand and Jean Acker published one such descriptive work, lavishly illustrated with photographs of landscape and oil installations, in 1957. "Ancient sea dried up for millions of years, symbol of absolute sterility, desert of fear and thirst, the Sahara opens itself to a new conquest," epitomized by the petrochemical facilities and uranium mines of their photographs.[38] However, the greatest conquest, they made clear, lay in the relation of people to the land itself. "'The Sahara remained uninhabitable because people did not know how—or did not want—to render it inhabitable.' But let's be just: did they have the possibility, before our époque that portions out miracles?"[39] Normand and Acker offered precise depictions of just what such miracles would entail, of their eventual results. They traveled to one locale with "an agronomist in shorts who ... let the sand run through his fingers. What do they demand of the mysterious soil of the desert? Geraniums, trellised roses? 'With water, nothing is impossible,' murmured the agronomist.... One day ... there will be bungalows for the families, with flowers all around."[40] Normand and Acker witnessed "management of the oases and technical equipment in the process of metamorphosing, not only the rhythm of life, but the entire native economy."[41] To their credit, the two saw this as a process, remaining quite aware of the physical dangers of thirst and death in the desert, and explaining their own fear at their automobile trip through it. Nevertheless, they expressed complete confidence in the ultimate triumph of the management of the desert environment through the manipulation of water resources.

The explanation of Normand and Acker offers a neat, clean interpretation of the environmental history of the Sahara as a passage from menace to management. In no way, however, can a history of water in the Sahara trace such a simplistic narrative line from the land of thirst and fear to the land of trucks and numbers: the Sahara, after all, remains a place where it is still eminently possible to die of thirst, a place of precious few bungalows and trellised roses. Contemporary with increasingly precise geological definitions of the desert emerged questions about the very nature of the Sahara itself in a time of technological change: a desert with roses and bungalows, after all, is not much of a desert. The potential for new technology, for Duval's "secrets of the future" to tame nature, threatened to call into question the very idea of a desert, rainfall measurements notwithstanding.

"The essential character of deserts," wrote Robert Capot-Rey, "is the disappearance of living beings."[42] The essential character of deserts is, of course, not the absence of people, but the absence of water, and Capot-Rey, professor at the university in Algiers and in the 1950s the foremost expert on the Algerian Sahara, knew this.[43] Especially in the Sahara, crossed by trade routes for millennia and dotted with oases, sites of pilgrimage, and a wide variety of ecological practices, the absence of people rarely, despite the absence of water, served as the quintessence of a definition of desert environments. Nevertheless, Capot-Rey struggled with how to define a desert whose ultimate defeat seemed imminent. "Human industry," wrote Edmond Sergeant, an Institut Pasteur d'Algérie employee, "intervenes to mitigate the indigence of nature and to maintain water in the land of thirst."[44]

Mitigating the indigence of nature—the very concrete attempts to remake the Saharan landscape and environment to conform to industrial or agricultural uses highly dependent on water—posed something of an epistemological problem. The question of what, exactly, is a desert that is no longer arid had wider repercussions in a political system that defined communities according to their place of residence, but also in relation to how they used the land: as nomads, as sedentary farmers, as potentially restive urban dwellers, as land pirates, as oil-rig workers. In a 1958 book published as part of the Que Sais-Je series, Bruno Verlet noted that, "geographically speaking, the Sahara possesses no natural frontier. The principal character of the desert being its aridity, the best definition geographically seems thus to rest on criteria on the order of vegetation."[45] He made clear, however, that he himself preferred a completely different definition, embedded not just in space, but in time.

> The Sahara undergoes at the present hour upsets of a considerable scope that are profoundly modifying its physiognomy. On its ground confront, clash, two civilizations, two worlds. On the one hand, an ensemble of millennial adaptations..., heritage of a long series of indigenous civilizations. On the other, a violent and rapid intrusion of technical and Western methods, fundamentally foreign to life in the desert, but seeking to surmount its difficulties by mechanical force. Between the two a fundamental difference: the Saharans of yore submitted to the law of the desert, those of today seek to impose their own upon it. On one side tradition, on the other evolution.[46]

Verlet interpreted the twentieth century as transformative, exaggeratedly so, in its potential for remaking desert environments. Technical change would replace adaptation and heritage. Lacking geographic boundaries, the Sahara would eventually vanish under the weight of "mechanical force." A desert without possibility of desiccation is no desert at all.

Inadvertently, even though they cast their ideas as revolutionary, proponents of those interventions echoed nineteenth-century descriptions of the desert. Just as Colomieu, Foureau, Daumas, and others had criticized the idea of an "ocean of sand" for neglecting the varied environments of the Sahara, so, too, did later writers. Guy Le Rumeur's *Le Sahara avant le pétrole* of 1960 recalled that the regions "without water and without people are called 'the land of thirst' or 'the land of fear.' ... No! The Sahara is not a 'no man's land,' for it is not entirely deserted."[47] In some senses, and without knowing it, Le Rumeur had attempted to reintroduce the Arabic distinction of water and land. Like Arabic-speaking Algerians, Le Rumeur did not deny the existence of expanses of emptiness and aridity, but underlined that they did not, in fact, encompass the entirety of Saharan environments. Le Rumeur, however, cast this understanding as part of the outcome of technological change, new forms of transportation and water technologies, not as part of a deeper knowledge of the desert. Thus, he situated this recognition of multiple Saharas not as greater comprehension of the environment, but of greater control over it.

This mooted transformation, this crucial addition of water to the landscape, like earlier plans for artesian wells, undermined the very idea of a desert. One law professor struggled, in a 1960 text titled *Sahara et communauté*, to define what, exactly, he took for the boundaries of his community. "One calls 'desert' all territory abandoned by man, all centrifugal land. . . . This arid zone is not and has never been but a relative desert where . . . man has always tried to maintain himself. There is, in this will of existence, something dramatic, a struggle of man against nature."[48] He defined the desert as land simultaneously abandoned and fought for by man, as deserted,[49] rather than primarily arid, because he saw the imminent end, he thought, of that struggle. "Water is the condition of all life and all development," he explained, and "the program of mise-en-valeur" that had constructed waterworks in parts of the Sahara made "the desert cede place to an oasis."[50] The lawyer literally redefined the Sahara as deserted rather than desert, as abandoned rather than uninhabitable, and capable of imminent restoration. The possibility of making the Sahara wet, impractical though it proved to be, seemed to presage a radical reconfiguring of the very idea of "desert" from thirst to utility.

At the same time, a curious kind of doublespeak emerges from such colonial texts. Although these projects never conceived of Saharan Algerians in relation to the project, their proponents cannot, of course, ignore the existence of people altogether. In short, Saharan Algerians emerged ambiguously connected to economic proposals cast almost exclusively in environmental terms. These analyses of the future of the peoples of the Sahara remain simultaneously divorced from and linked to various aspects of economic projects: not active, cogitating participants in the remaking of the Sahara, but bystanders acted upon, like the land they inhabit, by the French builders of railroads, inland seas, derricks.

Many portrayed Algerians as a vanishing presence, a silent absence, in the Sahara. Peyré contended that "this desert was abandoned to us like a realm of derision," yet congratulated the colonial state for not exterminating the "natives,"[51] who apparently remained in the "abandoned" desert. Similarly, Albert Sarraut, president of the Assemblée de l'Union Française, described Algerians as inert, in stasis, ultimately incapable of action or improvement without French activation, trapped in "a desert that could be animated, peopled, irrigated, fertilized, utilized to furnish to local populations" the benefits of agriculture and mineral exploitation.[52] Sarraut's very words underline the contradiction at the heart of plans for the Saharan mise-en-valeur: an inhabited desert nonetheless "fertilized" and "animated" solely through "peopling," inhabited yet simultaneously in need of people. Another politician soberly reminded the reader of "the role and importance of man for the mise-en-valeur of these abandoned territories."[53] The constant reassertions of the human emptiness of the Sahara, usually alongside acknowledgments of the very real people who did, in fact, make a living in the desert, demonstrates that, for many French writers and policymakers, Algerians simply did not or could not contribute to the potential use of the region. In short, for Peyré, Sarraut, and others, the desert remained empty of those who mattered, those who acted, those who built.

Indeed, Guy Le Rumeur, in his majestically titled *Le Sahara avant le pétrole* (1960), explicitly linked water, the romance of the desert, and the relative absence of people. "Gazelles," he wrote, "live there in bands, but people scarcely venture from rare points of water."[54] His image, though picturesque, sacrificed no small amount of accuracy in its pursuit of imagery: oasis communities, those "rare points of water," depended as much on nomadic populations passing, like gazelles, through that desert in bands, as upon settlers in the oasis town itself. Romances of the Sahara, both verdant and parched, did not die out in the petrochemical age.

Daniel Strasser, economist and political scientist at the Institut d'Etudes politiques in Paris, best summarized the political stakes behind such representations. "The Sahara, empty of people and rich with potential, appears as a privileged space for national grandeur."[55] The Sahara was not, of course, empty of people, but desires for "national grandeur" reserved its potential riches for those not inhabiting it. "This dynamism of the occidental type," he maintained, "is incumbent upon the French government to possess."[56] This depiction of the Sahara, empty, rich, and privileged, relied on environment and economics as modes of description to offer the Sahara up as a site of renewed colonial interest in a time when Algerian opposition made itself heard with increasing vehemence.

In an opinion submitted to the Assemblée de l'Union Française in favor of creating a desert territory, equivalent to the Afrique occidentale française or Afrique équatoriale française, called "l'Afrique saharienne française," Valerio Cianfarani neatly summarized the romance of an empty desert for colonial politicians: "Territories 'vacant and without masters'? . . . One could have said that before the French presence, one cannot anymore, since the bleached bones of the soldiers of France have staked out the trails of ergs and of hamadas, since French sacrifices of all sorts have generously multiplied to pacify, organize, administer the Saharan territories."[57] Only once the French arrived, the bureaucrat opined, did the Sahara cease its vacancy, its emptiness. At the same time, French sacrifices aimed at pacifying, organizing, administering ... whom? The empty desert? Or desert inhabitants constructed as absent? Cianfarani kept a strategic silence.

Capot-Rey went even further, organizing his seminal text to begin with a lengthy environmental discussion that excluded mention of people before moving on to addressing Saharan inhabitants in detail as functions of their environment. Capot-Rey remained throughout his work an ardent environmental determinist for whom only those "native" to the Sahara could adequately perform labor initiated and dictated by French interests.[58] Raymond Furon, the associate director of the French museum of natural history and internationally regarded hydrologist and geologist, further racialized questions of labor, contending that only "*noirs*" could work in the extreme environmental conditions of the desert.[59] Narratives about the Saharan environment, and especially about human needs for and projects regarding water, frequently took the form of ill-concealed polemics of environmental determinism.

Even environmental descriptions not wedded to mechanistic interpretations of ecological influences had difficulty reconciling economic development with the human component of the desert. Jean Dubief, a hydrologist living and working in Algeria, decried the state of colonial environmental policy in the desert in the 1950s. "To want to settle nomads by making them cultivators or mine workers," he fumed, "is in fact to seek out purely selfish goals under altruistic appearances." To do so, he continued, would "suppress in one blow the only mode of rational exploitation of the reaches not totally deprived of life in the desert."[60] As opposed to forced settlement and industrial labor as Dubief might have been, he could only ultimately subject Algerians to "rational exploitation," to increased production best facilitated, he argued, through the construction of additional wells. Dubief rejected mining, agriculture, forced settlement, but not the logic of economic maximization behind it. He, like those he criticized, still comprehended the Sahara as a place in which manipulation of water resources for economic purposes remained the primary goal. Rooted in environmental mastery, "rational exploitation" of Algerian bodies for unspecified work undergirded even Dubief's disavowal of forcible settlement.

Impracticality rarely fazed those interested in an economically useful Sahara. The very real challenges of the desert had, in many ways, not vanished in the 1950s and 1960s, and, as a result, neither had recourse to what, a century earlier, Duval had called the "secrets of the future." Furon attempted to argue for the mise-en-valeur of the Sahara in the 1950s: "There is water, minerals, and oil, but it is still necessary to be able to exploit them. We will leave aside technical difficulties that very generally find elegant solutions."[61] Arguing for the economic necessity of maintaining French control over the Sahara proved rather easier when the burden of furnishing technical solutions to the problem of water fell to others. Furon, like his contemporaries, presumed the resolution of the environmental challenges of the desert imminent, and proceeded to the hypothetical reconfiguring of the desert in its mooted future as no longer deserted.

Despite their vagueness, these purported resolutions also concentrated on the reorganization of desert communities. The changing character of the desert landscape implied, for some, changing the character of the people of the Sahara. In a 1960 special issue of *La Nef* titled "Sahara en questions," Daniel Plessis expressly cast these changes as communally based. "The mentality of the desert changes from week to week. Thanks to oil workers, a new infrastructure has imposed itself that permits dormant populations... to touch, brusquely, the marvels of mechanization."[62] Infrastructures and machines in the desert, Plessis argued, would awaken slumbering Algerians.

The colonial government similarly viewed its environmental interventions as social ones, as policies aimed at modifying communal life in the Sahara. "The French administration," claimed a 1954 government publication on the Territoires du Sud, "was preoccupied with finding a solution to the grave... social problems posed" in the desert. "New irrigation methods were tried and popularized there."[63] If irrigation offered the solution, then the "grave social problems" arose out of assumptions about agricultural uses of land and the sedentarization of nomadic populations. The drilling of wells and the creation of irrigation projects, although both rooted in water, imply very different uses and organizations of space. The colonial government argued that irrigation, and settled use of land, and not wells, with the potential for more episodic use, provided the only possible solution for reforming Saharan communities and resolving their "grave social problems."

No Man's Land

Other texts from the era of incipient independence movements and decolonization, written by a wide variety of experts, politicians, and popularizers of the Saharan mise-en-valeur, conceived of the Sahara first as an ecological landscape, relegating social questions to secondary importance or ignoring them altogether. Georges Le Fèvre and P. Mannoni attempted to frame the terms of the debate about the Sahara in 1956: "This Sahara ... [is] visibly arid.... Although some still claim that it is but a dead region, a sterile scrap of terrestrial crust, others ... are of the opposing opinion, persuaded that this no man's land of five hundred million hectares contains fabulous riches" in petrochemicals and possibilities for nuclear and atomic energy.[64] In neither arid wastes nor petrochemical wealth do the authors identify people: the definition of the Sahara remains essentially and quintessentially environmental, the realm of what Capot-Rey referred to as the "tyranny of water."[65] The lack of people, for Le Fèvre and Mannoni as for Capot Rey, did, in fact, characterize the desert environment and determine the boundaries of its potential use.

Raymond Furon, whose influential works appeared in multiple languages worldwide, discussed the wells, foggara, and qanat of Saharan Algeria—but not who built or used them.[66] The oasis-dwellers who built extensive irrigation or other kinds of waterworks vanish from Furon's account; the built environment of water infrastructure and technology becomes, instead, a landscape, a background of structures made without agency, emerging as if naturally. Proposals to turn the Sahara into what J.-C. Peyré called "a gargantuan Tennessee" purported to mimic the massive construction projects of the New Deal's Tennessee Valley Authority, yet shared none of the ideology of social welfare implicit, at least theoretically, in such projects' American analogs.[67] Even if the Sahara represented the new Tennessee, the numerous writers who made such comparisons never identified the Algerian equivalent of impoverished Appalachians or laborers in need of work. They merely wrote such proposals onto the land, mapping potential locations and placements, but never uses or builders.

Indeed, the mid-twentieth century did witness shifts in patterns of human settlement in the desert. Wrote one engineer, "the light yellow stain of the atlases of our youth that spoke to our spirit and made us imagine a Sahara, land of thirst and death, is now replaced by banal roadmaps on which one discovers, not without surprise, roads, trails, points of water, hotels."[68] These roads and oil derricks and new wells intensified, rather than transformed, human use of the Sahara. Settlements remained dotted in oases clustered around wells, whether oil wells or artesian wells, and more than one writer referred to petrochemical workers as the "new nomads." Plans to "green" the Sahara came to naught, and economic use of the desert emerged despite its environmental constraints, not through their obliteration. As one French government publication noted, "all drilling for oil follows a first drilling, that of the discovery of a point of water."[69]

Drilling for oil only partially answers a question first asked in the *Revue française* in an 1887 article titled "Excursions dans le Sahara" by one Edouard Gibert. "Colonization of the Sahara? Certainly, if one has nothing better to do. But why spend so much time and money on a land where it is necessary to create water and trees, and when trees and water abound on the other side of the mountains?"[70] Oil might explain drilling wells, but not the desire for bungalows and trellised roses.

In addition to the romance of the desert and conflicting, ideologically inflected debates about the nature, literal and figurative, of the human role in the Sahara emerged another form of colonial romanticism. Scholars have largely failed to investigate the emergence of discourses of economic Orientalism in the twentieth century. Indeed, Orientalism itself skips, in the words of Said, from "Renan, Sacy, and Lane" to "Orientalism now."[71] The technological romances of the Saharan mise-en-valeur at the end of empire, science fictions though they often proved to be, nevertheless represent new ways of configuring, of representing, the Sahara and Saharan peoples as objects for imperial intervention and domination, new methods that nevertheless proved congruent with previous tropes of Orientalism.

The economist Daniel Strasser succinctly articulated the emergence of these new strands of techno-Orientalism. Industrial capital, he argued, required a different representational life for the Sahara.

> The Sahara cannot be at the same time the expression of a captivating Orientalism and the hope of a future industrial zone, a poetic escape and the field of a new French expansion. These mirages that we condemn are moreover equally those that give rise to the prophets of a Saharan Eldorado. In fact, the modern Sahara will only be the work of a strong and resolute France.[72]

Strasser explicitly rejected the "captivating Orientalism" of the nineteenth century, of a Fromentin, as well as the foolhardy hopes of a Saharan economic miracle. He nevertheless never conceived of the Sahara as an object of politically interested representations. A "strong and resolute" France will create neither a poetic escape nor an Eldorado, but rather "a future industrial zone." Saharan industrial parks proved, indeed, far less captivating than desert escapes or riches, but also proved no less Orientalist: technological and economic interests in the desert at the end of empire never abandoned the genesis of politically interested representations of people and land as part of the pursuit of the maintenance of imperial monopolies on power and economy.

The expansion of Orientalist discourse to include mid-twentieth century economic and technological fetishism may seem a discursive stretch, but it did not seem so to those attempting to conceive of a French Sahara. In his "Quel visage le Sahara d'hier et d'aujourd'hui aura-t-il demain?" of 1960, Daniel Plessis remarked that, "on the margins of modernism, beside the Saharan unities and the commandos of petrol, still subsist the nomads, the people of yore, those whose silhouettes attest to the stagnation of the desert for centuries . . . pass[ing] from point of water to point of water."[73] The attempts at a technological reconfiguration of the Sahara implied varied and often contradictory, inescapably politically interested, representations of Saharan people as both separate from and involved in Saharan economics. Moreover, Strasser explicitly juxtaposed the romantic and the technological, noting that "after the second world war, the Government of the Republic intended to approach head on what was still the Saharan mystery . . . to determine the chances and conditions of a mineral, industrial, and strategic Sahara, in the place of the traditional, immutable, and sterile Sahara of sands."[74] That governmental approach, reflected in the metonym of water, reveals new forms of cultural representations, economic and ecological, marshaled in support of empire. The mystery of a French Sahara, asserted in the face of an increasingly restive Algeria and increasingly assertive anticolonial movements worldwide, began to replace the "mysterious Sahara" of previous representations.

Indeed, economic dreams in the Sahara did not vanish in the face of the Algerian War of Independence. As John Ruedy has noted, petrochemical discoveries in "the Sahara had stimulated, during the late 1950s, a frenetic rush of French businessmen, financiers, and investors hoping to share in the bonanza—a new commitment to Algeria that was totally out of phase with a politico-military reality that augured imminent disengagement."[75] Moreover, that reality, which Algerians articulated with increasing armed and discursive force in the 1950s and 1960s, existed alongside what Gabrielle Hecht has called a belief, entirely colonial in nature, that "technological prowess could be particularly important in helping France combat the crisis of grandeur brought on by the decolonization of the empire."[76] As a result, once independent, Algeria had to address terms of independence that had enshrined the interests of French capital in the Sahara (especially in the petrochemical industry), primarily through recourse to statist interventions in the industrial economy in the Sahara that in turn financed Algerian dependence on imports.[77] Declining oil prices and resistance to private exploitation of the Sahara in the 1970s and 1980s precipitated social, economic, and, in the 1990s and 2000s, political instability in Algeria.[78]

Contemporarily, Algeria has turned, not only to the European Union and the United States for investment in the Sahara, but to Russia and China, as well.[79] These economic interests in the Sahara imply a reliance on water as yet unarticulated, uninvestigated—a reliance, like water in the Sahara itself, largely concealed.

French conceptions of the Sahara as a colonial, economic, and technological space depended on the genesis of environmental understandings and misrepresentations of the desert. Water posed a particular problem of management, need, and access, in particular in the form of newly articulated, if often theoretical, political, commercial, and, later, industrial projects, and as a result functioned as a placeholder in economic debates, standing in for a wider variety of anxieties, hopes, and plans. Thus, the economic history of the Sahara, both colonially and after Algerian independence, depended on a congeries of primary environmental representations, less structured and totalizing than tentative, inchoate, and often contradictory. The indeterminacy of economic projects whose profits often proved illusory reflected an underlying uncertainty regarding the potential for mastering the desert environment itself.

"The desert is a pack of lies," wrote Suzanne Normand and Jean Acker. "This lie has enveloped so many people: nothing is real."[80] The desert is, in fact, "real," a real geography in Blackbourn's sense. People died in the desert of thirst, but also worked on oil derricks, and, for a moment in history, conceived of the possibility of an engineered end of the desert. The environmental constraints of desert life may have prohibited trellises and bungalows, but fear and thirst alone never succeeded in closing the Sahara from the realm of imagination. To the contrary; the superimposition, though often imperfect, of environmental and economic representations perpetuated colonial conceptions of the Sahara as the site of empire's final interventions.

Notes

1. 'Abd al-Qâdir, "Éloge du Sahara," in Eugène Daumas, *Mœurs et coutumes de l'Algérie* (1853; Paris: Sindbad, 1888), 278.

2. See, for example, Benjamin Claude Brower, *A Desert Named Peace: The Violence of France's Empire in the Algerian Sahara, 1844–1902* (New York: Columbia University Press, 2009); Allan Christelow, *Muslim Law Courts and the French Colonial State in Algeria* (Princeton, N.J.: Princeton University Press, 1985); Julia Clancy-Smith, *Rebel and Saint: Muslim Notables, Populist Protest, Colonial Encounters (Algeria and Tunisia, 1800–1914)* (Berkeley: University of California Press, 1994); Diana K. Davis, *Resurrecting the Granary of Rome: Environmental History and French Colonial Expansion in North Africa* (Athens:

Ohio University Press, 2007); Patrica M. E. Lorcin, *Imperial Identities: Stereotyping, Prejudice and Race in Colonial Algeria* (London: I. B. Tauris, 1995).

3. See my *An Empire of Facts: Colonial Power, Cultural Knowledge, and Islam in Algeria, 1870–1914,* Critical Perspectives on Empire, ed. Catherine Hall, Mrinalini Sinha, and Kathleen Wilson (Cambridge: Cambridge University Press, 2009).

4. Alfred W. Crosby, "The Past and Present of Environmental History," *American Historical Review* 100, no. 4 (1995): 1188.

5. David Blackbourn, "A Sense of Place: New Directions in German History," the 1998 annual lecture of the German Historical Institute London (London, 1999), in Frank Uekötter, "The Old Conservation History—and the New: An Argument for Fresh Perspectives on an Established Topic," *Historical Social Research* 29, no. 3 (2004): 189–90.

6. James C. McCann, *Green Land, Brown Land, Black Land: An Environmental History of Africa, 1800–1990* (Portsmouth, N.H.: Heinemann, 1999), 3. See also 4–5.

7. Ibid., 5.

8. Davis, *Resurrecting the Granary of Rome.*

9. Brower, *A Desert Named Peace;* Martin Thomas, *Empires of Intelligence: Security Services and Colonial Disorder after 1914* (Berkeley: University of California Press, 2008), 60–61.

10. Robert Vitalis, *America's Kingdom: Mythmaking on the Saudi Oil Frontier* (Stanford, Calif.: Stanford University Press, 2007), 18–26.

11. Jules Duval, *L'Algérie: Tableau historique, descriptif et statistique* (Paris: L. Hachette, 1859), 46–47.

12. Jules Duval, *Les Puits artésiens du Sahara* (Paris: Guillaumin, 1867), 29.

13. Daumas, *Mœurs,* 185.

14. Fernand Foureau, *Sahara, Soudan, Tchad, Congo* (Paris: Société d'Etudes Algériennes, 1901), 3.

15. V. Colomieu, *Voyage dans le Sahara algérien*, Le Tour du Monde (Paris: Hachette, 1862), 166.

16. Daumas, *Mœurs,* 262. On Daumas, see also Brower, *Desert Named Peace,* 200–202.

17. Colomieu, *Voyage,* 162.

18. Ibid., 171.

19. Daumas, *Mœurs,* 185.

20. James Richardson, *Notes du Sahara: Intinéraires dans l'intérieur du Grand Désert d'Afrique* (Paris: L. Martinet, 1850), 6.

21. Duval, *Puits artésiens,* 1–2.

22. Ibid., 21–22.

23. Gazeau de Vautibault, *Le Trans-Saharien: Chemin de fer d'Alger au Soudan à travers le Sahara* (Paris: La France coloniale, 1879), 8.

24. Ibid., 11.

25. M. Ville, *Notes d'un voyage d'exploration dans les basins du Hodna et du Sahara* (Paris: Dunod, 1865), 106.
26. Ibid.,
27. Ibid., 107–8.
28. Ibid., 109.
29. Duval, *Puits*, 39.
30. Brower, *Desert Named Peace*, 61.
31. Ibid., 6.
32. Trumbull, *Empire of Facts*, 209–61; Brower, *Desert Named Peace*, 222–38.
33. Jean Lartéguy, *Sahara: An I* (Paris: Gallimard, 1958), 29.
34. Ibid., 9.
35. Stéphane Désombre, *Aventures sahariennes* (Paris: Nouvelles editions latines, 1950), 51.
36. Edmond Sergent, *Le Peuplement humain du Sahara* (Algiers: Institut Paster d'Algérie, 1953), 4, 10–11; Daniel Strasser, *Réalités et promesses sahariennes* (Paris: Encyclopédie d'Outre-Mer, 1956), 13; also Robert Capot-Rey, *Le Sahara français* (Paris: Presses Universitaires de France, 1953), passim.
37. Jacques Britsch, *Perspectives sahariennes* (Paris: Charles-Lavauzelle, 1956), 14; Pierre Cornet, *Sahara: Terre de demain* (Paris: Nouvelle éditions latines, 1956), 10.
38. Suzanne Normand and Jean Acker, *Sahara* (Paris: Horizons de France, 1957), 6.
39. Ibid., 36.
40. Ibid., 72.
41. Ibid., 148–51.
42. Capot-Rey, *Sahara français*, 7.
43. Ibid., 162.
44. Sergent, *Peuplement*, 12.
45. Bruno Verlet, *Le Sahara*, Que Sais-Je? series, no. 766 (Paris: Presses Universitaires de France, 1958), 7.
46. Ibid., 9.
47. Guy Le Rumeur, *Le Sahara avent le pétrole* (Paris: Société continentale, 1960), 7–9, 15.
48. Marc-Robert Thomas, *Sahara et Communauté* (Paris: Presses Universitaire de France, 1960), 111.
49. This echoes the much earlier definition of *désert* in Old French as meaning precisely this: empty of people. Its first appearance, in the 1080 Chanson de Roland, and a subsequent thirteenth-century reference, attest to the original definition of *désert* as implying, not a lack of water, but a lack of people. By the twentieth century, however, the water-centered ecological definition of désert had largely eclipsed the earlier one. *Grand Dictionnaire étymologique et historique du français* (Paris: Larousse, 2005), 281.
50. Thomas, *Sahara*, 115, 117.

51. Joseph Peyré, *De Sable et d'or* (Paris: Flammarion, 1957), 211.

52. Cornet, *Sahara*, 10.

53. Jean Godard, *L'Oasis moderne: Essai d'urbanisme saharien*, Avant-Propos by Tony Socard (Algiers: La Maison des livres, 1954), 10.

54. Le Rumeur, *Sahara avant le pétrole*, 12.

55. Strasser, *Réalités et promesses*, 13.

56. Ibid., 193.

57. Valerio Cianfarani, *Avis présenté au nom de la commission des affaires économiques* ([Paris]: Assemblée de l'Union française, 1953), 9.

58. Capot-Rey, *Sahara*, 67.

59. Raymond Furon, *Le Sahara: Géologie. Ressources minérals. Mise en valeur* (Paris: Payot, 1957), 271–73.

60. Jean Dubief, *Essai sur l'hydrologie superficielle au Sahara*. Thèse pour le doctorat de l'Université d'Alger (Mention Sciences), soutenue publiquement le 29 Mai 1953 (Algiers: Jules Carbonel, 1953), 436.

61. Furon, *Sahara*, 252.

62. Daniel Plessis, "Quel visage le Sahara d'hier et d'aujourd'hui aura-t-il demain?" *La Nef*, 1, special issue: Le Sahara en Questions (1960): 33.

63. Gouvernement Général de l'Algérie, *Territoire du Sud de l'Algérie* (Algiers: Imprimerie officielle, 1954), 22.

64. Georges Le Fèvre and P. Mannoni, *Notre Sahara: Une terre morte qui ressuscite* (Paris: Éditions Denoël, 1956), 12.

65. Capot-Rey, *Sahara français*, 13.

66. Furon, *Sahara*1957, 212–19.

67. Strasser, *Réalités et promesses*, 97, 106; Britsch, *Perspectives*, 59; Peyré, *De Sable et d'or*, 199–204.

68. Godard, *Oasis moderne*, 11.

69. André Labarthe, *Document sur le pétrole* (Paris: Imprimerie centrale commerciale, 1957), 87.

70. Edouard Gibert, "Excursions dans le Sahara," *Revue française* 7 (1887): 12.

71. Edward W. Said, *Orientalism* (New York: Pantheon Books, 1978), 197–99.

72. Strasser, *Réalités*, 193.

73. Plessis, "Quel visage," 1.

74. Strasser, *Réalités*, 7.

75. John Ruedy, *Modern Algeria: The Origins and Development of a Nation* (Bloomington: Indiana University Press, 1992), 187.

76. Gabrielle Hecht, *The Radiance of France: Nuclear Power and National Identity after World War II* (Cambridge, Mass.: MIT Press, 1998), 39; 206–7; Phillip C. Naylor, *France and Algeria: A History of Decolonization and Transformation* (Gainesville: University Press of Florida, 2000), 20, 58–59.

77. Naylor, *France and Algeria*, 28–31, 65–69, 82–97, 118–19; Phillip C. Naylor, *North Africa: A History from Antiquity to the Present* (Austin: University of Texas Press, 2009), 219; Claire Spencer, "The Maghreb in the 1990s: Political

and Economic Developments in Algeria, Morocco, and Tunisia," *Adelphi Paper* 274 (February 1993):16.

78. Spencer, "Maghreb in the 1990s," 17, 38; Azzedine Layachi, "The Domestic and International Constraints of Economic Adjustment in Algeria," in *North Africa: Development and Reform in a Changing Global Economy*, ed. Dirk Vandewalle (New York: St. Martin's Press, 1996), 135–37.

79. Naylor, *North Africa*, 216–17.

80. Normand and Acker, *Sahara*, 126.

Bibliography

'Abd al-Qâdir. "Éloge du Sahara." 1853. In *Mœurs et coutumes de l'Algérie*, by Eugène Daumas, 278. Paris: Sindbad, 1888.

Blackbourn, David. "A Sense of Place: New Directions in German History." The 1998 annual lecture of the German Historical Institute London. London, 1999. In Frank Uekötter, "The Old Conservation History—and the New: An Argument for Fresh Perspectives on an Established Topic." *Historical Social Research* 29, no. 3 (2004): 171–91.

Britsch, Jacques. *Perspectives sahariennes*. Paris: Charles-Lavauzelle, 1956.

Brower, Benjamin Claude. *A Desert Named Peace: The Violence of France's Empire in the Algerian Sahara, 1844–1902*. New York: Columbia University Press, 2009.

Capot-Rey, Robert. *Le Sahara français*. Paris: Presses Universitaires de France, 1953.

Christelow, Allan. *Muslim Law Courts and the French Colonial State in Algeria*. Princeton, N.J.: Princeton University Press, 1985.

Cianfarani, Valerio. *Avis présenté au nom de la commission des affaires économiques*. [Paris]: Assemblée de l'Union française, 1953.

Clancy-Smith, Julia. *Rebel and Saint: Muslim Notables, Populist Protest, Colonial Encounters (Algeria and Tunisia, 1800–1914)*. Berkeley: University of California Press, 1994.

Colomieu, Victor. *Voyage dans le Sahara algérien*, Le Tour du Monde. Paris: Hachette, 1862.

Cornet, Pierre. *Sahara: Terre de demain*. Paris: Nouvelles éditions latines, 1956.

Crosby, Alfred W. "The Past and Present of Environmental History." *American Historical Review* 100, no. 4 (1995): 1177–90.

Daumas, Eugène. *Mœurs et coutumes de l'Algérie*. 1853, Paris: Sindbad, 1888.

Davis, Diana K. *Resurrecting the Granary of Rome: Environmental History and French Colonial Expansion in North Africa*. Athens: Ohio University Press, 2007.

Désombre, Stéphane. *Aventures sahariennes*. Paris: Nouvelles éditions latines, 1950.

Dubief, Jean. *Essai sur l'hydrologie superficielle au Sahara*. Algiers: Jules Carbonel, 1953.

Duval, Jules. *L'Algérie: Tableau historique, descriptif et statistique.* Paris: L. Hachette, 1859.

———. *Les Puits artésiens du Sahara.* Paris: Guillaumin, 1867.

Foureau, Fernand. *Sahara, Soudan, Tchad, Congo.* Paris: Société d'Etudes Algériennes, 1901.

Furon, Raymond. *Le Sahara: Géologie. Ressources minérales. Mise en valeur.* Paris: Payot, 1957.

Gazeau de Vautibault. *Le Trans-Saharien: Chemin de fer d'Alger au Soudan à travers le Sahara.* Paris: La France coloniale, 1879.

Gibert, Edouard. "Excursions dans le Sahara." *Revue française* 7 (1887): 1–16.

Godard, Jean. *L'Oasis moderne: Essai d'urbanisme saharien.* Avant-Propos by Tony Socard. Algiers: La Maison des livres, 1954.

Gouvernement Général de l'Algérie. *Territoire du Sud de l'Algérie.* Algiers: Imprimerie officielle, 1954.

Grand Dictionnaire étymologique et historique du français. Paris: Larousse, 2005.

Hecht, Gabrielle. *The Radiance of France: Nuclear Power and National Identity after World War II.* Cambridge, Mass.: MIT Press, 1998.

Labarthe, André. *Document sur le pétrole.* Paris: Imprimerie centrale commerciale, 1957.

Lartéguy, Jean. *Sahara: An I.* Paris: Gallimard, 1958.

Layachi, Azzedine. "The Domestic and International Constraints of Economic Adjustment in Algeria." In *North Africa: Development and Reform in a Changing Global Economy,* ed. Dirk Vandewalle, 129–52. New York: St. Martin's Press, 1996.

Le Fèvre, Georges, and P. Mannoni. *Notre Sahara: Une terre morte qui ressuscite.* Paris: Éditions Denoël, 1956.

Le Rumeur, Guy. *Le Sahara avant le pétrole.* Paris: Société continentale, 1960.

Lorcin, Patricia M. E. *Imperial Identities: Stereotyping, Prejudice and Race in Colonial Algeria* London: I. B. Tauris, 1995.

McCann, James C. *Green Land, Brown Land, Black Land: An Environmental History of Africa, 1800–1990.* Portsmouth, N.H.: Heinemann, 1999.

Naylor, Phillip C. *France and Algeria: A History of Decolonization and Transformation.* Gainesville: University Press of Florida, 2000.

———. *North Africa: A History from Antiquity to the Present.* Austin: University of Texas Press, 2009.

Normand, Suzanne, and Jean Acker. *Sahara.* Paris: Horizons de France, 1957.

Peyré, Joseph. *De Sable et d'or.* Paris: Flammarion, 1957.

Plessis, Daniel. "Quel visage le Sahara d'hier et d'aujourd'hui aura-t-il demain?" *La Nef,* 1, special issue: Le Sahara en Questions (1960): 24–34.

Richardson, James. *Notes du Sahara: Intinéraires dans l'intérieur du Grand Désert d'Afrique.* Paris: L. Martinet, 1850.

Ruedy, John. *Modern Algeria: The Origins and Development of a Nation.* Bloomington: Indiana University Press, 1992.

Said, Edward W. *Orientalism*. New York: Pantheon Books, 1978.
Sergent, Edmond. *Le Peuplement humain du Sahara*. Algiers: Institut Paster d'Algérie, 1953.
Spencer, Claire. "The Maghreb in the 1990s: Political and Economic Developments in Algeria, Morocco, and Tunisia." *Adelphi Paper* 274 (February 1993).
Strasser, Daniel. *Réalités et promesses sahariennes*. Paris: Encyclopédie d'Outre-Mer, 1956.
Thomas, Marc-Robert. *Sahara et Communauté*. Paris: Presses Universitaire de France, 1960.
Thomas, Martin C. *Empires of Intelligence: Security Services and Colonial Disorder after 1914*. Berkeley: University of California Press, 2008.
Trumbull IV, George R. *An Empire of Facts: Colonial Power, Cultural Knowledge, and Islam in Algeria, 1870–1914*. Critical Perspectives on Empire, edited by Catherine Hall, Mrinalini Sinha, and Kathleen Wilson. Cambridge: Cambridge University Press, 2009.
Verlet, Bruno. *Le Sahara*. Que Sais-Je series 766. Paris: Presses Universitaire de France, 1958.
Ville, M. *Notes d'un voyage d'exploration dans les basins du Hodna et du Sahara*. Paris: Dunod, 1865.
Vitalis, Robert P. *America's Kingdom: Mythmaking on the Saudi Oil Frontier*. Stanford, Calif.: Stanford University Press, 2007.

CHAPTER 4

From the Bottom Up

The Nile, Silt, and Humans in Ottoman Egypt

Alan Mikhail

THE NILE Delta and the Mediterranean have been pushing against each other for the past 10 million years since the river first began carrying dirt to the sea.[1] For most of the last 7,500 years though, the Delta has enjoyed the upper hand. As the fifth-century B.C.E. Greek traveler and historian Herodotus sailed toward Egypt's northern coast, he wrote of how "as you approach it and are still within one day's run from the land, and you drop a sounding line, you will bring up mud, though you are in eleven fathoms' depth."[2] For Herodotus, the presence of all this mud so far out at sea was evidence enough of how the Delta had been steadily made over the course of thousands of years by the accumulation of sand and dirt carried by the Nile.[3] In his words, "The Delta, according to the Egyptians themselves (and I certainly agree), is alluvial silt and, one might say, a contribution of the day before yesterday."[4] As evidence that the Delta was indeed a product of "the day before yesterday," Herodotus noted the region's absence of any of the ancient ruins responsible for bringing so many visitors like himself to Egypt.

Another of these travelers who wrote of the Nile Delta and its steady creation over millennia was an American named John Antes who lived in Egypt in the eighteenth century, the period of most immediate concern to us in this chapter. Of the Delta he wrote, "The large quantities of muscle and oyster beds, with other productions of the sea, which are to be found under ground in various places, even not far from Grand Cairo, made me sometimes think, that most probably the whole Delta was originally nothing but a shallow bay of the sea, of unequal depth.... Near Rosetta there seems to be striking proof that the country is still encreasing by the sediments of the river; by every appearance it seems that Rosetta was formerly situated close to the sea."[5] In addition to these fossilized remnants of the sea, Antes also observed how the yearly flood moved large amounts of dirt to grow the area of the Delta. "When I thus noticed what large pieces of ground were yearly carried away, and of course removed towards the sea, and considered that this must have been the case from the first existence of the river, it seemed to me a very strong argument ... that perhaps the greatest part, if not the whole of the Delta has been thus produced, and must still be encreasing by an encroachment upon the sea."[6] And like Herodotus many years before him, Antes also observed "that no monuments of very great antiquity are to be found in these low places, but only on some few elevated spots, and even these few do not seem to be so old as those found in the upper parts of the country."[7] Thus the period from Herodotus's visit to Egypt 2,500 years ago to Antes's observations at the end of the eighteenth century saw the steady expansion of the Delta into the Mediterranean. This reign of Egypt's northern coast over the sea, however, would soon begin to come to an end a few decades after Antes wrote his account.

Indeed on the basis of much more contemporary accounts, there is clear evidence that the multiple millennial domination of the Delta's dirt over the Mediterranean has slowly been coming to an end since about 1800.[8] Like other deltas around the world, Egypt's is slowly retreating. Some parts of the coastline are being eroded at a rate of 125 to 170 meters/year.[9] This is primarily a function of the detrimental effects of two hundred years of gigantic public works projects meant to manipulate the Nile's waters for what were stated at the time to be exigent political and economic needs. From the efforts of the early nineteenth-century Ottoman provincial governor Mehmet 'Ali to irrigate more of the Delta to President Gamal 'Abd al-Nasir's Aswan High Dam hydroelectric project in the mid-twentieth century, the ecology of the lower Nile was changed more rapidly and more fundamentally in the past two hundred years than ever before. One consequence of these changes to the river has been that the

Delta no longer receives the full impact of the yearly flood and the rich silt it contains (over 125 million tons of sediment a year).[10] These gifts of the Nile now pile up behind the Aswan High Dam. Thus unlike Herodotus, someone sailing toward the Nile Delta today would not find much mud in the sea at even a very close distance to the shore. Among the other regrettable environmental consequences of these public works projects—each of course with its own significant human costs as well—are salinization, coastal erosion, massive increases in the usage of chemical fertilizers, and extreme water loss due to evaporation from Lake Nasir behind the High Dam. These grand environmental stories of the creation of the Nile Delta and its current erosion are clear enough to anyone interested in Egypt and have received much attention from geologists, historians, environmental activists, hydrologists, and others.

Instead of these well-known millennial tales of creation and destruction, this chapter focuses in on some of the thousands of smaller scale daily interactions between Egyptians and the Nile Delta's silt in the seventeenth and eighteenth centuries—a few decades before the nineteenth and twentieth centuries' massive projects of river manipulation.[11] This history of human interaction with water and dirt in Ottoman Egypt (as elsewhere) is at its heart a story about the outlines of society—literally—and about how imaginaries of the rural landscape were formed and maintained through and by water. The yearly flood and the massive amount of sediment it brought ensured that the shape of Egypt in the Ottoman period and before was in constant flux. Water ebbed and flowed, embankments broke, canals were dredged, silt settled, water evaporated, and dams collapsed. These and other environmental and infrastructural realities of life in rural Ottoman Egypt meant that peasants and the imperial bureaucracy they were a part of had to adapt to a constantly changing physical landscape. The history of how peasants and the Ottoman state dealt with this environment in flux reveals how and why they conceived of, negotiated with, and tried to harness the dirt of their countryside.

The annual meeting of water with dirt was a process that fundamentally shaped Egyptian peasant and Ottoman imperial imaginaries of the rural environment. As is made clear in a seventeenth-century satirical Arabic literary account of the countryside, proximity to the Nile and the particular ways its flood waters settled in land created a hierarchy of rural spaces.[12] At the bottom of this hierarchy were swampy lands (*bilād al-malaq*) on the margins of the Nile watershed. These areas received water but not enough to properly irrigate agricultural fields to grow food. Next were villages very close to the river with highly sophisticated irrigation networks that fed water to very productive areas of cultivation. And at the top of this social ladder were Egypt's large towns and cities. That Egyptian peasants and the imperial bureaucracy equated relative levels of irrigation to social status, political and economic import, and cultural sophistication clearly indicates the centrality of water to the development of imaginaries of rural society and environment in Ottoman Egypt.

At the same time, an examination of both local and Ottoman imperial imaginations of the environment further suggests something of the cooperative nature of water management. Controlling, sharing, and using water both necessitated and fostered cooperation and compromise among all parties. As we will see below, many conceptions of how best to manage water were built on this cooperative ideal, one understood and cultivated by *both* the imperial bureaucracy and Egyptian peasants. This common acceptance of the cooperative nature of water utilization goes a long way in explaining the remarkable similarities of many of the shared imperial and local views of the rural Egyptian environment. As I show below, however, this is not to say that peasant and imperial interests and actions were always in lockstep. Taken together, these cooperative and contested negotiations over environmental resource management help delineate a set of environmental imaginaries at play in the early modern Ottoman Egyptian countryside that included notions of community, responsibility, precedent, and resource allocation.

Two aspects of life in rural Ottoman Egypt bring the imperial bureaucracy's and peasants' engagements with dirt and water into the starkest of reliefs—canal dredging and the changing shape of alluvial islands in the Nile and its tributaries. Canals had to be dredged regularly throughout Egypt to keep irrigated water flowing in the countryside, and likewise the vicissitudes of the Nile ensured that alluvial islands were constantly getting larger and smaller, reforging their spatial form, and connecting and disconnecting from canal banks. Both of these processes, among others, altered the physical landscape of Egypt, changed political and social relationships between peasant groups and between peasants and the Ottoman state, affected rural labor practices, challenged the abilities of rural Islamic courts to adjudicate complex disputes, and reshaped economic interests. In more specific terms, I will show below how canal dredging involved the establishment of legal precedents for the responsibility of maintaining properly functioning waterways and other irrigation works and how alluvial islands contributed to notions about what constituted evidence for the continuous use and cultivation of property. These ideals of community, precedent, sharing, and the establishment of responsibility were all integral facets of both imperial and local imaginaries of the rural Ottoman Egyptian environment.

Ideals in the Dirt

The water of Egypt's vastly complex irrigation network was forever in motion. This perpetual aqueous movement ensured that land as well was constantly appearing, disappearing, and changing shape. It also ensured that the Ottoman state had to address this continually shifting terrain through various bureaucratic and legal mechanisms. It did this largely by upholding in its network of legal courts certain notions of how communities shared and used water resources.

One of the most important factors determining how water flow shaped the banks of canals and the borders of land was the amount and character of silt on the bottoms of the beds of Egypt's waterways. A highly silted-up canal could, for example, force water to flow with more force and in considerably different directions than it usually did. This could in turn erode canal embankments or completely overtake them. Alternatively, such a canal could stop flowing altogether. To attempt to gain a semblance of control over how water changed the shape of the rural Egyptian environment, the Ottoman administration of the countryside in the early modern period relied on dredging as one of the most crucial elements in its management of rural spaces. Because cleaning canal beds greatly impacted the local environments of all villages sharing a particular waterway, the bureaucratic organization of dredging points to conceptions of ecological community and responsibility and to how these notions were established, maintained, and manipulated to manage Egypt's rural irrigation network.

Dredging is one of the most common issues in the archival record of irrigation in Ottoman Egypt.[13] Certain canals were notoriously susceptible to large buildups of silt and were therefore constantly in need of attention. One of these waterways was a canal branching off of a large central canal known as al-Baḥr al-Ṣaghīr in al-Manzala in the subprovince of al-Manṣūra in the northeast Delta.[14] Between 1684 and 1704, this auxiliary canal was dredged in every one of these twenty years to remove what were termed the many small "islands and steps" (*cezireler ü atebeler*) of underwater buildup that had formed on the canal bottom.[15] The regular opening and closing of smaller canals feeding off of this main canal allowed silt and debris to settle on its bed resulting in its nearly perennial state of siltation.

The dirt obstructing the canal's flow created all sorts of problems for peasants living in the forty villages along its length. In an effort to deal with these problems in a more permanent way so as to avoid the need to dredge the canal every year, the people (*ahali*) of these villages served by the waterway came to the court of al-Manṣūra in 1704 with village notables and engineers of the region to discuss what could be done about this situation. Not surprisingly, it was agreed by all that, in the words of this case, the canal should be cleaned of all the dirt clogging it up so as to repair it with maximum strength and sturdiness to ensure that funds and effort were not continually expended on its dredging and maintenance. Functionaries of the court were thus dispatched along with peasants living on the canal to determine the costs of such a repair. They returned to the court to report that this work would total 50,000 paras.[16] The twenty-three upstream villages near the mouth of the smaller canal at al-Baḥr al-Ṣaghīr were each to contribute 1,000 paras to this repair effort, and the other seventeen downstream villages were only to contribute 600 paras each (the remaining difference of 16,800 paras was to be made up by Ottoman state funds).[17]

This adjudication of the canal's dredging reflected an understanding by the Ottoman administration and by Egyptian peasants of how water flow and canal siltation affected communities differently based on their location along a waterway. Because downstream siltation was largely a byproduct of the opening and closing of upstream canals and of the water consumption of upstream villages, these villages had to pay more for the dredging of the canal. Undergirding this and other similar court settlements was an understanding shared by all parties involved that the collective usage of a canal tied them together into a community of water utilization and consumption. This reflected a conception of environmental resource management in which actions in any one part of this irrigated ecosystem were seen to affect and implicate all canal users. This principle of irrigation was a basic tenet of the shared rural environmental imaginary of Ottoman Egypt and was maintained in almost every dispute involving water in the countryside.[18] Included in this imaginary was the notion that clearly not all actions on a canal were equal. The water usage of upstream villages greatly impacted the quantity and character of the water and silt that reached downstream villages. The opposite was, however, obviously not true. Thus in dealing with the sediment carried by water it was always important to remember in which direction water flowed.

One of the best examples of the implementation of this principle in Egyptian irrigation was the management of the flow and dredging of the Ashrafiyya Canal that coursed through the subprovince of al-Baḥayra in the northwest Delta to connect Alexandria, Egypt's second city, to the Rosetta (western) branch of the Nile. As with the previous canal, the Ashrafiyya's flow was extremely weak owing both to its lack of incline from its mouth toward Alexandria and to the constant breaking of the canal's embankments by peasants seeking to siphon water off to their fields.[19] Unlike in other cases of communities of water in Egypt, however, with the Ashrafiyya it was obvious (at least from the perspective of the Ottoman state and Alexandria's residents) which of the populations served by the waterway was most important—those at the canal's terminus in Alexandria. The imperial bureaucracy therefore expended a great deal of energy attempting to prevent villages along the length of the canal from breaking into the waterway, since this removal of water from the canal made its problems of siltation all the worse.[20] The canal was shallow, had a weak current, was surrounded by very loose soil, and consistently lost water. All of these factors combined with the desire to have copious amounts of fresh and clean drinking water reach the people of Alexandria contributed to nearly constant dredging efforts.

In the middle of the eighteenth century, for example, there were several major dredging and cleaning initiatives designed to improve the canal's flow. In the summer of 1751, peasants from the village of Minyyat Ḥiṭṭiyya were charged by the Ottoman state to dredge the bed of the canal and to reinforce embankments near their village to prevent soil and debris from falling into the waterway.[21] Almost exactly a year later (in 1752), other villages along the canal were instructed to carry out similar infrastructural work on the Ashrafiyya.[22] The canal was divided into three sections to make its dredging and cleaning more orderly and efficient. In each section, one village was put in charge of overseeing work on that part of the canal. In this period as well, a large waterwheel was constructed at the mouth of the canal in the village of al-Raḥmāniyya in an additional attempt to quicken its flow.[23]

Despite these and other similar efforts, however, siltation and the collection of debris, rocks, and sand in the canal remained constant problems throughout the seventeenth and eighteenth centuries. In a firman (imperial order) sent from Istanbul to the vali (Ottoman provincial governor) of Egypt Mustafa Paşa in February 1738, for instance, the palace complained that the canal had been badly neglected over the previous few years and was currently so clogged up with sand and dirt that water was barely reaching Alexandria.[24] When the canal was clean and properly functioning, the normal flood height of 16 cubits was more than sufficient to fill Alexandria's 210 cisterns with water for the city's residents, which were estimated here to be sixty or seventy thousand.[25] In this year, however, the canal was in such a bad state that even the waters of the exceptionally high flood mark of 22 cubits did not reach Alexandria. Thus, the imperial divan ordered the immediate dredging and cleaning of the Ashrafiyya. Nevertheless a few decades later in the spring of 1763, Alexandrians living near the canal filed a petition with the Ottoman bureaucracy complaining that the waterway's flow was again being restricted by all the silt, thorny branches, and garbage that were collecting in it.[26] These petitioners continued on to say that this shortage of flowing water exposed them to great difficulty and hardship, and they thus implored the state to clean and dredge the canal as soon as possible. Realizing the urgency of this situation, the imperial capital issued a firman to its vali in Cairo to immediately undertake this work.

In these cases about the dredging of the Ashrafiyya and other canals, the Ottoman state and Egyptian peasants sought to preserve the flow of canals so that their water would serve as many people as possible all along the waterways. At play in these cases were attempts to balance the needs and desires of the upstream against the demands and necessities of the downstream—a fundamental aspect of the imagined ideal of how to manage the consumption of water by multiple parties. And in these cases, community welfare was always privileged over individual rights. This was one of the basic principles guiding the management of water and dirt in Ottoman Egypt. In establishing how to dredge canals and who was to be charged with this work, several other conceptions of environmental management were also at play. Foremost among them were notions of how proximity and shared usage determined responsibilities for the maintenance of irrigation works and the dredging of canal beds. Those in the immediate vicinity of an irrigation work who directly benefited from its presence and proper function were responsible for its upkeep; likewise, those who shared the water of a canal were also to share in the work of dredging and maintaining that canal. Telling examples of these ideals in action in the Egyptian countryside were instances of the dredging of canals shared between two or more villages on opposite sides of a waterway.

In June 1724, three villages—two from the subprovince of al-Daqahliyya (Kafr Ghannām and al-Jazīra Bākhir) and one from al-Sharqiyya (al-Hajārsa)—came to the court of al-Manṣūra (the subprovincial seat of al-Daqahliyya) to report on the successful dredging of a shared canal that served as the border between the two subprovinces.[27] The hakim (subprovincial governor) of each of these two subprovinces was responsible for dredging and cleaning the canal every year from the water's edge at the border of his subprovince to the middle of the canal.[28] In 1724, the court of al-Daqahliyya sent its representatives to villages near the canal to ask local village elders (*mashāʾikh*) whether or not their half of the canal had indeed been properly dredged. These local notables reported to the court's functionaries that the hakim of al-Daqahliyya had indeed carried out his required charge efficiently and properly. His men (*rijāl*) had worked for thirteen days to clean the canal and to reinforce its embankments, and its waters were now flowing quickly and without obstruction. The judge in this case then reminded these local village elders that the responsibilities to keep the canal properly functioning were now completely in their hands. The imperial bureaucracy had, in other words, carried out a major dredging operation on a canal and was now handing off its fate to villagers living around it. Moreover, the judge added that should these local notables fail to maintain the canal's proper function they would have to pay for this failure with their lives.[29]

Water and silt were thus literally matters of life and death. With this dramatically unambiguous threat of execution, the Ottoman bureaucracy clearly indicated its conceptions of irrigation and dredging as two of the most important aspects of its rule in the Egyptian countryside. Moreover, it was also making a strong declaration in this case, as in others like it, that ensuring the steady supply of irrigated water to dozens or scores of villages and thousands of peasants was of greater concern to the state than preserving the life of one or a few peasants. This ideal of resource management and access was, needless to say, one that only *some* Egyptian peasants benefited from and hence consented to and willingly implemented. Thus unlike previous cases, this was an instance in which various Egyptian peasants and the Ottoman bureaucracy obviously held very different environmental ideals. This disjuncture of outlook and priority aside, the fact remains that the Ottoman imperial imagination of the countryside consistently privileged the interests of the whole over the life of the individual.

Moreover, these examples of the sharing of a canal between multiple villages also illustrate how authority over dredging and irrigation was conceptualized, organized, and delegated in Ottoman Egypt. Proximity was again key to the empire's imagination of environmental management. Like the peasants and their village heads in the above case, those who directly benefited from a properly functioning canal were responsible for keeping it flowing. This authority invested in the local control of irrigation works was meant to serve as a preemptive measure against massive destruction and the repairs it would surely necessitate. Steady maintenance of canals by those directly served by them would ensure the overall health of Egypt's irrigation network. The Ottoman administration of Egypt calculated that if all peasants took control of their immediate surroundings, then the irrigation system would work together as a whole. The line of authority traced in this case makes this abundantly clear: from the Ottoman state through its imperial institution of the court, to subprovincial hakims, to representatives of the court, to local peasant elders, and finally to those peasants who actually carried out the canal's repairs. Cases like this one in many ways thus represented the ideal function and most efficient execution of the empire's conception of irrigation management.

In other cases, these privileged conceptions of proximity, shared authority, and communal welfare were again challenged by peasants attempting to gain some degree of advantage over their neighboring peasants through the manipulation of a canal's water or silt or both. As before, some of the most common and instructive of these disputes over water and dredging were those between upstream and downstream villages. In February 1682, the heads of two neighboring villages on the same bank of a shared canal came to the court of al-Manṣūra.[30] The head of the downstream village Nūb Ṭarīf complained to the court that the peasants of the upstream village Ṭummāy had failed to dredge and clean the section of the canal that ran past their village.[31] As a result, the canal's embankments were crumbling and silt mounds were beginning to peak through the water surface. An insufficient amount of water was thus reaching Nūb Ṭarīf causing many of its fields and those of other villages near it to become parched and dry. The representative of this village thus asked the judge to send state officials to inspect the situation so that they could see for themselves that the peasants of Ṭummāy had failed to clean and dredge the canal as was their duty "from times of old" (*min qadīm al-zamān*)—as the oft-repeated phrase went—and so that they could force these locals to fix the waterway.

The peasants of Ṭummāy in this instance either through choice, incompetence, or irresponsibility let their canal silt up, which in turn prevented water from reaching their downstream neighbors. This case gives no indication as to why the canal's dredging was ignored in opposition to the empire's idealized imaginary of environmental resource management. Perhaps the people of Ṭummāy had acquired some other source of water that made the older canal no longer relevant for their own irrigation purposes. Perhaps there was some crisis in the village that took peasants' attention away from the canal. Alternatively, perhaps a dispute between the two villages caused the people of Ṭummāy to use their more advantageous upstream position as a weapon against Nūb Ṭarīf. Whatever the case may be, the actions of the court instigated by the head of Nūb Ṭarīf upheld the ideal of proximity in determining responsibility for canal maintenance. Moreover, in a statement asserting the power of community above all else, the physical presence of the canal in Ṭummāy did not give its residents ultimate authority over the canal's usage, consumption, and management rights. The downstream village of Nūb Ṭarīf indeed exercised its authority as an invested member in a community of water to force peasants in another village to dredge a canal they all shared.

The constantly changing shape of rural Egypt caused by the movement of water and sand, siltation, the collapse of dams and embankments, and the various actions of users of canals and other irrigation works ensured that dredging was a central aspect of Ottoman rule in Egypt. As a site of regular cooperation and contestation between the empire and peasants and between different peasant communities, dredging indeed serves as a crucial indicator of how various challenges to the Ottoman imperial imaginary of the Egyptian environment were handled. Within this realm of negotiation over how to deal with silt, water, and their multiple and often unpredictable effects on rural life, ideals of community, proximity, and the sharing of responsibility were both developed and maintained to govern canal dredging and cleaning. This was accomplished through various legal institutions, infrastructural formations, and social principles that operated to uphold and reinforce these ideals and to protect the overall health and productivity of agriculture in the countryside. Nile sediment thus not only made Egypt the most lucrative agricultural and financial province of the Ottoman Empire, but it also shaped much of Ottoman rule in Egypt and much of both imperial and local social, ecological, and political understandings of the countryside and of how rural physical spaces were to be governed.

Dots on the River

Some of the best examples of how Ottoman imperial and local Egyptian imaginaries came to bear on the rural environment are the multiple ways in which the Nile and the dirt it carried altered the topography of the Egyptian countryside through the changing shape, size, and connectivity of islands in the Nile and its tributaries. The rise and fall of the Nile meant that islands were constantly getting bigger and smaller and often connecting and disconnecting from the mainland. This geographical flux challenged conceptions of terrestrial fixity, on which was built the whole edifice of ideas about responsibility, sharing, and communal governance. Even perhaps Egypt's most famous island—al-Rauḍa, whose prominence derived chiefly from the Nilometer (*miqyās al-Nīl*) on its southern tip, the device used to measure the official level of the annual flood for purposes of taxation and agricultural production—often found itself connected to Cairo's coastline due to the river's recession.[32] Such was the case in the spring of 1792 when the eastern portion of the Nile between al-Rauḍa and

Figure 4.1. Nile between al-Rauḍa and Mainland Cairo, late eighteenth century. Commission des sciences et arts d'Egypte, *État moderne I*, vol. 7 of *Description de l'Égypte, ou, recueil de observations et des recherches qui ont été faites en Égypte pendant l'éxpédition de l'armée française, publié par les ordres de Sa Majesté l'empereur Napoléon le Grand* (Paris: Imprimerie impériale, 1809–28), 36 (plate 17).

Cairo began to dry.[33] Huge piles of sand formed all along the channel and even further north, serving essentially to connect al-Rauḍa to the eastern bank.[34] Water levels in this season were so low that even to the west of the island, in the much wider portion of the river separating al-Rauḍa from Giza, land had begun to emerge from underneath the river, turning this western section into a pathetic trickling brook (*salsūl jadwal*) in which little children played and through which only the smallest boats could pass.[35]

With the river's rapidly changing water levels and its slower and faster currents, the amount of land available for cultivation on islands like al-Rauḍa was constantly fluctuating. As we saw with the example of dredging, because of erosion and other environmental changes, some areas of land along the banks of the Nile and its branches were exposed for parts of the year and submerged in others. Thus, some dirt formerly covered by water often became permanent agricultural land as a result of changes—humanly induced or otherwise—to the direction and flow of the river. This emergence and disappearance of cultivatable earth meant that there was a constant need to reimagine and redetermine the legal, social, and agricultural status of these new and old lands. The working out of resolutions to these administrative imperatives again shows us how the bureaucratic mechanisms of the Ottoman Empire in Egypt sought to maintain precedent as the empire's overriding conceptual framework for understanding and managing the persistently changing rural environment. And furthermore it also helps us see how Egyptian peasants attempted to harness these changes for their own local advantage.

In a dispute over an island from the late eighteenth century, a group of tax farmers (multazims) from the subprovince of al-Daqahliyya came to the court of al-Manṣūra to testify on behalf of the rights of the village of Ṭalkhā al-Gharbī over an island that had recently been seized by peasants from the neighboring village of Qūjindīma.[36] Whereas this island had historically been separated from the mainland by water on all sides, it had recently attached to the shoreline near the two villages due to the receding or shallowing of the river. Once connected to the mainland, the people of Qūjindīma moved quickly to take control of the former island by crossing over the newly formed land bridge. Although the peasants of Qūjindīma freely admitted to seizing the island, they refused to give up their claims to it, and thus the present quarrel between the two villages came to pass. All the tax farmers and other locals who came to court and everyone else mentioned in this case—other than the peasants of Qūjindīma of course—agreed that the island, no matter that it was now connected to the mainland, belonged to the peasants of Ṭalkhā since they had historically cultivated it. And thus on the basis of this testimony, the judge in this case ruled in favor of the peasants of Ṭalkhā. Unlike other disputes over islands in which the presence of irrigation works and other built features evidenced a history of cultivation, in this case no such structures existed, and hence the assertion of rights over the island rested purely on the testimony of various parties as to which group of peasants had historically farmed the island.[37]

For their parts, through their takeover of the island the peasants of Qūjindīma clearly prescribed a reimagination of its status. Not only had its new connection to the mainland fundamentally altered a particular local geography, but it also necessitated a completely different bureaucratic and legal configuration. Given the new land bridge, where were the new borders of the former island's cultivated space? To whom did the cultivation rights of the new land bridge belong? Did it belong to the people of Ṭalkhā since the land fell between two areas they farmed? Or was its status as yet undefined since it was a new piece of land that had never before had an assertion of rights applied to it? For the imperial court, the answers to these and other similar questions were reached through a determination of legal precedent—the precedent of the historic cultivation of the island by the people of Ṭalkhā. To this end, the court sought out the testimony of peasants from neighboring villages to help establish who had previously cultivated the island. Thus in this instance of their imagining of the rural Egyptian environment, the Ottoman state sought to reinstitute a system of resource management that had obtained before the island had attached to the mainland.

At the same time, the peasants of Qūjindīma wanted to establish their own new superseding precedent of cultivation on the island by moving quickly to take it over once it was connected to the shore. Theirs was thus an effort to create new facts on a new ground. They attempted to entrench a new physical reality so as to precipitate a reimagining of the island as their possession. In this case, however, the court upheld that the recent connection of the island to the shore did not change who enjoyed cultivation rights to the island. Thus even in the face of literally shifting geographies and challenges to established imaginations of the Egyptian countryside, here, as elsewhere in the Ottoman Empire, precedent continued to reign supreme.

What is not made explicitly clear in this case is the legal status of the new land that emerged from underneath the water. The judge made no determination in this regard. Thus here again it seems that there was resistance to reimagining this land as having a legal status other than the one that previously obtained. Perhaps establishing rights to cultivate this new piece of earth was considered unnecessary since all knew that land near the Nile and its canals regularly appeared and disappeared as the river rose and fell. It was only a matter of time, therefore, before this land was again flooded over, making the complexities of its legal status rather irrelevant. As we saw previously, however, in cases involving the dredging of canals between villages on opposite sides of a waterway, there was an imaginary line established down the center of canals splitting the responsibilities of cleaning and dredging them into equal parts. Was such a notion at play in this case that made the establishment of rights to the new land unnecessary since it was clearly that of the nearest village? These questions are at their base inquiries into how silt and dirt were imagined and legally assessed in rural Ottoman Egypt. Despite the lack of explicit answers to some of these questions, we should nevertheless not assume that these issues were somehow not debated or disputed in Ottoman Egypt. Clearly they were, as evidenced by the numerous court cases produced to deal with Egypt's ever-shifting rural terrain.

Another of these cases shows how conceptions of precedent and a notion of shared usage similar to that discussed previously came to govern the management of peasant actions precipitated by physical changes to alluvial islands. In the spring of 1792, a series of cases came to the court of al-Baḥayra about an island in a branch of the Nile between the villages of Nitmā and Kafr al-Gharīb.[38] From times of old (*min qadīm al-zamān*), these two villages had equally shared the island in sowing and cultivation.[39] Beginning a few years earlier, however, the tax farmer of the village of Nitmā started preventing the peasants of Kafr al-Gharīb from coming to cultivate their fields on the island. Moreover, because of the strength of the Nile's crashing waters, the river "ate" (*akala*) most of the section of the island that had historically been cultivated by the people of Kafr al-Gharīb. Thus, needless to say, this situation caused great hardship and concern for the peasants of Kafr al-Gharīb, since not only had the total area of their section of the island's agricultural land decreased because of the Nile's encroachment, but the whole of the lands that did remain were taken over by the peasants of Nitmā. In the face of this difficult state of affairs, the firman issued in this case directed the people of Kafr al-Gharīb to take back half of the reduced total area of the island so that, as before, both villages again cultivated equal halves of this bounded piece of land. Indeed, these cases cite the imperative to return to the precedent from times of old that the two villages were to split the island's area equally.[40] As such, these cases also end with an admonition, if even a formulaic one, to both villages to never again act against this principle of equal usage—one of the basic conceptual ideals shaping how the rural landscape was to be managed.

In this example, as in most, the set of strictures that determined how disputes over a shared island were to be resolved was precedent. Precedent, then, was the "law" as it came to be practiced in rural Ottoman courts. Over and over in these cases, judges, litigants, and witnesses underscore their ideas of environmental resource management by invoking the way things have always been done, again "from times of old" (*min qadīm al-zamān*), as a justification for why they should remain that way. Thus in the face of a rural topography that was constantly changing, the Ottoman bureaucracy of Egypt and the province's peasants sought to preserve a social order based on their understandings of the previous shape of the Egyptian countryside. Principally through its courts, the Ottoman imperial bureaucracy strove to make the countryside match its ideal imagining of the history and function of the rural Egyptian world. And through their recourse to these courts, groups of Egyptian peasants sought to preserve their history of cultivation and water usage rights.

To put it differently, the Ottoman state attempted to prevent environmental change from dictating its imperial rule. Although the empire could do very little to prevent the environmental impacts of erosion, siltation, or flood, it could attempt to prevent these natural forces from changing its management of the Egyptian countryside.[41] This is perhaps an obvious point—that existing political powers want to preserve the status quo of their rule. For their part, Egyptian peasants were likewise so invested in this imperial system of natural resource management that they too had a stake in its preservation. Nevertheless, neither Ottoman imperial power nor Egyptian peasant knowledge of local environments could prevent islands from becoming larger and smaller or from connecting and disconnecting from the mainland. Thus to preserve a sustainable rural social order given these constants of change, the state—through cooperation and contestation with Egyptian peasants—upheld and defended precedent, cultivated ideals of sharing and community, and financed and supported irrigation repair work in an effort to fashion the countryside in accord with its own imperial environmental imagination.

WHEN ANALYZING the environmental imaginaries and rule of political entities like the Ottoman Empire, it is essential to define the specific spatial demarcations within which such polities exist. In the case of Ottoman Egypt, the physical outlines and shape of this province were constantly changing. As the Nile's waters pushed silt along or allowed it to settle, some lands were submerged and others appeared. Canal embankments were eroded away, and islands often changed size or connected to the shore. Through a consideration of how precedent was defended and of the legal and social mechanisms used to establish responsibility over irrigation works, I have attempted in this chapter to outline part of the environmental imaginary of Ottoman state bureaucrats and Egyptian peasants as it emerged in their dealings with the rural environment's forever shifting terrain. In contemporary parlance, we would say that the Ottoman Empire's "environmental policy" in dealing with the dirt and water of early modern Egypt was to return irrigation works to their former states of functionality through dredging or some other means of environmental manipulation and to uphold previous local cultivation rights no matter the changes made to the land. In sum, the Ottoman Empire's goal was to maintain the physical parameters of the rural environment in accord both with local Egyptian imagined conceptions of its past and with perceived notions of its most efficient function in the present moment.

The twin examples of dredging and islands thus highlight two very different aspects of Ottoman rule in Egypt as it relates to local communities—respectively, peasant responsibilities of maintenance and peasant rights of cultivation. Whereas the former was an imposition on village communities, the latter was a privilege. Both however were ultimately derived from and sustained by notions of what proximity, shared usage, community, and precedent represented for the users of canals and the farmers of lands fed by these waterways. Such environmental ideals and the imaginations that underlay them—though often submerged under water and buried in the dirt—are fundamental to any understanding not only of the history of rural Ottoman Egypt, but also of the Ottoman Empire as a whole and of riparian communities more generally.

Notes

For their very useful comments on drafts of this essay, I thank Diana K. Davis, Beshara Doumani, Huri İslamoğlu, and Edith Sheffer. My sincere thanks as well to the very helpful staffs of the Prime Ministry's Ottoman Archive in Istanbul and the National Archives of Egypt in Cairo.

1. The sedimentary processes that formed the Nile Delta began during the Upper Miocene. Scot E. Smith and Adel Abdel-Kader, "Coastal Erosion along the Egyptian Delta," *Journal of Coastal Research* 4, no. 2 (1988): 245–55; Rushdi Said, *The Geological Evolution of the River Nile* (New York: Springer-Verlag, 1981).

2. Herodotus, *The History*, trans. David Grene (Chicago: University of Chicago Press, 1987), 2.5.

3. Approximately half of the total sediment load of 125 million tons carried by the river each year into Egypt was discharged to the Mediterranean. Smith and Abdel-Kader, "Coastal Erosion," 249. For a further analysis of these Delta sediments, see Janusz Dominik and Daniel Jean Stanley, "Boron, Beryllium and Sulfur in Holocene Sediments and Peats of the Nile Delta, Egypt: Their Use as Indicators of Salinity and Climate," *Chemical Geology* 104, no. 1–4 (1993): 203–16.

4. Herodotus, *History*, 2.15.

5. John Antes, *Observations on the Manners and Customs of the Egyptians, the Overflowing of the Nile and its Effects; with Remarks on the Plague and Other Subjects. Written During a Residence of Twelve Years in Cairo and its Vicinity* (London: Printed for J. Stockdale, 1800), 64–65. For a study of these fossilized mollusks in the Delta, see Maria Pia Bernasconi, Daniel Jean Stanley, and Italo Di Geronimo, "Molluscan Faunas and Paleobathymetry of Holocene Sequences in the Northeastern Nile Delta, Egypt," *Marine Geology* 99, no. 1–2 (1991): 29–43.

6. Antes, *Observations*, 74–75.

7. Ibid., 75.

8. Smith and Abdel-Kader, "Coastal Erosion"; Abdel-Aziz I. Kashef, "Salt-Water Intrusion in the Nile Delta," *Ground Water* 21, no. 2 (1983): 160–67; Omran E. Frihy, Alfy M. Fanos, Ahmed A. Khafagy, and Paul D. Komar, "Patterns of Nearshore Sediment Transport along the Nile Delta, Egypt," *Coastal Engineering* 15, no. 5–6 (1991): 409–29. See also J. R. McNeill, *Something New Under the Sun: An Environmental History of the Twentieth-Century World* (New York: W. W. Norton, 2000), 166–73.

9. Mohamed A. K. Elsayed, Nazeih A. Younan, Alfy M. Fanos, and Khalid H. Baghdady, "Accretion and Erosion Patterns along Rosetta Promontory, Nile Delta Coast," *Journal of Coastal Research* 21, no. 3 (2005), 413. From 1900 to 1964 (when construction of the Aswan High Dam began), the average rate of erosion was much lower: about 50 meters/year. As with most aspects of environmental or historical change, this was neither a completely linear nor

universal phenomenon. Even into the nineteenth century, some parts of the Delta continued to expand into the sea. For example between 1500 and 1900, sections of the Rosetta promontory advanced into the sea at an average rate of 25 meters/year.

10. Smith and Abdel-Kader, "Coastal Erosion," 249.

11. Much of the writing of environmental history has privileged the stories of very big changes to the natural world—coastal erosion, climate change, deforestation, species extinction, and so forth. As this chapter attempts to illustrate, however, the minutiae of these enormous ecological processes as well as other independent small-scale environmental changes are of no less historical and environmental significance and are thus equally deserving of our attention.

12. For the Arabic critical edition of this very important text and an English translation, see Yūsuf ibn Muḥammad al-Shirbīnī, *Kitāb Hazz al-Quḥūf bi-Sharḥ Qaṣīd Abī Shādūf*, ed. and trans. Humphrey Davies, 2 vols. (Leuven: Peeters, 2005–7).

13. In addition to the cases about dredging discussed here, see also Alan Mikhail, *Nature and Empire in Ottoman Egypt: An Environmental History* (New York: Cambridge University Press, 2011), 38–81.

14. On al-Manzala, see Muḥammad Ramzī, *Al-Qāmūs al-Jughrāfī lil-Bilād al-Miṣriyya min 'Ahd Qudamā' al-Miṣriyyīn ilā Sanat 1945*, 6 vols. in 2 parts (Cairo: al-Hay'a al-Miṣriyya al-'Āmma lil-Kitāb, 1994), part 2, vol. 1, 203–4.

15. Maḥkamat al-Manṣūra 16, p. 397 A, no case number (6 Za 1115/12 March 1704), Dār al-Wathā'iq al-Qawmiyya (National Archives of Egypt, Cairo; hereafter DWQ).

16. The para was the basic unit of currency in Ottoman Egypt. On its history, conversion, and usage, see Stanford J. Shaw, *The Financial and Administrative Organization and Development of Ottoman Egypt, 1517–1798* (Princeton: Princeton University Press, 1962), xxii.

17. For the breakdown of these payments by village, see Maḥkamat al-Manṣūra 16, p. 397 B, no case number (6 Za 1115/12 March 1704), DWQ.

18. Another case from the court of al-Manṣūra from late June 1692 concerned a community of water formed around the shared usage of a canal known as Ḥammām. One section of this canal was badly in need of dredging, and villages along its length therefore came to the court to push the Ottoman administration to dredge this part of the waterway because the earth near it was dry, hard, and stony. If immediate action was not taken to dredge this shared canal, water would not reach these villages' fields, and they would remain bare, unfit for cultivation, and destitute. The Ottoman imperial administration heeded these peasants' warnings in this case and appointed one of its local functionaries to oversee the dredging and cleaning of the canal. Maḥkamat al-Manṣūra 12, p. 447 A, no case number (10 L 1103/25 June 1692), DWQ.

19. For an example of the ease with which the canal could be drained, see 'Abd al-Raḥman ibn Ḥasan al-Jabartī, *'Ajā'ib al-Āthār fī al-Tarājim wa al-Akhbār*,

ed. ʿAbd al-Raḥīm ʿAbd al-Raḥman ʿAbd al-Raḥīm, 4 vols. (Cairo: Maṭbaʿat Dār al-Kutub al-Miṣriyya, 1998), 4:31. In this case, a group of soldiers dammed the canal in two places and was then able to siphon off all of the trapped water to ground its enemy's ships.

20. See, for example, Maḥkamat al-Baḥayra 7, p. 56, case 112 (2 Ra 1171/14 November 1757), DWQ.

21. Maḥkamat al-Baḥayra 5, pp. 9–10, case 15 (12 Ş 1164/6 July 1751), DWQ.

22. Maḥkamat al-Baḥayra 5, pp. 172–73, case 302 (10 Ş 1165/22 June 1752), DWQ.

23. For references to this waterwheel, see Maḥkamat al-Baḥayra 5, pp. 9–10, case 15 (12 Ş 1164/6 July 1751), DWQ; Maḥkamat al-Baḥayra 5, pp. 172–73, case 302 (10 Ş 1165/22 June 1752), DWQ. For descriptions of other kinds of irrigation works built at the mouth of the canal to aid its current, see Maḥkamat al-Baḥayra 5, p. 6, case 11 (30 B 1164/24 June 1751), DWQ; Maḥkamat al-Baḥayra 5, p. 314, case 389 (10 Ş 1165/22 June 1752), DWQ. On the village of al-Raḥmāniyya, see Ramzī, *Al-Qāmūs al-Jughrāfī*, part 2, vol. 2, 305.

24. Mühimme-i Mısır (hereafter MM), 5:393 (Evahir L 1150/10–20 February 1738), Başbakanlık Osmanlı Arşivi (Prime Ministry's Ottoman Archive, Istanbul; hereafter BOA).

25. There is no indication as to how the Sultan's imperial council reached this population figure, which seems rather exaggerated for the mid-eighteenth century. The consensus in the historical literature puts Alexandria's population in this period closer to ten or twenty thousand. See, for example, Daniel Panzac, "Alexandrie: Peste et croissance urbaine (XVIIe–XIXe siècles)," in *Population et santé dans l'Empire ottoman (XVIIIe–XXe siècles)* (Istanbul: Isis, 1996), 45–55; Michael J. Reimer, "Ottoman Alexandria: The Paradox of Decline and the Reconfiguration of Power in Eighteenth-Century Arab Provinces," *Journal of the Economic and Social History of the Orient* 37, no. 2 (1994): 107–46.

26. MM, 8:139 (Evasıt L 1176/25 April–4 May 1763), BOA.

27. Maḥkamat al-Manṣūra 24, p. 288, case 628 (28 N 1136/20 June 1724), DWQ. On the village of Kafr Ghannām, see Ramzī, *Al-Qāmūs al-Jughrāfī*, part 2, vol. 1, 199. On al-Hajārsa, see ibid., part 2, vol. 1, 128.

28. Cases like this one about the dredging of a shared canal seem to indicate that there was an imaginary line assumed to run down the middle of canals dividing them into two equal parts. We are given no indication as to how this line was established or how the complicated work of dredging only *half* a canal was organized and actually accomplished.

29. The operative phrase is *in ḥaṣala fīhi khalal . . . kāna dhālika muqābilan bi-arwāḥihim*. For another case that cites similar threats of execution, see Maḥkamat al-Manṣūra 9, p. 205, case 466 (Evail L 1100/19–28 July 1689), DWQ. The notion that a village head could be killed for failing to properly maintain irrigation works is one established in the founding Ottoman law code (*kanunname*) of Egypt promulgated in 1525, less than a decade after the Ottoman conquest of Egypt in 1517. For the relevant sections of this law code,

see Ömer Lûtfi Barkan, *Kanunlar,* vol. 1 of *XV ve XVIinci asırlarda Osmanlı İmparatorluğunda Ziraî Ekonominin Hukukî ve Malî Esasları,* İstanbul Üniversitesi Yayınlarından 256 (Istanbul: Bürhaneddin Matbaası, 1943), 360–61. For the Arabic translation, see Aḥmad Fu'ād Mutawallī, trans. and intro., *Qānūn Nāmah Miṣr, alladhī Aṣdarahu al-Sulṭān al-Qānūnī li-Ḥukm Miṣr* (Cairo: Maktabat al-Anjlū al-Miṣriyya, 1986), 30–31.

30. Maḥkamat al-Manṣūra 7, p. 310, case 767 (19 S 1093/27 February 1682) DWQ.

31. On Nūb Ṭarīf see Ramzī, *Al-Qāmūs al-Jughrāfī,* part 2, vol. 1, 196. On Ṭummāy see ibid., part 2, vol. 1, 192.

32. Its name meaning garden or meadow, the island of al-Rauḍa is a long, slender piece of land (approximately three kilometers long and half a kilometer wide at its thickest point) separated from the east bank of the Nile by a thin section of the river and from the west bank by a much wider section of the Nile. The most detailed account of the island and its history is the following fifteenth-century work: Jalāl al-Dīn al-Sayūṭī, *Kawkab al-Rauḍa,* ed. Muḥammad al-Shashtāwī (Cairo: Dār al-Āfāq al-ʿArabiyya, 2002).

The Ottoman historian Muṣṭafā ʿĀlī, who visited Egypt at the end of the sixteenth century, describes the Nilometer as "indeed one of the rare creations of the world and of the curious works resembling magical devices." Andreas Tietze, *Muṣṭafā ʿĀlī's Description of Cairo of 1599: Text, Transliteration, Translation, Notes* (Vienna: Verlag der Österreichischen Akademie der Wissenschaften, 1975), 30. More generally on the Nilometer, see William Popper, *The Cairo Nilometer: Studies in Ibn Taghrî Birdî's Chronicles of Egypt, I* (Berkeley: University of California Press, 1951); Amīn Sāmī, *Taqwīm al-Nīl,* 5 vols. in 3 parts (Cairo: Dār al-Kutub wa al-Wathā'iq al-Qawmiyya, 2003), part 1, 65–95; Nicholas Warner, *The True Description of Cairo: A Sixteenth-Century Venetian View,* 3 vols. (Oxford: Arcadian Library in association with Oxford University Press, 2006), 2:123–25.

33. al-Jabartī, *ʿAjā'ib al-Āthīr,* 2:363–64.

34. Ibid., 2:363.

35. Ibid., 2:363–64. A few decades later in May 1812 the Nile in Cairo dried to such an extent that it was possible to walk on the exposed riverbed nearly the entire width of the river from Būlāq to Imbāba. Ibid., 4:246.

36. Maḍābiṭ al-Daqahliyya 34, pp. 93–94, case 198 (21 S 1211/25 August 1796), DWQ. On the village of Qūjindīma, see Ramzī, *Al-Qāmūs al-Jughrāfī,* part 1, no vol. number, 354. On Ṭalkhā, see ibid., part 2, vol. 2, 88.

37. For cases in which the presence of irrigation works on an island was used as evidence of the continued cultivation of that island by a particular group of peasants, see Maḥkamat al-Manṣūra 7, p. 90, case 240 (3 Ca 1091/31 May 1680), DWQ.

38. Maḥkamat al-Baḥayra 21, p. 152, case 298 (12 Ş 1206/4 April 1792), DWQ; Maḥkamat al-Baḥayra 21, p. 480, case 943 (25 B 1206/19 March 1792), DWQ. On

Nitmā, see Ramzī, *Al-Qāmūs al-Jughrāfī*, part 2, vol. 2, 340. On Kafr al-Gharīb, see ibid., part 2, vol. 2, 169.

39. Of note here is the use of the colloquial Egyptian Arabic verb declension in the following passage: "*ahālī al-nāḥyatayn al-madhkūratayn biyazraʿū atyānahā*" (the people of the two aforementioned villages cultivate its [the island's] lands). Maḥkamat al-Baḥayra 21, p. 480, case 943 (25 B 1206/19 March 1792), DWQ. This and other instances of the use of colloquial Egyptian Arabic in the normally formal Arabic texts of Islamic court cases are important examples of the ways in which Egyptian peasants were able literally to interject their voices into the workings of the court and of other bureaucratic structures in rural Ottoman Egypt.

40. The operative phrase in the following case is "*ḥukm mā kānū ʿalayhi min qadīm al-zamān*" (in accordance with what they practiced from times of old): Maḥkamat al-Baḥayra 21, p. 152, case 298 (12 Ş 1206/4 April 1792), DWQ. In the other case, the phrase is: "*ḥukm mā kānū awwal ʿalā qadīmihim*" (in accordance with the precedent of their customary practice). Maḥkamat al-Baḥayra 21, p. 480, case 943 (25 B 1206/19 March 1792), DWQ.

41. As an example of these efforts on the part of the Ottoman state in Egypt, consider the speed with which the two court cases related to the previous island dispute were adjudicated and implemented. Only seventeen days elapsed between the date of the original petition and the date of the second case confirming that the orders of the firman issued in response to this petition were implemented. In other words, in two and a half weeks, a petition was written, delivered to Cairo, and heard by the high divan of Egypt; this petition was discussed and a decision was made; the piece of paper on which the divan's firman was written was transported from Cairo to al-Damanhūr, the seat of the court of al-Baḥayra (a distance of roughly 100 miles); it was then delivered to the appropriate representatives of the subprovince; these men discussed the best way to address the situation; their plan was implemented; the results of this implementation were heard by the court; and the case reporting these results was recorded in the registers of this legal body. On al-Damanhūr and its hinterland, see Ramzī, *Al-Qāmūs al-Jughrāfī*, part 2, vol. 2, 282–97. Not only does the speed with which all of this occurred suggest a very efficient process of Ottoman imperial rule that relied on networks of communication, roads, necessary material objects like paper, and the timely actions of administrators to undertake all the steps in these bureaucratic processes, but it also serves as further evidence of the imperative to quickly establish and uphold precedent.

Bibliography

Archival Sources

Maḍābiṭ al-Daqahliyya. Register 34. Dār al-Wathāʾiq al-Qawmiyya (National Archives of Egypt, Cairo; hereafter DWQ).

Mahkamat al-Baḥayra. Registers 5, 7, 21. DWQ.
Mahkamat al-Manṣūra. Registers 7, 9, 12, 16, 24. DWQ.
Mühimme-i Mısır. Registers 5, 8. Başbakanlık Osmanlı Arşivi (Prime Ministry's Ottoman Archive, Istanbul).

Published Primary and Secondary Sources

Antes, John. *Observations on the Manners and Customs of the Egyptians, the Overflowing of the Nile and its Effects; with Remarks on the Plague and Other Subjects. Written During a Residence of Twelve Years in Cairo and its Vicinity.* London: Printed for J. Stockdale, 1800.

Barkan, Ömer Lûtfi. *Kanunlar.* Vol. 1 of *XV ve XVIinci asırlarda Osmanlı İmparatorluğunda Ziraî Ekonominin Hukukî ve Malî Esasları.* İstanbul Üniversitesi Yayınlarından 256. Istanbul: Bürhaneddin Matbaası, 1943.

Bernasconi, Maria Pia, Daniel Jean Stanley, and Italo Di Geronimo. "Molluscan Faunas and Paleobathymetry of Holocene Sequences in the Northeastern Nile Delta, Egypt." *Marine Geology* 99, no. 1–2 (1991): 29–43.

Dominik, Janusz, and Daniel Jean Stanley. "Boron, Beryllium and Sulfur in Holocene Sediments and Peats of the Nile Delta, Egypt: Their Use as Indicators of Salinity and Climate." *Chemical Geology* 104, no. 1–4 (1993): 203–16.

Elsayed, Mohamed A. K., Nazeih A. Younan, Alfy M. Fanos, and Khalid H. Baghdady. "Accretion and Erosion Patterns along Rosetta Promontory, Nile Delta Coast." *Journal of Coastal Research* 21, no. 3 (2005): 412–20.

Frihy, Omran E., Alfy M. Fanos, Ahmed A. Khafagy, and Paul D. Komar. "Patterns of Nearshore Sediment Transport along the Nile Delta, Egypt." *Coastal Engineering* 15, no. 5–6 (1991): 409–29.

Herodotus. *The History.* Translated by David Grene. Chicago: University of Chicago Press, 1987.

al-Jabartī, ʿAbd al-Raḥman ibn Ḥasan. *ʿAjāʾib al-Āthār fī al-Tarājim wa al-Akhbār.* Edited by ʿAbd al-Raḥīm ʿAbd al-Raḥman ʿAbd al-Raḥīm. 4 vols. Cairo: Maṭṭbaʿat Dār al-Kutub al-Miṣriyya, 1998.

Kashef, Abdel-Aziz I. "Salt-Water Intrusion in the Nile Delta." *Ground Water* 21, no. 2 (1983): 160–67.

McNeill, J. R. *Something New Under the Sun: An Environmental History of the Twentieth-Century World.* New York: W. W. Norton, 2000.

Mikhail, Alan. *Nature and Empire in Ottoman Egypt: An Environmental History.* New York: Cambridge University Press, 2011.

Mutawallī, Aḥmad Fuʾād, trans. and intro. *Qānūn Nāmah Miṣr, alladhī Aṣdarahu al-Sulṭān al-Qānūnī li-Ḥukm Miṣr.* Cairo: Maktabat al-Anjlū al-Miṣriyya, 1986.

Panzac, Daniel. "Alexandrie: Peste et croissance urbaine (XVIIe–XIXe siècles)." In *Population et santé dans l'Empire ottoman (XVIIIe–XXe siècles),* 45–55. Istanbul: Isis, 1996.

Popper, William. *The Cairo Nilometer: Studies in Ibn Taghrî Birdî's Chronicles of Egypt, I.* Berkeley: University of California Press, 1951.
Ramzī, Muḥammad. *Al-Qāmūs al-Jughrāfī lil-Bilād al-Miṣriyya min ʿAhd Qudamāʾ al-Miṣriyyīn ilā Sanat 1945.* 6 vols. in 2 parts. Cairo: al-Hayʾa al-Miṣriyya al-ʿĀmma lil-Kitāb, 1994.
Reimer, Michael J. "Ottoman Alexandria: The Paradox of Decline and the Reconfiguration of Power in Eighteenth-Century Arab Provinces." *Journal of the Economic and Social History of the Orient* 37, no. 2 (1994): 107–46.
Said, Rushdi. *The Geological Evolution of the River Nile.* New York: Springer-Verlag, 1981.
Sāmī, Amīn. *Taqwīm al-Nīl.* 5 vols. in 3 parts. Cairo: Dār al-Kutub wa al-Wathāʾiq al-Qawmiyya, 2003.
al-Sayūṭī, Jalāl al-Dīn. *Kawkab al-Rauḍa.* Edited by Muḥammad al-Shashtāwī. Cairo: Dār al-Āfāq al-ʿArabiyya, 2002.
Shaw, Stanford J. *The Financial and Administrative Organization and Development of Ottoman Egypt, 1517–1798.* Princeton: Princeton University Press, 1962.
al-Shirbīnī, Yūsuf ibn Muḥammad. *Kitāb Hazz al-Quḥūf bi-Sharḥ Qaṣīd Abī Shādūf.* Edited and translated by Humphrey Davies. 2 vols. Leuven: Peeters, 2005–7.
Smith, Scot E., and Adel Abdel-Kader. "Coastal Erosion along the Egyptian Delta." *Journal of Coastal Research* 4, no. 2 (1988): 245–55.
Tietze, Andreas. *Muṣṭafā ʿĀlī's Description of Cairo of 1599: Text, Transliteration, Translation, Notes.* Vienna: Verlag der Österreichischen Akademie der Wissenschaften, 1975.
Warner, Nicholas. *The True Description of Cairo: A Sixteenth-Century Venetian View.* 3 vols. Oxford: Arcadian Library in association with Oxford University Press, 2006.

CHAPTER 5

Drafting a Map of Colonial Egypt

The 1902 Aswan Dam, Historical Imagination, and the Production of Agricultural Geography

Jennifer L. Derr

IN DECEMBER 1902, with much pomp and circumstance, Egypt's British and Egyptian elite celebrated the completion of the first Aswan dam. The 1902 Aswan dam (Khazan Aswan) represented a dramatic new foray in the colonial government's ability to manipulate the physical environment and allocate its most valuable resource. Egypt's economic livelihood had always depended on the annual Nile flood, and successive governments spearheaded irrigation works to best capitalize on this resource. Following their 1882 occupation of Egypt, the British were no exception. In the late nineteenth and early twentieth centuries, newly powerful forms of irrigation infrastructure facilitated the engineering of colonial geography through the spatial and temporal reconfiguration of the Nile. I argue that the significance of the 1902 dam lay in the manner in which it configured Egypt as a colony, specifically its environment, pursuing the following questions: First, how did colonial technocrats imagine and map the colonial Egyptian environment? Second, how did this particular imagination render possible the construction of the dam and its associated irrigation

Figure 5.1. The completed 1902 Aswan Dam, viewed from downstream. D. S. George and William E. Garstin, *The Nile Reservoir Works at Aswan and Asyut,* Cairo: 1902. *Reproduced with the permission of The Harry Ransom Humanities Research Center, The University of Texas at Austin.*

infrastructure? Finally, how did irrigation infrastructure rearticulate the colonial geography of Egypt, facilitating the emergence of a regionally differentiated agricultural landscape? The construction of the dam and the entrenchment of new irrigation regimes reflected a particular vision of the rural Egyptian environment as well as the potential of newly powerful infrastructural forms to transform colonial territory.

British Rule and the Construction of the Dam

The standard narrative of the 1902 Aswan dam explains its construction as the product of British industrial demand for Egyptian cotton.[1] Widespread cultivation of export-oriented cotton in Egypt began in the first portion of the nineteenth century during the rule of Mehmed Ali, Egypt's strong Ottoman governor. At the time of the British invasion, cotton represented Egypt's primary economic resource and the means by which this colony could be made productive within a colonial framework. The British colonial administration in Egypt was eager to construct a dam on the Nile to increase Egyptian cotton production and supplies to British mills. Discussions concerning possible locations for the dam and the technical aspects of the grandiose project began in the early years of the occupation. Evelyn Baring, the first Earl of Cromer and the British consul-general, requested £E500,000 from Egypt's reserve fund to pursue the project, only to find his request blocked by the French and Russian members of La Caisse de la Dette Publique (the Public Debt Commission).[2] In 1895, Cromer raised the issue to the powers in London, with the idea that the profits from a dam could help finance a British invasion of Sudan. After a period of indecision, the British opted to pursue a military campaign in Sudan instead of constructing the reservoir. However, Cromer and his business allies remained enthusiastic about the dam project, and the consul-general concocted a plan by which an English engineering firm, Sir John Aird and Co., would build a dam over a period of five years, and the "Egyptian" government would repay the cost of construction over a thirty-year period.[3]

Ernest Cassel, a German British businessman active in many facets of the Egyptian economy during the first three decades of British colonialism, came forward with the money to build the dam and a barrage at Asyut to control the release of stored water. The Asyut barrage was complemented by a series of similar barrages designed to increase the availability of water in specific regions of Egypt.[4] Following the completion of the initial dam, a debate began almost immediately concerning the demand for water.[5] As a result, the dam was raised twice: first between 1907 and 1912, and again between 1929 and 1933.

In the early twentieth century, Egypt possessed approximately six and half million irrigable acres. Following the construction of the Aswan dam, around four million of those acres were perennially irrigated. In *Modern Egypt*, Lord Cromer boasts of the achievements of British irrigation engineers, describing the irrigation infrastructure associated with the dam in glowing terms. He claimed that in the first ten years of British administration "the cotton crop was trebled, the sugar crop more than trebled, and the country was gradually being covered with a network of light railways and agricultural roads in order to enable the produce to be brought to market."[6] Cromer describes a decaying Egyptian irrigation system that was revived, expanded, and advanced by the work of British irrigation engineers in the early years of the occupation.[7] However, Cromer's enthusiasm for new infrastructure was limited to that which facilitated the expansion of Egyptian cash crop agriculture and moved goods to Mediterranean ports for transport to England. His conceptual map of the Egyptian colonial environment was simple, yet involved both temporal and spatial transformations: Water from the Nile would soak a larger surface area of Egyptian land with greater frequency to grow more cotton. For Cromer, the process of colonizing Egypt extended beyond politics to include the mastery and structuring of the raw material of its environment.

Engineers and Technocrats

The dam itself, as a showpiece of environmental infrastructure, was a fundamental component of the unfolding relationship between colonialism and environmental engineering within the context of British Empire. In British India, the practice of engineering the environment contributed to the processes of imagining and building colonies. During the nineteenth century, the profession of civil engineering evolved from a profession requiring little formal training, dependent on field experience and experimentation, to one characterized by a body of predictive theory, demanding more formal training.[8] In 1847, the Roorkee Civil Engineering College, later renamed the Thomason College of Civil Engineering, was founded on the Ganges Canal in India, and in 1871, the government of India established an engineering school at Cooper's Hill in England to train future generations of British, and eventually Indian, civil engineers. Notable members of Egypt's first generation of colonial engineers, including William Willcocks and William Garstin, were educated at Thomason and began their careers in India. Willcocks crafted the initial plans for the Aswan dam, and Garstin became the British "adviser" to the Ministry of Public Works in 1892.[9]

Exploring the work of Willcocks, one of Egypt's most noteworthy colonial engineers, highlights the positions of colonial technocrats in the projects of colonialism and civil engineering. Willcocks, the son of a British irrigation engineer, was born and raised in India. His father was posted to India after serving in the Bengal Horse Artillery and fighting in Afghanistan. At the age of eighteen, Willcocks enrolled in the Thomason Civil Engineering College at Roorkee. Following graduation, he was assigned to several different locations in India. With the British occupation of Egypt, another fellow engineer working in India, Sir Colin Scott-Moncrieff assumed the position of undersecretary of public works in Egypt. Scott-Moncrieff recruited irrigation engineers from India for the higher posts of the irrigation service, and in 1883, Willcocks accepted a post as an irrigation inspector in the regions of the Nile Delta that the Egyptian Ministry of Public Works classified as the "second circle of irrigation."[10]

Willcocks played an active role in Egypt's world of colonial governance. He emerged as an early critic of corvée, a practice that supplied the bulk of the labor force for the Ministry of Public Works, especially in clearing canals and maintaining irrigation infrastructure during the Nile's annual flood. In 1890, the British administration sent Willcocks on a mission to Italy, France, and England to investigate various irrigation technologies and plan for the construction of a dam at Aswan. At the request of Ernest Cassel, Willcocks accepted a position as the chairman of the Daira Sanieh Company in 1899. Composed of a prominent set of businessmen that dominated the Egyptian economy during this early British colonial period, the Daira Sanieh Company was charged with the sale of the former khedive's agricultural properties to private owners.[11] Willcocks's association with the company tied him closely to the matrix of elite business interests that helped fund colonial infrastructure and reaped its benefits through the distribution of more valuable agricultural property and the expansion of cash crop cultivation.

Although he eventually left Egypt and turned against the irrigation infrastructure that he helped build, Willcocks was, in many ways, emblematic of the colonial technocrats that engineered the British Empire. Although not all were born and raised in the far reaches of the empire, many ventured into this realm for technical education at relatively young ages and served as colonial administrators for much of their adult lives. Whereas political administrators managed one set of affairs in the empire, colonial engineers designed the physical infrastructure of the colony and this, in turn, determined patterns of agricultural production and the geography on which peasant agricultural life was lived. The historian of South Asia David Gilmartin reads Willcocks as the embodiment of imperial engineering and its association with the colonial state, and this characterization is largely suitable for the first portion of Willcocks's career.[12] However, Willcocks's ideology and public role underwent a transformation due to his critique of perennial irrigation and his subsequent estrangement from the British colonial establishment in Egypt. In his memoir, one senses the distance that separated engineers like Willcocks from political functionaries: Willcocks's attitude toward Cromer is lukewarm at best, and he argues that Kitchener, consul-general between 1911 and 1914, did not strive to improve the colony.[13] He viewed himself and the project of colonial engineering as distinct from political colonialism and administration. Although engineers represented vital components of the colonial project, they understood their mandate to be both related to and distinct from what we commonly consider the body of practices that constitute colonialism.

Reading the Egyptian Environment with Colonial Eyes

Although the British demand for Egyptian cotton fueled support for the dam's construction, that the project of damming the Nile was thought plausible reflected a colonial imagining of the Egyptian environment that extended beyond economic and political considerations. The idea that the Nile could be dammed was premised on a particular conceptualization of the "natural" environment associated with the Nile and the practice of agriculture within that environment. Reading the environment was a vital step in constructing conceptual maps of Egypt's historical landscape and tangible maps of its environment. Colonial technocrats assembled historical frames of reference to situate and contextualize the history of the Egyptian environment, the organization of the river within that geography, and the place of its human components. A voluminous body of literature describes the Egyptian environment of the late nineteenth and early twentieth centuries.[14] Whereas many colonial engineers focused on matters more directly technical, the work of William Willcocks ranged more widely. His conclusions and method are individual. However, they reflected broader assumptions, thought patterns, and practices among colonial officials. The construction of the dam and its articulation of the Egyptian environment made stark the significance of these visions.

One popular frame of reference among colonial technocrats concerned Egypt's significance within biblical history. For many Europeans, the process of discovering Egypt in the late nineteenth century was intimately connected to the imagining of a more ancient biblical landscape. This emotional relationship to the Egyptian environment, as the historical backdrop for an imagined biblical past, fueled the popularity of tours to Egypt and Palestine among wealthy Europeans during the nineteenth century. The desire to associate nineteenth-century Egypt with Christian beginnings was not limited to tourists; for colonial officials of many stripes, biblical history functioned as a touchstone for their encounters with nineteenth-century Egypt. These individuals sometimes doubled as amateur biblical scholars, dabbling in archeology, particularly its more speculative aspects. William Willcocks was no exception. In 1919, Willcocks published *From the Garden of Eden to the Crossing of the Jordan*. Portions of this text were originally given as a series of lectures to the Geographical Society of Cairo, the Egyptian Institute, and the Royal Geographical Society of London. *From the Garden of Eden* situates colonial endeavors in agriculture and irrigation within the context of the biblical histories of Egypt and Mesopotamia (Iraq). Willcocks juxtaposes a wide variety of late nineteenth- and early twentieth-century observations with interpretations of the biblical epoch.

> In Joseph's day, the Pyramids were standing, the basin irrigation of the Nile valley had been functioning for some 3500

years, the low lands of the Delta had been reclaimed 600 years before, and all this wealth had been insured against inundation by the Lake Moeris escape, one of the wonders of the ancient world. We to-day have not succeeded in reclaiming one-tenth of the low lands of the Delta, and that tenth is uninsured against inundation. Three thousand five hundred years ago the Egyptian question was the irrigation question, even more thoroughly than it is in our day.[15]

Although Willcocks's text was published two decades after the construction of the 1902 dam, situating Egyptian history within a biblical narrative was firmly entrenched within strands of the British historical imagination. Egypt's biblical past was not only imagined as technologically and agriculturally advanced; this vision was part and parcel of a larger historical imagining that emptied several millennia of Egyptian history of historical change. Cast in this light, colonial efforts in irrigation sought to recapture the historical glory of the biblical epoch.

An obsession with biblical Egypt correlated with a similarly intense focus on ancient Egypt. European fascination with ancient civilizations, especially as manifested by the profession of Egyptology and restoration of ancient Egyptian ruins, thrived in the late nineteenth century. As ancient Egypt formed the political backdrop for many biblical stories, the imagining of Egypt as a biblical scape and the fixation on a distant past were intertwined. During the colonial period, the ruins of this past were important attributes of the Egyptian environment. The colonial fixation on ancient Egypt resulted in the conversion of ruins into monuments. Most European tourists of the colonial period encountered Egypt through Nile cruises that stopped at various ancient Egyptian sites. Images of Egypt from the period, especially its south, present an Egyptian environment dotted by ruins and inhabited by peasants living through historical practices dating back thousands of years. Both Egyptologists working on restoration projects in the south and anthropologists of the period raced to record the lifestyles and habits of southern Egyptian peasants because they interpreted them as the living embodiments of an ancient Egypt.[16] This reading of Egypt's history and environment relegated Egyptian cultivators to an ancient past, erasing several millennia of political, economic, and cultural transformation.

Ancient Egypt was not only a historical reference point; restoration projects and tourism reinscribed these sites on contemporary colonial geography. When discussions of building a dam began, European Egyptologists fumed at the possibility that it would flood the Philae Temple that lay just

Figure 5.2. "The Island of Philae." D. S. George and William E. Garstin, *The Nile Reservoir Works at Aswan and Asyut*, Cairo, 1902. *Reproduced with the permission of The Harry Ransom Humanities Research Center, The University of Texas at Austin.*

upstream of the dam. In the lead-up to the dam's construction, Captain H. G. Lyons, an Egyptologist, surveyed the temples of Philae and published his findings. With money from the Public Debt Commission, the foundations of the temples were shored up in preparation for their partial flooding.[17] While Philae was ultimately flooded for portions of the year, the debate that unfolded about its possible destruction illustrated the integrality of ancient Egyptian ruins within the colonial Egyptian environment.

Whereas one prevalent conceptual map of colonial Egypt was marked by the re-presenting of biblical and ancient Egyptian history, other facets of the environment were relegated to a distant past. One such facet concerned the practice of irrigation. As most fertile land in Egypt was confined to those areas that bordered the Nile, Egyptian agriculture followed the rhythms of the Nile's annual flood. Until the nineteenth century, a form of irrigation known as basin irrigation predominated in Egypt. Basin irrigation spread the waters of the flood throughout stretches of agricultural land bordered by the Nile on one side and desert on the other. During the flood, the waters of the Nile were directed through large manmade canals connected to series of basins formed by earthen dikes running both parallel and perpendicular to the Nile. Regulated sluices directed water into each of the basins, where it soaked the soil in preparation for sowing. High dikes running parallel to the Nile protected against direct inundation while transverse dikes made possible regulated gradual inundation. Basins were filled with water for approximately forty-five days of the year with an average depth of one meter when each basin was full. When this period had elapsed, the remaining water was drained to another basin or canal and farmers planted their crops in the basins that had been evacuated.[18]

As the process of colonizing Egypt entailed the creation of a new geography of water and agriculture, colonial technocrats were first charged with understanding the map of existing practice and infrastructure. They deployed a historical frame of reference derived from an imagination of a biblical and ancient Egyptian past, and naturalized preexisting irrigation methods, specifically basin irrigation, and the practice of agriculture. Colonial technocrats elided the relationship between Ottoman provincial politics and irrigation management, describing the basins of Egypt as if they belonged to an ancient geography.

> Considering the times of flood and low supply, the climate of Egypt, the turbidity of the Nile flood, and the deltaic formation of the Nile Valley, no better system than basin irrigation as practiced in Egypt could possibly have been devised. If the flood had come in April or May and been followed by a burning summer, or if the actual autumn floods had been followed by the frozen winters of Europe or the warm winters of the Sudan, basin irrigation would have been a failure or a moderate success; but, given the Egyptian climate, basin irrigation has stood without rival for 7000 years. . . . King Menes made his first dyke when the Egyptian nation was in its infancy. Egypt, in Roman times, supported a population denser than that of to-day.[19]

Technocratic visions of Egypt rendered static the system of basin irrigation managed by the Ottoman and Mamluk regimes that predated Mehmed Ali's rise to power in the early nineteenth century. The effect of this reading of the Egyptian landscape was to renaturalize Egypt's landscape despite the existence of complex historical practices tied to irrigation and cultivation. During the three centuries of Ottoman-Mamluk rule, irrigation management was an important element of local provincial politics. Although ancient Egyptian civilizations practiced complex irrigation methods, these practices and the geographies that they produced evolved in the millennia separating the rise of Islamic polities in Egypt and Mehmed Ali's nineteenth-century state. A similar imagining of the agricultural population complemented this naturalization of basin irrigation. Descriptions of irrigation and agriculture were curiously devoid of human actors. As conceived in these narratives, agricultural geography was made up of fixed and passive crops, water usage patterns, and irrigation infrastructure. Agricultural communities, harvest, and consumption were absent, as they would have exposed the dynamism of this agricultural geography and the weaknesses of a static map.

Structuring a Colonial Agricultural Geography

A particular(ly) colonial imagination of the Egyptian environment framed the construction of the 1902 dam. This conceptualization not only understood the composition of the "natural" environment to contain and exclude certain components; it interpreted the Egyptian environment as fundamentally malleable and ripe for manipulation. Although the objective motivating the construction of the dam was increased cotton production, this manipulation also resulted in the production of a new, regionally differentiated map of water. Because cotton was centered in Egypt's northern half, perennial irrigation as associated with the state did not spread into southern Egypt until the 1930s. Although the dam was at Aswan, near Egypt's southernmost border, the land that benefited from the newly available water lay in northern and central Egypt. Of the areas that remained under basin irrigation (not irrigated by the dam), Lord Cromer estimated in 1904 that 750,000 of the two million acres lay in Egypt's south, between Asyut in central Egypt and Qina to its south.[20] During this same period, none of the lands lying between Qina and Egypt's southernmost city of Aswan were perennially irrigated by the state. The situation of the south with respect to irrigation water remained much the same in 1915 after the first heightening of the dam. Sir Murdoch MacDonald, a prominent colonial engineer, reported that while water was available during the summer months to the agricultural regions lying between Cairo and Asyut, the 560,000 feddans lying between Asyut and Baliana (south of Asyut), did not have access to summer water.[21] In short, the initial construction of the dam and its first heightening only provided perennial irrigation to those regions that lay to the north of Asyut. The project to irrigate the remaining areas of southern Egypt via state infrastructure did not become a priority until the dam was raised for a second time (1929–33) and a barrage constructed at Naj' Hammadi (1927–30), which facilitated the watering of the region between Asyut and Baliana without the use of privately funded mechanized irrigation.[22]

The 1902 Aswan dam transformed water from a local resource into one that could be controlled and allocated at the level of the central state. The agricultural economy structured by the dam was intimately tied to the colonial state's capacity to employ newfound environmental infrastructure to reconfigure its environment and physical territory in dramatic new ways. The fact of Egypt's intimate relationship with cotton under Cromer's rule is well documented.[23] What this story omits is the impact of this agricultural formation on regions of the country spatially situated outside the geography of cotton and perennial irrigation. As one traveled south along the Nile in Egypt, export-oriented cotton cultivation decreased dramatically until it eventually became nonexistent.[24] Limited by climate and geography, most experiments cultivating long-staple exportable cotton south of Asyut did not succeed. Those areas that did not cultivate cotton remained on the periphery of Egypt's agricultural economy in the early years of the century. The overwhelming dominance of cotton in Egypt's agricultural economy produced an irrigation infrastructure in which southern Egypt (between Asyut and Aswan) was the last region to be watered by the state.

The new map of irrigation not only included temporal changes related to the frequency of cultivation and watering; it plotted an expansion of the overall agricultural surface area. One explicit objective underlying the dam outlined by colonial irrigation engineers was to expand the area of cultivable land through land reclamation.[25] A number of land reclamation companies formed in the early twentieth century and sought to reap the profits of an expanding agricultural economy. At the end of World War I, the capitalization of land mortgage companies amounted to 45 percent of the total capitalization of joint-stock companies operating in Egypt.[26] One of the most successful land reclamation schemes was the Wadi Kom Ombo Company. Purchased in 1904, the Kom Ombo plain, located north of Aswan, became a center of sugarcane cultivation and industry in Egypt's southernmost region. However, while the boom in land reclamation illustrated the primacy of agriculture as profitable business, it also demonstrated a flawed understanding of the environmental processes framing agricultural production. At first, when land reclamation processes were still being tested, faulty procedures and techniques caused the majority of these ventures to fail. However, by 1913, the failure of most rural land reclamation companies was due to a complex set of causes that included technical difficulties, such as the absence of proper drainage systems, and social and economic issues.[27] In order to effectively progress through the process of reclamation, tracts of land needed to be populated as a means of providing agricultural labor. Many companies did not offer adequate compensation for peasants to move and settle new land. Moreover, the eagerness to extract a quick profit doomed a number of these schemes as companies sold peasants partially reclaimed land that subsequently reverted to its uncultivable status.

Irrigated, crop-producing land was the raw material for Egypt's colonial economy. However, the colonial map of Egypt's agricultural geography extended beyond concrete physical elements like cultivation patterns and irrigation practice to include a more abstract landscape of capital flow. In assessing Egypt's potential productivity, William Willcocks estimated that one billion cubic meters of water could convert half a million acres to perennial irrigation and that the newly irrigated land would produce £15,000,000 of profit.[28] British administrators and engineers also employed measures of land and crop value to assess the regional gradations of Egypt's economy.

> Again, from the broader point of view of the general riches of Egypt, the importance of cultivation in the Delta stands far ahead of that of Upper Egypt. Cotton, and especially cotton grown in the Delta, is by far our most valuable crop and the tracts which may be reclaimed in Lower Egypt will be far more valuable, feddan for feddan, than those in the southern part of the country. The best land in the Delta is now worth L.E. 150–200 per feddan while the best land in Upper Egypt is worth, if it has perennial irrigation, L.E. 100–160 per feddan, and if basin, L.E. 50–60.[29]

As the intention motivating the dam's construction was never to diversify Egypt's agricultural economy but rather to expand cash crop production, measures of land value directly correlated with the flow of irrigation water and the potential for cotton production.[30] Thus, the geography of irrigation that emerged after 1902 was also marked by a new terrain of value.

As preference was given to Egypt's north, much of the south continued to follow the system of basin irrigation with its single annual crop. In some respects, this was preferable for peasant cultivators. In the Nile Delta, cotton production was associated with the consolidation of property under elite landowners and the trend toward sharecropping among increasing numbers of once independent peasants. The *'izba* system, in which peasants provided the labor necessary to cultivate cash crops on large estates in exchange for a small plot of land, represented the dominant unit of production in cotton-growing areas of the Nile Delta.[31] In southern Egypt, land tenure patterns varied depending on the crop grown and the local history of property sales. In south Minya and north Asyut (central Egypt), large landowners held more than 50 percent of the cultivable land, peasant wage labor on large farms was prevalent, and cotton covered more than 30 percent of farmland. Much of this land belonged to the former khedivial estates, the Daira Sanieh, and was purchased by large landowners in colonial auctions in the early twentieth century. However, as one moved south of Asyut and the colonial irrigation frontier, cotton cultivation decreased dramatically, eventually becoming nonexistent. Property ownership and labor patterns in southern Egypt were mixed: In some areas, sugarcane was cultivated as a monoculture, and property ownership was characterized by small holdings. In others, landowners possessing large estates predominated.[32]

Although the two regions were separate in many respects, the demands and fluctuations of the northern cotton economy influenced the economic realm of southern Egypt. The manpower that fueled the northern cotton economy was in part supplied by southern laborers.[33] In the second half of the nineteenth century, the expansion of cash crop production, industrialization, and construction associated with growth in Cairo and Alexandria attracted southerners to northern Egypt in search of wage labor as comparable projects in southern Egypt were relatively sparse. Because many southern peasants cultivated crops according to the seasons of basin irrigation, the agricultural calendar facilitated a certain amount of labor migration in the dry season preceding the flood. An interconnected colonial economy developed, in which cash crop production depended on migrant labor from the south. However, the coalescence of this broader economy did not extinguish local economic networks, especially as they thrived in peripheral areas of the state. Portions of Egypt's south cultivated sugarcane and a distinct economic realm associated with sugarcane cultivation and industry emerged in this region.[34]

The New Colonial Environment

For technocrats and political administrators, the dam served as a tool with which to rearticulate the colony as a physical territory, mapped according to irrigation patterns, cotton cultivation, and capital flow. In this sense, the dam represented a means of colonizing the Egyptian environment, partially through its organization of a cash-crop producing economy. The production of colonial geography was also colored by a series of unanticipated interactions among pieces of infrastructure, environmental forces, cultivation patterns, and Egyptian peasants. The irrigation frontier that divided more northern cotton-producing regions from Egypt's deep south demarcated regional differences in the character of the land itself, including its relationship with peasant cultivators. A shift in the temporality of irrigation—cultivators now watered the land more frequently throughout the year—literally soaked the Nile Delta with irrigation water. The land did not respond with the anticipated increased productivity as technocrats failed to account for the importance of drainage and the impact of the changed relationship between water and soil. The spread of perennial irrigation in the Delta meant that canals that once functioned as drains for lands under perennial irrigation before the dam's construction were now filled with water and no longer facilitated drainage.[35] The absence of drainage mechanisms resulted in a rising subsoil water table in the north of Egypt. The continuous presence of water on perennially irrigated lands interfered with processes that had promoted soil fertility. In the dry season associated with the seasons of flood agriculture known as *sharaqi*, fallow lands had heated, dried, and cracked. These processes aerated the soil, broke up colloids, and promoted the growth of nitrifying bacteria.[36] However, colonial technocrats believed that *sharaqi* lands reflected wasted agricultural productivity and thus discouraged the practice through new irrigation regimes.[37] Finally, as it was no longer rinsed by periodic flooding over the higher banks of the Nile, the salinity of the soil increased. Problems with drainage, soil fertility, and salinity not only stunted agricultural production;[38] as these problems especially plagued the Nile Delta, they signaled the extension of a regionally differentiated colonial geography to the character of the land itself.

The reconfiguration of agriculture stemming from new irrigation patterns also involved the severing of relationships between cultivators and local agricultural environments. The construction of the first Aswan dam initiated a pattern of land expropriation from predominantly Nubian villages that culminated with the High Dam and the destruction of historical Nubia in 1964. In 1902, the Egyptian government issued a decree declaring particular villages part of the public domain. The primary victim of this initial expropriation was the village of Shallal—reconstituted under the same name at a nearby site in the 1930s—and portions of other neighboring villages.[39] A special commission composed of a representative from the Ministry of Finance, two representatives from the district, and an additional appointed member assessed individual holdings and compensation payments. Entirely expropriated by the state, the inhabitants of Shallal were compensated for the value of their land, in addition to buildings, date palms, and henna plants. The inhabitants of villages only partially incorporated into the public domain were offered compensation for land and property both inside and outside of the new state domain.[40] The process of expropriation and isolation that began with the 1902 dam continued with future projects to heighten the dam. Some villages were totally submerged by the Nile's new geography near Aswan, but many others faced decreasing agricultural opportunities as portions of their farmland were partially submerged, only accessible for both sowing and harvesting for brief periods of the year.[41]

The archival trail mapping displacement emphasizes its significance as a process of geographic reconfiguration rather than community rupture. In colonial thought, Egyptian peasants were conceptually figured as either agricultural producers or as vessels of ancient tradition. They possessed specificity of neither time nor place. For technocrats like Willcocks, the imagining of a historically stunted rural Egypt facilitated the conceptual transformation of Egyptian peasants into the simplest of agricultural producers. The absence of debate concerning the 1902 displacement of Shallal stood in marked contrast to the controversy surrounding the Philae Temple. Whereas international outrage erupted at the prospect of destroying an ancient monument, Egyptian peasants existed as mobile pieces of an agricultural landscape. Although the landscape itself was locally differentiated, the imagined simplicity of Egyptian peasants prevented colonial technocrats from grasping the significance of the human components of that landscape.[42] Following the construction of the dam, financial compensation was meant to erase the pain of displacement in communities like Shallal, but colonial officials did not recognize the importance of localized agricultural relationships associated with specific plots of land.

Changes in irrigation practice also sparked new struggles with disease. In an April 11, 1927, address to l'Institut d'Egypte, Willcocks attributed rising subsoil water levels to increases in the prevalence of particular diseases, specifically bilharzia and "anklyostoma," among peasants in northern Egypt farming land under perennial irrigation.[43] Bilharzia, also known as schistosomiasis, is a parasitic infection that results from the exposure of skin to infected freshwater containing aquatic snails. "Ankloyostoma" (ancylostoma), or hookworm infection, is transmitted by direct contact with contaminated soil. Willcocks argued that the incidence of both of these conditions among peasants working the land had increased dramatically since the construction of the 1902 dam and the spread of perennial irrigation. He claimed that 95 percent of the peasants working perennially irrigated land in the Delta were infected with ancylostoma and 65 percent with bilharzia.[44] Although the accuracy of Willcocks's statistics is questionable, that the dam and the spread of perennial irrigation resulted in the increased prevalence of waterborne infections among rural populations is not.

Despite the fact that perennial irrigation was uncommon in southern Egypt, peasants in this region faced the threat of malaria. The damming of the Nile produced changes in the physical composition of the river and its annual cycles. The river's ecosystem consequently evolved. Curly pondweed (*Potamogeton crispus*) thrived in this new environment and large traveling islands of weeds formed on the river. The *Anopheles gambiae* mosquitoes that transmitted malaria laid eggs on these mobile islands, thus moving the disease along the river.[45] Because of shifts in the physical environment of the dammed river, malaria moved easily into southern Egypt where it found a vulnerable human population. In 1942, there was a large malaria outbreak in southern Egypt centered in regions devoted to sugarcane cultivation. Timothy Mitchell argues that a changing natural environment, market changes produced by World War II, specifically the shortage of artificial fertilizers, malnutrition among Upper Egyptian peasants, and the consumption of sugarcane lay at the root of this epidemic.[46]

These environmental changes and their effects on rural communities highlight the failure of irrigation engineers to fully appreciate the impact that the dam would have on the ecosystems of the Nile and the lands that bordered it. This stemmed, in part, from their conceptualization of the dam and the ecosystem in which it was constructed. The engineers who built the dam envisioned it as a piece of technology designed to control and augment a natural, that is, nonhuman, environment. Therefore, the dam was represented by sets of technical diagrams composed of pressures, angles, strains, and materials. This abstraction resulted from an active process of conceptually emptying Egypt's geography of complicating and dynamic variables. As the relationships between different human communities and the Nile could not be expressed and stabilized in quantifiable terms, they were excluded from the conceptualization of the project. However, above and beyond this conceptual absence, the engineers who built the dam did not grasp the complexity of the river's ecosystems and the transformative potential of slight changes to the environment. The "natural" ecosystem associated with the river included many factors outside of the river itself. In this case, the dam's construction did not cause a minor environmental change, but rather dramatically altered the river and its riparian environment. Intended as a demonstration of humankind's ability to harness science to manipulate the environment to its own advantage, this project ultimately demonstrated this ecosystem's infinite complexity and its interconnectedness with a more broadly defined environment.

Producing the Colony

The history of the 1902 dam illustrates the complex set of relationships binding colonial practice to the physical territory of the colony. Just as Egypt was imagined culturally and politically, it was also conceptualized as a distinct natural and agricultural environment. The technocratic imagining of the Egyptian environment rendered particular manipulations of this environment plausible: Altering the flow of the Nile across the space of the colony was premised on a distinct, if problematic, understanding of the relationship between the river, the practice of agriculture, and the human communities that inhabited this space. Interpreting this matrix of relationships was rooted in a reading of the Egyptian environment, including its human components, that included a certain history, or in this case, an ahistoricity. As increased cotton production fueled the project to build the dam, regionally differentiated shifts in cultivation patterns, capital flows, and levels of agricultural productivity resulted. Finally, the separation of north and south within colonial geography was reinforced by an evolving physical geography in the north driven by new irrigation practices. The processes constituting the production of colonial geography in Egypt extended beyond cultivation patterns and the concentration of irrigation water to include the physical transformation of the land itself.

The practice of the colonial state in Egypt intersected with that of the natural environment. Infrastructure and irrigation regimes configured the Nile's flow and its relationship to cultivation. The experience of colonialism was, for many cultivators, tied to their interactions with the environment, especially as framed by agriculture. Irrigation infrastructure was not a passive manifestation of colonial policy. Rather, this infrastructure played an active role in rearticulating the physical territory of the colony and the agricultural spaces with which Egyptian cultivators interacted. As infrastructure modified the river and its interactions with the lands and communities along its banks, the experience of colonial authority interfaced with larger environmental and agricultural trends.

Notes

1. This narrative is reflected by the British archival trail concerning the dam as well as monographs discussing the British colonial administration in Egypt. See, for example, Robert Tignor, *Modernization and British Colonial Rule in Egypt, 1882–1914* (Princeton: Princeton University Press, 1966), 219–20.

2. As the Egyptian government was unable to repay its loans, European countries saw an opportunity to intervene in Egyptian politics. In 1876, a French-led effort resulted in the formation of La Caisse de la Dette Publique (the Public Debt Commission) to manage the Egyptian state's finances.

3. John Marlowe, *Cromer in Egypt* (New York: Praeger, 1970), 226.

4. Each barrage ensured water availability to a particular region. The Rosetta and Damietta barrages were the first barrages built on the Nile. Begun

under Mehmed Ali and completed in 1861, the state intended these barrages as a means of increasing water availability in the Nile Delta, Egypt's primary cotton-growing region. Still concerned about water availability for cotton and the security of the barrages, the British colonial government completed a series of renovations in 1890. The 1902 Asyut barrage ensured that 1,250,000 acres of Middle Egypt could be perennially irrigated. The Zifta barrage in the Delta also opened in 1902. In 1906, the government completed another contract with Messrs. Aird and Co. for the construction of a barrage at Esna. First used in 1909, this barrage improved the irrigation of the Qina province during the summer flood. A fifth barrage, designed to increase water availability in southern Egypt, was completed at Naj' Hammadi in 1930. William Willcocks and J. I. Craig, *Egyptian Irrigation*, vol. 2 (London: E. and F. N. Spon, 1913), 642, 656; 9 May 1921, FO 141-550-1, British National Archives (BNA).

5. Newly available water had already been dedicated to designated tracts of land, and the government refused all new applications for water. 28 April 1923, FO 141-658-7, BNA.

6. Evelyn Baring, First Earl of Cromer, *Modern Egypt*, part 2 (London: Macmillan, 1908), 460.

7. Ibid., 462.

8. David Gilmartin, "Imperial Rivers: Irrigation and British Visions of Empire," in *Decentering Empire: Britain, India and the Transcolonial World*, ed. Dane Kennedy and Durba Ghosh (London: Orient Longman, 2006), 79, 81.

9. While Egyptian ministers usually headed the different Egyptian ministries, a British adviser who informally dictated policy was appointed to each.

10. At the start of the British occupation, the Ministry of Public Works divided Egypt into eight irrigation circles or districts. Eight hydraulic engineers were brought from India and put in charge of a circle. The duties of each inspector included distributing water from the headworks of the main canal to smaller canals, the maintenance of canals and drains, and the protection of his district from flood. They also settled disputes over water, determined how often land would be watered, and decided whether private canals could be constructed and pumping stations installed. Tignor, *Modernization and British Colonial Rule in Egypt*, 115.

11. The British pushed Khedive Isma'il out of office in 1879. This followed the seizure and management of Isma'il's properties in 1878 by an "international" commission. The prominent businessmen active in the Egyptian economy during this period included Ernest Cassel, the Qattawi family, Ernest Cronier, and Raphael Suarès. Cronier, a Frenchman, first become involved in Egyptian business in 1892 as managing director of the Paris-based sugar company, Henri Says et Cie. The Suarès and Qattawi families dominated Egypt's economic life during the late nineteenth and early twentieth centuries with ventures in finance, industry, and agriculture. Unlike other prominent investors who drove Egyptian commerce and industry during this period, these families primarily

confined their economic activities to Egypt. Within Egypt, Ernest Cassel's investments and business ventures often overlapped with those of Suarès.

12. Gilmartin, "Imperial Rivers," 90–101.

13. William Willcocks, *Sixty Years in the East* (Edinburgh; London: W. Blackwood, 1935), 116–17, 270–71.

14. Among Willcocks's works describing the Egyptian environment are William Willcocks and J. I. Craig, *Egyptian Irrigation*, 3rd ed. (London: E. and F. N. Spon, 1913); William Willcocks, *The Assuan Reservoir and Lake Moeris: A Lecture Delivered at a Meeting of the Khedivial Geographical Society, Cairo, 16 January 1904* (London: Messrs E. and F. N. Spon, 1904); *Egyptian Irrigation and the Public Health, Information presented at the Institut d'Egypte at its meeting on 11 April 1927* (Cairo: Nile Mission Press, 1927); and *The Wadi Rayan Reservoir and the Drainage of Egypt* (Cairo, 1932).

15. William Willcocks, *From the Garden of Eden to the Crossing of the Jordan* (London: E. and F. N. Spon, 1929), 54. The Lake Moeris escape was reported by Herodotus in 450 B.C.E. when he visited Egypt and reported seeing the waters of an artificially controlled lake filling the Fayum depression. Gertrude Caton-Thompson and E. W. Gardner, "Recent Work on the Problem of Lake Moeris," *Geographical Journal* 73, no. 1 (1929): 20.

16. Winifred Blackman's *The Fellahin of Upper Egypt* is the most notable of these works. Between 1920 and 1926, Blackman spent a considerable portion of each year in Egypt performing fieldwork near Asyut, in central Egypt, and in the oasis of Fayum. In *The Fellahin of Upper Egypt,* Blackman argues that peasant practices derive from "ancient" tradition. The last chapter of her text is devoted exclusively to discussing the parallels between early twentieth-century peasant life and ancient Egyptian customs. Winifred Blackman, *The Fellahin of Upper Egypt* (1927; Cairo: American University in Cairo, 2000).

17. D. S. George and W. E. Garstin, "Descriptive Note," in *The Nile Reservoir Works at Aswan and Asyut* (Cairo, 1902).

18. Willcocks and Craig, *Egyptian Irrigation*, 1:301.

19. Ibid., 299.

20. Note by the Egyptian Ministry of Public Works, 21 March 1915, FO 141-550-1, BNA.

21. "Conversion of basin lands in Upper Egypt," Sir Murdoch MacDonald, Office of the Undersecretary of State, Khartoum, 22 February 1915, FO 141-531-5, BNA.

22. Large companies and private landowners used mechanized pumps to raise water from the Nile and irrigate their land by means other than basin irrigation.

23. See Roger Owen, *Cotton and the Egyptian Economy, 1820–1914* (Oxford: Clarendon Press, 1969).

24. There are several possible reasons that cotton cultivation in southern Upper Egypt was not a real option for cultivators: As one moved south along the Nile, the amount of cultivable land bordering each side of the river became

increasingly narrow, and soil composition changed. Moreover, without perennial irrigation in these regions, even if cotton could technically be grown, it could not be produced in the same quantities.

25. George and Garstin, "Descriptive Note."

26. Rural land companies amounted to 5 percent of the total capitalization. Robert Tignor, "The Economic Activities of Foreigners in Egypt, 1920–1950: From Millet to Haute Bourgeoisie," *Comparative Studies in Society and History* 22, no. 3 (1980): 419.

27. Among the reasons that Willcocks and Craig cite for the failure of land reclamation schemes was "the presence of large numbers of careless, shifty Arabs in the waste lands" and the conflicts between these populations and the settled peasant, or "fellahin," populations that were recruited to settle and farm the newly reclaimed land. The authors' perspective reflects a pervasive colonial disdain for unsettled populations and the historical, and often overemphasized, conflict between settled peasant populations and nomadic groups of Bedouin. Willcocks and Craig, *Egyptian Irrigation*, 2:833–37.

28. Willcocks does not specify the amount of investment that was required to produce this amount of profit or include a context-specific correlation between money invested and profit gained. Willcocks, *Assuan Reservoir and Lake Moeris*, 6.

29. A report written by an adviser to the Ministry of Public Works, signature illegible, 21 March 1915, FO 141-550-1, BNA.

30. Cotton's impact on the cultivation of foodstuffs within Egypt was not worrisome for British administrators until the onset of World War I and as a result of Egypt's role as a supplier of raw materials to the British war effort. Following the war, Egyptian and European industrialists bemoaned cotton's dominance within the Egyptian economy in the 1917 *Report of the Commission of Commerce and Industry*. This unease was a result of periodic crashes in the price of cotton, which affected Egypt's landowning class. Nonetheless, the issue did not become a matter of real concern until the 1930s with the onset of declining agricultural yields, an expanding population, and an economic downturn.

31. As of 1910, large landowners predominated in both the north and south Delta. The *'izba* was especially widespread in the north Delta. See Reinhard Schulze, "Colonization and Resistance: The Egyptian Peasant Rebellion, 1919," in *Peasants and Politics in the Modern Middle East*, ed. Farhad Kazemi and John Waterbury (Miami: Florida International University Press, 1991), 173–74.

32. Ibid., 176.

33. Alan Richards, "Land and Labor on Egyptian Cotton Farms, 1882–1940," *Agricultural History* 52, no. 4 (1978): 506.

34. In my dissertation, I explore the development of sugarcane-producing colonies in southern Egypt and their historical relationship to colonial capital, irrigation, and the dominant cotton economy. Jennifer L. Derr, "Cultivating the State:

Cash Crop Agriculture, Irrigation, and the Geography of Authority in Colonial Southern Egypt, 1868–1931" (PhD diss., Stanford University, 2009), 173–230.

35. Alan Richards, "Technical and Social Change in Egyptian Agriculture, 1890–1914," *Economic Development and Cultural Change* 26, no. 4 (1978): 728.

36. Ibid., 729.

37. One of the numerous examples of this colonial attitude to *sharaqi* land is found in Majlis al-Wutharaʾ, Nithara al-Ashghal, Maslaha al-Ray, al-Nil, 2/4/j, "Notes on the Nile Flood," September 1904, Dār al-Wathāʾiq al-Qawmiyya (DWQ).

38. Richards, "Technical and Social Change in Egyptian Agriculture," 728.

39. British Embassy, Cairo, to R. S. Scrivner, North and East African Department, Foreign Office, London, 16 May 1964, FO 371-178650, BNA.

40. Majlis al-Wuzaraʾ, Nitharat al-Ray, 22 January 1881–31 August 1920, al-Nil, 2/4/b, DWQ.

41. British Embassy, Cairo, to R. S. Scrivner, North and East African Department, Foreign Office, London, 16 May 1964, FO 371-178650, BNA.

42. This dynamic began to shift in the 1930s when a debate concerning a much larger Nubian displacement emerged as a result of the second project to heighten the dam. In this debate, at least two members of the Egyptian chamber of deputies, although eventually outvoted, objected to the ease with which the Egyptian government sought to uproot and relocate Nubian communities. Despite this limited official objection, communities were displaced in 1933, and much of historical Nubia destroyed after the construction of the High Dam. Report of the meeting on 13 February 1933, Chambre des Députés, FO 141-699-3, BNA.

43. Willcocks, *Egyptian Irrigation and the Public Health*, 3.

44. Ibid.

45. Timothy Mitchell, *Rule of Experts: Egypt, Techno-Politics, Modernity* (Berkeley: University of California Press, 2002), 24. For an in-depth discussion of the politics surrounding the treatment of the 1942 malaria epidemic, see Nancy Gallagher's *Egypt's Other Wars: Epidemics and the Politics of Public Health* (Syracuse, N.Y.: Syracuse University Press, 1990).

46. Mitchell, *Rule of Experts*, 23–25.

Bibliography

Archival Sources

The British National Archives, Kew Gardens, United Kingdom.
The Egyptian National Archives, Dar al-Wathaʾiq al-Qawmiyya, Cairo, Egypt.
Primary and Secondary Sources

Baring, Evelyn, First Earl of Cromer. *Modern Egypt*. London: Macmillan, 1908.
Blackman, Winifred. *The Fellahin of Upper Egypt*. 1927. Cairo: American University in Cairo, 2000.

Caton-Thompson, Gertrude, and E. W. Gardner. "Recent Work on the Problem of Lake Moeris." *Geographical Journal* 73, no. 1 (1929): 20–58.
Derr, Jennifer L. "Cultivating the State: Cash Crop Agriculture, Irrigation, and the Geography of Authority in Colonial Southern Egypt, 1868–1931." PhD diss., Stanford University, 2009.
Gallagher, Nancy. *Egypt's Other Wars: Epidemics and the Politics of Public Health*. Syracuse, N.Y.: Syracuse University Press, 1990.
George, D. S., and W. E. Garstin. "Descriptive Note." In *The Nile Reservoir Works at Aswan and Asyut*. Cairo, 1902.
Gilmartin, David. "Imperial Rivers: Irrigation and British Visions of Empire." In *Decentering Empire: Britain, India and the Transcolonial World*, edited by Dane Kennedy and Durba Ghosh, 76–103. London: Orient Longman, 2006.
Marlowe, John. *Cromer in Egypt*. New York: Praeger, 1970.
Mitchell, Timothy. *Rule of Experts: Egypt, Techno-Politics, Modernity*. Berkeley: University of California Press, 2002.
Owen, Roger. *Cotton and the Egyptian Economy, 1820–1914*. Oxford: Clarendon Press, 1969.
Richards, Alan. "Land and Labor on Egyptian Cotton Farms, 1882–1940." *Agricultural History* 52, no. 4 (1978): 503–18.
———. "Technical and Social Change in Egyptian Agriculture, 1890–1914." *Economic Development and Cultural Change* 26, no. 4 (1978): 725–45.
Schulze, Reinhard. "Colonization and Resistance: The Egyptian Peasant Rebellion, 1919." In *Peasants and Politics in the Modern Middle East*, edited by Farhad Kazemi and John Waterbury, 171–202. Miami: Florida International University Press, 1991.
Tignor, Robert. "The Economic Activities of Foreigners in Egypt, 1920–1950: From Millet to Haute Bourgeoisie." *Comparative Studies in Society and History* 22, no. 3 (1980): 416–49.
———. *Modernization and British Colonial Rule in Egypt, 1882–1914*. Princeton: Princeton University Press, 1966.
Willcocks, William. *The Assuan Reservoir and Lake Moeris: A Lecture Delivered at a Meeting of the Khedivial Geographical Society, Cairo, 16 January 1904*. London: Messrs E. and F. N. Spon, 1904.
———. *Egyptian Irrigation and the Public Health, Communication présenté à l'Institut d'Egypte dans sa séance du 11 Avril 1927*. Cairo: Nile Mission Press, 1927.
———. *From the Garden of Eden to the Crossing of the Jordan*. London: E. and F. N. Spon, 1929.
———. *Sixty Years in the East*. Edinburgh; London: W. Blackwood, 1935.
———. *The Wadi Rayan Reservoir and the Drainage of Egypt*. Cairo, 1932.
Willcocks, William, and J. I. Craig. *Egyptian Irrigation*. London: E. and F. N. Spon, 1913.

CHAPTER 6

Remapping the Nation, Critiquing the State

Environmental Narratives and Desert Land Reclamation in Egypt

Jeannie Sowers

IN 1998, the Mubarak regime announced that it would build the largest water-pumping station in the world, taking Nile water from behind the Aswan High Dam reservoir to irrigate portions of the southwestern desert. The government declared it would convert millions of acres from desert to arable land, transforming the largely arid New Valley province into cultivated fields. The goal of this massive exercise in land reclamation was ostensibly to attract Egypt's multiplying population from the densely populated "old" Nile River Valley and Delta to the desert periphery. The New Valley Project, or *Toshka* Project as it was usually called in the Arabic press, was thus justified in terms of a perceived demographic imperative.

The "Mubarak Pumping Station" began operation in 2005, with twenty-four turbines capable of pumping 1.2 million cubic meters of water per hour.[1] By winter 2008, however, demand for irrigation water was so limited that only one of the installed turbines was in use at a time. Out of an initial 540,000 acres targeted for reclamation, agribusiness managers in the area reported that only a few thousand were under cultivation.[2] Far from being a celebrated achievement of the Mubarak government, the New Valley Project increasingly embodied its failures. The New Valley Project came to be seen as the paradigmatic example of corruption, inefficacy, and squandered national resources under Mubarak's rule. As such, the project served as another nail in the coffin of the regime's exhausted, hollow claims to act in the interests of ordinary Egyptians. By January 2011, the depth of this mass discontent became clear when popular protest broke out across Egyptian cities, and Mubarak's thirty-year reign ended in a mere eighteen days.

While senior figures of the Mubarak era have been deposed, debates over how to allocate land and water in the context of Egypt's growing population remain. As this chapter explores, state and private initiatives to "green the desert" have long been central to popular and elite conceptions of Egypt's developmental options. Nor has Egypt been alone in this emphasis on land reclamation. Converting desert land to cultivation has figured centrally in nation-building projects in countries as disparate as the United States, Australia, India, Pakistan, China, Central Asia, and the former Soviet Union.[3] Colonial and nationalist regimes alike have attempted to "green the desert" for a variety of political, economic, and social reasons. In the Middle East, Egypt, Israel, Turkey, Libya, and Saudi Arabia established generous incentives for land reclamation to promote economic development and national integration.[4]

In Egypt, land reclamation was a long-standing practice in the colonial period, producing significant revenue for land-holding elites from crops such as cotton, sugarcane, and rice. By the postcolonial era, state discourse increasingly portrayed land reclamation not simply as an economic investment, but as a social endeavor and a political imperative. New agricultural land would provide employment and physical space for Egypt's rapidly expanding population. Although Egyptian nationalists and social reformers articulated key elements of this demographic imaginary during the colonial period, it was not until the construction of the Aswan High Dam in the 1960s that the government began to conceive of large-scale, state-run land reclamation projects. The High Dam offered the Egyptian government the ability to store the full flow of the Nile River, without relying on a system of barrages in upstream states. More water storage capacity meant the possibility of converting more desert land to irrigated acreage. Reliance on large-scale infrastructure and state-driven development planning in Egypt thus echoed the faith in "high modernist" development schemes prevalent across developing and industrial countries alike.[5]

Even in its heyday during the 1960s, however, the gap between the government's lofty rhetoric and the realities of land reclamation were significant. Whereas state narratives about land reclamation were hegemonic in official propaganda, the situation on the ground—as documented in reports by various government agencies, international donors, and field studies—identified recurrent challenges. Problems with salinity, rising water tables, inadequate drainage, and poor water quality compounded inadequate provision of education and other services.[6] State-sponsored land reclamation efforts thus never attracted large numbers of people away from existing urban areas.

When the Mubarak government announced the Toshka Project in 1998, many Egyptian water experts, public intellectuals, and journalists were skeptical of resurrecting land reclamation as a solution to Egypt's grave developmental dilemmas. Most of these concerns, however, were voiced either in private, for fear of political reprisal, or in the pages of sanctioned opposition papers. These critical voices argued that the decision to undertake the Toshka Project epitomized the regime's opaque, unaccountable, and sclerotic system of rule. These critical accounts were eventually amplified by the independent media[7] and aired in a variety of public forums, including parliamentary debates, international book fairs, and university symposia. In recent years, agribusiness managers tasked with actually reclaiming land in the New Valley have produced their own critical claims about the state's role in land reclamation. The proliferation and amplification of critical narratives regarding the New Valley Project were thus part of a broader, cumulative critique of the Mubarak regime's development policies that emerged during the 1990s and 2000s.

This chapter examines the evolution of Egyptian narratives about environment, population, and development through the prism of land reclamation. I show how different actors—state officials, environmental experts, and agribusiness managers—created distinctive yet interrelated story-lines around the notion of converting desert land to irrigated cropland. For Maarten Hajer, story-lines are discursive constructions that combine different (often highly specialized and complex) discourses into legible, simplified framings of an environmental problem that appeal to differently situated actors.[8]

The dominant story-line in Egyptian environmental history and policy, as outlined in the next section of this chapter, has been an ecological-demographic narrative of crisis, in which limited arable land and the pressure of an increasing population require ongoing horizontal expansion of arable lands. This narrative still infuses governmental planning and investment, but I suggest it is increasingly dissociated from two key developments. First, Egyptian water experts circulate a parallel crisis narrative, highlighting Egypt's scarce and polluted water resources. These water crisis narratives have in the past few years sparked questions about using such a scarce resource to cultivate desert land. Second, while official discourse highlights the role of the state in promoting land reclamation, reclaiming desert land has instead proceeded largely through the cumulative investments of agribusiness firms and peasant farmers, not the state.

In order to explain the staying power of the official demographic-ecological crisis narrative despite these dissonances, the third section of this chapter explores the historical construction of this foundational environmental imaginary as it was elaborated during the interwar and early postcolonial period. For Egyptian reformers, land reclamation would remake the lives of the peasantry by physically relocating them to a new cultural, social, and natural "environment." This populist and paternalistic framing of land reclamation persisted in official discourse through the Sadat period. In the fourth section, I show how key elements of this narrative were recast in the Mubarak era, as modern environmental idioms were introduced into the old neo-Malthusian narrative about a demographic crisis. These official justifications for the New Valley Project, however, encountered critiques launched by environmental scientists, journalists in opposition papers, and leading officials, which are traced in the fifth section.

Whereas in the Nasser period, newly irrigated lands were to benefit poorer peasants directly through ownership, in Mubarak's New Valley Project, agribusiness was to be the principal beneficiary of newly irrigated land. These firms were supposed to conserve water through the use of new technologies and produce high-quality, organic products for export. In the sixth part of the chapter, I turn to the largely private narratives produced by agribusiness managers, who link the problems of desert land reclamation with the government's opaque policy-making and unclear commitment to property rights.

Despite the proliferation of critical narratives since the inception of the New Valley Project in 1998, however, the long-standing ecological-demographic *imaginaire* remains a key element of political discourse in Egypt. At the end of this essay, I note how the story-lines produced by officials, scientists, public intellectuals, and journalists continue to share some key assumptions about the desirability of reclaiming desert land. I then sketch the key elements that might inform a more fundamental rethinking of Egypt's dominant environmental imaginary.

Narratives of Ecological-Demographic Crisis, Policies of Complacency

Most Egyptians live in the increasingly urbanized Nile Delta and Nile Valley. The Egyptian government maintains that moving people to the desert is essential to deal with urban encroachment on old agricultural lands and high rates of population growth.[9] From 1975 to 2005, Egypt's population expanded from 39.599 million to 77.154 million.[10] As a result, by the 1990s, per capita arable land was among the lowest in the world, at 0.12 *feddan* (slightly over 1 acre) per person.[11]

The New Valley Project was the most ambitious but not the only large land reclamation project initiated by the Mubarak regime during the late 1990s. Together, projects in the northern Sinai and southwestern desert aimed to increase Egypt's total arable land by 3.4 million feddans by 2017.[12] Maps produced for the Cabinet of Ministers report "Egypt's Development Strategy until 2017" graphically portray these future irrigated areas as new bands of green space cutting dramatically across Egypt's desert peripheries (See map 6.1).

Several scholars have critiqued the substance and representation of this demographic-environmental *imaginaire*. Timothy Mitchell showed how aid agencies and the Egyptian government reproduce a pervasive visual imagery in reports and documents, in which a burgeoning population is confined within a narrow habitable river valley amid vast deserts.[13] Ray Bush captured the essence of this imaginary when he noted that "Egyptian environmental policy discussion focuses almost exclusively on the relationship between population pressure, scarce water resources and limited cultivable land.[14] These and other critics have suggested that focusing on an imminent ecological-demographic crisis allows the government to avoid grappling with the more difficult social problems of rural poverty and unequal landholdings.[15]

A parallel crisis narrative has also been circulating in Egypt. This narrative focuses on the scarcity and degradation of Egypt's water resources, highlighting the country's dependence on the Nile River. Egyptian water experts have long argued that Egypt's 55 billion cubic meters quota of Nile water is fully utilized and that with population growth, Egypt will soon face significant water scarcity. Not surprisingly, in light of these assertions, Egypt has adamantly refused to renegotiate the 1959 treaty that reaffirmed the British colonial allocation of the full flow of the Nile River to Egypt and Sudan. Upstream states have declared their intention to reallocate Nile flow, with or without Egypt's participation, producing acrimonious exchanges in the World Bank–sponsored fora of the Nile Basin Initiative.[16]

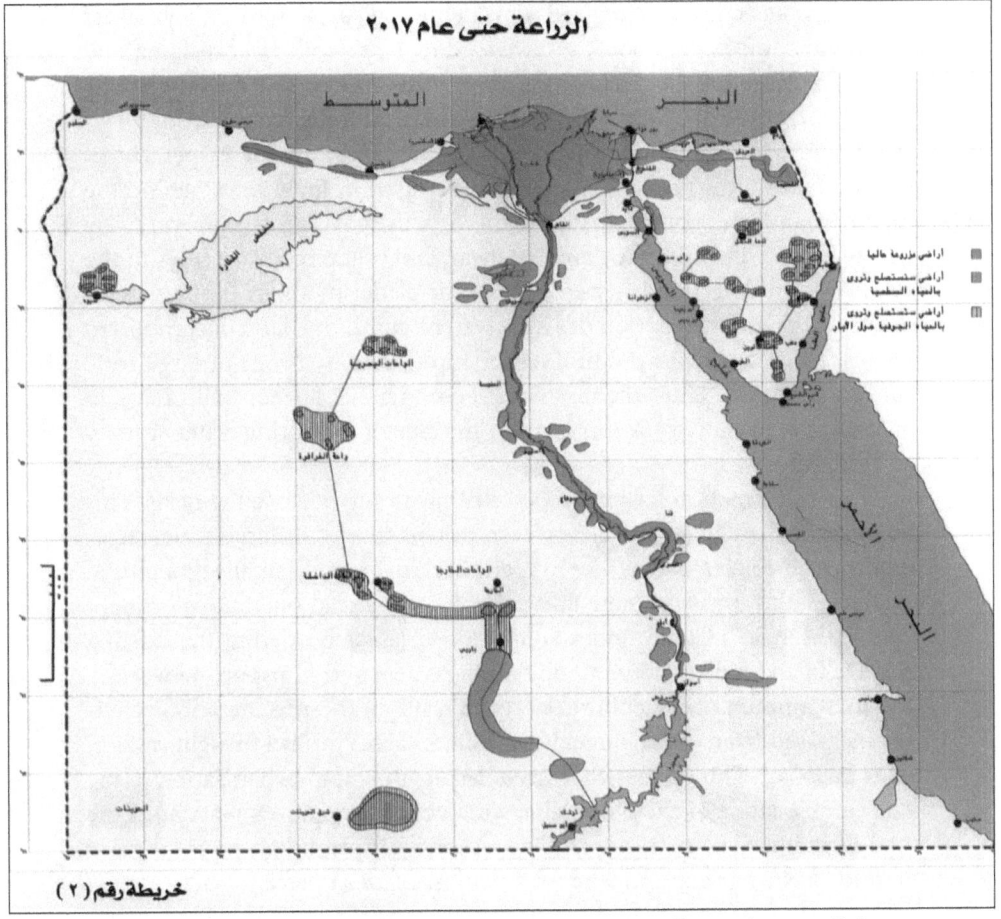

Map 6.1. Land reclamation in Egypt's master plan until 2017. "Agriculture until the year 2017," in *Egypt and the Twenty-First Century* (Cairo: Arab Republic of Egypt, Cabinet of Ministers, 1997), map no. 2, p. 191 (in Arabic).

In arid lands, water is the principal constraint on the expansion of irrigated land. Yet there has been little serious public debate and few policy shifts regarding limiting water for agricultural use in Egypt. As Tony Allen has argued, the global trade in food, especially cereals, allowed Middle Eastern political economies to quietly address water deficits through food imports.[17] Importing virtual water perpetuated a myth in which "economies have enjoyed stability and expansions because of efforts by farmers and managers to manage an adequate supply."[18] The perception that supply was manageable, and that existing uses could be made more efficient through water conservation and new technologies, allowed policymakers to remain complacent about, and wedded to, large-scale land reclamation.

Perceptions of adequate water supply were reinforced during the late 1990s, when the New Valley Project was announced. Historically high levels of rain in the Ethiopian highlands (which accounts for 85 percent of the Nile's flow) during the prior decade resulted in high flows behind the Aswan High Dam. For the first time, in 1997, the government preemptively released water through the dam's spillway, creating temporary lakes in the southwestern desert and sparking domestic criticism about the "wasteful" use of water. The perception of rising water behind the dam, like imported cereals, allowed Egypt's political leadership to retain visions of large-scale land reclamation. Thus, the regime and commercial farmers alike have, in practice, been relatively complacent in the face of mounting water scarcity in subsequent years.

Land reclamation has proceeded steadily in Egypt since the 1950s. This reclamation has taken place, however, not primarily in large-scale, state-sponsored projects in the desert peripheries. Instead, small agricultural producers and a mix of state and private commercial operations brought significant areas of land under cultivation in areas bordering the existing Nile Delta and Valley, close to population centers and transport networks.[19] The total amount of agricultural land as a result of these reclamation activities increased from approximately six million acres in 1972 to eight million acres in 2003.[20] This increase occurred despite the rapid urbanization of the "old" arable lands of the Nile Delta, which constitute 60–65 percent of the total agricultural land in Egypt.[21] One recent study put urban encroachment on "old" Delta agricultural lands at a net loss of 28.43 percent (32,236 acres) between 1972 and 2003, with an annual loss of 1,040 acres.[22] Predictably, urban expansion has been most rapid around Cairo and its satellite cities.

Not surprisingly, newly reclaimed lands are not as productive as the old lands of the Delta; these show less biomass in remote sensing analysis than old Delta land or land under reclamation for decades.[23] The expansion of irrigated agriculture to new lands has accelerated the depletion, salinization, and pollution of groundwater resources, requiring donor and state interventions to deal with deteriorating groundwater quality and aquifer subsidence.[24] Both "new" and "old" reclaimed lands thus require ongoing government, multilateral, and private investment to ensure that cultivation remains viable.[25] The principal issue for Egyptian officials, peasants, and donors is thus not whether the state should support land reclamation, but in what ways, where, and for whose benefit.

Land Reclamation: Building a New Rural Society Under Nasser

Land consolidation in large-scale estates and along the fringes of the Nile Delta expanded in the wake of the construction of the first dam at Aswan, built between 1899 and 1902. The dam facilitated perennial irrigation in the Old Delta, while the stored floodwaters could also be used for land reclamation. The European and Egyptian investors involved in land reclamation were considered at the forefront of reclamation technologies and practices. In the early 1900s, for instance, a soil scientist from the U.S. Bureau of Soil published detailed descriptions of experimental techniques used in Egypt to address problems of salinization of reclaimed land under perennial irrigation, arguing that similar techniques could work in the arid West of the United States.[26]

During the interwar period, wealthy elites and political parties began to focus on land reclamation as a means to address rural poverty and "overpopulation" in the Nile valley by expanding the arable land base of Egypt. The precarious position of much of the peasantry in the wake of World War I, the rural revolt in Egypt in 1919, and further impoverishment during the Great Depression served to fuel an interest in "peasant studies" abroad and an array of social reform proposals targeting the peasantry within Egypt.[27]

In the interwar period, liberal reformers called for more extensive land reclamation to solve the shortages of arable land vis-à-vis a burgeoning population, while avoiding calls for significant redistribution of the highly inequitable landholdings concentrated in large estates.[28] Foreshadowing contemporary developments, private business groups undertook land reclamation on a modest scale throughout this period, particularly in the northern and western Delta provinces.

With the advent of Nasser's military regime in the 1950s, land reclamation was increasingly elevated as part of a new populist "contract" with the peasantry, even as new institutions such as cooperatives sought to demobilize the rural population.[29] In 1958, Nasser used his speech commemorating the 1956 Suez crisis to announce that the government was undertaking land reclamation projects in the New Valley governorate.

> Today, brethren, we turn to the Western Desert to establish there a New Valley, parallel to the valley of the Nile. We are endeavoring to utilize the water of the wells in order to create new lands.... [T]here are cultivable lands there estimated at 3 million *feddans* which are being left uncultivated.[30]

In May 1959, the regime created a new government agency, the Egyptian Public Organization for Desert Reclamation; one of its first approved budgetary expenditures was in the New Valley.[31] These projects relied on wells accessing large fossil groundwater aquifers, as does much of the ongoing land reclamation in the oases of the western desert.

It was the construction of the Aswan High Dam, however, that made large-scale land reclamation in the desert more promising to Egyptian engineers and agronomists, since the Aswan High Dam made multiyear storage of the Nile flood possible.[32] Leading government technocrats disagreed about the extent of land reclamation the dam made possible. Rosy projections of the amount and quality of land to be reclaimed, however, prevailed, and military officials established land reclamation companies expecting to capitalize on a bonanza in land creation.[33]

The most ambitious of these plans envisioned building a "parallel Nile," diverting the waters of the Nile River from the newly created Lake Nasser to the southwestern desert. This idea became the core of the New Valley Project undertaken under Mubarak. When initially circulated in the late 1960s, however, the parallel Nile project was deemed infeasible and uneconomical, consigned to the files of the Ministry of Planning.[34] In 1978, the idea was briefly revived, when the ministry estimated that 1.3 million feddans could be reclaimed through diverting Nile water via a canal to the New Valley.[35] These project proposals generated soil classification studies, surveys of groundwater and drainage issues, and other planning documents produced by a variety of governmental institutions, including the National Water Research Center, the Academy of Scientific Research, the Agricultural Research Center, and the Desert Research Center.[36] In several of these reports, Egyptian experts accurately highlighted many of the profitability, administration, and ownership issues that would plague state-promoted land reclamation efforts.[37]

Official discourse of the Nasser period suggested that land reclamation would transform workers and peasants by changing their environments. Model communities established by the government in newly reclaimed lands would create new citizens by granting them land ownership, imbuing residents with modern mentalities and work ethics, and providing training and support services.[38] These themes echoed notions made decades earlier by Labor Zionists in Palestine, in which new citizens would be forged through the conquest of desert land.[39] Whereas early Zionists, drawing on their roots in reformist socialism, emphasized collectively owned communal labor to green the desert, Egyptian planners invoked a significant role for the state along Soviet lines, first in establishing model communities and then, by the late 1960s, by creating large state-owned farms.

One of the largest government-owned projects was Tahrir (Liberation) Province, where the regime envisioned large-scale "modern" farms employing mechanization and scientific planning, staffed by model settlers living in modern communities.[40] Settlers were required to attend lessons in hygiene, religious instruction, physical exercise, and familial and personal responsibility; Western dress was compulsory.[41]

As in the Soviet system, central directives for land reclamation often focused on bureaucratic units achieving fixed numerical quotas, regardless of the quality or viability of the land reclaimed. By 1965, for instance, the end of Egypt's first "Five-Year Plan," only 47 percent of reclaimed land was actually under cultivation.[42] This prompted the government to largely abandon plans for extending model communities.

The pace of land reclamation further slowed as a result of the 1967 and 1973 wars. However, in 1978, Nasser's successor, Anwar Sadat, called for an "invasion" of the desert to ease population pressures in the Delta. "Why should we not emerge from this narrow valley to new horizons in the land where there is space and water?" Sadat asked rhetorically in 1978 in the pages of the *World*, the monthly publication of the oil company Saudi Aramco.[43]

Land reclamation remained costly and difficult to sustain in the Western desert, however. In his memoir, the well-known Egyptian geologist Rushdi Said recalled the effects of shifting political priorities—and overextraction of groundwater—on efforts to reclaim land in some of the oases of western desert: "I have seen thousands of *feddans* that were abandoned and the dozens of wells that dried up or suffered a substantial decrease in their discharge."[44] He also enumerated a set of problems that continue to make desert agriculture costly: the high costs of groundwater extraction and delivery, ineffective drainage systems, increasing salinity, moving sand dunes, harsh winds, and a lack of effective support services for new residents.

When state-owned farms proved inefficient and costly, the government established a program to allocate reclaimed land to unemployed university graduates in the late 1970s. This program was extended to high school and non-university graduates after 1981.[45] Privatization of the remaining, highly indebted state-owned farms accelerated during the 1980s. The 56,810-acre Salhiyya land reclamation project, another project begun during the Nasser period, was 250 million LE (Egyptian pounds) in debt when it was finally transferred from the Ministry of Agriculture in 1992 to its public-sector creditors. No private sector investor stepped forward to pay the government's asking price.[46]

The New Valley Project and the Mubarak Regime

Given past experience with state-sponsored land reclamation, many Egyptian public intellectuals and technocrats were surprised when the Mubarak regime announced the New Valley Project. Until then, the government had focused its rhetoric and finance on the Al Salaam (Peace) Canal project to expand arable land in northern Sinai, with little attention to the western desert.[47] Many suggested that the project was an attempt by Kamal Ganzouri, then prime minister, and Yousef Wali, then minister of agriculture, to provide the president with a monumental legacy.[48]

While the project's location and scale were surprising to observers, many of the key tropes employed by the regime were familiar staples of Egyptian environmental narratives. These were recast, however, in the idioms of contemporary environmentalism. State rhetoric attempted to construct diametrically opposed visions—a polluted, crowded Old Valley versus a pristine, pure, and unpolluted "New Valley." This framing sought to capitalize on widespread public concern with contaminated drinking water, pesticides, dirt, garbage, and industrial pollution in the Delta contrasted with the tabula rasa of desert areas to be reclaimed. As the pro-government columnist Ibrahim Nafie wrote, the New Valley was far away from the "over-population, environmental pollution and the consequent attrition on our current urban, industrial and agricultural infrastructure."[49] The government-owned weekly *Roz al-Yusuf* justified the project's remote location far from the inhabited Valley in similar terms: "The strategic Egyptian chooses a site in which the environment is not polluted."[50] Government papers also carried personal testimonials from visitors to the New Valley attesting to the pure drinking water obtained from wells and organic crops produced without fertilizers or chemicals.[51]

As in colonial discourses about the peasantry, the Mubarak regime's propaganda linked a clean and sanitary environment with the creation of a new citizenry.[52] This theme was reiterated in numerous government speeches and publications. President Mubarak, at the opening of a main canal, stated: "The New Valley Project will create new lives, cities, villages and societies for Egyptians. . . . The environment does not carry one iota of pollution—the water is clear and the land is untouched by fertilizers. It is the project of the future." Similarly, a journalist for the state-owned daily *Al Ahram* echoed these sentiments on a visit to the area in 2003.

> When I sampled the organic crops growing on the farms there, they were like nothing I had ever tasted before. . . . I also saw a new kind of Egyptian citizen. . . . The Toshka resident believes

Figure 6.1. The Sheikh Zayed (Toshka) Canal conveys Nile water from the Aswan Dam reservoir (Lake Nasser) to the New Valley land reclamation project. *Photo by Jeannie Sowers.*

in his work, gives his best according to a clear and organized plan, puts his patriotism at the service of the project, and wants to live in Toshka once it is completed.[53]

The government's campaign to stress the environmental cleanliness and amenities of the New Valley targeted domestic and international investors as much as ordinary Egyptians. The General Authority for Investment touted the area as "pristine and free from pests. The water supply is of the highest quality, without any pollutants."[54] Yousef Wali, then the long-time minister of agriculture and general secretary of the National Democratic Party (NDP), called for keeping the area "free from pollution by insecticides" to facilitate exports to Europe.[55] Mubarak reiterated this theme in the New Valley at a ceremony for the pumping station, noting that "Toshka's products are ideal for exporting to Europe because they are organic crops grown in healthy, unpolluted soil."[56]

The government further sought to contrast the "wasteful" excess of water by small farmers in the old Delta lands with the "efficient" use of water by large-scale investors planned for the New Valley. In governmental framings, small cultivators applied excess water because they lacked access to modern technologies, did not pay for the resource, and were risk averse, accustomed to "traditional" methods of basin irrigation. These claims were reiterated, for instance, in a public relations campaign launched by the Ministry of Public Works and Water Resources and United States Agency for International Development (USAID) in 1997 to educate farmers about water scarcity. The goal, noted one of the project publications, "was to transform farmers from being the 'problem' to being the solution to water scarcity concerns."[57]

The government argued that "wasteful" water use by cultivators in the Delta allowed for improvements in water efficiency, to make water available for use in the New Valley Project. Egyptian officials were adamant that water for land reclamation could be found within Egypt's legal allotment of Nile water. The government accordingly touted a range of measures to increase water efficiency, including fines and bans on exports of water-intensive crops such as sugarcane and rice, reusing ever more drainage water, and investing in modern irrigation technologies and drainage systems. Domestic critics of the New Valley project, however, questioned whether Egypt could save enough water to warrant large-scale expansions in irrigated agriculture.

Controversies and Criticisms of the New Valley Project

Many water experts, like public intellectuals and journalists for opposition newspapers, saw the New Valley Project primarily as an example of closed, nontransparent decision-making by the Mubarak regime. However, at the inception of the project, many of these critiques were aired privately or in the pages of opposition newspapers, as the regime embarked on a sustained propaganda campaign to market the project. This section explores the critiques that circulated when the project was announced in the late 1990s, when the regime's rhetoric and expenditures on the New Valley Project took center stage in Egyptian political life.

Egyptian experts and intellectuals shared the conviction of state officials that some land reclamation was necessary. At the same time, however, experts called for limiting plans for land reclamation given scarce and increasingly polluted water resources. Upper-level bureaucrats within the Ministries of Irrigation and Agriculture privately expressed doubt in interviews with the author about the New Valley Project's feasibility and costs. They stress their limited access to information and exclusion from policy-making. These doubts were often expressed by commenting on the political origins of the project versus more objective considerations of technical feasibility. As a top adviser to then minister of irrigation Mahmud Abu Zeid commented:

> There was a strong political push for the Toshka (New Valley) Project. It was part of a policy decision taken by the Cabinet to develop the Western Desert, Sinai, and Upper Egypt. We have some technical studies, which are not public information, but even I don't have that much information. If we were deciding on cost-benefit grounds, I would be reluctant to pursue it. If it's just agricultural, the project will fail. If there are no investors, it will fail.[58]

Egyptian critics generally argued that scarce water and limited financial resources would be better spent on land reclamation or other economic activities near existing centers of transport and population. "It is true that the Nile Valley is overcrowded," argued an outspoken former chairman of the parliamentary housing committee. "But why this project, and why now? Toshka will be a sponge, a sponge for investment funds that could have been used more productively elsewhere in the country."[59]

During the project's inception, environmental scientists were publicly circumspect in their criticisms about the possible environmental implications of the project. In professional journals and in private discussions, however, several cited common concerns. The Ministry of Public Works and Water Resources initially estimated the amount of water required by the New Valley Project to be 5.5 billion cubic meters (BCM) annually, which constituted 9–10 percent of Egypt's annual Nile water allocation. Water and agriculture experts argued that this water should be used more productively elsewhere, particularly as drainage and salinity problems would undermine large-scale land reclamation efforts.[60] They argued that using water to grow crops in the western desert offered few opportunities for reuse, unlike using water in the Delta, which is typically recycled as it flows through the system.[61] More cost-effective approaches should focus on improving the old lands, they suggested, and include substantive efforts to provide rural sanitation, control industrial pollution, and implement further technical improvements to the irrigation system.[62]

The opposition press incorporated some of these expert critiques but emphasized the authoritarian nature of decision-making. They depicted the New Valley Project as yet another example of exclusionary and irrational decision-making by an increasingly ossified circle of political insiders. Opposition papers and journalists challenged the regime's cost estimates for the project and argued that these projects were marred by high-level corruption, enriching contracting and construction firms close to the regime. The daily *Al-Wafd* newspaper embarked on a vociferous campaign attacking the project on the grounds that the government had presented no budgetary information to Parliament and had not released feasibility, cost, and environmental impact studies to the public.[63] Throughout 1998 and 1999 *Al-Wafd* escalated its criticism of the project as a slush fund for government contractors and their affiliates close to the regime. The government's response was swift: it arrested an *Al-Wafd* editor and several journalists under a new and restrictive Press Law (#93).[64]

Leading Egyptian intellectuals and former officials also criticized the costs and uncertain returns associated with the New Valley Project in interviews and specialized reports. One external estimate put the costs for water infrastructure at approximately LE5.5 billion, with total costs estimated between LE300 and 500 billion (US$90–150 billion).[65] For 1999–2000, official figures show that planned investment in the New Valley Project accounted for 53 percent of the state's total budget for the Ministry of Agriculture, and 63 percent of the total planned expenditures of the Ministry of Agriculture.[66]

The Mubarak regime financed these costs through the state-owned National Investment Bank, a $100 million contribution from Sheikh Zayed, the ruler of Abu Dhabi, and using additional funds for land reclamation provided by Gulf-funded development institutions.[67] Egyptian critics argued that these funding sources did not meet the relatively rigorous standards used by the World Bank, and pointed to the numerous technical and feasibility studies produced by international consulting firms and aid agencies for other megaprojects, such as the Aswan High Dam and the Al-Salaam Canal. "The decision should be discussed openly, and a neutral committee should be formed to decide its economic feasibility," observed a former prime minister who helped author the 1974 investment liberalization laws.[68]

The Mubarak regime widely publicized that the World Bank had undertaken an environmental impact assessment (EIA), and that it had contracted for its own EIA with CEDARE, the Center for Environment and Development in the Arab World.[69] Neither impact assessment was publicly released, however, nor did the Egyptian environmental experts I interviewed succeed in obtaining copies. Similarly, domestic cost-benefit analyses were not available. A few were attempted by outside experts: one U.S. academic calculated the infrastructure and investment costs per feddan of the New Valley Project at $4,337, while expected revenues over twenty-five years were projected at $2,589 per feddan.[70] As the author noted, private firms would invest in such a scheme only if the government subsidized the full infrastructure costs.

In the absence of cost-benefit analyses or impact assessments, the New Valley Project was quickly linked in Egyptian political life with the reluctance of the Mubarak regime to democratize. The late public intellectual Tahsin Bashir christened the New Valley Project the "stealth project," arguing that Mubarak and his appointees embarked on a colossal national project rather than acquiesce to a democratic transition.[71] In 2008, a respected environmental scientist asked, "How, in Egypt, can the decision to do a 20–30 billion dollar project have been taken by only a few people? Only because high-ranking persons have tried to stay in power forever."[72]

Agribusiness Narratives in the New Valley

Environmental experts, opposition journalists, and public intellectuals were not the only actors critical of the New Valley Project. Unlike the state-sponsored reclamation projects of the Nasser period, which targeted small farmers as beneficiaries, Mubarak's New Valley Project was supposed to attract large-scale private investment in commercial farms. The state promised large-scale engineering works to the borders of private land, but the task of leveling land, building irrigation and drainage networks, and cultivating crops was delegated to agribusiness. As a 2004 World Bank paper noted, these projects "renew the nineteenth-century tradition of close cooperation with the state by national and foreign investors to develop export-based agricultural production."[73] The key difference, however, was the source of external capital. Rather than European firms, external investment largely flowed from the Gulf region, particularly Saudi Arabia and the United Arab Emirates.

Prioritizing large-scale investors was congruent with the regime's larger macroeconomic policies of privatization and neoliberal restructuring. As in tourism and industrial zones, the government offered investors a twenty-year tax holiday, cheap land prices, long-term concessions, tax exemptions on imported equipment, and guaranteed allocations of irrigation water.[74] Officials justified the privileged position accorded to large-scale investors by arguing that they would employ water-conserving irrigation technologies, such as pivot irrigation.

While promoting agribusiness in the New Valley, the Mubarak government dismantled Nasser-era policies supporting small-scale peasant agriculture in the old Delta during the 1980s and 1990s. Land tenure protections were repealed, subsidies on fertilizers, pesticides, and diesel fuel were reduced, and the system of cooperatives was left largely unfunded.[75] These changes put significant pressures on Egypt's small-scale farmers, many of whom have limited access to credit, cannot afford sufficient quantities of fertilizers, gypsum, and other soil amendments, and who are not consulted in the planning or delivery of government-sponsored rehabilitation and drainage projects.[76]

This neoliberal restructuring of Egyptian peasant agriculture reflected broader regional trends. Egyptian and Arab agribusiness firms pursued consolidation among agricultural companies and sought vertical integration of supply chains to enhance competitiveness during the 1990s and 2000s. New investment vehicles for private and public capital, such as private equity firms and sovereign wealth funds, also began to target the

Egyptian agricultural sector.[77] As a result, foreign companies accounted for 37 percent of agro-industrial investment in Egypt in 2008.[78]

Despite government incentives and increasing foreign investment in agriculture, private investors were reluctant to invest in the New Valley Project.[79] By 2008, only five companies had acquired plots in Toshka, and of these, only three firms were cultivating crops.[80] With rapidly increasing global food prices in 2007–8, a number of Saudi and Gulf investment groups were reportedly interested in acquiring land in the New Valley Project, but few details of finalized deals emerged.[81] Eager to deflect criticism, the government declared that it would start selling 2,900 feddans in the Toshka area to new graduates and young peasants as early as 2002,[82] yet few of these transfers have been evident.

Of the three companies cultivating crops in the New Valley Project, two were privately owned and one was majority state-owned. The state-owned South Valley Company for Development, created in 1999, was allocated 160,000 acres and had reportedly cultivated about 7,000 of these by 2006.[83] One of the private companies, Green Valley Association, was an Egyptian joint-stock company established in the early 1990s. It owned a total of 7,000 acres devoted to peanut cultivation for export and served as the local agent for multinational manufacturers of pivot and drip irrigation systems.[84]

The second private company, Kingdom Agricultural Development Company (KADCO) was wholly owned by Prince Al-Waleed bin Talal Al-Saud of Saudi Arabia, the first private investor in the New Valley Project. The nephew of King Fahd of Saudi Arabia, Prince Al-Waleed's holdings included ownership of the Saudi Kingdom Holding Company, and significant shares of such global conglomerates as Apple, Citigroup, the Four Seasons hotel chain, and others. Al-Waleed had a reputation for business acumen by investing in well-known companies during hard times and then reaping the benefits as companies restructured and stock prices climbed.[85] In 2009, he was ranked as the twenty-second wealthiest person in the world, despite steep declines in his net worth as the result of the global banking and financial crisis.[86]

KADCO, incorporated as an Egyptian joint-stock company, initially planned to cultivate 100,000 acres over a seven-year period, investing US$500–650 million total. The acquisition was part of what Al-Waleed described as a limited investment strategy in Egypt targeting only "real estate, tourism, and agriculture, all fields with high rates of return."[87] Al-Waleed already had significant investments in Egypt's tourism and real estate sectors when he purchased land in the New Valley Project.[88]

KADCO's reclamation efforts in the New Valley began with an experimental farm, drawing groundwater from wells in order to determine the viability and profitability of export agriculture. Al-Waleed also sought to link KADCO with global agro-industrial firms through joint ventures. KADCO sought to create a joint venture with CADIZ, a subsidiary of the California-based agro-industry firm Sun World International, one of the largest vertically integrated agricultural development companies in California. The venture collapsed, however, when CADIZ declared bankruptcy in 2002.[89]

By the winter of 2008, when the author visited KADCO's fields, the company had cultivated 600 acres out of their initial 100,000 target.[90] They employed 70–100 permanent workers, and at peak packing and harvesting times employed 250–1000 temporary laborers. Even permanent workers, however, commuted from the nearby city of Aswan, and no permanent settlement had been created.

These modest acreage and employment figures troubled the Mubarak government. For the regime, Al-Waleed's investment was a crucial marketing device to justify their estimated LE5.5 billion (US$1.6 billion) investment in the pumping station and main canals. The slow pace of land reclamation in the New Valley had become fodder for parliamentary debates,[91] newspaper editorials, satirical cartoons, and public jokes. As a result, the government threatened to suspend KADCO's operations and revoke their land title.

Although managers admitted that Al-Waleed's commitment and investment in KADCO had fluctuated, their story-lines about land reclamation focused on obstacles created by weak domestic markets, poor governance, inadequate infrastructure, and unpredictable policies. In short, they argued that poor economic returns on land reclamation were in large part the result of government policies and practices.

Farm managers took the inadequacies of government planning as the starting point for their narratives. Investors like Al-Waleed bought New Valley land based on government soil classifications that proved inaccurate. In the case of KADCO, only half of their 100,000-acre parcel could be cultivated, according to their soil surveys. Both KADCO and the state-owned firm reported encountering a stratified salty clay layer, locally termed *tafla*, that was difficult to cultivate. One of the expatriate agronomists working for KADCO noted:

> Our land was supposed to be class one and two agricultural soils, but the government didn't get the topography and the

soil right. This was because the layout and design of the branch canals was done from an engineering perspective, not an agricultural one. The canal layouts were designed to take advantage of gradients, to go down into the Toshka depression. But as you go down, you encounter more *tafla*. From an agronomist's perspective, it is better to pump the water up to better soils.[92]

The state-owned company reportedly shifted to flooding fields, in the old style of basin cultivation, as well as growing salt-tolerant rice, in order to cope with *tafla* in their soils. Rice is a water-intensive crop, and thus the Mubarak government's claims about conserving water in New Valley agriculture rang increasingly hollow.

Some Egyptian experts involved in planning the irrigation infrastructure had anticipated such problems. These employees of governmental research institutes published articles in academic journals describing alternative routes for the canal system to access better quality soils in the New Valley.[93] Yet their recommendations went unheeded.

Agribusiness managers highlighted a number of other difficulties. The government failed to provide needed infrastructure and transport investments, which made it difficult to get horticultural produce to overseas markets in a timely fashion. Faced with difficulties in export opportunities, KADCO managers found that their certified organic, labor-friendly produce was too costly for domestic markets. Cold nights in winter require greenhouses, and blisteringly hot days in summer require shaded cultivation with the ongoing use of sprinklers, but neither export nor domestic prices were sufficient to recoup these kinds of production costs. KADCO and other farms in the area have thus increasingly turned to growing forage and fodder crops, particularly alfalfa.[94] Alfalfa is salt tolerant, breaks up clay soils, and produces a crop every twenty to twenty-two days.

Most important, demand for fodder from the United Arab Emirates and Saudi Arabia has escalated rapidly in recent years. To conserve depleting fossil groundwater aquifers, Saudi Arabia imposed limits on extracting groundwater in recent years, while subsidizing the import of fodder to sustain existing dairy and meat operations.[95] Other Saudi investors see similar opportunities for cereal production in the New Valley Project. Suleiman Al Rahji, who controls Saudi Arabia's largest publicly traded bank, Al Rahji Bank, reportedly acquired 100,000 acres in the New Valley for wheat and corn production.[96]

Shifting to fodder for export, however, poses a significant risk: namely, that the Egyptian government, with its own needs for domestic fodder and cereals, will impose export bans. Export duties on wheat and corn exports were already in place, and in 2008, faced with skyrocketing global food prices, the government imposed an export ban on rice, one of the most lucrative crops for Egyptian farmers.[97]

Given these issues, agribusiness firms have dramatically lower estimates for economically viable land reclamation than the government. In interviews, one manager noted, "The New Valley Project will not even reach half of the 540,000 acres that the government has been touting as its first phase." Another noted that "we have been telling this to the ministers, but they don't believe us. The Minister of Agriculture threatened to take our land back, even though we have paid for it, because we have not cultivated it. I told him, 'I will give half of it back to you, for free, because you cannot grow anything!' And that is when I think he started to listen."[98]

The Prince and the President: Land Reclamation as Political Theater

Managers at KADCO and the handful of other New Valley firms were well aware that their firms were not established purely on economic rationales, and that their land reclamation activities were periodically invoked as set pieces in larger dramas of political theater.[99] Managers recounted periodic visits by cabinet ministers, Prince Al-Waleed, and President Mubarak with a mixture of humor, resentment, and dismay. One supervisor recalled that "for the official visits, the Ministry of Irrigation built a six-helicopter pad, so that the prince and the president could arrive by helicopter. They paved the farm roads for the Mercedes to come through; they didn't care what they destroyed." Another remarked, "We don't like when officials come, especially during harvests, because they bring 1,000 soldiers who strip the harvest. The soldiers do it quickly because they know they are stealing, so in their haste they destroy the plants. Last time, by the time President Mubarak arrived, much of the crop had been destroyed by security forces, so we had to transplant anything into the area around the platform they had built for media appearances."[100]

As these accounts suggest, private investors faced political as well as economic challenges in the New Valley Project. As a result, many agribusiness firms chose to locate outside the New Valley.

> ALL ENVIRONMENTAL-ECOLOGICAL arguments are arguments about society, and therefore, complex refractions of all sorts of struggles being waged in other realms.
> —David Harvey, "The Environment of Justice"

ANALYZING EGYPTIAN land reclamation through the prism of the New Valley Project reveals change as well as continuity in environmental narratives. Key elements of state-produced discourses about land reclamation have remained prominent since the Nasser period, though the extent to which the regime pursued land reclamation in practice waxed and waned with changing financial resources and political priorities. The 1990s marked a new intensification of land reclamation efforts, as the Mubarak government positioned the New Valley Project and other megaprojects as a solution to Egypt's enduring environmental imaginary, in which population outstrips available arable land. The Mubarak government recast this narrative in modern environmental idioms, contrasting the pollution of the old agricultural lands with the prospects for cultivating organic, clean, and high-value crops for export in the New Valley. Land reclamation retains a prominent place in Egyptian agricultural policy, particularly with recent increases in the prices of basic foodstuffs. These spikes in global food prices have reinvigorated long-standing concerns about food security in Egypt and much of the Middle East.[101]

From its inception in 1998, the New Valley Project catalyzed dissenting views from Egyptian water and agricultural experts, opposition party members, and journalists. These actors argued that water is scarce and would be used by more people, more productively, elsewhere than in the uninhabited parts of the southwestern desert. And indeed, the Mubarak government's megaprojects failed to attract sufficient private investment or significant settlement to justify their significant costs. As presciently suggested in the critical discourses of the late 1990s, the New Valley Project came to represent the flaws of Mubarak's reign, rather than his crowning achievement.

During the 2000s, agribusiness firms and their workers were the primary actors actually present in the New Valley Project lands. Managers at these farms framed land reclamation in terms of how to cope with various kinds of political and economic costs. In addition to conventional economic costs, such as those associated with transport, input, and production, they emphasized how unpredictable policies, poor infrastructure design, uncertain property rights, and political spectacle decreased returns to desert agriculture.

Although critical of large-scale state projects, neither expert nor business narratives about land reclamation addressed broader questions of rural development, ecological degradation, and social equity. Instead, critical narratives around land reclamation generally promoted "repairing" it, rather than transforming the terms of debate.[102] For environmental experts, "repairing" land reclamation entails making more efficient use of water at the farm level and throughout the irrigation system. For agribusiness firms, international donors, and government officials, repair entails accelerating agricultural restructuring in favor of larger firms and consolidated landholdings in order to compete in changing regional markets. Firms and experts alike thus favor water/agricultural policies that privilege capital-intensive, large-scale technologies to "conserve" water and produce crops competitively. This approach is clearly at odds with the rhetorical focus of the government on generating rural employment, yet is fully consonant with liberalizing agricultural production. In contrast, little governmental attention has been paid to enacting social insurance or welfare policies to assist Egypt's thousands of small agricultural producers, buffeted by price volatility, rising costs of inputs, and mounting environmental problems.

Ecological critiques, derived from the perspective of the Nile River basin as a whole, have similarly made little discernible headway in domestic narratives of land reclamation. River basin considerations, across the ten riparian countries of the Nile, suggest that governments limit land reclamation, tackle increasingly grave problems of water pollution, ensure that water goes to high value uses after satisfying basic needs, and maintain sufficient flows and adequate water quality to sustain ecosystem services.

During the 2000s, however, local concern and activism around water scarcity and pollution became more prominent in Egypt. A diversified public sphere and independent media increasingly linked pollution and public health crises to authoritarian rule and centralized, opaque decision-making. Critiques of government initiatives, such as the New Valley Project, once aired principally in conversation and on the pages of opposition newspapers, circulated in national and regional satellite broadcasts, independent daily papers, university forums, and parliamentary debates.[103] Similarly, protests about low wages, high prices, water shortages, labor conditions, foreign policy, and other grievances became commonplace. The revolutionary moment that spread across Egypt in 2011 was thus an intensification of existing dynamics of protest, overturning Mubarak's rule and starting a significant restructuring of the political order.

With the ouster of the president and the imposition of military rule, it is far from certain, however, whether deeper changes in Egypt's environmental narratives will emerge. Government ministries in Cairo will likely continue to issue centralized plans for remaking the nation's landscape through land reclamation, with little reference to existing patterns of urbanization or agricultural practice and little communication with farmers or agribusiness. Should the military council eventually oversee relatively free national elections, one may see more effective parliamentary oversight of the costs and benefits of large-scale, state-sponsored projects. Devolution of authority to provincial governments, however, may well result in a proliferation of land reclamation projects, spun off to well-connected agribusiness interests. If political reform allows cities, towns, and rural communities to articulate local priorities, raise and spend funds, and experiment with various innovative approaches to land reclamation, we may eventually see significant change in Egypt's dominant environmental narratives.

Notes

Research and writing was facilitated by fellowships from the Center for Humanities at the University of New Hampshire, and the Dubai Initiative, Belfer Center for Science and International Affairs, Harvard University. My sincere thanks to both institutions.

1. "Toshka Project—Mubarak Pumping Station/ Sheikh Zayed Canal, Egypt," http://www.water-technology.net/projects/mubarak/specs.html.

2. Author interview with Kingdom Agricultural Development Company (KADCO) manager, New Valley, 28 November 2008.

3. For an overview, see François Molle, Peter Mollinga, and Philippus Wester, "Hydraulic Bureaucracies and the Hydraulic Mission: Flows of Water, Flows of Power," *Water Alternatives* 2, no. 3 (2009): 328–49.

4. For Israel, see Avner De-Shalit, "From the Political to the Objective: The Dialectics of Zionism and the Environment," *Environmental Politics* 4, no. 1 (1995): 70–87. For Israel and Palestine, see Jan Selby, *Water, Power, and Politics in the Middle East: the Other Israeli-Palestinian Conflict* (London: I. B. Tauris, 2003).

5. James Scott captured the zeitgeist of postwar development trends with his discussion of high modernism and landscape modification in *Seeing Like a State* (New Haven: Yale University Press, 1999).

6. Desert Development Center, *Institutional Framework for Alleviating Poverty and Preventing Land Degradation in Egypt's New Lands* (Cairo: American University in Cairo, 2003), 4.

7. For an overview of expanding public sphere in the Arab world, see Marc Lynch, *Voices of the New Arab Public: Iraq, Al-Jazeera, and Middle East Politics Today* (New York: Columbia University Press, 2006).

8. Maarten A. Hajer, *The Politics of Environmental Discourse: Ecological Modernization and the Policy Process* (New York: Clarendon Press, 1995), 61–68.

9. See, among many examples, statements by the head of the Horizontal Expansion Sector, Ministry of Water Resources and Irrigation, in an article by Neil Ford, "Greening Egypt's Desert," *Middle East* 330 (2003): 42–46.

10. World Population Prospects Database, United Nations Department of Economic and Social Affairs, Population Division, http://esa.un.org/unpp/p2kodata.asp.

11. A feddan equals 1.038 acres or 0.42 hectars. World Food Programme, "Settlement on Newly Developed Land in Upper Egypt" (Cairo, 1996).

12. Ray Bush, "Politics, Power and Poverty: Twenty Years of Agricultural Reform and Market Liberalisation in Egypt," *Third World Quarterly* 28, no. 8 (2007): 1599–615.

13. Timothy Mitchell, "America's Egypt: Discourse of the Development Industry," *Middle East Report* 169 (1991): 18–36; and "Object of Development," in *Rule of Experts: Egypt, Techno-politics, Modernity* (Berkeley: University of California Press, 2002).

14. Ray Bush and Amal Sabri, "Mining for Fish," *Middle East Report* 216 (2000), http://www.merip.org/mer/mer216_bush-sabri.html.

15. Official narratives about land and population also typically gloss over the complex socioeconomic changes under way in Egypt that have dramatically transformed most rural areas into peri-urban spaces. In "rural" Egypt, the "peasantry" is increasingly linked to broader national and regional labor markets, surviving by undertaking diverse activities and migration.

16. Laila Reem, "Water Matters," *Al Ahram Weekly*, 30 July–5 August, 2009, http://weekly.ahram.org.eg/print/2009/958/eg2.htm.

17. Tony Allen, *The Middle East Water Question: Hydropolitics and the Global Economy* (London: I. B. Tauris, 2001); A. Y. Hoekstra and P. Q. Hung, "Globalisation of Water Resources: International Virtual Water Flows in Relation to Crop Trade," *Global Environmental Change* 15, no. 1 (2005): 45–56.

18. Allen, *Middle East Water Question*, 164.

19. Ibid. See also Abdulaziz M. Abdulaziz, J. Jose, M. Murtado, and R. Al-Douri, "Application of Multitemporal Landsat Data to Monitor Land Cover Changes in the Eastern Nile Delta Region, Egypt," *International Journal of Remote Sensing* 30, no. 11 (2009): 2977–96.

20. Mohamed El-Desoky Hereher, "Monitoring Spatial and Temporal Changes of Agricultural Lands in the Nile Delta and Their Implications of Soil Characteristics Using Remote Sensing" (PhD diss., University of Arizona, 2006).

21. The quality of Delta soil is decreasing, and the Delta as a whole is considered an eroding, subsiding coastal plain, as it no longer receives silt and soil accumulation from Nile flooding. Daniel Jean Stanley and Andrew Warne, "Nile Delta in Its Destruction Phase," *Journal of Coastal Research* 14, no. 3 (1998): 794–825.

22. Hereher, "Monitoring Spatial and Temporal Changes."

23. Ibid.

24. See, for example, Ministry of Water Resources and Irrigation, *West Delta Water Conservation and Irrigation Rehabilitation Project: Draft Resettlement Policy Framework* (Cairo: Ministry of Water Resources and Irrigation, 2007).

25. Ibid., 4–5.

26. Thomas H. Means, *Reclamation of Alkali Lands in Egypt as Adapted to Similar Work in the United States*, Bureau of Soils, Department of Agriculture, Bulletin No. 21 (Washington, D.C.: Government Printing Office, 1903).

27. Omnia S. El Shakry, *The Great Social Laboratory: Subjects of Knowledge in Colonial and Postcolonial Egypt* (Stanford: Stanford University Press, 2007).
28. Ibid.
29. John Waterbury, *The Egypt of Nasser and Sadat: The Political Economy of Two Regimes* (Princeton, N.J.: Princeton University Press, 1983).
30. United Arab Republic. *The New Valley* (Cairo: Maslahat al-Isti'lamat, 1964), 1.
31. Nazih Ayubi, *The State and Public Policies in Egypt Since Sadat* (Reading, UK: Ithaca Press, 1991), 210.
32. John Waterbury, *Hydropolitics of the Nile Valley* (Syracuse, N.Y.: Syracuse University Press, 1979).
33. Robert Springborg, *Family, Power, and Politics in Egypt* (Philadelphia: University of Pennsylvania Press, 1982), 157.
34. Ayubi, *State and Public Policies in Egypt*, 210.
35. Ibid.
36. Nagy G. R. Yakoub and Mona El Kady. "Using GIS for Planning and Water Management of the Southern Egypt Development Project," unpublished report, 1998, 5.
37. See, for instance, the transcript of discussions held in 1958, at the Arab Centre for Political and Economic Studies, "Seminar on Land Reclamation and Exploitation in the United Arab Republic" (Cairo: Al Ahram, 1958).
38. Omnia S. El Shakry, *The Great Social Laboratory: Subjects of Knowledge in Colonial and Postcolonial Egypt* (Stanford: Stanford University Press, 2007).
39. Yael Zerubavel, "The Conquest of the Desert and the Settlement Ethos," in *The Desert Experience in Israel: Communities, Arts, Science, and Education in the Negev*, ed. A. Paul Hare and Gideon Kressel (Lanham, Md.: University Press of America, 2009), 33–44.
40. Jon Alterman, *Egypt and American Foreign Assistance, 1952–1962: Hopes Dashed* (New York: Palgrave Macmillan, 2002), 80.
41. Ibid.
42. Sarah P. Voll, "Egyptian Land Reclamation since the Revolution," *Middle East Journal* 34, no. 2 (1980): 127–48.
43. Elias Antar, "Farming by the Nile: Egypt," *Saudi Aramco World* 29, no. 3 (1978).
44. Rushdi Said, *Science and Politics in Egypt: A Life's Journey* (Cairo: American University in Cairo Press, 2004), 188.
45. Desert Development Center, *Institutional Framework*, 3.
46. Guenter Meyer, "The Impact of Liberalization and Privatization on the Agricultural Sector in Egypt," in *Economic Liberalization and Privatization in Socialist Arab Countries*, ed. H. Hopfinger (Nahost and Nordafrika: Studien zu Politik und Wirtschaft, Neuerer Geschichte, Geographie und Gesellschaft 1, 1996), 132.
47. John Waterbury, *The Nile Basin: National Determinants of Collective Action* (New Haven: Yale University Press, 2002), 84.

48. Author interviews with environmental experts, Cairo, June 1999.

49. Ibrahim Nafie, "A Pioneering Spirit," *Al Ahram Weekly* 10, 29 January 1998.

50. Mohamed Abdel Moneim, "The Battle of Toshka," *Roz al-Yusuf*, 25 January 1999, 7 (in Arabic).

51. 'Asem Rifaat, "Excellent Toshka," *Al Ahram Al Iqtisadi*, 1 February 1999 (in Arabic).

52. See Timothy Mitchell, *Colonising Egypt* (Berkeley: University of California Press, 1991).

53. Ali El Samman, "Toshka Is TOPs," *Al Ahram Weekly*, 9 January 2003, http://weekly.ahram.org.eg/2003/620/ec2.htm.

54. General Authority for Investment, Arab Republic of Egypt, *The South Valley Development Project* (Cairo: General Authority for Investment, 1997), 11.

55. "Dr. Yousef Wali Clarifies the Need to Keep the Toshka Area Free from Pollution by Insecticides," *Al Ahram*, 21 March 1998 (in Arabic).

56. Nevine Khalil, "A New Life in the South," *Al Ahram Weekly*, 18 February 1999.

57. GreenCom, "Water Scarcity Campaign Targets Egyptian Farmers," *Human Nature* 2, no. 2 (1997), 1, http://www.greencom.org/greencom/pdf/Hnenaug97.pdf.

58. Author interview with senior consultant to the minister of irrigation, Ministry of Public Works and Water Resources, Cairo, 2 February 1999.

59. Author interview with Milad Hanna, housing expert, Cairo, 1 May 1999.

60. Interviews with, among others, technical consultant to minister of Agriculture, Cairo, 9 February 1999; adviser to the minister of Water Resources and Irrigation, Cairo, 20 February 1999; environmental engineer, University of Alexandria, 30 October 1997; environmental scientist, Cairo, 21 May1998; professor, Sadat Academy, Cairo, 5 February 1999.

61. Interviews with the author. See also Mohsen Elarabawy and Paul Tosswell, "An Appraisal of the Southern Valley Development Project in Egypt," *Journal of Water Supply, Research, and Technology-Aqua* 47, no. 4 (1998): 172. Reuse is limited, however, by increasing salinity and contamination.

62. Mohsen Elarabawy, Bayoumy Attia, and Paul Tosswell, "Integrated Water Resources Management for Egypt," *Journal of Water Supply, Research, and Technology-Aqua* 49, no. 3 (2000): 111–25.

63. See issues of *Al-Wafd*, especially January to March 1999. Representative articles and editorials include Medhat Khafagi, "The Kings of Business and the Toshka Project," 9 April 1999; Abbas Tarabili, "The Toshka Project: Violating the Constitution and the Law!" 14 November 1999 (all in Arabic). For coverage of opposition to Toshka in other newspapers, see Mahoud Salem, "Ask Them! The Opposition Requests the Government to Pile Up the Dirt on the Toshka Project," *Akhbar Al-Yom*, 16 January 1999 (in Arabic); Sa'ad Kamil, "Toshka . . . And Democracy," *Al-Akhbar*, 7 February 1999 (in Arabic); and Gamal Essam El-Din, "Toshka in the Crossfire," *Al Ahram Weekly* 466, 27 January 2000.

64. Simon Apiku, "Wafd Set for Head-on Collision with State," *Middle East Times*, 15 February 1999, 9.

65. Rachel Noeman, "Egypt Pours Money into Desert Reclamation," Reuters News Service, 17 January 2000, http://www.planetark.org/avantgo/dailynewsstory.cfm?newsid=9340.

66. Calculated from figures provided by the Ministry of Planning, *State Development Plan for 1999–2000*, 1999.

67. "Arabs Pledge 1.6 Billion in Soft Loans," *Cairo Times*, 29 April 1999.

68. Author interview with former Prime Minister Abdel Aziz Hegazi, Cairo, 10 February 1999.

69. CEDARE is a quasi-governmental organization funded by the Egyptian government, UNDP (the United Nations Development Program), and the Arab Fund for Economic and Social Development (AFESD).

70. Dennis Wichelns, "Moving Water to Move People: Evaluating Success of the Toshka Project in Egypt," *Water International* 28, no. 1 (2003): 52–56.

71. Author interview with Tahsin Bashir, Cairo, 5 May 1999.

72. Author interview with prominent environmental scientist, Alexandria, 5 December 2008.

73. Ton Van Achthoven, Zohra Merabet, Karim S. Shalaby, and Frank van Steenbergen, "Balancing Productivity and Environmental Pressure in Egypt," Agriculture and Rural Development Working Paper #13, World Bank (Washington, D.C., 2004), 27.

74. Sahr El-Bahr, "Two Years of Aspirations," *Al Ahram Weekly* 17, 11 February 1999.

75. Ray Bush, *Civil Society and the Uncivil State: Land Tenure Reform in Egypt and the Crisis of Rural Livelihoods* (Geneva: United Nations Research Institute for Social Development, 2004).

76. For an insightful discussion of the interlocking effects of poverty and land degradation, see M. A. Kishk, "Poverty and Land Degradation: Prospects and Constraints for Sustainable Land Use in Rural Egypt" (Minia: Department of Agriculture, Minia University, undated).

77. These investment vehicles pool the capital of high-worth individuals and institutional investors, mostly from Egypt, Saudi Arabia, and the UAE. Fueled by oil revenues and increasingly liberalized economies, equity firms have been increasingly active in creating larger, more vertically integrated agribusiness companies in Egypt, with regional ambitions and scope. Ayman Ismail, "Private Equity and Venture Capital" (PhD diss., MIT, 2009); Cynthia Johnston, "Egypt's Citadel to Invest $200–$400 Million in 2010," Reuters, 29 September 2009; Maha El Dahan, "Egypt Firm Says Investing in Sudanese Farmland," Reuters, 29 September 2009.

78. The agribusiness sector, worth $4.7 billion and accounting for 21 percent of total industrial output, represents only 3.65 percent of total GDP. However, low wages continue to make the sector attractive to investors: the General

Authority for Investment reported that in the food processing sector alone, average annual wages declined from $2,403 in 2001 to $1,729 in 2007. General Authority for Investment, *Agribusiness*, 1.

79. The few Egyptian businessmen who invested in land reclamation in the New Valley governorate focused largely on the area of East Oweinat, where some thirteen investors from the most prominent family business groups bought 5 percent each in some 130,000 feddan. American Chamber of Commerce in Egypt, *The South Valley Development Project* (Cairo: American Chamber of Commerce, 1998), 33. East Oweinat's water is derived from groundwater pumping of the Nubian aquifer underlying parts of the western desert. Unlike in Toshka, therefore, water supply is not contingent on Nile flow, a fact that Egyptian investors may have taken into account.

80. Author interview with KADCO manager, New Valley, 28 November 2008.

81. See Eckart Woertz, "Outward Agricultural FDI by GCC Countries," 2nd rev. draft paper (Dubai: UNCTAD, 2009); Eckart Woertz, Samir Pradhan, Nermina Biberovic, and Chan Jingzhong, *Potential for GCC Agro-Investments in Africa and Central Asia* (Dubai: Gulf Research Center, 2008).

82. Karima Al Serougi, "The Minister of Irrigation Announces Groundwater Land for Sale in Toshka in the Coming Month," *Al Akhbar*, 2 July 2002 (in Arabic).

83. "South Valley Company for Development Born Huge," *Akhbar Al-Yom*, 17 April 1999 (in Arabic); Niveen Wahish, "Marketing Toshka," *Al Ahram Weekly*, 16–22 February 2006.

84. http://www.greenvalley-egypt.com/RA_HT/RA_H_page_1.htm. Last accessed 15 May 2010.

85. Andy Serwer, "The Prince of Tech Investors," *Fortune* 40, no. 11 (1999): 116.

86. http://www.forbes.com/lists/2009/10/billionaires-2009-richest-people_Prince-Alwaleed-Bin-Talal-Alsaud_0RD0.html.

87. Aziza Sami, "Big Boost for Toshka," *Al Ahram Weekly*, 24 September 1998, www.ahram.org.eg/weekly/1998/396/ec2.htm. Last accessed 5 May 2010.

88. Prince Al-Waleed's estimated LE2 billion investment in Egypt included the purchase of the San Stefano hotel in Alexandria and two Four Seasons hotels in Cairo and Sharm Al Sheikh, as well as stakes in Talaat Mustapha's Alexandria Real Estate Company and an electronics company with the Ahmed Bahgat Group.

89. "Sun World Agricultural Operations: Cadiz' Partnership in Southern Egypt," 2001, http://www.cadizinc.com/b/b3.htm; "Cadiz Announces Proposed Combination of Sun World with Kingdom Agricultural Development Company (KADCO)," 15 January 2002, http://www.cadizinc.com/a/articles/Jan16–02.html; and Vic Pollard, "Planned Merger Fails for Bakersfield, Calif., Farming Company and Saudi Firm," *Bakersfield Californian*, 12 July 2002.

90. Interview with the author, KADCO, New Valley, 28 November 2009.

91. Francesca de Châtel, *Water Sheikhs and Dam Builders: Stories of People and Water in the Middle East* (New Brunswick, N.J.: Transaction, 2007); Maher Chmaytelli and Abeer Allam, "Pharaonic Pump Sits Idle as Egypt Fails to Lure Investors to the Desert," *Bloomberg L.P.*, 19 February 2008.

92. Interview with the author, KADCO, New Valley, 28 November 2008.

93. See, for example, Yakoub and El Kady, "Using GIS for Planning and Water Management," 1998.

94. Author interviews with KADCO managers, 28 November 2008.

95. Eckart Woertz, Samir Pradhan, Nermina Biberovic, and Christian Koch, *Food Inflation in the GCC Countries* (Dubai: Gulf Research Center, 2008); Woertz, "Outward Agricultural FDI by GCC Countries," 25.

96. Chmaytelli and Allam, "Pharaonic Pump Sits Idle," 2/19/2008, *Bloomberg L.P.*

97. "Egypt Says Rice Export Ban to Oct. 2011," Reuters Africa, http://af.reuters.com/article/investingNews/idAFJOE68K04120100921, 21 September 2010. Last accessed 29 September 2010.

98. Author interview with KADCO manager, New Valley, 28 November 2008.

99. Author interview with KADCO chief executive officer, New Valley, 28 November 2008.

100. Author interviews with managers at KADCO, New Valley, 27 November 2008.

101. Andrew Martin, "Mideast Facing a Choice between Crops and Water," *New York Times*, 21 July 2008, http://www.nytimes.com/2008/07/21/business/worldbusiness/21arabfood.html?_r=1&scp=1&sq=MidEast%20Faces%20Choice%20Betwen%20Crops%20Water%20Andrew%20Martin&st=cse.

102. Christopher Hencke argues that irrigated agriculture, like other complex systems of social and material networks, can be understood as an institutional ecology in which actors may pursue "repair" strategies to reinforce and protect established meanings and boundaries, or challenge them, reframing problems in terms of existing hierarchies and power relations. *Cultivating Science, Harvesting Power: Science and Industrial Agriculture in California* (Cambridge, Mass.: MIT Press).

103. For the increasingly important role played by independent newspapers and parliamentarians in environmental activism, see Sharif Elmusa and Jeannie Sowers, "Damietta Mobilizes for Its Environment," *Middle East Report Online*, 21 October 2009, http://www.merip.org/mero/mero102109.html.

Bibliography

Abdulaziz, Abdulaziz M., J. Jose, M. Murtado, and R. Al-Douri. "Application of Multitemporal Landsat Data to Monitor Land Cover Changes in the Eastern Nile Delta Region, Egypt." *International Journal of Remote Sensing* 30, no. 11 (2009): 2977–96.

Al Serougi, Karima. "The Minister of Irrigation Announces Groundwater Land for Sale in Toshka in the Coming Month." *Al Akhbar,* 2 July 2002. Arabic.

Allen, Tony. *The Middle East Water Question: Hydropolitics and the Global Economy.* London: I. B. Tauris, 2001.

Alterman, Jon. *Egypt and American Foreign Assistance, 1952–1962: Hopes Dashed.* New York: Palgrave Macmillan, 2002.

American Chamber of Commerce in Egypt. *The South Valley Development Project.* Cairo: American Chamber of Commerce, 1998.

Antar, Elias. "Farming by the Nile: Egypt." *Saudi Aramco World* 29, no. 3 (1978).

"Arabs Pledge 1.6 Billion in Soft Loans." *Cairo Times,* 29 April 1999.

Apiku, Simon. "Wafd Set for Head-on Collision with State." *Middle East Times,* 15 February 1999, 9.

Arab Centre for Political and Economic Studies. "Seminar on Land Reclamation and Exploitation in the United Arab Republic." Cairo: Al Ahram, 1958.

Ayubi, Nazih. *The State and Public Policies in Egypt since Sadat.* Reading, UK: Ithaca Press, 1991.

Bush, Ray. *Civil Society and the Uncivil State: Land Tenure Reform in Egypt and the Crisis of Rural Livelihoods.* Geneva: United Nations Research Institute for Social Development, 2004.

———. "Politics, Power and Poverty: Twenty Years of Agricultural Reform and Market Liberalisation in Egypt." *Third World Quarterly* 28, no. 8 (2007): 1599–615.

Bush, Ray, and Amal Sabri. "Mining for Fish." *Middle East Report* 216 (2000). http://www.merip.org/mer/mer216_bush-sabri.html.

Chmaytelli, Maher, and Abeer Allam. "Pharaonic Pump Sits Idle as Egypt Fails to Lure Investors to the Desert." *Bloomberg L.P.,* 19 February 2008.

de Châtel, Francesca. *Water Sheikhs and Dam Builders: Stories of People and Water in the Middle East.* New Brunswick, N.J.: Transaction, 2007.

Desert Development Center. *Institutional Framework for Alleviating Poverty and Preventing Land Degradation in Egypt's New Lands.* Cairo: American University in Cairo, 2003.

De-Shalit, Avner. "From the Political to the Objective: The Dialectics of Zionism and the Environment." *Environmental Politics* 4, no. 1 (1995): 70–87.

"Dr. Yousef Wali Clarifies the Need to Keep the Toshka Area Free from Pollution by Insecticides," *Al Ahram,* 21 March 1998. Arabic.

"Egypt Says Rice Export Ban to Oct 2011." Reuters Africa, 21 September 2010. Last accessed 29 September 2010. http://af.reuters.com/article/investingNews/idAFJOE68K04120100921.

El-Bahr, Sahr. "Two Years of Aspirations." *Al Ahram Weekly* 17, 11 February 1999.

El Dahan, Maha. "Egypt Firm Says Investing in Sudanese Farmland." Reuters, 29 September 2009.

El-Din, Gamal Essam. "Toshka in the Crossfire." *Al Ahram Weekly* 466, 27 January 2000.

El Samman, Ali. "Toshka Is TOPs." *Al Ahram Weekly*, 9 January 2003. http://weekly.ahram.org.eg/2003/620/ec2.htm.

El Shakry, Omnia S. *The Great Social Laboratory: Subjects of Knowledge in Colonial and Postcolonial Egypt*. Stanford: Stanford University Press, 2007.

Elarabawy, Mohsen, Bayoumy Attia, and Paul Tosswell. "Integrated Water Resources Management for Egypt." *Journal of Water Supply, Research, and Technology-Aqua* 49, no. 3 (2000): 111–25.

Elarabawy, Mohsen, and Paul Tosswell. "An Appraisal of the Southern Valley Development Project in Egypt." *Journal of Water Supply, Research, and Technology-Aqua* 47, no. 4 (1998): 172.

Elmusa, Sharif, and Jeannie Sowers. "Damietta Mobilizes for Its Environment." *Middle East Report Online*, 21 October 2009. http://www.merip.org/mero/mero102109.html.

Ford, Neil. "Greening Egypt's Desert." *Middle East* 330 (2003): 42–46.

General Authority for Investment, Arab Republic of Egypt. *Agribusiness: A Value Proposition*. Cairo: General Authority for Investment, 2008.

———. *The South Valley Development Project*. Cairo: General Authority for Investment, 1997.

GreenCom. "Water Scarcity Campaign Targets Egyptian Farmers." *Human Nature* 2, no. 2 (1997). http://www.greencom.org/greencom/pdf/Hnenaug97.pdf.

Hajer, Maarten A. *The Politics of Environmental Discourse: Ecological Modernization and the Policy Process*. New York: Clarendon Press, 1995.

Harvey, David. "The Environment of Justice." In *Living with Nature: Environmental Politics as Cultural Discourse*, edited by Frank Fisher and Maarten A. Hajer, 159. New York: Oxford University Press, 1999.

Hencke, Christopher. *Cultivating Science, Harvesting Power: Science and Industrial Agriculture in California*. Cambridge, Mass.: MIT Press, 2008.

Hereher, Mohamed El-Desoky. "Monitoring Spatial and Temporal Changes of Agricultural Lands in the Nile Delta and Their Implications of Soil Characteristics Using Remote Sensing." PhD diss., University of Arizona, 2006.

Hoekstra, A. Y., and P. Q. Hung. "Globalisation of Water Resources: International Virtual Water Flows in Relation to Crop Trade." *Global Environmental Change* 15, no. 1 (2005): 45–56.

Ismail, Ayman. "Private Equity and Venture Capital." PhD diss., MIT, 2009.

Johnston, Cynthia. "Egypt's Citadel to Invest $200–$400 Million in 2010." Reuters, 29 September 1999.

Kamil, Sa'ad. "Toshka … And Democracy." *Al-Akhbar*, 7 February 1999. Arabic.

Khafagi, Medhat. "The Kings of Business and the Toshka Project." *Al-Wafd*, 9 April 1999. Arabic.

Khalil, Nevine. "A New Life in the South." *Al Ahram Weekly*, 18 February 1999.

Kishk, Mohamed A. "Poverty and Land Degradation: Prospects and Constraints for Sustainable Land Use in Rural Egypt." Minia: Department of Agriculture, Minia University, undated.

Lynch, Mark. *Voices of the New Arab Public: Iraq, Al-Jazeera, and Middle East Politics Today.* New York: Columbia University Press, 2006.
Martin, Andrew. "Mideast Facing a Choice between Crops and Water." *New York Times,* 21 July 2008. http://www.nytimes.com/2008/07/21/business/worldbusiness/21arabfood.html?_r=1&scp=1&sq=MidEast%20Faces%20Choice%20Betwen%20Crops%20Water%20Andrew%20Martin&st=cse.
Means, Thomas H. *Reclamation of Alkali Lands in Egypt as Adapted to Similar Work in the United States.* Bureau of Soils, Department of Agriculture, Bulletin No. 21. Washington, D.C.: Government Printing Office, 1903.
Meyer, Guenter. "The Impact of Liberalization and Privatization on the Agricultural Sector in Egypt." In *Economic Liberalization and Privatization in Socialist Arab Countries,* edited by H. Hopfinger. Nahost and Nordafrika: Studien zu Politik und Wirtschaft, Neuerer Geschichte, Geographie und Gesellschaft 1, 1996.
Ministry of Planning. *State Development Plan for 1999–2000.* Cairo: Ministry of Water Resources and Irrigation, 1999.
Ministry of Water Resources and Irrigation. *West Delta Water Conservation and Irrigation Rehabilitation Project: Draft Resettlement Policy Framework.* Cairo: Ministry of Water Resources and Irrigation, 2007.
Mitchell, Timothy. "America's Egypt: Discourse of the Development Industry." *Middle East Report* 169 (1991): 18–36.
———. *Colonising Egypt.* Berkeley: University of California Press, 1991.
———. "Object of Development." In *Rule of Experts: Egypt, Techno-politics, Modernity.* Berkeley: University of California Press, 2002.
Molle, Francois, Peter Mollinga, and Philippus Wester. "Hydraulic Bureaucracies and the Hydraulic Mission: Flows of Water, Flows of Power." *Water Alternatives* 2, no. 3 (2009): 328–49.
Moneim, Mohamed Abdel. "The Battle of Toshka." *Roz al-Yusuf,* 25 January 1999. Arabic.
Nafie, Ibrahim. "A Pioneering Spirit." *Al Ahram Weekly* 10, 29 January 1998.
Noeman, Rachel. "Egypt Pours Money into Desert Reclamation." Reuters News Service, 17 January 2000. http://www.planetark.org/avantgo/daily-newsstory.cfm?newsid=9340.
Pollard, Vic. "Planned Merger Fails for Bakersfield, Calif., Farming Company and Saudi Firm." *Bakersfield Californian,* 12 July 2002.
Reem, Laila. "Water Matters." *Al Ahram Weekly* (July 30–August 5, 2009). http://weekly.ahram.org.eg/print/2009/958/eg2.htm.
Rifaat, Asem. "Excellent Toshka." *Al Ahram Al Iqtisadi* (1999). Arabic.
Said, Rushdi. *Science and Politics in Egypt: A Life's Journey.* Cairo: American University in Cairo Press, 2004.
Salem, Mahoud. "Ask Them! The Opposition Requests the Government to Pile Up the Dirt on the Toshka Project." *Akhbar Al-Yom,* 16 January 1999. Arabic.

Sami, Aziza. "Big Boost for Toshka." *Al Ahram Weekly*, 24 September 1998. http://www.ahram.org.eg/weekly/1998/396/ec2.htm.
Scott, James. *Seeing Like a State*. New Haven: Yale University Press, 1999.
Selby, Jan. *Water, Power, and Politics in the Middle East: The Other Israeli-Palestinian Conflict*. London: I. B. Tauris, 2003.
Serwer, Andy. "The Prince of Tech Investors." *Fortune* 40, no. 11 (1999): 116.
"South Valley Company for Development Born Huge." *Akhbar Al-Yom*, 17 April 1999. Arabic.
Springborg, Robert. *Family, Power, and Politics in Egypt*. Philadelphia: University of Pennsylvania Press, 1982.
Stanley, Daniel Jean, and Andrew Warne. "Nile Delta in Its Destruction Phase." *Journal of Coastal Research* 14, no. 3 (1998): 794–825.
"Sun World Agricultural Operations: Cadiz' Partnership in Southern Egypt," 2001, http://www.cadizinc.com/b/b3.htm; "Cadiz Announces Proposed Combination of Sun World with Kingdom Agricultural Development Company (KADCO)," 15 January 2002, http://www.cadizinc.com/a/articles/Jan16–02.html.
Tarabili, Abbas. "The Toshka Project: Violating the Constitution and the Law!" *Al-Wafd*, 14 November 1999. Arabic.
"Toshka Project—Mubarak Pumping Station/ Sheikh Zayed Canal, Egypt," http://www.water-technology.net/projects/mubarak/specs.html.
United Arab Republic. *The New Valley*. Cairo: Maslahat al-Isti'lamat, 1964.
Van Achthoven, Ton, Zohra Merabet, Karim S. Shalaby, and Frank van Steenbergen. "Balancing Productivity and Environmental Pressure in Egypt." Agriculture and Rural Development Working Paper #13, World Bank. Washington, D.C., 2004.
Voll, Sarah P. "Egyptian Land Reclamation Since the Revolution." *Middle East Journal* 34, no. 2 (1980): 127–48.
Wahish, Niveen. "Marketing Toshka." *Al Ahram Weekly*, 16–22 February 2006.
Waterbury, John. *The Egypt of Nasser and Sadat: The Political Economy of Two Regimes*. Princeton, N.J.: Princeton University Press, 1983.
———. *Hydropolitics of the Nile Valley*. Syracuse, N.Y.: Syracuse University Press, 1979.
———. *The Nile Basin: National Determinants of Collective Action*. New Haven: Yale University Press, 2002.
Wichelns, Dennis. "Moving Water to Move People: Evaluating Success of the Toshka Project in Egypt." *Water International* 28 no. 1 (2003): 52–56.
Woertz, Eckart. "Outward Agricultural FDI by GCC Countries." Dubai: UNCTAD, 2009.
Woertz, Eckart, Samir Pradhan, Nermina Biberovic, and Chan Jingzhong. *Potential for GCC Agro-Investments in Africa and Central Asia*. Dubai: Gulf Research Center, 2008.

Woertz, Eckart, Samir Pradhan, Nermina Biberovic, and Christian Koch. *Food Inflation in the GCC Countries.* Dubai: Gulf Research Center, 2008.

World Food Programme. "Settlement on Newly Developed Land in Upper Egypt." Cairo, 1996.

World Population Prospects Database, United Nations Department of Economic and Social Affairs, Population Division, http://esa.un.org/unpp/p2kodata.asp.

Yakoub, Nagy G. R., and Mona El Kady. "Using GIS for Planning and Water Management of the Southern Egypt Development Project." Unpublished report, 1998.

Zerubavel, Yael. "The Conquest of the Desert and the Settlement Ethos." In *The Desert Experience in Israel: Communities, Arts, Science, and Education in the Negev,* edited by Paul Hare and Gideon Kressel, 33–44. Lanham, Md.: University Press of America, 2009.

CHAPTER 7

Salts, Soils, and (Un)Sustainabilities?

Analyzing Narratives of Environmental Change in Southeastern Turkey

Leila M. Harris

SEVERAL THOUSAND years after salinization led to the abandonment of irrigated agriculture among the early settlements of upper Mesopotamia, irrigation is emerging anew.[1] With a host of technologies now available, and careful monitoring of soil and water conditions, planners and scientists are hopeful that a similar fate for contemporary irrigation efforts can be avoided and that emergent agro-ecologies will be "sustainable" now and into the future. Irrigation is a key component of the massive GAP project (Southeastern Anatolia Project), referred to by Turkish planners as an "integrated regional sustainable development program."[2] Guarding such optimism, major issues of concern have captured the attention of the international scientific community. Indeed, preliminary evidence suggests that salinization, soil erosion and degradation, and agricultural pests are all possible issues that might point to the potential "unsustainability" of irrigated agriculture in this context.

This chapter maps diverse environmental imaginaries connected to irrigation-related changes under way in Turkey's Southeastern Anatolia region. Although some attention is given to scientific imaginaries and assessments, the focus is on local voices and interpretations of irrigation-related changes. How are ongoing changes and key threats to sustainability for irrigation variously narrated, assessed, and attributed? What is the significance of the multiplicity of assessments and narratives of change that circulate in the region, and more broadly? Bringing scientific evaluations of ongoing changes together with narratives invoked by those living and working in the region, my aim is to analyze the diverse, contested, *and convergent* environmental imaginaries related to change in southeastern Turkey in the contemporary moment. In brief, while many other works have sought to highlight local narratives in order to counter top-down scientific or state knowledges,[3] here I consider why might it be meaningful to analyze diverse narratives relationally rather than positing them as distinct or even oppositional (based on positionality, situatedness, or some other typology). My argument is that there is value in thinking through diverse environmental imaginaries by paying close attention to their multiplicity, their tensions, as well as their key resonances. Mapping out and thinking through key points of *divergence and convergence* bring out novel possibilities for understanding how and why narratives are invoked, how they might be strategically deployed given a particular contextual field, and how various environmental imaginaries are constituted (or contested) as hegemonic in particular times and places.

Contributing to a wider field of interest on environmental imaginaries, here I emphasize a narrative approach that calls attention to stories that are told about environmental issues, allowing analysis of ways that changes are attributed as positive or negative, or of the ways that environmental conditions are often discussed in relation to other issues—highlighting the embeddedness of environmental issues in broader power relations, histories, and contexts.[4] Thus, a narrative approach shares focus of work on "environmental imaginaries" in that both highlight meanings and systems of signification related to environmental issues, including how those imaginaries are mobilized in environmental politics. Within this broader framework, a focus on narrative calls particular attention to the plot and story-line of stories that circulate, including issues of attribution and causality. Who is positioned as causing observed changes? Who is to blame for the change? And by extension, who or what might be called for to overcome or respond to particular environmental conditions? Do particular story-lines enroll well-known plots that may hold meaning in a particular context, or replicate familiar notions of who the heroes or victims might be?[5] Tracking narratives of change also enables consideration of how various actors may situate their own understandings against broader environmental imaginaries. Do various actors accept hegemonic environmental imaginaries and fit their stories within a given plot and set of actors? Do they tell stories in order to contest those imaginaries, and thus, to contest the power relations that might inhere in them? As this chapter makes clear, stories we tell about environments are not always easily predictable but rather need to be assessed, evaluated, and understood in relation to key contextual issues—whether identity politics or in relation to key political-economic, cultural, or other historical-contextual issues.[6]

It is critical to underscore that an interest in environmental imaginaries and narratives is somewhat distinct from attempts to assess the "truth" of changes under way, or to validate the veracity of one claim over another. Regardless of whether stories are "accurate," they are nevertheless important for conditioning responses and mitigation strategies, future environmental conditions, or potential for sustainability. Indeed, I argue that meanings and associations of changes assigned by those who transform, negotiate, and interpret environments on a daily basis are as crucial for agro-ecological sustainability, if not more so, than understanding the contours of changing agro-ecological conditions themselves.[7] To make this case, the analysis provided pays particular attention to divergences and convergences between environmental narratives and emphasizes contextual factors that may help account for this complex mapping. Specifically, I argue that narratives of environmental change in evidence cannot be understood without an appreciation of broader geographical imaginaries that hold importance for this region—whether they be imaginaries related to the Kurdish southeast that has been forgotten as part of Turkish modernization efforts, or imaginaries related to the need for Turkey to "catch up" to the West that have been present since before the establishment of the Turkish republic in 1923 and remain salient today as frequent refrains in ongoing debates related to possibilities for Turkish accession to the European Union.

Before launching into the case study, a few additional notes on the context of southeastern Turkey may be helpful. The southeast region, a border region between Turkey, Syria, and Iraq, is one of Turkey's most impoverished areas. It is also inhabited by several of Turkey's significant minority populations, including Kurdish and Arabic speakers. This part of the country has also been at the center of several decades of intense conflict, largely associated with Kurdish separatist movements and state response. There are many other features of the region that are notable;[8] however, these brief notes highlight a few key features of the context that will be further elaborated below. I now turn to a treatment of diverse narrations of change in the region and more generally, beginning with the ways that

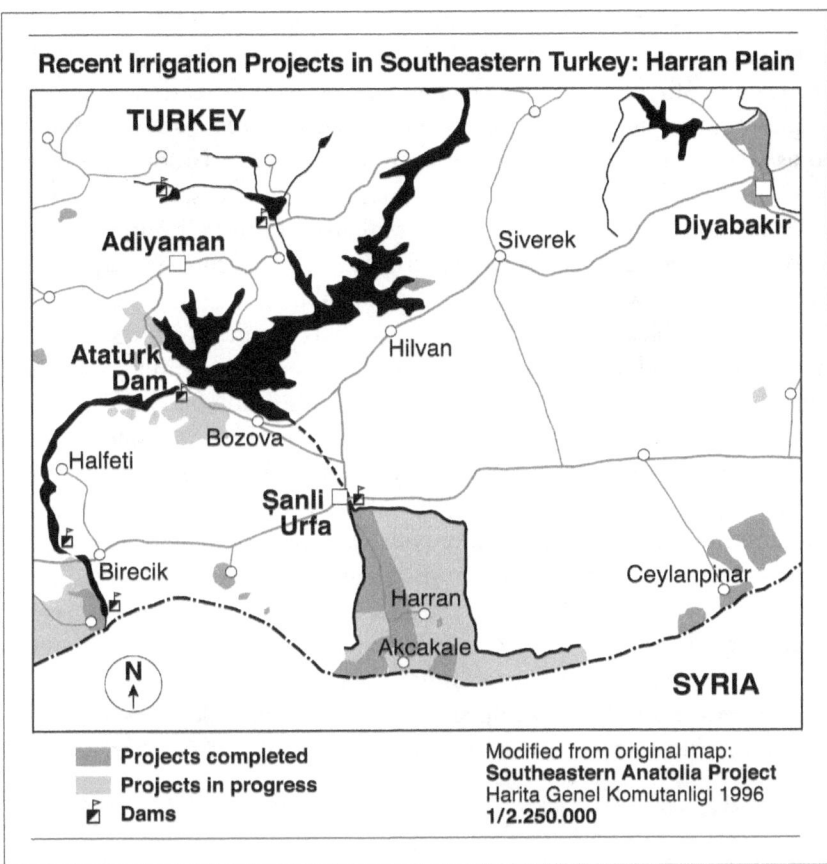

Map 7.1. The Harran Plain, pilot irrigation area for the Southeastern Anatolia Project (GAP). Modified from original map in *Southeastern Anatolia Project* (Ankara: Harita Genel Komutanligi, 1996).

ongoing changes have been discussed and attributed by scientists, then turning to narrations and understandings more common to those living and working in the affected region.

Contested and Multiple Environmental Imaginaries: Divergent Narratives of Change, and Assessing Sustainabilities through Science

In the first decade since irrigation implementation in the Harran plain in the 1990s (see map 7.1), it is estimated that salinization has already forced retirement of as much of 15 percent of agricultural lands, most notably in the plain's southern reaches.[9] Exacerbating such trends, the cropping pattern is now estimated to be 90 percent cotton, leading to difficulties associated with near monocropping, and also issues specific to cotton as an input-intensive crop (see figure 7.1). The overapplication of irrigation water has further contributed to salinization as well as soil erosion and degradation. Given the topography of the plain, this has also led to the creation of pools of stagnant water in many villages during the irrigation season (referred to as lakes, see figure 7.2), contributing to increased risk of malaria and other water-related diseases. Understanding these issues, among others,[10] is clearly critical for any attempt to evaluate future irrigation potential, associated health risks, livelihood securities, or other concerns commonly brought to light with evaluations of "sustainability."

It is notable, however, that even with recognition of these issues, many planning documents and scientific assessments maintain a spirit of optimism with respect to the potential for the sustainability of irrigation in the region. In an evaluation of water use based on remotely sensed data Mutlu Ozdoğan writes of the need to decrease rates of evaporation in future projects: "Incorporating this decrease in overall planning of the irrigation projects currently under construction should lead to improved management [and], by extension, sustainability of water resources in the region."[11] Analysis of this type recognizes vulnerabilities of the region related to histories of irrigation, soil conditions, topography, and even climate change, yet remains optimistic about the potential of engaging science and technology to improve outcomes and avoid worsening degradation. University economists Fikret Adaman and Gokhan Özertan

Figure 7.1. Cotton bales brought back to a village following harvest in the Harran plain. *Photo by Leila M. Harris.*

Figure 7.2. Rising groundwater due to heavy application of irrigation water forms "lakes" such as this in many villages in the southern part of the Harran plain, inundating houses and posing health risks from stagnant water. *Photo by Leila M. Harris.*

similarly provide a comprehensive treatment of threats to sustainability in irrigated areas of the GAP region from a socioeconomic perspective, pointing to difficulties associated with virtual monocropping of cotton, the lack of price signals to discourage overuse of irrigation water, and the inadequacy of furrow irrigation techniques, among other factors.[12] Nevertheless, they suggest that with the proper education of farmers, water pricing, incentives for crop diversification, the establishment of democratic water-user associations, and modernization of irrigation techniques, many of these issues can be countered. Although these types of assessments offered by independent scientists are less rosy than the pictures often painted by GAP planners and government agents,[13] they still share an identifiable story line: degradation is occurring, yet, better understanding and science together with adaptation of new technology can minimize threats to sustainability and improve success of such projects over the long term. Consequences of this shared story-line are to validate several related interlinked efforts: to observe, monitor, and assess ongoing changes, to implement improved technology, and to teach farmers or provide incentives to conduct appropriate farming to achieve sustainability. This story thus validates a strong role for the scientific community and for the Turkish state as entities that must continue to monitor conditions and encourage particular changes.

Fixities of Place: Sociocultural Attributes and Unsustainable Farming Practice

Although sharing similarities with scientific assessments, somewhat different narratives circulate among actors living and working in the Southeastern Anatolia region. In an interview with sociologists at the GAP administration regional offices in Urfa, one state agent explained ongoing difficulties related to irrigation adoption in the plain:[14] "The people there used to be nomads, and then they earned a living as seasonal workers, picking cotton in Çukurova. No pre-study has been carried out about the people of Harran and how they will adapt to living with water. Before they didn't even have drinking water, now they have (irrigation) water and they can grow their own cotton. However, they are not prepared to live with water, and to earn big money."

In this narrative, residents of the Harran plain are portrayed as facing difficulties with irrigation, unable to adapt to new conditions. In the same meeting, it was noted that local people "don't change easily; it is not clear how this will proceed." Another said, "They don't want to change. One reason might be that they have doubts toward the state, since the state never brought them any service prior to the water development projects." In another conversation, a state engineer summed up the obstacles related to crop diversification this way: "People know how to grow cotton; they are not eager to learn any new crop, and this shows how closed the society is to change." In all such statements, emphasis is given to the idea that farmers are resistant or unable to change, even as recognition is given that this might stem from skepticism toward the state. In narratives of this type, threats to sustainability are attributed to the people or cultures of the region. Following such logic, if sustainability is not achieved, it can be readily attributed to the obstinacy or the ignorance of the local farmers. Such narratives of change (and the inability of farmers themselves to change) are necessarily read through long histories of inequality between the Turkish state and the Kurdish and Arabic-speaking populations in the southeast region. Thus, the way that these issues are narrated is as much about cultural politics as it is about environmental conditions or irrigation technologies.[15] Narratives along these lines also clearly demonstrate consistencies with "expert" and "state" narratives that have been evaluated in other contexts, "blaming" local populations and attributing degradation to local culture or livelihood practices.[16]

Another narrative of degradation that is fairly common relates environmental problems to high percentages of sharecropping among farmers, which is directly linked to high rates of landlessness. State agents, technicians, and landowners explain that because sharecroppers do not own the land, they have no interest in maintaining long-term soil productivity or in learning appropriate irrigation techniques. As one state agent explained, referring to sharecroppers, "They don't have the initiative to implement a new program for the land." As part of such explanations, the fact that sharecroppers often farm different land parcels from year to year is invoked to demonstrate that they have little investment and interest in protecting the soil and mitigating further damage.

Related to these discourses, outreach efforts of state extension agents currently focus on "teaching" local farmers, for instance, by telling them to use less water, or by investing in demonstration farms to show farmers the value of planting orchards, tomatoes, or other crops. These portrayals and policy directives often cast farmers inter alia as practicing inappropriate agriculture, having insufficient knowledge, or suffering from illiteracy or other conditions that might impede sustainable agricultural potential. In a focus group of irrigation engineers employed at irrigation unions similar ideas were reinforced. The engineers note, for instance, that not knowing any better, farmers add water in excess of what is needed to grow the crops, leading to degradation.[17] In other narratives, the overreliance on cotton was directly connected to high rates of illiteracy among farmers.

Although sociocultural obstacles and farmer illiteracy are often blamed for inappropriate farming, narratives also frequently emphasize the know-how and good intentions of the state. For instance, one irrigation extension agent said: "We tell people the aim of the project. Our aim is to invest in people, to benefit from natural and human resources in the best way. However, because of wrong irrigation practices, the most fertile layers of soil are degraded and carried to Syria. Four hundred years are required for the formation of a one-centimeter-thick layer of fertile soil. What we are trying to do is implement sustainable use of water resources."

With this statement, the planner asserts his own scientific understanding of soil fertility, suggesting that state agents have the knowledge to make "sustainable use of water resources" possible. Here it is of interest not only that farmers lack the knowledge of appropriate farming or familiarity with science, but that the state in general, and irrigation engineers in particular, would be able to achieve sustainability were it not for this deficit. Through a litany of similar statements encoded in state planning documents and conveyed in interviews, the kernel that is common to these narratives is that again *sustainability is possible* and could be achieved through further reliance on state agents or investment in scientific knowledge and practices.

On the flip side, lack of agricultural knowledge, landlessness, and illiteracy are all discursively linked to *un*sustainabilities, connecting contemporary environmental imaginaries to long histories and policies related to sociocultural attributes of this "backward" region dominated by Kurdish and Arabic speakers.[18]

It is important to note that farmers too echo such narratives, for instance highlighting their own ignorance or identifying the need for more farmer training, illustrating that these narratives are not exclusive to state agents and scientists.[19] This type of hybridized knowledge is of particular interest, both to illustrate that farmer and state knowledges are not discrete categories[20] as well as to consider how hegemonic environmental imaginaries are consolidated, in part through support, iteration, and buy-in from diverse agents.

Although some farmers reinforce these narratives, others expressly contest such framings, demonstrating awareness that their knowledge of farming and irrigation is actively questioned. Consider the statement made by an Arabic-speaking farmer in the southern reaches of the Harran plain.

> Many agricultural engineers and others come to talk with us about water use, fertilizer, etc. . . . but every farmer is as knowledgeable as an engineer right now. The engineers just study with the books in his hand, but we, the farmers, live with the soil. So, we know better than the engineer what the soil needs.

Quite apart from commonly accepted framings of sustainability as contingent on soil or water conditions, these narratives clearly affirm that "environmental politics are always entangled with a cultural politics of knowing,"[21] with contestations over what constitutes appropriate knowledge, or farming, at the core.

Farmer's Narrations: Recognizing Change and Complex Drivers

> What is needed is to ensure that the irrigation lasts a long time. I don't know how many years the state has assumed for this irrigation system to last, but I expect that it will be fifty years. Then we will see what will happen. There is a lack of infrastructure, such as drainage canals. Also, the slope of the canalets is incorrect in some places, creating places where the water flows over. (Subyan, irrigation technician and farmer)

This quotation, by a rural resident employed as an irrigation technician for one of the irrigation unions, provides a worthwhile starting point to consider narratives of environmental change more common to rural residents living in the plain. Subyan accepts that irrigated agriculture in the plain may have finite possibilities. Consistent with other assessments already noted, yet in contrast to the idea that farmers need to be told that degradation is occurring, rural residents demonstrate considerable recognition of environmental degradation occurring with irrigation implementation. A strong majority of survey respondents identified issues related to agricultural pests, soil erosion, rising ground water, salinization, and other issues as problems in their village (over 65 percent of survey respondents identified these issues). Validating claims made by engineers, farmers also generally recognize environmental degradation associated with overreliance on cotton and heavy irrigation application. For instance, Subyan (the same technician quoted above) explained that at first farmers applied excessive irrigation water. Noticing their harvest didn't do well, that the fields degraded, and the groundwater table rose, he explained, farmers responded by applying less and requesting that drainage canals be installed. Despite these changes, Subyan notes that problems persist.

In terms of other convergences between narratives, one village headman echoed statements made by several state agents, blaming cotton monocropping on farmers' illiteracy. He said, "It is because of the farmers' illiteracy that they only plant cotton since 1997." In the next breath, however, he added, "It is a problem though because the state lends support when you plant cotton," thereby relating another cause for heavy reliance on cotton production among farmers—state crop subsidies. At the time of initial research, the state provided both a nine-cent per kilo subsidy for cotton (U.S. dollar terms, in 2001) and support for cotton-related pesticides, not necessarily available for other crops. In repeated interviews with state agents the issue of state subsidies for cotton was offered unprompted only once, and this was off the record. By contrast, when farmers spoke about environmental changes in the plain, the issue of state subsidies was noted readily. When a DSİ (State Hydraulic Works) engineer was asked directly about the subsidy, he noted: "The subsidy for cotton is a political issue. The government says it does not want people to grow cotton here but still provides the subsidy; they should change this; I'm not sure why they do it."

In terms of the implications of the subsidy, it was mentioned at several points that the predominance of cotton is a result of state support, and without it, some mentioned they would prefer to grow wheat or some other less demanding crop. One farmer complained, "The state only gives us support for cotton, so we grow only cotton." Another explained, "Surely, the subsidy becomes a secondary income for cotton. We don't receive subsidy for any other crop. . . . [Also] cotton is better because it is useful to the country's economy." These and similar statements clearly attribute predominance of cotton not to the ignorance of the farmers but to specific state policies.[22] As such, these stories offer different dimensions to assessments of emergent irrigated agro-ecologies of the plain. With respect to cotton pesticide subsidies, one farmer noted: "We don't have white fly or green worm this year, but nearby villages are struggling with it . . . the state gives us 30 percent toward the bill for pesticides associated with cotton. . . . We don't like pesticides if there are not too many pests because it destroys 5 to 10 percent of the product and decreases the harvest." Not only are subsidies encouraging cotton production, they are also contributing to the use of certain pesticides, with the implicit suggestion that this is how appropriate agriculture is practiced.

With respect to multiscalar considerations, these types of statements made by farmers clearly connect their local practices (e.g., crop choice or pesticide use) to state practices, as well as to scales and notions of nationalist belonging (e.g., the idea of benefiting the national economy through cotton production). As such, although perhaps counterintuitive, it is interesting to note that themes among narratives offered by rural residents tend to situate changes under way within wider fields of political, economic, and ecological processes, offering a challenge to what is meant by "local knowledges." By contrast, a number of the portrayals by state agents tended to fix these problems geographically, defining them in terms of particularities of place (e.g., in relation to local sociocultural attributes or soil characteristics).[23] Such tendencies further challenge neat binaries separating local from expert knowledge, particularly confounding common scalar and spatial associations with each.

Exploring diverse narratives of ongoing changes provides some initial insights to enrich our understanding of the complex issues at play with respect to crop choice, water use, changing soil conditions, and other key dimensions of environmental change in Turkey's southeast. The issues that come to light by evaluating diverse narrations of change clearly displace attention from the need to convince farmers to grow other crops (and to explain to farmers why monocropping is detrimental, as many state agents and independent scientists suggest), to the need to more actively encourage other types of agro-industrial investment or create flexible scheduling arrangements to enable alternative cropping choices.[24] Juxtaposing these narratives, which highlights certain points of tension and overlap, also reaffirms other research that has suggested that that categories of local, farmer, or state knowledge are much more elusive and hybridized than we may assume. Although it might appear that previous sections have replicated artificial separations between categories of state, expert, or local knowledge, in the next section I consider hybridities and elisions across these categories more fully. Part of the purpose of the next section is also to consider broader geographical and environmental imaginaries through which these narratives must be understood and evaluated.

Multiple and Overlapping Narratives: Toward Understanding Divergences and Convergences

To some, reading the above sections might seem frustratingly familiar—many others have convincingly brought local knowledges to bear to enrich understanding of socioecological changes, for instance drawing on farmers' or herders' knowledge to contest statist narratives of peasant backwardness,[25] or drawing on historical and ecological data to correct biases inherent in colonial environmental narratives.[26] Resonant with studies of this type, the work here validates that attention to diverse and contested knowledges is crucial in assessing environmental or developmental changes. As I have shown, without incorporating multiple knowledges, and especially local knowledges, an understanding of potential for (un)sustainabilities of irrigated agriculture is at best incomplete, and at worst misdirected. Without considering how farmers assess and narrate these issues, the state is likely to continue misdirected policies of "teaching" appropriate agriculture, without considering marketing, state subsidies, or other key issues. My goal is to move beyond these insights. I ask: What can be gained by more fully considering diverse environmental imaginaries relationally, focusing on the complex interplay, and points of *convergence and divergence* between different narratives of environmental change? How might evaluation of environmental imaginaries not only provide insight related to environmental conditions or changes but also provide valuable lenses through which to better understand the broader sociocultural or economic context in which environmental imaginaries are necessarily embedded, especially power dynamics across scales?

The analysis above reveals that there are indeed key points of divergence across the narratives of change, only some of which might be anticipated by positionality of the actors. More important, I argue, there are also key *convergences* and shared elements across the narratives that also require attention. Although situated knowledge approaches appear to suggest an infinite array of possibilities,[27] I am suggesting here that it is crucial also to explicitly theorize key convergences among environmental knowledges and imaginaries. How and why do certain elements of plot, story-line, or attribution hold together across narratives from diverse actors, or why do narratives tend to diverge in some ways, but not others? What do these convergences and divergences suggest with respect to the range and scope of environmental imaginaries that might be possible in particular times and places? And relatedly, how do different actors reinforce or contest elements of familiar or hegemonic environmental imaginaries?

Across the narratives from southeastern Turkey, notable convergences include the fact that most people living and working in the region recognize that considerable degradation is under way—awareness of the issues is not lacking. Another key convergence that is perhaps more illuminating is that even with this widespread recognition, few if any of those living and working in the region appear to question the suitability of irrigated agriculture in this context. Indeed, for most, irrigation is long overdue, and any problems relate mostly to the need to continue implementation (e.g., with land leveling and drainage). Across diverse imaginaries, sustainability is maintained as *possible,* even if there are significant hurdles to be overcome in getting there (whether implementing new technologies, getting the prices right, or teaching farmers). As such, the evidence from southeastern Turkey appears to validate insights offered elsewhere[28] whereby farmers do not cast off technoscientific interventions as inappropriate for local lifeways or as ecologically devastating,[29] but rather they insist on the need for continued engagement with technoscientific approaches. It is particularly striking that even initial evidence related to environmental degradation is not taken as a reason to question the appropriateness of statist or technoscientific interventions. The opposite appears to be true—narratives reveal that farmers *and* state agents engage the evidence of environmental degradation to argue for *more* technoscience,[30] and *more* state intervention, *not less.* This convergence across narratives reveals an intriguing puzzle: Why is it that precisely when there is broad recognition of losses and degradation associated with irrigated agricultural implementation that those living and working in the region appear to valorize and retrench technoscientific and statist solutions and approaches?

Unlikely Convergences: Recognizing Degradation yet Valorizing Technoscience?

The widespread valorization of technoscientific approaches, of irrigation, and of state implementation invites further elaboration, even if only speculative. Unlike other accounts of similar processes,[31] farmers and state agents in this region do not appear to long for a return to traditional livelihoods prior to irrigation.[32] Further, as noted, the evidence of degradation is not taken to question the appropriateness of irrigated agriculture or to challenge state practices and development efforts in the region (over 80 percent of respondents assess irrigation-related changes as "very positive" or "positive," in contrast to less than 10 percent of respondents who consider changes to be "very negative" or "negative").[33] Instead, farmers in the Harran plain request new and better seeds, more effective pesticides, irrigation training, land leveling, and drainage works—all amounting to demands for more state involvement, and more technoscientific engagement.[34]

Considered together, a foundational aspect of many narratives from southeastern Turkey is that they appear to maintain faith that the appropriate scientific knowledge is available and only needs to be more effectively conveyed and implemented. Even though degradation is observed, hegemonic and shared environmental imaginaries convey an implicit faith that the appropriate technology can, and will, be applied. Thus, a common theme is that sustainability remains possible, even if elusive for the moment. For many state agents, it is a matter of teaching appropriate techniques to farmers. For many farmers, it is a question of the state following through on land leveling, drainage works, or other applications.[35]

The convergences between lay-knowledges and state or expert opinion in this case study also raise the question of situated knowledges beyond the acknowledgment that there are diverse knowledges, dependent on social or physical location or positionality to consider what factors, processes, and relations account for, or enable, differential, and shared, environmental imaginaries and representations. For farmers in the Harran plain, many have no choice but to remain hopeful about the potential for irrigation to bring improvement to their lives. The relative poverty and underdevelopment in the region, as well as histories of Kurdish and Iraqi conflicts that have plagued the region, bring this possibility into relief.[36] The southeast has long been one of the poorest regions of the country, and these retrenched differences have long contributed to tensions between east and west in Turkey (as well as between notions of Kurd and Turk that map onto those geographies). To garner support for their cause Kurdish separatists have long invoked discourses about the southeast being "left out" of Turkish state efforts. [37]

This background may help, in part, to situate and understand why farmers in the region appear to welcome Turkish state intervention, viewing it as long overdue and perhaps even key to stemming the long-term conflict and associated problems in the region.[38] Thus, the current receptivity to state intervention may be understandable precisely given the field of conflictual relations that have existed previously, particularly given discourses that have circulated about the need for greater state attention to the southeast and for modernist development in particular. Consistent with this, after decades of conflict and the associated underdevelopment, some environmental degradation may also be understood as a small cost to pay in contrast with other costs that have been borne in the region.[39] To take this a step further, perhaps the situation is one where ongoing degradation simply cannot translate into skepticism or distrust more generally. To consider these development efforts as unsustainable or ineffective would constitute a loss of hope and even greater uncertainty about future possibilities for survival and well-being. A loss of hope might be too much to ask of a population that has suffered through decades of conflict and other hardships. In sum, the fact that the Turkish state is finally investing in modernist development in the Kurdish southeast has a great deal of symbolic value, and indeed, this symbolism may overshadow any particular evidence related to degradation associated with irrigation and associated changes.

For state agents as well, given that it was the Turkish state that implemented delivery of irrigation to the region, it is perhaps not surprising that the negative effects of irrigation are not taken as referenda on the suitability of irrigated agriculture. Thus, while farmers and state agents appear to focus on divergent obstacles to sustainable irrigated agriculture in the region, neither appears to take the evidence of degradation to mean that one should be pessimistic about irrigated agricultural potential in general.

Related to these striking convergences between narratives, it is also notable that at times while talking with residents in southeastern Turkey, irrigation and technology seem to be elevated to mythic proportions. Farmers made statements that conveyed a sense that irrigation was a change that was a long-awaited improvement in their lives. As one farmer said, "When water came to the village, life came as well. . . . [B]ut we will have to work hard. Then we will be rich, but we will need to work hard." As mentioned above, and discussed in more detail elsewhere,[40] despite many negative effects of irrigation, an overwhelming majority of farmers view irrigation on the whole very positively (with over two-thirds of farmers on the survey noting that irrigation has been either "beneficial," or "very beneficial"). Clearly, irrigation technology is taken for more than the ability to water fields and grow different crops; it is also considered to be a point of entry for other possibilities, perhaps even viewed as an opening for broader associations with modernity or wealth. Indeed, before widespread canalet irrigation in the plain, only those farmers who were already well-off were able to afford pumped irrigation water to grow cotton. As such, irrigation generally and cotton cropping specifically appear to remain symbolically linked to wealth and prestige. Thus many living and working in the region now believe that since irrigation is available to everyone, wealth and prestige will surely follow.[41] This adds yet another layer to the contextual specificities of the region that matter to how ongoing environmental changes are understood and interpreted.

These types of associations also point to the possibility that irrigation and associated technology are symbolic of modernity and rapprochement with the West. Specifically, irrigation in this region appears to symbolically transgress divides between the West and non-West, industrialized and nonindustrialized, developed and nondeveloped, or European and non-European (both within Turkey and more generally). These constellations of difference and related associations with progress and wealth have long marked Turkish cultural politics and the relative underdevelopment of the Kurdish southeast in particular. Given the centrality of these constructions to the history and geography of Turkey, and to the southeast region, the potential of these binaries to mark contemporary environmental and developmental imaginaries cannot be understated. Indeed the frequency with which these types of binaries continue to be invoked in Turkey-EU discussions only adds further to the saliency of these constructions to contextualize environmental imaginaries that circulate, and take hold, among diverse actors in the contemporary moment. Certain types of degradation may be considered the necessary price on the path to realizing certain lifestyles and systems of production more in line with those of the West.[42] In this sense, environmental imaginaries of state agents and farmers are certainly distinct but also very similar to the extent that they share identification and investment in transcending notions of West–non-West or other divides that have been so central to the histories and geographies of Turkey and of the southeast.

Toward Contextualized Understanding: Situating Environmental Imaginaries

With the analysis offered here, I have endeavored to take seriously Cronon's suggestion that we need to tell not only the stories about nature but also the stories about stories about nature.[43] While we invest millions of dollars to measure and assess biophysical dimensions of ongoing changes, calculating rates of change, or endeavoring to predict future conditions under climate change scenarios, too often we ignore the complex terrain of environmental imaginaries. From the analysis above, and from the literature generally, it is increasingly clear that rates of salinization or measurements of soil runoff hold little relevance for sustainability debates without a sense of how those changing agro-ecological conditions are understood, interpreted, negotiated, and conveyed by farmers, irrigation engineers, or others living and working in affected regions. Given the complex interpretations and meanings attached to changes in southeastern Turkey, it is clear that sustainability of irrigation is dependent on meanings attached to ongoing changes at least as much, if not more so, as it is on the soil and water characteristics of the region.[44] Further, these narratives overlap in key ways to reveal how environmental conditions and changes are necessarily inflected with meaning, symbolism, and other complex associations.

I have also argued for a contextual approach, attentive to social, cultural, and economic processes as crucial for interpreting the complex mapping of narratives and imaginaries (including their overlap and dissonance). As Proctor warns with respect to the need to more fully situate our knowledges of environments with respect to the particularities of context and in relation to the sociopolitical dimensions of knowledge production, "Alarming biophysical facts and seemingly self-evident values concerning nature do not stand outside of a social context, and that context itself must be interrogated, even in what appears to be an incontrovertible case."[45] In the case examined, we can only begin to appreciate the shared faith in technoscience, and the shared interest among actors in state involvement, when we evaluate narratives in relation to broader power dynamics, histories, and contextual issues. These include specificities regarding the Southeastern Anatolia region and the ongoing Kurdish conflict, as well as contemporary EU accession debates. As such, changing agro-ecologies in Turkey's southeast cannot be abstracted from histories of difference: West–non-West, European–non-European and industrialized–non-industrialized divides and the uneven relations of power implicit in each.

Apart from attempts to bring in local knowledges that have been the currency of political, ecological, anthropological, and developmental literatures over the past several decades, I have also argued for an analytic that explicitly theorizes key *convergences and divergences* between narratives of change. It is only by doing so that we can begin to understand the construction and consolidation of particular environmental imaginaries and their effects. The case adds force to calls to focus more precisely on the portrayals of environments themselves as objects of analysis, and what sort of insights analysis of this type might afford.[46] Among other insights, consideration of diverse narratives of change in this region offers a stark contrast to general crisis narratives, including those imaginaries that cast the Middle East as arid, water scarce, degraded, or unsuitable for agriculture. Although analysts may read ongoing degradation and unsustainabilities as suggestive of the need to abandon irrigated agriculture in this context, it is clear that this interpretation is not shared by many living and working in the region. It is only by taking seriously the seeming consensus across narratives told by scientists, state agents, and farmers that we can begin to consider the complex meanings assigned to changing conditions. In this case, notions of modernity, technoscience, and crises linked to conflict and underdevelopment together underwrite shared commitments to particular environmental imaginaries, and thus particular agro-ecological possibilities and futures.

Notes

Elements of this chapter were previously published as L. Harris, "Contested Sustainabilities: Assessing Narratives of Environmental Change in Southeastern Turkey," *Local Environment* 14, no. 8 (2009): 699–720.

1. Sandra Postel, *Pillar of Sand: Can the Irrigation Miracle Last?* New York: W. W. Norton, 1999.

2. E.g., I. H. Olcay Ünver, "Southeastern Anatolia Project (GAP)," *Water Resources Development* 13, no. 4 (1997): 453–83; I. H. Olcay Ünver, "Southeastern Anatolia Integrated Development Project (GAP), Turkey: An Overview of Issues of Sustainability," *Water Resources Development* 13, no. 2 (1997): 187–207.

3. Cf. James C. Scott, *Seeing Like a State: How Certain Schemes to Improve the Human Condition Have Failed* (New Haven: Yale University Press, 1998).

4. See Frank Fischer, *Reframing Public Policy: Discursive Politics and Deliberative Practices* (Oxford: Oxford University Press, 2003); William Cronon, "A Place for Stories," *Journal of American History* 78, no. 4 (2002): 1347–76.

5. Cf. Richard Peet and Michael Watts, *Liberation Ecologies: Environment, Development and Social Movements* (London: Routledge, 1996); Richard Cowell and Huw Thomas, "Managing Nature and Narratives of Dispossession: Reclaiming Territory in Cardiff Bay," *Urban Studies* 39, no. 7 (2002): 1241–60, in addition to the other chapters in this volume.

6. See other chapters this volume, particularly those by Alatout, Davis, and Cohen.

7. See also Saskia M. Visser, Jeannette K. Leenders, and M. Leeuwis, "Farmers' Perceptions of Erosion by Wind and Water in Northern Burkina Faso," *Land Degradation and Development* 14, no. 1 (2003): 123–32; Serge Cartier van Dissel and Jan de Graaff, "Differences between Farmers and Scientists in the Perception of Soil Erosion: A South African Case Study," *Indigenous Knowledge and Development Monitor* 6, no. 3 (1998): 8–9; William M. Adams and Elizabeth E. Watson, "Soil Erosion, Indigenous Irrigation and Environmental Sustainability, Marakwet, Kenya," *Land Degradation and Development* 14, no. 1

(2003): 109–22; and H. F. Lee and D. D. Zhang, "Perceiving Desertification from the Lay Perspective in Northern China," *Land Degradation and Development* 15, no. 6 (2004): 529–42.

8. See L. Harris, "Modernizing the Nation: Postcolonialism, (Post)Development, and Ambivalent Spaces of Difference in Southeastern Turkey," *Geoforum* 39, no. 5 (2008): 1698–1708; and Carl Dahlman, "The Political Geography of Kurdistan," *Eurasian Geography and Economics* 43, no. 4 (2002): 271–99, for more detail.

9. Mehmet Ali Çullu, Ahmet Almaca, Yüksel Şahin, and Salih Aydemir, "Application of GIS for Monitoring Salinization in the Harran Plain, Turkey," in *Proceedings of the International Conference on Sustainable Land Use and Management* (Çanakkale, Turkey, 2002), 326–31. Using satellite imagery, Çullu estimates that the salinized area doubled in the first five years since surface irrigation was introduced to the plain.

10. A longer list would include pollution risk of underground drinking water reserves, dietary changes, and concerns related to pesticide exposure among residents.

11. Mutlu Ozdoğan, "Changes in Summer Irrigated Crop Area and Water Use in Southeastern Turkey 1993 to 2002: Implications for Current Use and Future Water Resources," *Water Resources Management* 20, no. 3 (2006): 467.

12. Fikret Adaman and Gokhan Özertan, "Perceptions and Practices of Farmers towards the Salinity Problem: The Case of Harran Plain, Turkey," *International Journal of Agricultural Resources, Governance and Ecology* 6, no. 4/5 (2007): 533–51.

13. See Ünver, "Southeastern Anatolia Project (GAP)," and Ünver, "Southeastern Anatolia Integrated Development Project (GAP)," for prime examples.

14. Although I indicate statements as direct quotations, most often interviews with farmers were not recorded. Quotations were noted in field notebooks or were transcribed immediately following interviews. Interviews with state agents, by contrast, were most often recorded.

15. See L. Harris, "Water and Conflict Geographies of the Southeastern Anatolia Project," *Society and Natural Resources* 15, no. 8 (2002): 743–59 for discussion of the importance of the Kurdish question to evaluations of water related changes in this context.

16. Another example is the herders who were blamed for degradation in Morocco, as described in Diana K. Davis, "Indigenous Knowledge and the Desertification Debate: Problematising Expert Knowledge in North Africa," *Geoforum* 36, no. 4 (2005): 509–24. See similar examples from Niger in Matthew D. Turner, "No Space for Participation: Pastoralist Narratives and the Etiology of Park-Herder Conflict in Southwestern Niger," *Land Degradation and Development* 10, no. 4 (1999): 345–63. See also other chapters, this volume.

17. This is often noted especially given the relatively inexpensive access to irrigation water (approximately US$4.00 per decare for an entire season

for cotton, regardless of amount of water used). In one study of this issue conducted by agricultural economists, it was estimated that farmers apply 12 percent more than the actual amount of water needed for cotton. F. Şelli and A. Koral, *Adaptation of New Technologies and Socio-Economic Changes in the Agricultural Plains of Sanliurfa Harran Plain after Irrigation and Possible Problems* (Sanliurfa: Village Services General Management Research Institute Publication, 2000).

18. See also Harris, "Modernizing the Nation."

19. In our survey of rural households in the Harran plain nearly 83 percent of respondents noted a "problem with insufficient agricultural training and education" in their village. The vast majority of respondents, 79 percent, also noted that they had never attended an irrigation-related course or read informational materials. The 2001 survey of 124 rural households in the Harran plain was conducted cooperatively with Professor Karahan Kara of Harran University. Survey respondents included nonfarmers, such as schoolteachers. As such, participation of these respondents must be considered when evaluating responses such as the ones noted above (that they are likely not to have attended irrigation training). The survey dealt with sociocultural, economic, and environmental consequences associated with irrigated agriculture and other GAP-related changes. See L. Harris, "Water Rich, Resource Poor: Intersections of Gender, Poverty and Vulnerability in Newly Irrigated Areas of Southeastern Turkey," *World Development* 36, no. 12 (2008): 2643–62; and L. Harris, "States at the Limit: Tracing Evolving State-Society Relations in the Borderlands of Southeastern Turkey," *EJTS: European Journal of Turkish Studies* 10, no. 1 (2009): 1–19.

20. See also Akhil Gupta, *Postcolonial Developments: Agriculture in the Making of Modern India* (Durham, N.C.: Duke University Press, 1998); and Paul Robbins, "The Practical Politics of Knowing: State Environmental Knowledge and Local Political Economy," *Economic Geography* 76, no. 2 (2000): 126–44.

21. Bruce Braun and Joel Wainwright, "Nature, Poststructuralism, and Politics," in *Social Nature: Theory, Practice and Politics*, ed. Noel Castree and Bruce Braun (London: Blackwell, 2001), 41.

22. Similar processes have been documented in other contexts; for instance, Karl S. Zimmerer, "Discourses on Soil Loss in Bolivia: Sustainability and the Search for Socioenvironmental 'Middle Ground,'" in *Liberation Ecologies: Environment, Development and Social Movements*, ed. Richard Peet and Michael Watts (London: Routledge, 1996), 110–24, describes how peasants and herders are blamed for soil erosion in Bolivia, with emphasis on education to address perceived ignorance of farmers. He notes that peasants also adopt these discourses, often blaming themselves for the degradation. Similar trends are demonstrated in the GAP region, though the degree to which farmers blamed themselves was less strong than statements related to partial or incomplete state attention to particular issues (e.g., drainage works or land leveling).

23. Yet another example is that farmers often discuss marketing constraints that restrict options for what can be grown. Here again, farmers seem to be able to situate their choices within a broader political economic field. By contrast, the approach of the local research station to explore alternative crop possibilities tests crop suitability in relation to local climatic and soil conditions, seemingly abstracting these conditions from the broader context that is crucial to understand what crops might be economically viable.

24. The current system reinforces tendencies toward monoculture as the delivery schedule is largely determined by needs for cotton production. With this system, it would be very difficult for a small number of farmers to grow something other than the predominant crop.

25. E.g., Thomas J. Bassett and Donald Crummey, *African Savannas: Global Narratives and Local Knowledges of Environmental Change* (Portsmouth, N.H.: Heinemann, 2003).

26. E.g., Davis, "Indigenous Knowledge and the Desertification Debate."

27. Cf. Donna Haraway, "Situated Knowledges: The Science Question in Feminism and the Privilege of Partial Perspective," in *Simians, Cyborgs, and Women: The Reinvention of Nature* (New York: Routledge, 1991), 183–201.

28. E.g., with respect to hybridized seeds, see Lakshman Yapa, "Improved Seeds and Constructed Scarcity," in *Liberation Ecologies: Environment, Development and Social Movements,* ed. Richard Peet and Michael Watts (London: Routledge, 1996), 69–85; with respect to promotion of green revolution technologies in Ecuador, see Anthony Bebbington, "Modernization from Below: An Alternative Indigenous Development?," *Economic Geography* 69, no. 3 (1993): 274–92, and Anthony Bebbington, "Movements, Modernizations, and Markets: Indigenous Organizations and Agrarian Strategies in Ecuador," in *Liberation Ecologies: Environment, Development and Social Movements,* ed. Richard Peet and Michael Watts (London: Routledge, 1996), 86–109.

29. Cf. Arturo Escobar, *Encountering Development: The Making and Unmaking of the Third World* (Princeton: Princeton University Press, 1995); Vandana Shiva, *The Violence of the Green Revolution: Third World Agriculture, Ecology and Politics* (Penang: Third World Network, 1993).

30. Recognizing the difficulty of a term such as "technoscience," I use it here to refer to the ways that tools, practices, and techniques undertaken in the Harran plain are embedded in larger fields of technoscientific practices and principles, specifically scientific norms and principles developed from research and study across contexts that serve to underwrite the complex of changes in the southeast: from dam building on the Tigris-Euphrates to irrigation delivery and changing agricultural techniques.

31. Cf. Escobar, *Encountering Development;* Shiva, *Violence of the Green Revolution;* Scott, *Seeing Like a State.*

32. Among rural residents of the Harran plain, a notable exception might be those who previously engaged in animal husbandry and nomadism, as some

respondents did talk fondly of food and livelihoods prior to settled irrigated agriculture, and before cotton in particular (see Harris, "Water Rich, Resource Poor," for analysis along these lines).

33. See ibid. for further discussion.

34. Cf. Haripriya Rangan, "From Chipko to Uttaranchal: Development, Environment, and Social Protest in the Garhwal Himalayas, India," in *Liberation Ecologies: Environment, Development and Social Movements*, ed. Richard Peet and Michael Watts (London: Routledge, 1996), 205–26; Bebbington, "Modernization from Below"; Bebbington, "Movements, Modernizations, and Markets."

35. It is worth noting that Adams and Watson, "Soil Erosion, Indigenous Irrigation and Environmental Sustainability," draw parallel assessments from their work on irrigation in Kenya. These authors also note that while outside observers often point to soil erosion as part of broader crisis narratives to suggest that irrigation in the Marakwet region of Kenya is unsustainable, farmers of the region demonstrate very little concern in this regard. Worsening erosion is recognized by farmers and is viewed as a result of inefficient or poor application of anti-erosion methods, but not taken as evidence that problems associated with erosion or irrigation are insurmountable and should be abandoned. Farmers accept soil erosion as part of the dynamic environment in which they live and farm, and give no indication that evidence of degradation calls into question their approach to agriculture, or the suitability of irrigation in this context (see also van Dissel and de Graaff, "Differences between Farmers and Scientists in the Perception of Soil Erosion," for an example from Burkina Faso).

36. See Harris, "Modernizing the Nation"; Harris, "Water and Conflict Geographies"; Resat Kasaba, "Kurds in Turkey: A Nationalist Movement in the Making," in *Ethnopolitical Warfare: Causes, Consequences, and Possible Solutions*, ed. Daniel Chirot and Martin E. P. Seligman (Washington, D.C.: American Psychological Association, 2001), 164–77.

37. Harris, "States at the Limit."

38. See also Harris, "Modernizing the Nation," and "States at the Limit."

39. Kirisci and Winrow, "The Kurdish Question in Turkey"; Kasaba, "Kurds in Turkey."

40. Harris, "Water Rich, Resource Poor."

41. Ibid.

42. Cf. Arjun Appadurai, *Modernity at Large: Cultural Dimensions of Globalization* (Minneapolis: University of Minnesota Press, 1996); see also Harris, "Modernizing the Nation" for discussion.

43. Cronon, "Place for Stories."

44. Cf. Anita Veihe, "Sustainable Farming Practices: Ghanian Farmers' Perception of Erosion and Their Use of Conservation Measures," *Environmental Management* 25, no. 4 (2000): 393–402; A. Warren, "Land Degradation

Is Contextual," *Land Degradation and Development* 13, no. 6 (2002): 449–59; Nathan F. Sayre, "Viewpoint: The Need for Qualitative Research to Understand Range Management," *Journal of Range Management* 57, no. 6 (2004): 668–74.

45. James D. Proctor, "Solid Rock and Shifting Sands: The Moral Paradox of Saving a Socially Constructed Nature," in *Social Nature: Theory, Practice and Politics*, ed. Noel Castree and Bruce Braun (London: Blackwell, 2001), 229.

46. Cf. Andrea Nightingale, "A Feminist in the Forest: Situated Knowledges and Mixing Methods in Natural Resource Management," *Acme: An International E-journal for Critical Geographies* 2, no. 1 (2003): 77–90.

Bibliography

Adaman, Fikret, and Gokhan Özertan. "Perceptions and Practices of Farmers towards the Salinity Problem: The Case of Harran Plain, Turkey." *International Journal of Agricultural Resources, Governance and Ecology* 6, no. 4/5 (2007): 533–51.

Adams, William M., and Elizabeth E. Watson. "Soil Erosion, Indigenous Irrigation and Environmental Sustainability, Marakwet, Kenya." *Land Degradation and Development* 14, no. 1 (2003): 109–22.

Appadurai, Arjun. *Modernity at Large: Cultural Dimensions of Globalization*. Minneapolis: University of Minnesota Press, 1996.

Bassett, Thomas J., and Donald Crummey. *African Savannas: Global Narratives and Local Knowledges of Environmental Change*. Portsmouth, N.H.: Heinemann, 2003.

Bebbington, Anthony. "Modernization from Below: An Alternative Indigenous Development?" *Economic Geography* 69, no. 3 (1993): 274–92.

———. "Movements, Modernizations, and Markets: Indigenous Organizations and Agrarian Strategies in Ecuador." In *Liberation Ecologies: Environment, Development and Social Movements*, edited by Richard Peet and Michael Watts, 86–109. London: Routledge, 1996.

Braun, Bruce, and Joel Wainwright. "Nature, Poststructuralism, and Politics." In *Social Nature: Theory, Practice and Politics*, edited by Noel Castree and Bruce Braun, 41–63. London: Blackwell, 2001.

Cowell, Richard, and Huw Thomas. "Managing Nature and Narratives of Dispossession: Reclaiming Territory in Cardiff Bay." *Urban Studies* 39, no. 7 (2002): 1241–60.

Cronon, William. "A Place for Stories." *Journal of American History* 78, no. 4 (2002): 1347–76.

Çullu, Mehmet Ali, Ahmet Almaca, Yüksel Şahin, and Salih Aydemir. "Application of GIS for Monitoring Salinization in the Harran Plain, Turkey." In *Proceedings of the International Conference on Sustainable Land Use and Management*, 326–31. Çanakkale, Turkey, 2002.

Dahlman, Carl. "The Political Geography of Kurdistan." *Eurasian Geography and Economics* 43, no. 4 (2002): 271–99.

Davis, Diana K. "Indigenous Knowledge and the Desertification Debate: Problematising Expert Knowledge in North Africa." *Geoforum* 36, no. 4 (2005): 509–24.

Escobar, Arturo. *Encountering Development: The Making and Unmaking of the Third World.* Princeton: Princeton University Press, 1995.

Fischer, Frank. *Reframing Public Policy: Discursive Politics and Deliberative Practices.* Oxford: Oxford University Press, 2003.

Gupta, Akhil. *Postcolonial Developments: Agriculture in the Making of Modern India.* Durham, N.C.: Duke University Press, 1998.

Haraway, Donna. "Situated Knowledges: The Science Question in Feminism and the Privilege of Partial Perspective." In *Simians, Cyborgs, and Women: The Reinvention of Nature,* 183–201, New York: Routledge, 1991.

Harris, Leila M. "Contested Sustainbilities: Assessing Narratives of Environmental Change in Southeastern Turkey" *Local Environment* 14, no. 8 (2009): 699–720.

———. "Modernizing the Nation: Postcolonialism, (Post)Development, and Ambivalent Spaces of Difference in Southeastern Turkey." *Geoforum* 39, no. 5 (2008): 1698–1708.

———. "States at the Limit: Tracing Evolving State-Society Relations in the Borderlands of Southeastern Turkey." *EJTS: European Journal of Turkish Studies* 10 (2009): 1–19.

———. "Water and Conflict Geographies of the Southeastern Anatolia Project." *Society and Natural Resources* 15, no. 8 (2002): 743–59.

———. "Water Rich, Resource Poor: Intersections of Gender, Poverty and Vulnerability in Newly Irrigated Areas of Southeastern Turkey." *World Development* 36, no. 12 (2008): 2643–62.

Kasaba, Resat. "Kurds in Turkey: A Nationalist Movement in the Making." In *Ethnopolitical Warfare: Causes, Consequences, and Possible Solutions,* edited by Daniel Chirot and Martin E. P. Seligman, 164–177. Washington, D.C.: American Psychological Association, 2001.

Kirişci, Kemal, and Gareth M. Winrow. *The Kurdish Question in Turkey: An Example of Trans-state Ethnic Conflict.* London: Frank Cass, 1997.

Lee, H. F., and D. D. Zhang. "Perceiving Desertification from the Lay Perspective in Northern China." *Land Degradation and Development* 15, no. 6 (2004): 529–42.

Nightingale, Andrea. "A Feminist in the Forest: Situated Knowledges and Mixing Methods in Natural Resource Management." *Acme: An International E-journal for Critical Geographies* 2, no. 1 (2003): 77–90.

Ozdoğan, Mutlu. "Changes in Summer Irrigated Crop Area and Water Use in Southeastern Turkey 1993 to 2002: Implications for Current Use and Future Water Resources." *Water Resources Management* 20, no. 3 (2006): 467–88.

Peet, Richard, and Michael Watts, eds. *Liberation Ecologies: Environment, Development and Social Movements.* London: Routledge, 1996.

Postel, Sandra. *Pillar of Sand: Can the Irrigation Miracle Last?* New York: W. W. Norton, 1999.
Proctor, James D. "Solid Rock and Shifting Sands: The Moral Paradox of Saving a Socially Constructed Nature." In *Social Nature: Theory, Practice and Politics,* edited by Noel Castree and Bruce Braun, 225–40. London: Blackwell, 2001.
Rangan, Haripriya. "From Chipko to Uttaranchal: Development, Environment, and Social Protest in the Garhwal Himalayas, India." In *Liberation Ecologies: Environment, Development and Social Movements,* edited by Richard Peet and Michael Watts, 205–26. London: Routledge, 1996.
Robbins, Paul. "The Practical Politics of Knowing: State Environmental Knowledge and Local Political Economy." *Economic Geography* 76, no. 2 (2000): 126–44.
Sayre, Nathan F. "Viewpoint: The Need for Qualitative Research to Understand Range Management." *Journal of Range Management* 57, no. 6 (2004): 668–74.
Scott, James C. *Seeing Like a State: How Certain Schemes to Improve the Human Condition Have Failed.* New Haven: Yale University Press, 1998.
Shiva, Vandana. *The Violence of the Green Revolution: Third World Agriculture, Ecology and Politics.* Penang: Third World Network, 1993.
Şelli, Ferhat, and A. Ihsan Koral. *Adaptation of New Technologies and Socio-Economic Changes in the Agricultural Plains of Sanliurfa Harran Plain after Irrigation and Possible Problems.* Sanliurfa: Village Services General Management Research Institute Publication, 2000.
Turner, Matthew D. "No Space for Participation: Pastoralist Narratives and the Etiology of Park-Herder Conflict in Southwestern Niger." *Land Degradation and Development* 10, no. 4 (1999): 345–63.
Ünver, I. H. Olcay. "Southeastern Anatolia Integrated Development Project (GAP), Turkey: An Overview of Issues of Sustainability." *Water Resources Development* 13, no. 2 (1997): 187–207.
———. "Southeastern Anatolia Project (GAP)." *Water Resources Development* 13, no. 4 (1997): 453–83.
Van Dissel, Serge Cartier, and Jan de Graaff. "Differences between Farmers and Scientists in the Perception of Soil Erosion: A South African Case Study." *Indigenous Knowledge and Development Monitor* 6, no. 3 (1998): 8–9.
Veihe, Anita. "Sustainable Farming Practices: Ghanian Farmers' Perception of Erosion and Their Use of Conservation Measures." *Environmental Management* 25, no. 4 (2000): 393–402.
Visser, Saskia. M., Jeannette K. Leenders, and M. Leeuwis. "Farmers' Perceptions of Erosion by Wind and Water in Northern Burkina Faso." *Land Degradation and Development* 14, no. 1 (2003): 123–32.
Warren, Andrew. "Land Degradation Is Contextual." *Land Degradation and Development* 13, no. 6 (2002): 449–59.

Yapa, Lakshman. "Improved Seeds and Constructed Scarcity." In *Liberation Ecologies: Environment, Development and Social Movements,* edited by Richard Peet and Michael Watts, 69–85. London: Routledge, 1996.

Zimmerer, Karl S. "Discourses on Soil Loss in Bolivia: Sustainability and the Search for Socioenvironmental 'Middle Ground.'" In *Liberation Ecologies: Environment, Development and Social Movements,* edited by Richard Peet and Michael Watts, 110–24. London: Routledge, 1996.

CHAPTER 8

Hydro-Imaginaries and the Construction of the Political Geography of the Jordan River

The Johnston Mission, 1953–56

Samer Alatout

SHORTLY AFTER the establishment of the state of Israel in 1948, disputes over unilateral plans for utilizing the Jordan River and its tributaries erupted between Israel and the riparian Arab states of Jordan, Lebanon, and Syria. Conflict became especially intense between Syria and Israel when the latter began construction on its drainage project on Lake Huleh in 1950 and, more so, when Israel began its construction of the National Water Carrier in the demilitarized zone in 1953. Compounding these problems was the seemingly explosive situation of more than 800,000 Palestinians who became refugees as a result of the 1948 war and who settled, for the most part, along the Jordan River banks. Interventions on their behalf for repatriation to their homes in Palestine were rejected by the Israeli state. In addition, their permanent resettlement in the Arab states where they took refuge was resisted by the refugees themselves and their political organizations, fearing the dissolution of their political rights of return.

Both of these problems became especially critical in the early 1950s. In response, then U.S. President Dwight Eisenhower dispatched his personal envoy, Eric Johnston, to the Middle East to negotiate a water development plan among the Jordan River riparian states. With such a plan, the U.S. administration wanted to address three issues at once: conflict over the water resources by promoting a regional approach to water management, the Palestinian refugee problem by encouraging the settlement of Palestinian refugees in host countries, and underdevelopment by providing a regional development plan funded by the United States and other members of the international community. In order to negotiate such an agreement, Johnston visited the area four times between 1953 and 1955. The context of this episode of international diplomacy, the actors behind it, its politico-environmental imaginaries, assumptions, and representations, the debates that surrounded it, and its conclusion constitute the story of this essay.[1]

In a nutshell, Johnston and his team constructed the water resources of the region as a self-evident, *unified watershed* and used that conception to underwrite the political project of building a *cooperative region*. Articulating the watershed with the region in such a way, Johnston did not only *naturalize* and thus *legitimize* the emergence of cooperative regional politics; he also *naturalized* the very politics of containment toward the Soviet Union, at the heart of American diplomacy during the 1950s. This politico-environmental imaginary based on the conflation of a watershed (nature) and a region (politics) was met by resistance, or counterimaginaries, in both the Arab states and Israel. Not only was the regional politics of Johnston disputed, but also his very understanding of regional water resources. Upon arrival, Johnston faced two different politico-environmental imaginaries that rested on two different conceptions of the hydrology of the water resources in the area, overlapping with two drastically different political imaginaries. One of those was the Arab Technical Committee's articulation of the Jordan River with the primordial nation and its territorial expression and the other was an Israeli imaginary that situated the Jordan River within the narrow confines of the nation-state.[2]

These three different politico-environmental imaginaries of the river and its management proved incommensurable. Hence, it only makes sense that the final agreement was not formally ratified. However, despite that, the argument of this essay, consistent with much scholarship on the subject, is that the final *revised* Johnston agreement, which resulted from three years of negotiation, was not a total failure either. As a matter of fact, the revised agreement became the de facto framework followed by all states in the region until the war of 1967. The revised plan was instrumental in depoliticizing the Palestinian question and in defining the Palestine refugees issue in economic and humanitarian terms. This particular outcome was immensely important for all of the states in the region, most particularly Israel and Jordan.³

The argument of this essay rests on two decades of scholarship in science studies that emphasize the co-production of science and politics.⁴ Along those lines, particular understandings of the natural order (e.g., how scientists define the watershed, what constitutes evidence in the production of knowledge, what are the facts about water resources, and what interventions are deemed necessary) often overlap with particular understandings of the political order (e.g., what political units are appropriate for the management of water resources and what scale is appropriate for political intervention). In the case of the Johnston mission, we had three competing politico-environmental imaginaries that respectively linked a watershed approach with a political region (the original Johnston plan), differentiated water resources with a primordial nation (Arab plan), and a river with the nation-state (the Israeli plan).⁵

In what follows, I discuss all three plans (Johnston, Arab, and Israeli) with special attention to the ways each of these plans conceptualized the water resources and articulated that conceptualization with a particular political vision. I conclude by bringing the themes of the chapter together and by briefly describing current water-sharing regimes, or lack thereof.

The Johnston Plan

In September 1953, Israeli construction started at a point on the Jordan River known as Jisr Banat Ya'aqub to divert the river away from its course to Lake Tiberias.⁶ This was the initial stage of diverting the Upper Jordan River to the Negev Desert in the south of Israel. However, the point of diversion was within the demilitarized zone between Syria and Israel and thus without clear sovereignty status.⁷ Within a few days the Syrian government protested to the Security Council of the United Nations, which issued an order to the Israeli government to halt construction work. Even though the Israeli government rejected the order, an American threat of freezing financial aid to Israel forced the Israeli government to halt its operations. In October, a little more than a month later, work on the diversion canal stopped.

Although the United Nations Security Council decided to look into the matter at a later stage, it never did. Given the fact that the United States was preparing for a mission of negotiations, the Security Council opted to wait for the results of this intervention. The U.S. president dispatched Eric Johnston, the chairman of the U.S. International Development Advisory Board, as a special envoy to the Middle East with a mission to "explore with the governments of the countries of that region certain steps which might be expected to contribute to an improvement of the general situation in the region."[8] As mentioned previously, there was an agreement by all parties that the main cause for tension was the Palestinian refugees situation, which was subsequently defined as an essentially economic problem.[9] The Johnston plan, therefore, centered on an economic development program for the Jordan Valley and, more particularly, on reaching an agreement on a water-sharing regime among riparian states of the Jordan River—Jordan, Israel, Syria, and Lebanon.[10]

Johnston and his teams visited the Middle East four times between October 1953 and October 1955.[11] During his first visit, Johnston offered the development plan sponsored by the Tennessee Valley Authority that came to be known as the Main Plan of 1953, after the consulting firm C. T. Main. This plan proved to be only a starting point for negotiations. The Arab Technical Committee, composed of water experts from each of the four Arab countries, and the Israeli Technical Team each offered a counterproposal, the Arab and the Cotton plans respectively.[12] These proposals were negotiated back and forth until the beginning of 1956, when all technical teams agreed on one plan that came to be known as the Johnston Unified Plan.

Even though all teams agreed on the technical merits of the plan, the Arab states decided to turn the plan back to the technical team for further study. Many considered this move a rejection of the plan for political reasons. The important point to recognize, though, is that the Johnston Unified Plan became the de facto sharing regime for the Jordan River, even though it was never ratified.[13] All the states in the region limited their water use to their share of the plan until the war of 1967 when all the headwaters of the Jordan River came under the control of the Israeli forces.

Water Bodies in Question?

Let us begin with a brief description of the bodies of water with which the Johnston negotiations were concerned.[14] To begin with, the Jordan River has four main tributaries, of which three form the Upper Jordan: the Banias originating in Syria; the Hasbani in Lebanon; and the Leddan, which originates and runs its whole course within the boundaries of Israel.[15] These tributaries converge and form the Upper Jordan about 25 kilometers north of Lake Tiberias. The Jordan then flows into Lake Huleh and, later on, into Lake Tiberias. Before the river flows out of Lake Tiberias, it loses some of its waters to evaporation.

Another tributary of the Jordan River, indeed the largest, is the Yarmuk River, which originates in Syria and forms the boundary between Jordan and Syria for more than 90 percent of its course. More than six kilometers south of Lake Tiberias, the Yarmuk joins with the River Jordan. Before discharging into the Dead Sea, the Jordan River gains some water from wadis and perennial flows along its route. The Litani River, which runs its full course within the Lebanese boundaries and which discharges in the Mediterranean, was not included in the Johnston plan. As will become clear in later sections, Israel requested that the Litani River be part of any regional agreement.

The Johnston Plan: Naturalizing the Region

Johnston adopted in full the Main plan for the development of the Jordan River basin. The Main plan was supervised by the Tennessee Valley Authority in response to a request by the United Nations Relief and Works Agency for Palestine Refugees in the Near East (UNRWA). Rephrasing the UNRWA directive, Gordon Clapp, the chairman of the TVA, argued that the plan was "to establish, *disregarding political boundaries,* a broad plan for the effective and efficient use of the water resources of the *Jordan Valley* emphasizing, first, irrigation and, second, the production of hydroelectric power."[16] He went even further in distancing the plan from any political meaning: "The report describes the elements of an *efficient arrangement* of water supply within the watershed of the Jordan River System. *It does not consider political factors or attempt to set this system into the national boundaries now prevailing.*"[17] It was assumed, of course, that this *disregard* of political boundaries produced the most *objective* technical plan possible. The "engineer," "observing and using the lay of the land and the *natural* and potential storage areas in the watershed, gathers, saves, adds to, and divides the available water of the system economically and *lets* water run to the areas where it can be made useful for human beings."[18] The assumption was that any politics resulting from this objective study of nature should be fair politics. Clapp told us what exactly that politics ought to be: "The *optimum* development utilization of the water resources of the Jordan-Yarmuk watershed could only be achieved by *cooperation* among the states concerned."[19]

This should be surprising given the fact that the reverse position was taken by Clapp himself earlier in 1949, when he was the chairman of the United Nations' Economic Survey Mission (ESM). His mandate then was to survey Palestine and the broader region for possible economic recovery projects. Then, the report of the ESM argued against regional cooperation in river development: "The region is not ready, the projects are not ready, the people and Governments are not ready for large-scale development of the Region's basic river systems or major undeveloped land areas. To press forward on such a course is to pursue folly and frustration and thereby delay sound economic growth."[20]

Nevertheless, regional cooperation as reflected in Clapp's letter of transmittal, claimed to be the natural outcome of engineering practices that observe and gather data—in this scheme, the engineer is never active in constructing a natural phenomenon; s/he merely observes it. Regional cooperation was legitimized not as a political strategy, which is by definition disputable; it was legitimized by the constant reference to a nature that is undisputable, to a Jordan-Yarmuk watershed that makes regional cooperation the only natural (read rational) politics to be had. So, what are the properties of this nature that produced regional cooperation as a natural outcome? What is it about the natural order, as perceived by Johnston and his team, that made the politics of regional cooperation preferable or perhaps even necessary? And, how did the plan articulate the watershed with regional cooperation in a way that produced the former as a natural hydrological boundary and the latter as legitimate political practice?

The Depoliticization of Watershed Boundaries[21]

As mentioned above, the plan proclaimed its nonpolitical character from the start: "Political boundaries have been completely ignored and legal limitations involving water rights have not been considered."[22] Even more significant, the plan was to become the basis for political intervention; as the report noted, the "*facts* presented in this study should assist in solving these [political] problems."[23] In fact, the plan was to become a source of legitimacy for a certain political imagination—an imagination that was at once regional and cooperative.[24]

First and foremost, the plan constructed the Jordan-Yarmuk watershed as a unit of study and intervention (see map 8.1). As can be seen from the map, the watershed includes "the drainage area of the Jordan River including the inflow to Lake Huleh and Lake Tiberias, and all the tributaries and wadis entering the Jordan River."[25] It spans an area of 17,300 square kilometers that is distributed among all states of the region: Israel, Jordan, Syria, and Lebanon.

Included in the watershed were the river basins of the Hasbani, Leddan, Banias, and Yarmuk. However, it is clear from the map that constructing a Jordan-Yarmuk watershed that includes all of these river basins was far from necessary. Engineering interventions could have been limited to many notions of watershed that were smaller, or larger, in scale. These interventions, in turn, would have entailed different political consequences with respect to resource use.[26]

For example, one intervention could have taken the Yarmuk watershed as its basic unit, which was exactly what the Bunger plan did in

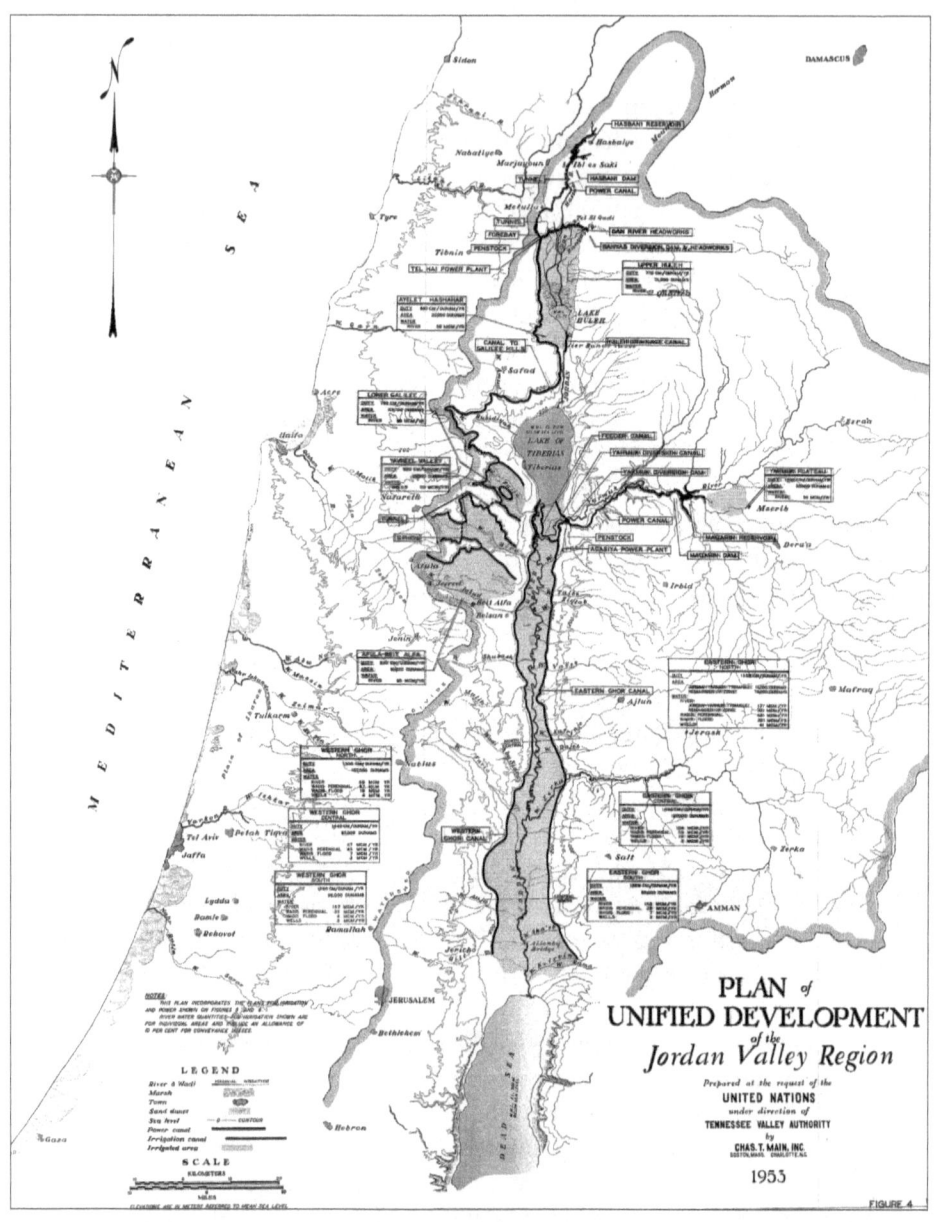

Map 8.1. The Jordan River watershed as seen by the Johnston mission. Chas. T. Main, *The Unified Development of the Water Resources of the Jordan Valley Region* (Boston: Chas. T. Main, 1953). *With permission of Parsons Corporation.*

1952. Mills E. Bunger was an engineer from the United States working for the Technical Cooperation Agency (TCA) in Amman, Jordan. During one of his trips to the United States, flying over the Yarmuk River, he noticed a suitable site for a dam on the Jordanian side that could be used in order to feed a suggested East Ghor Canal. This would have eliminated the need to cooperate with Israel in the development project. Jordan, the UNRWA, and the TCA each provided some funds in order to carry out the necessary studies.[27] The rejection of the plan was immediate from the Israeli side, arguing that Israel was a riparian on the Yarmuk River and that it deserved a share of its waters. What might be surprising for some, however, is the fact that the most vocal opposition to the plan came from the United States, with the immediate result of killing it. The main objections were that the plan was neither economic nor practical. For example, the secretary of state, John Foster Dulles, who visited the area in May 1953, later commented that available funds "can well be spent in large part on a coordinated use of the rivers which run through the Arab countries and Israel" instead of unilateral development plans.[28] Others at the State Department pointed to the fact that a regional approach to water development would be substantially cheaper.[29] U.S. intervention against the Bunger plan seems to have come at the time when news of the Main plan came out. It seems the United States, faithful to the notion of regional cooperation in post–World War II politics, chose to give the Main plan a chance. On the other side of possibilities, one could have imagined including the Litani River itself as part of the watershed, which is what the Israeli plan tried to achieve.[30]

Another example of this seemingly arbitrary construction of the watershed is the Main plan's exclusion of groundwater resources that lie within the boundaries of the watershed. Many, especially in the Arab technical committee, questioned the legitimacy of such a move.[31] In a word, conceptualizing the Jordan-Yarmuk watershed as the basic unit of intervention was an active process that involved a large degree of selections, inclusions, and exclusions. The watershed was, however, claimed to be a natural scale that came out of disinterested observation that was neither political nor conscious. This supposed depoliticization legitimized the plan, at least for those who put the plan together, as natural and thus politically neutral.

Even though the proclamation was otherwise, this construction of the boundaries of the watershed also depoliticized the problem of the Palestine refugees—and its resolution. In particular, the United Nations, and the United States as the major funding party, tried to resolve the problems within the area "where more and more souls are crowding a scant water supply, [where] there is a tragic need to develop, conserve, and dispense the waters of the Jordan Valley on a unified and impartial basis."[32] This neutral description of the problem, as if the "bodies" involved were void of ethnic, national, and political identities, compounded with the neutral construction of the boundaries of the watershed, removed the plan, or such was the hope, from dealing head-on with the politics of the region.[33]

One of the main effects of this politico-environmental imaginary was that the plan left out the Negev desert, which was out of the reach of the watershed. The watershed was the basic unit of analysis rather than the state. If one is to carry the Johnston mission's hydro-imaginary to its conclusion, then the connection between the Galilee Hills in the north of Israel was much stronger with the eastern and western Ghor, at the time part of Jordan, than with the Negev desert.[34] The sovereignty was established as one of nature, not one of politics. In this sense, the watershed naturalized the union between many lands and waters spanning Israel, Syria, Lebanon, and Jordan. The watershed provided the legitimacy needed to create a politically cooperative region.

Nature as Potential and the Engineer as a Facilitator of Potential

One of the contested points in the report turned out to be its "fundamental" principle: to utilize "the *topography* of the watershed advantageously to conserve the surface water yield by *natural storage* where possible, together with *gravity* transportation of irrigation water."[35] The report's preoccupation with the topography of the watershed and, especially, the use of gravity becomes obvious in the following quote:

> As a *problem* of *engineering* the most economic and the quickest way to get the most use from the waters of the Jordan River System requires better organization of the headwaters on the Hasbani and in the Huleh area to serve the lands by *gravity* flow within that part of the Jordan watershed and use of Lake Tiberias as a storage reservoir for the flood flows of the Jordan and Yarmuk Rivers. From Lake Tiberias these waters would be made available by *gravity* flow to irrigate lands on the east and west sides of the Jordan Valley to the south. *Gravity flow* eliminates expensive pumping facilities. . . . A quantity of water is suggested for each area of use within *gravity* reach of the supply made available and at the lowest cost.

However, there was no reason why economic efficiency through gravity, so dear to American participants, should have been respected more or less than efficiency through other means, such as irrigating the most fertile lands or those lands that required a lesser water duty.³⁶ In fact, this was precisely the critique leveled against the plan by the Israeli technical team, which argued for considering other routes to efficiency.³⁷

What needs to be emphasized here is the fact that gravity was as much, if not more, a politically efficient construct as it was a technically efficient one. It functioned in mysterious ways not only to convey water from one area to another, but also to connect, to suture together many disparate lands. Gravity naturalized the construction of a region. Literally and figuratively, gravity worked for the conveyance of water and the construction of a region. In a word, gravity was the force behind the political necessity of a cooperative region.

Although the Main plan advocated a series of concepts that attempted the naturalization and depoliticization of the plan, nature was not an easy ally. In order to achieve the maximum benefits of the project (to irrigate all the arable lands within the watershed using the force of gravity), the planners had to resort to the engineer. Many dams, canals, structures, storage areas and diversion canals needed to be constructed in order for nature to play the part of nature. In order for the force of gravity to work, another force was essential, that of diversion.

Naturalizing Water Storage Areas

Rainfall varies in the area from north to south, from season to season, and from year to year.³⁸ In order to deal with this complexity and to regulate such variations, all water management schemes in the region came up with plans to increase existing storage capacity.

The Main plan *insisted* on using Lake Tiberias as the regional storage reservoir in which not only seasonal and annual variations could be regulated, but also the Yarmuk winter floodwaters could be stored.³⁹ One stipulation to this arrangement, however, was the establishment of an international water authority, a water master, that would be responsible for the execution of the plan. At the same time, the Israeli interim plans, until 1956, repeatedly focused on the use of a "natural reservoir" at a place called Beit Nattaufa in order to regulate the flow of water in the Israeli system,⁴⁰ especially from the Jordan River in the north to the Negev desert in the south.

Even though the Israelis had no immediate plans for the use of Lake Tiberias, they vehemently rejected the Johnston plan's intention to use it as a regional storage area. Given the suggestions of the water master, the immediate concern was that of sovereignty. The Israeli side argued repeatedly that the use of Lake Tiberias as a regional storage site would threaten Israeli sovereignty over the lake.

American insistence on storing winter floodwaters from the Yarmuk in Lake Tiberias envisioned constructing a diversion dam on, and a diversion canal between, the Yarmuk River and the lake. In addition, the plan also envisioned the release of water to the west and east Ghor Canals during the summer dry months. From the point of view of the Johnston team, this would have been a truly regional project as well, for it would have connected Jordan, Israel, and Syria through the material interdependencies of machinery, pipelines, and water transport and irrigation works.

The Arab Plan of 1954

It is important to stress that the Arab plan was a negotiated settlement on the local and regional levels. Its design reflected and embedded the struggle over many visions of what the Arab world should look like, what the Palestinian problem meant, and how a legitimate politico-environmental imaginary in the area should be constructed.

The United States' rejection of the Bunger plan mentioned earlier meant that the ability of the Arab states to finance the project was almost nonexistent. To start with, the policies of the Bank of Development and Reconstruction prevented it from funding unilateral development projects on shared water systems, unless other riparians acquiesced. Second, the United States had already announced its commitment to a regional approach to water development and was therefore unwilling to pay for unilateral development projects. However, the United States also committed itself to paying most of the costs involved in constructing the regional project, estimated at more than $135 million.[41]

Water development, meanwhile, was successfully constructed as the only answer to the economic stress felt by the Arab countries. However, some Arab states were more eager to participate in a regionally negotiated scheme than others. For example, Jordan and Egypt were in favor of trying out the negotiation route, more so than Syria and Lebanon. In the end, an Arab League technical committee was established in 1953 with members from the four concerned Arab countries and headed by the secretary-general of Egypt's National Production Council, Muhammed Salim. From the very beginning, oppositional voices were strong. The Arab League Refugee Office in Beirut, for example, did not see any reason why the Arab states should share their waters with Israel, especially given the fact that water resources could more or less easily be diverted away.[42]

The technical committee submitted its report in January 1954. The Arab plan walked a fine line that conditionally accepted the Johnston plan, while posing three challenges: first, redefining the concept of the watershed;

second, stressing the legitimacy of the concept of gravity; and, third, adjusting the water duty determined by the Johnston plan.

Reintroducing Political Boundaries: From a Watershed to an Arab Nation

As was demonstrated in the previous section, the Johnston plan constructed, deployed, and articulated the category of a watershed and extended its boundaries as was deemed necessary for a regional plan to be workable. One important consequence of this politico-environmental imaginary was that all the lands within the watershed were deemed equal in terms of their access to irrigation water—as long as the gravity principle held true. The Arab plan agreed on the gravity principle, namely, that water should be used to irrigate lands that can be reached by gravity. However, it also insisted that water resources that originate in an Arab state belong to the Arab nation. In this sense, the Jordan River headwaters that originate in Lebanon or Syria and flow into Israel were deemed Arab property that could be diverted by those Arab states as they saw fit—particularly away from Israel and into Jordan, for example.[43]

The Arab plan argued that the watershed should be understood according to the political boundaries that already existed. However, it had a different, nonstatist conception of political boundaries that differentiated between the Arab nation and its other, in this case Israel. Water that falls within Israel, on the one hand, and Jordan, Syria, and Lebanon, on the other, should be identified as Israeli and Arab, respectively. The source of water defined priorities of irrigation. In that sense, the plan imagined a hierarchy of lands whose access to irrigation water was relative to their national contribution to the rivers in the form of rainfall. The following example might make this point clearer. As can be seen in table 8.1, the Johnston plan distributed the Jordan River water (according to its watershed and gravity principles) in the following fashion (1,213 million cubic

Table 8.1. Water distribution from each plan
Quantities in million cubic meters

Plan	Israel	Jordan	Syria	Lebanon	Total
Johnston (1953)	394	774	45	0	1,213
Cotton (1954)	1,290	575	30	451	2,346
Arab (1954)	182	698	132	35	1,047

Source: Data compiled by the author from the three proposals: Johnston 1953, Cotton 1954, and Arab Technical Committee, 1954.

meters per year—mcmy): Jordan, 774; Israel, 394; Syria, 45. This translated into a different calculation in the Arab plan: 819 mcmy for the Arab nation (constituting three countries) and 394 to Israel. This distribution was deemed unfair, given national contributions to the river.[44] Even more, what was important for the Arab plan was not the watershed argument. Rather, the important issue was the political identity of the water: "Most of the sources of the Jordan River waters come from Arab districts (Lebanon, Syria, and Jordan) and from other springs and sources that lie on the two banks of the river (most of which are in Jordan)."[45] The Arab plan went on to claim that of the 1,213 mcmy of Jordan River, 1057 mcmy came from Arab sources and thus should be reflected in water distribution.[46]

Conceptualizing Lake Tiberias as an Enemy Space

The Johnston plan included a project aimed at diverting water from the Yarmuk River and storing it in Lake Tiberias. Then water was to be transported back to Jordan during the summer months to the east and west Ghor canals for the irrigation of lands on both banks of the lower Jordan Valley. The Arab plan, by contrast, rejected the idea of storing the Yarmuk waters in Lake Tiberias. One of the main reasons was the different salinity between the Yarmuk waters (88 particles per million, ppm) and that of Lake Tiberias (more than 300 ppm), which threatened to decrease Yarmuk's water quality.

The Johnston plan estimated water loss to evaporation from Lake Tiberias at 300 mcmy. It further argued that the Jordan-Yarmuk plan would not increase that loss. However, the Arab plan countered that even though water loss would be almost the same as before, it would come after the diversion of the Banias and the Hasbani waters for the irrigation of the Galilee Hills. In other words, the loss would be added to that of the Hasbani and the Banias Rivers, at least inasmuch as the lower Ghor was concerned. The alternative, according to the plan, was the construction of a dam on the Yarmuk River on a site called Maqarin, which would have no significant increase in water loss to evaporation (7 mcmy).

In addition to what were deemed technical objections to establishing Lake Tiberias as a regional storage space, there was the political issue of sovereignty over Lake Tiberias and the project. Lake Tiberias was, and still is, located within the boundaries of Israel. Control over the diversion schemes was of much importance to the Arab side: "This condition will place Jordan under the mercy of the Jews and their Government in as much as storage and diversion to the Ghor is involved" (28). This situation was not to be allowed in any form, for it would confirm the legitimacy of Israeli control over Palestine, its waters, and its lands.

The Arab plan constructed a clearly demarcated region, one in which there was, on the one hand, a clear, interstate Arab identity that spans populations, rivers, lands, and even states and, on the other, there was a clear Other, what was considered the *illegitimate* Israeli state.

However, the Arab plan agreed with the Johnston plan on one important issue: limiting irrigation projects to land within the watershed that could be served by the force of gravity. This, from the Arab perspective, meant casting a shadow of illegitimacy over the Israeli National Water Project to divert the Jordan River water to the Negev. Only natural forces construct and link legitimate political boundaries. Pipes, plants, and physical constructions are a sign of artificiality that diminishes political legitimacy. In his elaboration on the Arab plan, Kahhalah gave this position the force of the obvious: "The Arab project, given the fact that its waters run in the *comfortable contours* of nature, is the *natural* one, while the Israeli project that needs, in order to deliver its waters, hundreds of meters of canals is the *unnatural* one."[47] He went on to argue that "Israel's diversion of any of the basin's water out of its geography constitutes stark aggression on the Arabs' rights and the stealing of their waters, which justifies all actions that preserve these rights and regain what was stolen of their waters."[48]

The Israeli (Cotton) Plan of 1954

Each of the previously discussed plans conceptualized a different politico-environmental imaginary in the region. Whereas the Johnston plan constructed a *politically* cooperative region the basis of which lay in its *naturalized* conception of the Jordan-Yarmuk watershed, the Arab plan constructed a hierarchy of lands within the watershed, based on articulating the source of water and irrigable lands with national identities—Arab or Other.

The Israeli plan, known as the Cotton Plan of 1954, constructed a wholly different politico-environmental world that was based on the nation-state.[49] The legitimacy of such a world rested on the constant reference to efficient utilization of water and land resources within the state: the guiding principle for water distribution should be the "careful determination of the location of the most suitable lands for irrigation regardless of location or *watershed*, with a view of *optimum combined utilization of land and water resources.*"[50] Water planning for irrigation not only should optimally combine land and water resources, it should also "insure optimum crop production from the available water resources."[51] By deploying a technical-rational argument of efficiency, the Israeli plan paved the way for legitimizing the nation-state as the basic political category in a water-sharing regime, rather than the region, as the Johnston plan envisioned, or the nation, as the Arab plan envisioned. How was that done and what functions did it achieve and serve?[52]

Constructing the Nation-State as Necessary while Expanding the Watershed

The Johnston mission started at a time when Israeli attempts at diverting the Jordan River to the Negev had already been halted.[53] However, the Johnston plan's construction of a cooperative region and a certain conception of the watershed met with strong Israeli resistance, which was based on political as well as technical-rational reasoning.[54]

The first Israeli objection was critical of the exclusion of the Litani River from the plan: "This report, although it claimed to offer an unbiased regional solution benefiting all the Jordan Valley *States*, had neglected to include the utilization of one of the principal water resources of the area, i.e., the Litani river."[55] The strategic significance of including the Litani River notwithstanding,[56] it is important to notice the way in which the Cotton plan redefined the Johnston plan's objective as "benefiting all the Jordan Valley *States*." In fact, the Johnston plan constructed a watershed empty of political boundaries, one that was ruled by topographic constructs rather than political ones.[57] It was precisely the absence of political boundaries of nation-states that gave the Johnston plan its definitive character.[58] However, the Cotton plan was determined to articulate the watershed of the Johnston plan with the nation-states within the watershed at every step of the way.[59] In fact, the Cotton plan stressed the following feature as most important: "It respects operational independence of the participant states."[60]

Another Israeli objection had to do with one of the material effects of the Johnston plan's construction of the watershed: excluding the Negev as a potential beneficiary of the regional plan. This meant that the main focus of Israeli water policymaking and immigrant settlement planning was in danger.[61] Those were never exclusively technical matters for the Israeli team—they were significantly imbued with politics, especially with the politics of legitimacy.

Taking these two critiques of the Johnston plan into account, the Cotton plan claimed to be based "upon the basic principle that in a water deficiency area *all water and power resources* should be utilized without undue waste, and that the volume of crops that can be grown in the region should be the paramount criterion of desirability."[62] However, in order to do just that, the plan needed to engage what the Johnston plan called the water duty of agricultural lands, i.e., the annual water requirement for the irrigation of one dunam of land. In estimating water needs of each type of land, the Johnston mission followed historic practices. The Israeli plan, however, was more interventionist: it envisioned the construction of a new, "modern," agriculture that depends on new irrigation technologies and new crop regimes. In a word, the Israeli plan envisioned redefining agriculture, and thus the economic and social orders of the area, in technical-rational terms.

From an Insignificant Technical Detail to a Worldview: Water Duty, Efficiency, Land Salinity, and Water Use

In order to decide the water requirement for irrigable lands within the watershed, the Johnston plan classified those lands into nine types and assigned each type a specific water duty (table 8.2). The classification of lands into types depended on many categories: the salinity of soil, the crops grown, and the hydrographic conditions.

In its classification scheme, the Johnston plan used historic and current agricultural practices as a yardstick for the measure of water duty. In that sense, the Johnston plan was not prescriptive, it did not demand a change in the agricultural practices of the present population—at least insofar as water duties were involved, the Johnston plan chose to err on the side of contemporary practices.

The Cotton plan, in contrast, was based on the primacy of *efficiency* for water utilization in agricultural development. The most important function of agricultural planning thus was to determine the best possible combinations of lands, crops, and water. Because of these different priorities, the Cotton plan contested the Johnston plan's water duties (see table 8.2). If

Table 8.2. Water duty according to the Johnston and the Israeli plans

Location	Water duty according to the Johnston plan	Water duty according to the Israeli plan
Lower Jordan Valley, North (Jordan and Israel)	1,330	1,000
Lower Jordan Valley, Central (Jordan)	1,440	1,250
Lower Jordan Valley, South (Jordan)	1,860	1,250
Upper Huleh (Israel)	770	1,000
Ayalet Hashahar (Israel)	890	1,150
Lower Galilee (Israel)	780	1,150
Yavneel Valley (Israel)	930	1,150
Afula-Beit Alfa (Israel)	930	1,150
Yarmuk Plateau (Jordan and Syria)	1,500	800
Negev	—	600

Source: Data compiled by the author from the plans: Johnston 1953 and Cotton 1954.

efficiency were to be the most important technical measure, the Israeli side argued, then it could hardly be based on present, "primitive" practices.

To give a concrete example, the Cotton plan was critical of Johnston's measures of water duty because they were "in part, based on the type of farming which was actually practiced at the time of writing his report. In the Jordan-Yarmuk Triangle Area, 15–20% of the irrigated area was used for banana growing, and another 25% for alfalfa, *both heavy consumers of water.*"[63] In a water deficient area, the Cotton plan concludes, "this kind of crops cannot be regarded as typical for the whole valley when fully developed."[64] The plan goes on to suggest that a new regime of crops should be utilized, depending on the market value of different crops: grains, vegetables, potatoes, and miscellaneous fruits. The line between the technical-rational measure of water duty and its potential to dictate agricultural practices is no longer clear. The technical-rational becomes prescriptive; it reconstructs the political economy of the whole region by restructuring its agricultural practices.

For the most part, the Cotton plan was concerned with including the Negev desert within the spatial imaginary of any development plan for the Jordan River. It was also concerned with establishing the territorial-sovereign rights of the Israeli state over the Jordan River waters. This is at a time when the very legitimacy of the Israeli state was in question. In addition, however, Israeli water experts that were engaged in the negotiations were also concerned about water scarcity. For those experts, efficiency should be redefined as a measure of water not a measure cost.[65] The Cotton plan thus articulated together in one politico-environmental imaginary the sovereignty of the state and its control over its water and territorial resources, the expansion of the watershed to include the Negev desert, and the redefinition of efficiency as a measure of resource use per unit of land not of cost.

Table 8.3. Comparing different plans' land distribution. Areas in dunam

Plan	Israel	Jordan	Syria	Lebanon	Total
Johnston (1953)	416,000	490,000	30,000	0	936,000
Cotton (1954)	1,790,000	430,000	30,000	390,000	2,640,000
Arab (1954)	234,000	490,000	119,000	35,000	878,000

Source: Data compiled by the author from the three proposals.

Remaking the Political Geography of the Jordan River Basin

By the end of his mission, Johnston's revised plan did not work as a watershed-wide, unified development project as he wished it would when he first visited the area. In this sense, the United States' political program of creating a politically and economically cooperative region in the Middle East that can defeat perceived Soviet threats failed. However, the plan did work on a number of levels.

First, all riparian states agreed to limit their withdrawals from the watershed system to the amounts specified in the final technical agreement. This meant that tensions between riparian states eased, at least relative to 1953. I have to qualify my statement here: I am not arguing that disputes over the distribution of water resources disappeared altogether, rather that those tensions took a backseat until 1964 when they resurfaced after Israel started diverting the Jordan River waters to the south. The commitments given to the revised plan, however, worked more or less until the 1967 war, when Israel occupied the Golan Heights and thus controlled all the headwaters of the river system. Second, the revised plan worked in the sense that it allowed each of the states to proceed with its unitary development plans. For Jordan, this meant more agricultural development along the banks of the river, which would create jobs and settlement opportunities for the Palestinian refugees in the area. For Israel, this meant that water could be used out of the Jordan River watershed. Diverting water to the Negev allowed the Israeli state to carry out its commitment for the spatial dispersal of new Jewish immigrants and their settlement in agricultural cooperatives in the south or border towns. Probably more important, at least on the symbolic level, is the perceived legitimacy of the state as an autonomous actor and as the basic unit of regional politics: it can survey its water resources, identify their legitimate uses, and distribute those resources throughout its territory as it sees fit. Third, the revised plan still treated the Palestinian refugees as a humanitarian and an economic problem, thus indefinitely suspending the urgency of dealing with the political and explosive question of Palestine.

This is on the substantive level. On the conceptual level, this essay argues that technically framed hydro-imaginaries are always and by necessity based on, deploy, negotiate, and underwrite political, cultural, and ideological conceptualizations of the world we live in.

Upon landing in the area on his first visit, Johnston faced three distinctly different politico-environmental imaginaries, each of which articulates a different understanding of the hydrological system and the politics that surrounds it. There was Johnston's own initial plan that advocated for the watershed, ruled by gravity, as the appropriate, *natural* scale for managing water resources, that in turn depoliticized water management, and legitimized cooperation in constructing a regional development plan. The Arab plan deployed a different understanding of the watershed that rejected the watershed as a framework for water management and the cooperative region as a political concept. In the process, the plan deployed a certain understanding of water, territory, nation, and nation-state in order to argue for Arab national rights in water that falls on or originates within Arab territories. The Israeli plan, in contrast, underscored the importance of the state and political boundaries in deciding water distribution and use, the sovereignty of the state in choosing its use of its water resources, and emphasized that under conditions of scarcity, water efficiency would be the most important technical detail.

The negotiations that lasted for three years resulted in the revised unified Johnston plan. The different riparian states negotiated a quota for each. They also accepted the Israeli demand of allowing each state to use its waters as it sees fit, even if away from the watershed. This resolved the question of efficiency, which became state-specific: while water efficiency remained more important than financial efficiency in Israeli politics,[66] financial demands for water-efficient projects (cost of power for diversion schemes and construction costs for infrastructure) remained a hurdle for Jordan and other Arab states.

However, it is also important to acknowledge the fact that while the revised agreement gave something to each of the parties to celebrate, it did that at the cost of depoliticizing the Palestinian refugee problem and turning it into a humanitarian and economic one. In this sense, the consensus that emerged, even in its informal and tenuous status, produced a new politico-environmental imaginary that was patched up of different frameworks, but that fully excluded the Palestinian perspective. This is in part a conceptual lesson: consensus does not always mean the rightful resolution of a technical or a political problem; sometimes it means the successful negation and silencing of dissenting voices. But it is also a practical problem: even though the revised Johnston plan does not hold any legal authority since it was never ratified nor was it even functioning since the war of 1967, it still is the only frame of reference in negotiations over shared water resources.

Although the Jordanian-Israeli peace treaty in the 1990s resolved the water dispute between the two parties, it did so again by ignoring Palestinian rights to the Jordan-Yarmuk water.[67] Since Palestine, the occupied Palestinian territories since 1967, is a riparian party to the Jordan River, it has a claim over some of the water from that river. Jordan, however, insists that Palestine has no claim over the water that was allotted it through the Johnston negotiations. Israel, on the other hand, claims that since the West Bank was part of Jordan during the Johnston negotiations, then the Palestinian share has already been allotted to and should be claimed from Jordan, not Israel. The Palestinians claim that they have a right to 180 mcmy from the Jordan River system, and many water experts in the region concur with that assessment.[68] The question that will have to be examined in the coming years is how to resolve this issue while at the same time dealing with the Johnston plan as the de facto historical precedent.

Notes

1. In using the term "politico-environmental imaginaries," I build on the concept of "co-production" in political and sociological studies of science. Specifically, I use it to emphasize the fact that every technical-rational conception of environmental issues necessarily implies, rests on, invokes, and underwrites a political framework for ordering and organizing our lives in the world. See Sheila Jasanoff, ed., *States of Knowledge: The Co-production of Science and Social Order* (London: Routledge, 2004).

2. I need to clarify a couple of concepts used throughout this chapter that might not be familiar to nonspecialists. Arab nationalism is based on the premise that all inhabitants of the Arab states belong to one nation and that their division into a number of states is the legacy of colonialism. Unlike other cases, such as Germany or France, where the assumption is that the nation and the state are coterminous (although this also has been contested), in pan-Arab ideological frameworks the Arab states are seen as obstacles for the nation to express itself fully, i.e., in one nation-state. Different Arab states, according to this line of thought, should be subsumed under one state that unifies the nation and extends from Iraq in the east to Morocco in the west. In this story, therefore, Arab formal discourse distinguishes between an Arab nation and the Arab states, then called districts. In this context, water resources belong to the Arab nation in the broader sense, not to one state or another.

3. See for more: Miriam R. Lowi, *Water and Power: The Politics of a Scarce Resource in the Jordan River Basin* (Cambridge: Cambridge University Press, 1993); and Aaron T. Wolf, *Hydropolitics along the Jordan River: Scarce Water and Its Impact on the Arab-Israeli Conflict* (Tokyo: United Nations University Press, 1995). The revised plan, as will become clearer in the essay, combined some elements of the Arab and Israeli plans, as well as some of the original Johnston plan. However, by incorporating the Israeli plan's vision of a state-centered river management scheme, the Johnston Unified Plan supported the Israeli geopolitical imaginary in which nation-states, rather than the region, were the basic units of political relations.

4. For an excellent review of co-production and its relationship to other science studies concepts, see Jasanoff, *States of Knowledge*.

5. One of the logical extensions of this argument is that recent trends toward watershed management in environmental discourse, for example, should always be investigated for their political implications. In theorizing water imageries, it is probably important to point to an article by Stefan Helmreich. Helmreich talks about the ways water imageries are deployed through tropes, in his case "currents, flows, and circulations"—tropes which are "more common in the talk of globalization." He suggests that such talk can also be reframed as "oceanization." What Helmreich does for the ocean, linking it with the political economy of globalization through water tropes, suggests that creative linkages between knowledge, objects, and politics are constantly on the move. In the case I cover here, similar processes, but certainly different tropes, can be gleaned in the creation of these three different politico-environmental imaginaries of the river and its management (think of watersheds, gravity, and soil). All of these tropes, tweaked here and there, deployed wholly or partially, used alone or mixed in hybrid tropes, define the horizons of possible politics, all the while grounding that politics in nature. See Stefan Helmreich, "Nature/Culture/Seawater," *American Anthropologist* 113, no. 1 (2011): 132–44.

6. In Hebrew that point of diversion is called "Gesher B'not Yaakov," and in English it is "Bridge of Jacob's Daughter."

7. After the war of 1948, Syria was in control of a small triangle of land that was part of Palestine before the war. As part of the Armistice Agreement of 1949, the Syrian government agreed to withdraw its forces from the area in exchange for designating the area as a demilitarized zone. See United Nations, *Israeli-Syrian General Armistice Agreement* (New York: United Nations, 20 July 1949), document number S/1353.

8. U.S. Department of State communiqué of 17 October 1953, quoted in the *Jerusalem Post*, 18 October 1953.

9. This was especially true under the influence of the Economic Survey Mission of the United Nations. For a critique of the economic approach of the state department, to which Lowi attributes the ultimate failure of the Johnston mission, see Miriam Lowi, *Water and Power: The Politics of a Scarce Resource in the Jordan River Basin* (Cambridge: Cambridge University Press, 1993). The notion that water sharing was crucial for the area was, at the time, ubiquitous. Witness what the secretary-general, Dag Hammarskjöld, said on one occasion: the "development of water resources was a 'key problem' which was reflected in particularly every 'Palestine' issue." Quoted in the *Jerusalem Post*, 25 February 1954.

10. Even though Egypt is not a riparian to the Jordan River, it was included in the diplomatic efforts for its strategic importance in the area.

11. His visits took place in October 1953, June 1954, January 1955, and October 1955.

12. John S. Cotton was an American engineer who functioned as a consultant for Zionist and, later on, Israeli water projects. All the Israeli plans were published by his firm. For the details of the Arab plan see Arab Technical Committee, *Arab Plan for the Utilization of the Waters of the River Jordan and Its Tributaries* (Cairo: Arab Technical Committee, 1954 [in Arabic]); see also *Egyptian Economic and Political Review* (1955). For details of the Israeli plan see John S. Cotton, *Plan for the Development of the Water Resources of the Jordan and Litani River Basins* (Jerusalem: Water Department of the Ministry of Agriculture, 1954).

13. The Arab states feared that a formal ratification of the agreement would imply the political recognition of the Israeli state—a hazardous proposal at the time, to say the least. For the Arab states, recognition of Israel would have had to be tied up with other important issues like the Palestinian refugee problem, Palestinian rights to repatriation, etc. The path of least resistance was chosen: the Johnston Unified Plan was technically sanctioned and the parties agreed to abide by its provisions.

14. Almost all works on the Jordan River agree on this description of the bodies of water involved. See Helena Lindholm, "Water and the Arab-Israeli Conflict," in *Hydropolitics: Conflicts over Water as a Development Constraint*, ed. L. Ohlsson (London: Zed Books, 1995) , 55–90; Lowi, *Water and Power*; Georgiana Stevens, *Jordan River Partition* (Stanford, Calif.: Hoover Institution, 1965); Aaron Wolf, "Guidelines for a Water-for-Peace Plan for the Jordan River Watershed," *Natural Resources Journal* 33, no. 3 (1993): 797–839; Aaron Wolf, *Hydropolitics along the Jordan River: The Impact of Scarce Water Resources on the Arab Israeli Conflict* (Tokyo: United Nations University, 1995).

15. For consistency's sake, Arabic names are used throughout the essay. Hebrew translations are as follows: Banias is Nahal Senir; Hasbani is Nahal Hermon; and Leddan is Nahal Dan.

16. Gordon Clapp, in a letter of transmittal addressed to the director of the UNRWA. A copy of the letter can be found in C. T. Main, *The Unified Development of the Water Resources of the Jordan Valley Region* (Boston: Chas. T. Main, 1953).

17. Ibid., emphasis added.

18. Ibid.

19. In the plan, there is even a visual presentation of this cooperative region which is hard to reproduce here. Clapp describes how "boundary lines are not shown on the maps in this report, but for the purpose of depicting the relationship between boundary lines and the Jordan River System a transparent overlay has been added at the back of this volume. This overlay can be placed over the maps to show the Armistice and national boundary lines. Thus the reader may see the political setting in which the engineering plan must be visualized. The present location of national boundaries suggests that the optimum development utilization of the water resources of the

Jordan-Yarmuk watershed could only be achieved by cooperation among the states concerned." Ibid.

20. United Nations Economic Survey Mission, *Final Report* (New York: United Nations Publications, Document Number A/AC25/6/28, December 1949), 3.

21. The depoliticization of public action has been on the minds of analysts for a while. Witness how Yaron Ezrahi describes the importance of such practices: "The uses of science and technology to 'depoliticize' action have been among the most potent political strategy in the modern state" (Yaron Ezrahi, *The Descent of Icarus: Science and the Transformation of Contemporary Democracy* [Cambridge: Harvard University Press, 1990], 51). In fact most of the literature on boundary work in science studies, which conceptualizes the very distinction between science and politics as an active political practice in itself, could be seen as literature on depoliticization practices. See Thomas Gieryn, "Boundary-Work and the Demarcation of Science from Non-Science: Strains and Interests in Professional Ideologies of Scientists and on Boundary," *American Sociological Review* 48, no. 6 (1983): 781–95; Thomas Gieryn, *Cultural Boundaries of Science: Credibility on the Line* (Chicago: University of Chicago Press, 1999); Sheila Jasanoff, *The Fifth Branch: Science Advisers as Policymakers* (Cambridge: Harvard University Press 1990); Sheila Jasanoff, *Science at the Bar: Law, Science, and Technology in America* (Cambridge: Harvard University Press, 1995). In development studies literature one can also find depoliticization theorized. See James Ferguson, *The Anti-Politics Machine: "Development," Depoliticization, and Bureaucratic Power in Lesotho* (Minneapolis: University of Minnesota Press, 1990), especially 251–77.

22. Main, *Unified Development of the Water Resources of the Jordan Valley Region*, 3.

23. Ibid.

24. The use of imagination in this context follows the work of Benedict Anderson. Most essential about this use is that imagining denotes "invention," it is an active process of construction. Benedict Anderson, *Imagined Communities: Reflections on the Origin and Spread of Nationalism* (New York: Verso, 1983), 6.

25. Main, *Unified Development of the Water Resources of the Jordan Valley Region*, 3.

26. For more on the intersection of the politics of scale with hydropolitics, see Samer Alatout, "'States' of Scarcity: Water, Space, and Identity Politics in Israel, 1948–1959," *Environment and Planning D: Society and Space* 26, no. 6 (2008): 959–82; Samer Alatout, "Bringing Abundance into Environmental Politics: Constructing a Zionist Network of Abundance, Immigration, and Colonization, 1918–1949, *Social Studies of Science* 39, no. 3 (2009): 363–94; Leila Harris, "Water and Conflict Geographies of the Southeastern Anatolia Project," *Society and Natural Resources* 15, no. 8 (2002): 743–59; Leila Harris and Samer Alatout, "Negotiating Hydro-Scales, Forging States: Comparison of the Upper Tigris/Euphrates and Jordan River Basins," *Political Geography* 29, no. 3 (2010): 148–56; Christopher Sneddon, "Water Conflict and River Basins: The

Contradictions of Comanagement and Scale in Northeast Thailand," *Society and Natural Resources* 15, no. 8 (2002): 725–41.

27. Stevens, *Jordan River Partition*.

28. U.S. Department of State, *Report on the Near East*, bulletin, vol. 28, no. 729 (Washington, D.C., 1953), 832.

29. Stevens, *Jordan River Partition*.

30. Cotton, *Plan for the Development of the Water Resources of the Jordan and Litani River Basins*.

31. As will be clear later on, including groundwater resources did not promise to make the construction of a cooperative region any easier. If at all, it would have made the Johnston mission more difficult.

32. Gordon Clapp, in a letter of transmittal addressed to the director of the UNRWA. A copy of the letter can be found in Main, *Unified Development of the Water Resources of the Jordan Valley Region*.

33. Rashid Khalidi argues, similarly, that the Johnston plan was an attempt at assimilating Palestinian refugees in the Arab countries, especially along the Jordan River in the Kingdom of Jordan. See Rashid Khalidi, *Palestinian Identity: The Construction of Modern National Consciousness* (New York: Columbia University Press, 1997).

34. In this context I use hydro-imaginaries in order to point to the technical and rational frameworks with which scientists and policymakers understand hydrological systems, design policies for their management, and intervene in their dynamics. However, I use the term hydro-imaginaries rather than hydro-rationalities, for example, in order to underscore the political embeddedness of any technical imagination of watersheds.

35. Main, *Unified Development of the Water Resources of the Jordan Valley Region*, 2, emphasis added.

36. Water duty is the annual amount of water needed for the irrigation of one dunam of land.

37. It should be obvious that this critical examination of the gravity principle does not imply agreement with the Israeli critique. As will be clear in what follows, the same critique can be offered to the Israeli alternatives. The point to emphasize here is that technical legitimacy of the project is always mixed with political constructions.

38. Annual rainfall varies from more than 1,000 mm in the North to less than 100 mm in the Negev. Most of the rainfall occurs during the winter months with very dry summer months (virtually nil). In addition, there is the yearly variation from wet to dry years.

39. Main argued that "Lake Tiberias, as far as our engineering program is concerned, must be used as a part of the storage of the River." Main, *Unified Development of the Water Resources of the Jordan Valley Region*, 33.

40. Within the Israeli water community, contentions were high regarding the suitability of this site. See Alatout, "'States' of Scarcity."

41. This figure increased with time. It was about $200 million toward the end of the mission. See Munther Haddadin, *Diplomacy on the Jordan: International Conflict and Negotiated Resolution* (Norwell, Mass.: Kluwer Academic, 2001).

42. Stevens, *Jordan River Partition*.

43. In international water law principles, this doctrine is often called the "absolute sovereignty doctrine" and is territorially based. For details, see Stephen C. McCaffrey, *The Law in International Watercourses: Non-Navigational Uses* (New York: Oxford University Press, 2001).

44. Arab Technical Committee, *Arab Plan for the Utilization of the Waters of the River Jordan and Its Tributaries* (Cairo: Arab Technical Committee, 1954 [in Arabic]).

45. Notice the use of the concept of "district" rather than state in this document. Ibid., 26.

46. Ibid.

47. S. Kahhalah, *Water Problem in Israel and Its Reflections on the Arab-Israeli Conflict* (Beirut: Institute of Palestine Studies, 1980), 31, emphasis added.

48. Ibid.

49. This is how the Cotton plan describes some of its priorities: "(a) The water and power resources of the Jordan and Litani river basins are considered in this report. Water resources outside of these basins are not considered. (b) Boundaries of the States, i.e., Lebanon, Israel, Syria or the Kingdom of Jordan, are taken into account. (c) Utilization of water resources for irrigation and power production are not limited by topographic boundaries of river basins. (d) Water from high elevation sources are used to irrigate high elevation irrigable lands. Irrigation supply is by gravity, except in a few cases where pumping is necessary or desirable." Cotton, *Plan for the Development of the Water Resources of the Jordan and Litani River Basins*, 6.

50. Ibid., 40, emphasis added.

51. Ibid.

52. The claim then, of course, was that other plans were strongly political while the Israeli plan used a technical-rational approach. Lowdermilk described it in an editorial in the *Jerusalem Post* on 19 July 1955: "Engineering founded on politics of the hour cannot promise as much as diplomacy founded on down-to-earth engineering."

53. As mentioned above, the Israeli plans for the utilization of water resources were halted under extreme pressure from the Security Council and the United States.

54. As early as 20 October 1953, it was clear to the Israeli establishment that the United States was delegitimizing diverting the Jordan River to the Negev. In a cable (X65/594) addressed to the Israeli prime minister at the time, Moshe Sharett, the Israeli ambassador to the United States, Abba Eban, pointed to the fact that the United States' plan envisages "the irrigation of the north rather than the south." Document can be found in F3688–11, Israel National Archives (INA).

55. Cotton, *Plan for the Development of the Water Resources of the Jordan and Litani River Basins,* 66.

56. The inclusion of the Litani River would have meant increasing the annual water potential of Israel (at least according to the Israeli plan) by more than 400 mcmy. However, this is not the concern at this point.

57. At one point, Johnston countered that the American project was not a regional project and thus should not involve the Litani River. Rather, this project was a "watershed development project." Press release from the *USIS—Daily News Bulletin* vol. 6, no. 129, 7 July 1954, F3688–12, INA.

58. Of course the absence of political boundaries from the Johnston plan in no way makes it apolitical. After all, as we have seen, the absence of political boundaries of nation-states made possible the construction of a region, which is also a political category, just as the nation-state is.

59. See, for example, what Cotton, *Plan for the Development of the Water Resources of the Jordan and Litani River Basins,* 6, argues in another location: "The objective of this plan is to develop and utilize, without undue waste, the large quantities of water now not being utilized in the Jordan and Litani river basins, for optimum irrigation and power development in the States of Lebanon, Israel, Syria and the Kingdom of Jordan."

60. Ibid., 85.

61. Alatout, "'States' of Scarcity."

62. Cotton, *Plan for the Development of the Water Resources of the Jordan and Litani River Basins,* 66.

63. Ibid., 45, emphasis added.

64. Ibid.

65. Alatout, "'States' of Scarcity."

66. For the sake of brevity I did not elaborate on the intense politics of water within Israel itself, or on the complicated story of the relationship between local and regional water politics and how each shaped the other. For more on that see Alatout, "'States' of Scarcity."

67. Neither did Israel and Jordan deal with the question of Syria's rights to the Yarmuk-Jordan waters. In the past few years, Syria, as the upstream riparian on the Yarmuk River, responded by increasing its water extraction from the Yarmuk River. Interview, Jordan Water Authority, July 2006.

68. For more on this question, see Samer Alatout, "Water Balances in Palestine, Regional Cooperation, and the Politics of Numbers," in *Water Balances in the Eastern Mediterranean,* ed. D. Brooks and O. Mehmet (Ottawa: International Development Research Centre, 2000), 59–84.

Bibliography

Alatout, Samer. "Bringing Abundance into Environmental Politics: Constructing a Zionist Network of Abundance, Immigration, and Colonization, 1918–1949." *Social Studies of Science* 39, no. 3 (2009): 363–94.

———. "'States' of Scarcity: Water, Space, and Identity Politics in Israel, 1948–1959." *Environment and Planning D: Society and Space* 26, no. 6 (2008): 959–82.

———. "Water Balances in Palestine, Regional Cooperation, and the Politics of Numbers." In *Water Balances in the Eastern Mediterranean*, edited by David Brooks and Ozay Mehmet, 59–84. Ottawa: International Development Research Centre, 2000.

Anderson, Benedict. *Imagined Communities: Reflections on the Origin and Spread of Nationalism*. New York: Verso, 1983.

Arab Technical Committee. *Arab Plan for the Utilization of the Waters of the River Jordan and Its Tributaries*. Cairo: Arab Technical Committee, 1954 [in Arabic].

Clapp, Gordon. "Letter of Transmittal to the Director of the UNRWA." In C. T. Main, *The Unified Development of the Water Resources of the Jordan Valley Region*. Boston: Chas. T. Main, 1953.

Cotton, S. *Plan for the Development of the Water Resources of the Jordan and Litani River Basins*. Jerusalem: Water Department of the Ministry of Agriculture, 1954.

Egyptian Economic and Political Review (1955).

Ezrahi, Yaron. *The Descent of Icarus: Science and the Transformation of Contemporary Democracy*. Cambridge: Harvard University Press, 1990.

Ferguson, James. *The Anti-Politics Machine: "Development," Depoliticization, and Bureaucratic Power in Lesotho*. Minneapolis: University of Minnesota Press, 1990.

Gieryn, Thomas. "Boundary-Work and the Demarcation of Science from Non-Science: Strains and Interests in Professional Ideologies of Scientists and on Boundary." *American Sociological Review* 48, no. 6 (1983): 781–95.

———. *Cultural Boundaries of Science: Credibility on the Line*. Chicago: University of Chicago Press, 1999.

Haddadin, Munther. *Diplomacy on the Jordan: International Conflict and Negotiated Resolution*. Norwell, Mass.: Kluwer Academic, 2001.

Harris, Leila. "Water and Conflict Geographies of the Southeastern Anatolia Project." *Society and Natural Resources* 15, no. 8 (2002): 743–59.

Harris, Leila, and Samer Alatout, "Negotiating Hydro-Scales, Forging States: Comparison of the Upper Tigris/Euphrates and Jordan River Basins." *Political Geography* 29, no. 3 (2010): 148–56.

Helmreich, Stefan. "Nature/Culture/Seawater." *American Anthropologist* 113, no. 1 (2011): 132–44.

Israel National Archives (INA) F3688–11; F3688–12.

Jasanoff, Sheila. *The Fifth Branch: Science Advisers as Policymakers*. Cambridge: Harvard University Press 1990.

———. *Science at the Bar: Law, Science, and Technology in America*. Cambridge: Harvard University Press, 1995.

———, ed. *States of Knowledge: The Co-production of Science and Social Order.* New York: Routledge, 2004.
Kahhalah, S. *Water Problem in Israel and Its Reflections on the Arab-Israeli Conflict.* Beirut: Institute of Palestine Studies, 1980.
Khalidi, Rashid. *Palestinian Identity: The Construction of Modern National Consciousness.* New York: Columbia University Press, 1997.
Lindholm, Helena. "Water and the Arab-Israeli Conflict." In *Hydropolitics: Conflicts over Water as a Development Constraint,* edited by L. Ohlsson, 55–90. London: Zed Books, 1995.
Lowi, Miriam R. *Water and Power: The Politics of a Scarce Resource in the Jordan River Basin.* Cambridge: Cambridge University Press, 1993.
Main, C. T. *The Unified Development of the Water Resources of the Jordan Valley Region.* Knoxville: Tennessee Valley Authority, 1953.
McCaffrey, Stephen C. *The Law in International Watercourses: Non-Navigational Uses.* New York: Oxford University Press, 2001.
Sneddon, Christopher. "Water Conflict and River Basins: The Contradictions of Comanagement and Scale in Northeast Thailand." *Society and Natural Resources* 15, no. 8 (2002): 725–41.
Stevens, Georgiana. *Jordan River Partition.* Stanford: Hoover Institution, 1965.
United Nations. *Israeli-Syrian General Armistice Agreement.* New York: United Nations, 20 July 1949. Document number S/1353.
United Nations Economic Survey Mission. *Final Report.* New York: United Nations Publications, Document Number A/AC25/6/28, December 1949.
United States Department of State. Communiqué of 17 October 1953. Quoted in the *Jerusalem Post,* 18 October 1953, 18e.
———. *Report on the Near East.* Bulletin, vol. 28, no. 729. Washington, D.C., 1953.
Wolf, Aaron T. "Guidelines for a Water-for-Peace Plan for the Jordan River Watershed." *Natural Resources Journal* 33, no. 3 (1993): 797–839.
———. *Hydropolitics along the Jordan River: Scarce Water and Its Impact on the Arab-Israeli Conflict.* Tokyo: United Nations University Press, 1995.

CHAPTER 9

Environmentalism Deferred

Nationalisms and Israeli/Palestinian Imaginaries

Shaul Cohen

THERE ARE many different ways to think about environmentalism; it can be examined sociologically, politically, scientifically, and so on. Perhaps the most common themes in relation to Palestinian and Israeli environmental issues have to do with the overarching question of power and ideology,[1] and to a lesser extent technical or attitudinal approaches to problem solving.[2] Both of these orientations begin from the premise that there *is* an Israeli environmentalism, and that there *is* a Palestinian environmentalism. Although this is certainly so in the sense that there are NGOs, government agencies, regulatory mechanisms, curricular models, and manifestations of engagement with the environment, it is my argument that these indicators are in some respects a "false positive," and that for both communities there is, at this time, only one fundamental question, and that is the national one. Environmentalism in Palestine/Israel operates within a context that is bounded by existential concerns, and, as such, it is subsumed by a metanarrative that makes it marginal in impact and, in many respects, irrelevant in the context of discourses of land, resources, and power. It isn't that environmental voices aren't heard, but rather that they are measured against a metric of nationhood that can make them significant in symbolic ways but politically lacking in power and subject to expedience. Moreover, when there are competing needs *within* the perceived national agendas, the environment rarely gets top priority. It is therefore instructive to ask: "Is there an Israeli environmentalism? Is there a Palestinian environmentalism? Is there a shared environmentalism?" Superficially, at least, the answer is "of course," but at a more complex level it seems that possible answers would include "not yet" or "not much." Thus attention must be directed to the functioning of separate imaginaries that guide action—and inaction—in a land that is fractured politically, and both rich and fragile in terms of environment.

In this chapter I discuss the compatibilities and incompatibilities of national and environmental aspirations that rub against one another amid the contest for hegemony on the ground and the validation of national imaginaries that frame the Israeli-Palestinian struggle. To do this, I briefly address the place of the environment as a political factor in the past, the incorporation of environmental issues in narratives of national aspiration, and the fate of environmental efforts during the era of the peace process. There are, of course, distinct and noncoincidental stages of development—political and material—for Palestinians and Israelis, and multiple interests and ideologies within each community. For both sides, there is a relevant and often romanticized past, a contentious present, and a future that blends both pragmatic and idealized aspirations with an evolving anxiety about how present actions compromise and circumscribe opportunities for a better future. A fundamental aspect of my analysis of environmentalism in Palestine/Israel is that I argue that neither side is in a position to construct its ideologies and policies free from the shadow of statelessness and the fear of annihilation. Though Israelis and Palestinians are in a very different place of power and statehood, notions of intrinsic environmental value seem to be an unaffordable luxury to all concerned, save, perhaps, for a small number of idealists who offer prophetic visions of doom and salvation from the sidelines. Indeed, the environmental imperative is a utilitarian one, in that resources must serve the national cause *now*. Issues of land, air, water, sprawl, pollution, sewage, and other constituents of the environment press upon both communities with growing urgency, but they cannot compete with the chronic obsession with statehood that dominates politics and identities in the region and leaves the environment as a zero-sum arena.

Palestinians and Israelis are bound up in imaginings. Many of their imaginings are exclusive, others are mutual, and some are parallel. For both communities, existential concerns suffuse and dominate many issues that, in other places, are not inextricably linked to questions of nation, sovereignty, and legitimacy. Elements in the environment play key roles in both constituting identity and metering the practicalities of survival, and yet they are backgrounded in relation to other factors that trump the environment when identity and survival are challenged. Such challenges can be real or fanciful, but either way, the metanarratives of nationalism for Israelis and Palestinians deploy the environment as a tool for claiming a moral high ground vis-à-vis the other, but also for claiming the mantle of the victim. Victimhood in terms of the environment obviously plays a lesser role when compared to the violence that each community has brought upon the other and upon itself. So long as the permanent status of Israel and Palestine are open to question, and violence is a primary tool of the struggle, issues of the environment will be consigned to a secondary status (at best), unless and until they forge a productive role in the respective metanarratives.

Inasmuch as land is at the heart of the conflict, it would seem that the environment would be a critical arena for contestation and possibly accommodation. Instead, its treatment by both sides has, so far, been largely two-dimensional. Much of the scholarship on the environment of Palestine/Israel treats the national question in a two-dimensional manner as well. The obvious condition is that Israel is a sovereign and powerful state, whereas Palestinians languish in their frustrated nationalism and are at the mercy of the Israeli state. This characterization is accurate, and yet it obscures two aspects that have salience in relation to the environment. First, for Palestinians, the absence of sovereignty has been narrated as an aberration that does not erase their rightful claim to the land, nor their historic and future role managing it better than Israelis/Jews do.[3] Israelis narrate their current position of strength as something that cannot be taken for granted, and their stewardship as both historically legitimate and conferring of a current moral claim to be sovereign. Analyses that examine Palestinians solely in the present tense and those that treat Israel as a confident hegemon miss critical forces that shape and suppress nascent environmentalism on both sides.

For Israelis, generally speaking, the environment has been the stage upon which the Zionist enterprise has been built, and its features are opportunities to showcase good stewardship and the prowess of Jewish agriculture, infrastructure development, and the "normalization" of the state.[4] In Zionist ideology, redemption of the self comes through redemption, i.e., rehabilitation, of the land, an early precursor to the link between environmental health and group rights.[5] For Palestinians, the environment is a vessel for the idyll of Palestinian independence and a place that has been despoiled by Israeli (de)construction.⁶ It is also an hourglass that shows the erosion of opportunity for (re)creating a garden of Eden that Palestinian nationalism has promised will materialize upon the termination of the occupation.⁷ Indeed, it has been argued that Palestinians live in a sort of suspended animation, unable to realize a life in place.⁸ In such a condition, caring for the environment can seem to be an abstraction, a diversion, or a pathetic consolation.

Early Environmental Orientations

A shared component in Israeli and Palestinian narratives is that the other community has treated the land poorly. For Israelis, this argument chiefly characterizes the period of the Ottoman empire, but it simultaneously draws a connection between the landscape of the Bible and the settlement efforts of the Zionist movement in the early twentieth century. Stemming from such texts as the travel diaries of Mark Twain,⁹ there was a general perception that the Holy Land was degraded under the Ottomans, a view confirmed by British forestry experts such as Richard St. Barbe Baker who observed in 1931 that "the barren hills of Judea sadly need to be planted.¹⁰ Their rain-washed slopes are bare of humus." Thus the early builders of the state were able to cast their efforts as restoring a lost and rightful fertility that had been squandered through neglect and abuse. In a 1951 address to the Knesset (Parliament), Prime Minister Ben Gurion issued the following call:

> We must wrap all the mountains of the country and their slopes in trees, all the hills and stony lands that will not succeed in agriculture, the dunes of the coastal valley, the dry lands of the Negev to the east and south of Baer Sheva, that is to say all of the land of Edom and the Arava until Eilat. We must also plant for security reasons, along all the borders, along all the roads, routes, and paths, around public and military buildings and facilities. . . . We will not be faithful to one of the two central goals of the state—making the wilderness bloom—if we make do with only the needs of the hour. . . . We are a state at the beginning of repairing the corruption of generations, corruption which was done to the nation and corruption which was done to the land.¹¹

Thus, from a very early stage in the implementation of Zionism, land and politics—and security—were indivisible, and the quasi-governmental agency charged with land purchase, the Keren Keyemet L'Yisrael (referred to in English as the Jewish National Fund) became the chief architect and executive body for both the development of infrastructure and care of the environment. The conflation of development and stewardship made sense in terms of the ethos of the national movement, which asserted the overlap of independence and the praxis of state building: to wit, if you did it properly, it validated your right to do it.[12] From this perspective, the Arab subjects of Ottoman rule shared in the responsibility for neglect and abuse of the land, and thereby yielded whatever interest they may have had in determining the fate of the territory. Ben-Gurion, perhaps the preeminent architect of the state, had an enduring and close relationship with Yosef Weitz, the head of the Keren Keyemet L'Yisrael, and together they shaped their construction of environment as an integral part of the national enterprise.

For Palestinians, a formal agenda of self-rule came later, and under the Ottoman empire and the early British Mandate, they were not organized in such a way as to develop institutions or an ideology in relation to land and environment.[13] Instead, they were reactive, and conditioned to suspect the role of regimes of outsiders whose interest in the land was largely economic, and whose practices blended a mixture of interfering regulation and distant lack of interest. The salient feature for the Palestinian peasantry was the dynamic of taxation, which imposed a significant burden, on the one hand, but allowed for the casual expansion of land holdings to bolster the tax base, on the other. The environment was a venue of subsistence, but it was also a theater of contention. Under Ottoman administration, tax rates for some of the different land rights categories, including the communal *musha'a* system, encouraged an extractive approach, with little regard for the long-term welfare of the land.[14] The regulatory approach of the British followed a colonial model which, as in other places, sought to minimize indigenous land rights in favor of an aggregating system of specific classifications and bans that put resources at the disposal of the government.[15] The result of Ottoman and British policies was that Palestinians, for whom land holding was a matter of cultural significance as a source of honor, viewed the environment as something to be mediated locally and utilized economically. The political connotations of that dynamic gained in importance only with the rise and success of the Zionist movement. As the two communities followed their overlapping yet increasingly separate paths during the Mandate years, the environment, still viewed as a tool for advancing individual and communal needs, became increasingly polarized and polarizing.

The Environment as a National Inventory

In the move toward and the transition to statehood, the environment represented for the Zionist movement a series of projects, challenges, and, most of all, opportunity. Indeed, the challenges *were* the opportunity, in that they could help forge and showcase the renewed Jewish spirit of independence and prowess. This spirit has been dubbed "technological optimism," a particular brand of Zionist romanticization of the environment and its potential to be harnessed into the national cause.[16] The draining of the Hula swamps, creation of the National Water Carrier to further the development of the Negev region, and reforestation of different parts of the country were seen as testimony to a productive and harmonious relationship with nature. That attitude would be tested in later decades, but in the period of nascent state building, the costs of these types of activities were not yet visible.

For Palestinians, however, those costs were very much evident in the landscape, albeit in a retrospective manner. With Israel's declaration of statehood in 1948 and the ensuing assumption of control in the remaining Palestinian lands by Egypt and Jordan, there began a process of memorializing what had been lost that was part "factual" and part mythical. By the factual component, I mean those events related to political developments such as the resolutions of the United Nations, the warfare, and the armistice of 1949 that shaped the territorial status and access for Palestinians. The mythical component related, in part, to the character of the land and lifestyle that had been lost or disrupted as a result of the Zionist endeavor. The pain of loss led to a romanticization on the Palestinian side that suggested that the turn of political events had not only cost them their right of self-rule, but also an idealized homeland in which the environment was part of a broader Palestinian idyll.[17] In many respects this didn't correspond with Palestinian experience prior to 1948, as conditions under the Ottoman and British Mandatory authorities were not seen as particularly uplifting according to contemporaneous accounts, but Hobsbawm observes that links are typically forged to a "suitable" past.[18] Parmenter notes that in their cultural expression Palestinians often enlist "nature in general, and the land in particular, as their last and strongest ally."[19] Thus, with the Zionist/Jewish influence and its changes on the land given an overwhelmingly negative valence in Palestinian discourse, all that "was not" subject to that influence, whether in the present or the remembered/imagined past, came to have a more positive patina by default. Thus a Palestinian "Eden" was created and lost as a process of memory, a more proximate version of

Zionist recovery of image and context from biblical descriptions of nature and land in an earlier era.[20]

During the transitional period from the late Mandate years through the early state building period of 1950s, events were wrenching, rapid, and engrossing. Though profound changes were still to come for both peoples, in some respects the templates for discursive patterns were formed in relation to self, nation, and the other. The environment was a part of these discourses, as described above. Indeed, one of the challenges facing both communities is that the fundamental orientations toward the environment have remained static. As will be discussed below, significant developments in the political realm signaled the potential for a new and possibly joint environmental ethos, but the lack of successive breakthroughs that could lead to an agreed settlement of the conflict left environmental attitudes at the status quo ante.

In such circumstances, the environment serves as a mythic inventory of deeds and virtues, triumph and victimization, containing stories for the Palestinians of what they have lost, and for the Israelis of what they accomplished. The significance of national(ist) narratives of the environment is that they help forge identities and provide explanations and justifications for actions that might otherwise remain apart from the metanarratives of nationhood. A helpful concept here is that of Benedict Anderson's "imagined communities."[21] Ideas of connection that allow for people to see themselves as having a common bond can include narratives of the environment and the ways in which people act or respond in the context of struggles for the disposition of land and stewardship of the environment. Thus to be Israeli is to subscribe to the hubris of technology and development that is part of the Zionist ethos,[22] and to be Palestinian is to identify with the loss of a prelapsarian relationship that was to embody the nobility of the relationship of the people to the land.[23]

Behaving Like a State?

According to Alatout, "Israeli [environmental] narratives . . . sidestep questions of property rights and sovereignty."[24] This suggestion posits a measure of confidence in the physical and political security of the state, and dovetails with a period that some have termed "post-Zionist." From this perspective, Israel has fulfilled the goal of Zionism—in that it has achieved independence and a sovereign Jewish state—and its government and people are beyond the existential questions that drove its early policies and ethos. Were this to be the case, then questions of the environment could exist alongside, but separate from, issues of national security and identity. Those issues, while still relevant, would not automatically trump environmental concerns inasmuch as they would be normalized priorities rather than stark choices between life and death. Yet it seems that Israel has not managed to separate its current strength from its past—and present—anxieties, and as a result, it continues to pursue development as a justification for statehood and a method of survival.

A number of examples shed light on the continuing imperatives that bracket environmental questions in Israel. On one hand, they show that there is an environmental constituency that is serious, dedicated, and persistent. On the other hand, they confirm that environmentalism, per se, must accede to appeals to the dominant metanarrative of nationalism. Indeed, at times Israelis advocating on behalf of the environment seek to tap into the pervasive discourse of the state in order to gain an audience or prevent the erosion of support for their cause. To date, however, major skirmishes around issues of environmental concern have not resulted in significant successes and, indeed, have yielded some symbolically important defeats. This illustrates what Newman terms "a form of environmental 'schizophrenia' where the society and its institutions are aware of the ecological problems, discuss them in great detail, but fail to act accordingly to prevent further environmental degradation."[25]

One case that shows this tension revolved around the allocation of land in the Negev desert. Settlement of the Negev by Jewish Israelis was one of Prime Minister Ben Gurion's signal ambitions, and it led, in part, to the construction of the National Water Carrier that created a conduit for water from the north to be used for agricultural expansion in the south. There are competing interests in the Negev, however, including open areas used for military training and wild and scenic areas that may merit preservation. A further matter of contention in the Negev is the future herding patterns of Bedouin communities that Israel has tried to limit in part by settling them in towns, and in part through the development of large rural land holdings for individual Jewish families. For opposing this settlement policy, the very mainstream Society for the Protection of Nature in Israel (SPNI) was accused of being anti-patriotic for its attempts to limit a measure that was depicted as preserving a resource for Jewish use by limiting Arab access to the land.[26] That accusation had to be taken seriously by the SPNI despite its stellar credentials as an institution that had contributed to the stewardship of the environment. Indeed, in another Negev dispute, the organization had overtly appealed to Israeli security concerns (and by implication national patriotism) when it opposed development of a Voice of America transmitter in the desert by arguing that construction and operation of the facility would have an adverse impact on the training activities of the air force.[27]

In the first Negev case, Israelis were attempting to limit development by other Israelis against a background of an international threat, and in the second case, from competition from a local Arab community. At other times, the challenge has come from competing visions held by other Israelis in regard to what Israel should be like. Open space is often the issue, as one version incorporates a more biblical vision that has a more nature-friendly approach to milk and honey, whereas the more powerful model is of a robust, industrialized, and prosperous land, despite the associated impacts on the land. In a case that I have discussed elsewhere,[28] a coalition of green interests attempted to check the development of Jerusalem at the expense of its urban greenbelt. In order to do so, opponents of sprawl depicted the incursion on the forested lands at the city's margins as being akin to terrorist attacks. Their language was fairly typical in its use of martial terms and a binary of attack and defense, as is the case in many other parts of the world, but the images deployed in the public materials designed by the coalition members were taken from common representations of violence carried out against Israeli civilians as part of a political attack against the state itself. That effort was part of an explicit recognition that security issues had an automatic salience, and that a successful case for environmental concerns could not be made on the merits of quality of life issues alone.

In perhaps the highest-profile case of an environmental dispute in Israel, opponents organized to block construction of the Trans-Israel (north-south) highway. The scope of the project rivaled the massive infrastructural developments of the early state period, and would leave its mark on much of the country in terms of day-to-day practicalities and a permanent imprint on the landscape. According to Garb, "Opposition to the project was keen, and in many ways constituted a landmark in the maturation of Israel's environmental movement."[29] Yet Mazlish notes that "the paving of the highway and its subsequent operations are perceived by many as proof of the total failure of environmental organizations in their struggle against it."[30]

It is not surprising that the green interests proved impotent in their effort to block construction of the highway. Quality of life certainly had a voice in the discussion and provided a strong appeal (both pro and con, for instance shorter travel time, less aggravation, etc. versus prevention of sprawl and maintenance of open spaces).[31] The notions of progress and modernization are part and parcel of the Israeli economy and are viewed by many as a measure of the stature of the state and as a reflection of its citizenry. It should also be noted, however, that moving the army rapidly and efficiently on a north-south axis was part of the official justification for the project, and the security question once again was available to those who, for sincere or opportunistic reasons, sought to defang environmental objections through the gravity of military necessity.

Waiting for a State

In relation to the environment, Palestinians have had little agency beyond the local decisions of individuals, and even these have been circumscribed in some respects since Ottoman times. In the breach, there have been efforts to write and narrate things as they were, as noted above, and to describe what ought to and may be in the present and future. Popular culture has been the venue for such imaginings, with a primary focus, understandably, on the land. Both formally and informally Palestinians have created a tradition of narrating Palestine, with poetry, theater, art, education, historiography—all contributing to a general oeuvre that posits a more perfect Palestine. Prior to the closure of Israeli territory to Palestinians from the West Bank and Gaza, individuals, families, and groups sometimes undertook unofficial "nostalgia tours," visiting sites such as Sahne (Gan HaShlosha), Bohayrat Tabaraya (the Sea of Galilee or Yam Kinneret) or the coastal plain, sharing or implanting reminiscences of what had been and hopes for what might yet come.[32] Whether they live on the land or elsewhere, Palestinians engage in activities in which their homes are "revitalized and their existence celebrated."[33]

One of the few ways in which Palestinians could act politically in relation to the environment was through acts of resistance. Their first iterations may have come during the Ottoman period, when peasants uprooted their own trees rather than see the entirety of their profit confiscated by tax authorities. A more overt and political manifestation was during the period of the Arab Revolt in Palestine, from 1936–39. During the Mandate period the British had undertaken afforestation projects and created (sometimes phantom) forest reserves that served to alienate a considerable amount of land and further restrict use by both Palestinians and Jews.[34] The forests were thus seen as markers of a restrictive governmental presence. Though they could also serve as sources of fuel, forage, cover, and recreation, Palestinians chose to destroy some of these symbols of the British role through politically motivated acts of arson.

In the period after 1948, Palestinians had no jurisdiction over their own land, and little to no voice in the disposition of their resources and development of the environment. In the West Bank, the Jordanians maintained a number of afforestation projects, primarily to the east of Jerusalem and in the northern areas near Jenin and Nabulus, but the significant changes were those occurring within the Green Line. It was evident that water was a key to the viability of Israel, and disputes with Lebanon, Syria, and Jordan accompanied the birth of the state and the ensuing years. It is notable that the first attack of the Fatah movement—later a leading power in the PLO—was carried out in 1965 against Israel's National Water Carrier. On the Israeli side, this affirmed the link between environmental issues and national security. On the Palestinian side, the mobilization of water for the massive expansion of infrastructure and community building was evidence that Israel's existence came at the expense of and was mediated through resource use in what was perceived as a zero-sum situation.[35] Overall, the period between the founding of Israel and the inception of the peace process was marked by exclusive agendas that concentrated on the dynamics of nationalism, and there was little room for protection of the environment—for differing reasons—on either side.

The Rise and Fall of Environmentalism

In the heady days following the Oslo Accords, there was a rush to create and facilitate joint projects that would foster Palestinian-Israeli cooperation and benefit both communities. The environment was an obvious arena for such endeavors. Support of various kinds and outside funding agencies and states embraced new partnerships between academics and NGOs, bureaucrats and technicians. Issues such as sewage processing, aquifer management, wildlife protection, pollution mitigation—all were attractive opportunities to move the process forward. Indeed, the environment was seen as a passive object that could be tended to by both sides (and the adjacent Arab states as well) as a confidence-building measure that would provide momentum for dealing with the "more difficult" subjects that needed to be addressed.[36] The Green Line receded as a barrier to environmental planning/mitigation, and plans for resource sharing were bandied about as part of an "emergent regional environmentalism."[37] The mood was optimistic, and the tone was somewhat celebratory. Politicians inclined toward lofty rhetoric, such as Shimon Peres of Israel, called for a new Middle East that would change the region from brown to green.[38] Activists on both sides were able to imagine a future in which the environment would not compete with nationalism, and a shared environment would improve in tandem with good relations.

Unfortunately, the peace process gave way to the difficulties of negotiation and the complexities of the conflict. As the honeymoon period

Figure 9.1. *Olive Columns.* 1991. By Ran Morin. The sculpture marks the landscape near the Green Line dividing Israel and Palestine at Ramat Rachel, Jerusalem. Intended as a statement on "natural existence in artificial conditions," it shows living olive trees dissociated from—yet still connected to—the earth. With the obvious symbolisms of the olive, its use in this context invites commentary on the peace process and the state of the environment. The olive trees are eighty years old and are kept alive via drip irrigation. *Photograph by Shaul Cohen, 2008.*

began to fade, the environmental issues maintained their status as a problem that had an inherent logic for cooperation, given the physical limitations of the small shared territory of Israel/Palestine. Yet to the dismay of many and the surprise of some, environmental projects and partnerships became increasingly problematic and isolated. According to Chaitlin et al., "Palestinian[s] . . . do not see the point of 'talking environment' without 'talking occupation.'"[39] The Israelis, however, tend to see "talking conflict" as a detour from "talking environment." Moreover, the outbreak of the al-Aqsa Intifada in 2000 led to increasing practical difficulties for both Palestinian and Israeli partners, complicating efforts to foster collaborative work, both applied and academic. Each community continued to inflict its own particular toll on the environment, and the blame for the damage in that polarizing dynamic accompanied feelings of abandonment and even betrayal that characterized the broader cooperative framework during these years. The derailment of a shared environmental agenda wasn't complete, and NGOs and some academic partnerships endure. But in the main, the demise of the peace process took the momentum out of environmental projects, which, as noted by Feitelson and Levy, had never been central to the agreements reached by the various sides.[40]

Environmentalism Deferred

For now, Israelis and Palestinians see a chauvinistic zero-sum situation as the defining characteristic of their relationship. Both sides, albeit in different ways, are insecure and feel themselves to be victimized. Whatever their commonalities and differences may be, neither side believes that the other relates to the environment in good faith, and each feels the other to be an untrustworthy—indeed an *unworthy*—partner for moving forward to a joint resolution of the conflict. The one issue that is clearly critical to both communities, the supply of water for domestic, agricultural, and industrial purposes, is viewed in the context of politics and security, with each side leveling accusations against the other for endangering a resource that is critical to both sides.

The environment is thus added to the victimology of the conflict, and the damage that is both increasing and increasingly evident is seen as a material strike against the welfare of the respective communities, and indicative of their moral failing as well. Yet, while violence against people is seen as a barometer of the state of relations between the two, actions that affect the environment, such as the urban sprawl that can be found throughout Palestine/Israel, is viewed differently. The use of land falls back to the nationalist tropes, and building is seen as supporting or undermining discourses of national legitimation, depending on who is offering the commentary. A senior official of Israel's Nature Reserves Authority observed that "the damage to the environment is a tragedy, and yet this is what we aspired to: a developed state with cities and roads, like anywhere else, so you have to see it as a success."[41]

Given the violence that seems an inherent part of the situation, questions of open space, the plight of migratory birds, and air quality seem, to most, rather pedestrian. Even for many of those who care about such matters, environmental issues take a backseat to the pressing concerns of the day. Dawson points out that environmental challenges are increasingly bundled with issues of environmental justice and, although there is potential to unite people around such problems, they can also be divisive in and of themselves.[42] Moreover, she notes that environmental problems may seem ephemeral, whereas the underlying identity problems of the broader conflict may seem much more enduring. As Tal observes, "In the inevitable clash between security and environmental values, it is no surprise that the environment comes out the loser."[43]

I believe that Tal makes a critical contribution in specifying environmental *values* as distinct from environmentalism. Such values can be found on both sides of the Palestinian-Israeli divide, but they cannot successfully bridge it, at least for now. Indeed, in the light of the evidence, it is clear that environmental issues give way before other needs, and a shared environmental discourse is marginal at best. Separate environmental discourses are themselves vulnerable to partisanship and operate only as subsets of the overarching nationalist metanarratives.

Returning to the question posed above concerning the existence of Palestinian, Israeli, and shared environmentalisms, I suggest that, although the question is pertinent, the answer has yet to emerge. In saying that, I argue that neither community has attained the degree of security necessary for there to be a *meaningful* environmentalism, that is, a movement that engages environmental challenges without defaulting to security or identity concerns along parochial lines. Land is a central facet of identity for Palestinians and Israelis, albeit in somewhat differing ways. Alongside the idea of the land, however, has always been its utilitarian value. Palestinian culture holds the land, and connectedness with the land, as a *national* value,[44] but also as a way to feed one's family, and, at both levels, land is equated with honor. Israelis embrace the land as refuge, but also as a way of shedding the confines of the diaspora experience: to have the land is to *be* Israeli. Both Israelis and Palestinians speak of the rest of the world as being "outside" of The Land. There is, however, space between the notional and the concrete in both communities, as evidenced by the practicalities of living day by day in and on the sacred, and population growth and economic development have inevitable impacts.

There continues to be a cultural celebration of the environment on both sides of the divide. Despite this, it seems that the land has little active voice. Yet, at some point, acknowledging the very right of the other to exist may compel cooperation of a sort that seems to be a forlorn aspiration of a "green" minority or a brief mirage of the peace process. The Palestinian poet Husayn Fa'ur wrote that he "made a promise to a beautiful dream, certain that your dream is the ruling dream. The path we have chosen will bring us to a haven."[45] There are dreams of the past and dreams of the future that posit an idyllic environment. A future haven, however, cannot be the exclusive territory of one side alone, for that vision has yielded the ongoing crisis that is Israel/Palestine. Perhaps it can only be that when security and identity concerns have been addressed for both Palestinians and Israelis that the existential pressures of a small and bounded space can become a priority for both communities, and a shared imaginary of the environment can begin to emerge.

Notes

1. Samer Alatout, "Towards a Bio-territorial Conception of Power: Territory, Population, and Environmental Narratives in Palestine and Israel," *Political Geography* 25, no. 6 (2006): 601–21; Avner De-Shalit, "From the Political to the Objective: The Dialectics of Zionism and the Environment," *Environmental Politics* 4, no. 1 (1995): 70–87; Deborah Shmueli, "Environmental Justice in the Israeli Context," *Environment and Planning A* 40, no. 10 (2008): 2384–401.

2. Alon Tal, "Enduring Technological Optimism: Zionism's Environmental Ethic and Its Influence on Israel's Environmental History," *Environmental History* 13, no. 2 (2008): 275–305.

3. Susan Slyomovics, *The Object of Memory: Arab and Jew Narrate the Palestinian Village* (Philadelphia: University of Pennsylvania Press), 172.

4. David Vogel, "Israeli Environmental Policy in Comparative Perspective," *Israel Affairs* 5, nos. 2 and 3 (1999): 246–64.

5. Jane Dawson, "The Two Faces of Environmental Justice: Lessons from the Eco-nationalist Phenomenon," *International Politics* 9, no. 2 (2000): 22–60.

6. Salim Tamari, "Narratives of Exile: How Narratives of the Nakba Have Evolved in the Memories of Exiled Palestinians," *Palestine-Israel Journal of Politics, Economics and Culture* 9, no. 4 (2002), accessed online August 2009; Julia Chaitlin et al. "Environmental Work and Peace Work: The Israeli-Palestinian Case," *Peace and Conflict Studies* 9, no. 2 (2002): 64–94.

7. Shaul Cohen, "An Absence of Place: Expectation and Realization in the West Bank," in *Cultural Encounters with the Environment: Enduring and Evolving Geographic Themes.* ed. Alexander Murphy and Douglas Johnson (Lanham, Md.: Rowman and Littlefield, 2000), 283–303.

8. Edward Said, *The Question of Palestine* (New York: Vintage Books, 1980).

9. Mark Twain, *Innocents Abroad; or, The New Pilgrims' Progress* (New York: Heritage Press, 1962).

10. Richard St. Barbe Baker, *Proceedings of the First Meeting of the Men of the Forests: Palestine* (1931), 7.

11. Yosef Weitz, *Forest and Afforestation in Israel* (Israel: Masada Press, 1970), 295. (In Hebrew; author's translation.)

12. Mark LeVine, *Overthrowing Geography: Jaffa, Tel Aviv, and the Struggle for Palestine. 1880–1948* (Berkeley: University of California Press, 2005), 24.

13. Rashid Khalidi, *Palestinian Identity* (New York: Columbia University Press, 1998).

14. In the *musha'a* system village lands were collectively owned but worked by families according to a periodic rotation of plots. As a result, there was little incentive for good stewardship practices, as the upcoming rotation would deny any direct benefit to the individual who made improvements. Peter Sluglett and Marion Farouk-Sluglett, "The Application of the 1858 Land Code in Greater Syria: Some Preliminary Observations," in *Land Tenure and*

Social Transformation in the Middle East, ed. Tarif Khalidi (Beirut: American University of Beirut Press, 1984); Shaul Cohen, *The Politics of Planting: Israeli-Palestinian Competition for Control of Land in the Jerusalem Periphery* (Chicago: University of Chicago Press, 1993).

15. Roza El-Eini, *Mandated Landscape: British Imperial Rule in Palestine, 1929–1948* (London: Routledge, 2006); Diana K. Davis, "Desert 'Wastes' of the Maghreb: Desertification Narratives in French Colonial Environmental History of North Africa," *Cultural Geographies* 11, no. 4 (2004): 359–87.

16. Tal, "Enduring Technological Optimism."

17. Slyomovics, *Object of Memory*.

18. Eric Hobsbawm, "Introduction: Inventing Traditions," in *The Invention of Tradition*, ed. Eric Hobsbawm and Terrence Ranger (Cambridge: Cambridge University Press, 1992), 1.

19. Barbara Parmenter, *Giving Voice to Stones: Place and Identity in Palestinian Literature* (Austin: University of Texas Press, 1994), 286–87.

20. Yael Zerubavel, *Recovered Roots: Collective Memory and the Making of Israeli National Tradition* (Chicago: University of Chicago Press, 1995).

21. Benedict Anderson, *Imagined Communities* (London: Verso, 1983).

22. Tal, "Enduring Technological Optimism"; De-Shalit, "From the Political to the Objective."

23. Walid Khalidi, *All That Remains: The Palestinian Villages Occupied and Depopulated by Israel* (Washington, D.C.: Institute for Palestine Studies, 1992); Ghazi Falah, "The 1948 Israeli-Palestinian War and Its Aftermath: The Transformation and De-signification of Palestine's Cultural Landscape," *Annals of the Association of American Geographers* 86, no. 2 (1996): 256–85; Cohen, "Absence of Place."

24. Alatout, "Towards a Bio-territorial Conception of Power," 610.

25. David Newman, "In the Name of Security: In the Name of Peace—Environmental Schizophrenia and the Security Discourse in Israel/Palestine," *Third AFES-PRESS GMOSS Workshop on Reconceptualising Security in an Era of Globalisation* (The Hague, 2004), 2.

26. Jeremy Benstein, "Between Earth Day and Land Day: Palestinian and Jewish Environmentalisms in Israel," in *Palestinian and Israeli Environmental Narratives*, ed. Stuart Schoenfeld (Toronto: Centre for International and Security Studies, York University, 2005), 65.

27. Avner De-Shalit and Moti Talias, "Green or Blue and White? Environmental Controversies in Israel," *Environmental Politics* 3, no. 2 (1994): 277.

28. Shaul Cohen, "As a City Besieged: Place, Zionism, and the Deforestation of Jerusalem," *Environment and Planning D: Society and Space* 20, no. 2 (2002): 209–30.

29. Yaakov Garb, "Constructing the Trans-Israel Highway's Inevitability," *Israel Studies* 9, no. 2 (2004): 180–217.

30. Michal Maizlish, *The Struggle against the Trans Israel Highway: Documenting an Environmental Struggle* (Jerusalem: Jerusalem Institute for Israel Studies, Center for Environmental Policy, 2005), 9.

31. Alatout, "Towards a Bio-territorial Conception of Power."
32. Diane Baxter, "Living the Uprising: Palestinian Lives during the Intifada" (PhD diss., University of California at Los Angeles, 1991).
33. Slyomovics, *Object of Memory,* xii.
34. Cohen, *Politics of Planting;* El-Eini, *Mandated Landscape.*
35. Miriam R. Lowi, *Water and Power: The Politics of a Scarce Resource in the Jordan River Basin* (Cambridge: Cambridge University Press, 1993); Jan Selby, *Water, Power, and Politics in the Middle East: The Other Israeli-Palestinian Conflict* (London: I. B. Tauris, 2003).
36. Eran Feitelson and Nitsan Levy, "The Environmental Aspects of Reterritorialization: Environmental Facets of Israeli-Arab Agreements," *Political Geography* 25, no. 4 (2006): 459–77.
37. Stuart Schoenfeld, Introduction to *Palestinian and Israeli Environmental Narratives,* ed. Stuart Schoenfeld (Toronto: Centre for International and Security Studies, York University, 2005), 1.
38. Shimon Peres and Arye Naor, *The New Middle East* (New York: Henry Holt, 1993).
39. Chaitlin et al., "Environmental Work and Peace Work," 83.
40. Feitelson and Levy, "Environmental Aspects of Reterritorialization."
41. Tzvika Avni, Jerusalem Region Director, Society for the Protection of Nature in Israel, personal interview, 11 April 1988, Jerusalem.
42. Dawson, "Two Faces of Environmental Justice."
43. Tal, "Enduring Technological Optimism," 92.
44. Ted Swedenburg, "The Palestinian Peasant as National Signifier," *Anthropological Quarterly* 63, no. 1 (1990): 18–30.
45. Slyomovics, *Object of Memory,* 177.

Bibliography

Alatout, Samer. "Towards a Bio-territorial Conception of Power: Territory, Population, and Environmental Narratives in Palestine and Israel." *Political Geography* 25, no. 6 (2006): 601–21.

Anderson, Benedict. *Imagined Communities.* London: Verso, 1983.

Baxter, Diane. "Living the Uprising: Palestinian Lives during the Intifada." PhD diss., University of California at Los Angeles, 1991.

Benstein, Jeremy. "Between Earth Day and Land Day: Palestinian and Jewish Environmentalisms in Israel." In *Palestinian and Israeli Environmental Narratives,* edited by Stuart Schoenfeld, 51–73. Toronto: Centre for International and Security Studies, York University, 2005.

Chaitlin, Julia, et al. "Environmental Work and Peace Work: The Israeli-Palestinian Case." *Peace and Conflict Studies* 9, no. 2 (2002): 64–94.

Cohen, Shaul. "An Absence of Place: Expectation and Realization in the West Bank." In *Cultural Encounters with the Environment: Enduring and Evolving*

Geographic Themes, edited by Alexander Murphy and Douglas Johnson, 283–303. Lanham, Md.: Rowman and Littlefield, 2000.

———. "As a City Besieged: Place, Zionism, and the Deforestation of Jerusalem." *Environment and Planning D: Society and Space* 20, no. 2 (2002): 209–30.

———. *The Politics of Planting: Israeli Palestinian Competition for Control of Land in the Jerusalem Periphery.* Chicago: University of Chicago Press, 1993.

Davis, Diana K. "Desert 'Wastes' of the Maghreb: Desertification Narratives in French Colonial Environmental History of North Africa." *Cultural Geographies* 11, no. 4 (2004): 359–87.

Dawson, Jane. "The Two Faces of Environmental Justice: Lessons from the Eco-nationalist Phenomenon." *International Politics* 9, no. 2 (2000): 22–60.

De-Shalit, Avner. "From the Political to the Objective: The Dialectics of Zionism and the Environment." *Environmental Politics* 4, no. 1 (1995): 70–87.

De-Shalit, Avner, and Moti Talias. "Green or Blue and White? Environmental Controversies in Israel." *Environmental Politics* 3, no. 2 (1994): 273–94.

El-Eini, Roza. *Mandated Landscape: British Imperial Rule in Palestine, 1929–1948.* London: Routledge, 2006.

Falah, Ghazi. "The 1948 Israeli-Palestinian War and Its Aftermath: The Transformation and De-signification of Palestine's Cultural Landscape." *Annals of the Association of American Geographers* 86, no. 2 (1996): 256–85.

Feitelson, Eran, and Nitsan Levy. "The Environmental Aspects of Reterritorialization: Environmental Facets of Israeli-Arab Agreements." *Political Geography* 25, no. 4 (2006): 459–77.

Garb, Yaakov. "Constructing the Trans-Israel Highway's Inevitability." *Israel Studies* 9, no. 2 (2004): 180–217.

Hobsbawm, Eric. "Introduction: Inventing Traditions." In *The Invention of Tradition*, edited by Eric Hobsbawm and Terence Ranger, 1–14. Cambridge: Cambridge University Press, 1992.

Khalidi, Rashid. *Palestinian Identity.* New York: Columbia University Press, 1998.

Khalidi, Walid. *All That Remains: The Palestinian Villages Occupied and Depopulated by Israel.* Washington, D.C.: Institute for Palestine Studies, 1992.

LeVine, Mark. *Overthrowing Geography: Jaffa, Tel Aviv, and the Struggle for Palestine, 1880–1948.* Berkeley: University of California Press, 2005.

Lowi, Miriam R. *Water and Power: The Politics of a Scarce Resource in the Jordan River Basin.* Cambridge: Cambridge University Press, 1993.

Maizlish, Michal. *The Struggle against the Trans Israel Highway: Documenting an Environmental Struggle.* Jerusalem: Jerusalem Institute for Israel Studies, Center for Environmental Policy, 2005.

Newman, David. "In the Name of Security: In the Name of Peace—Environmental Schizophrenia and the Security Discourse in Israel/Palestine." *Third AFES-PRESS GMOSS Workshop on Reconceptualising Security in an Era of Globalisation.* The Hague, 2004.

Parmenter, Barbara. *Giving Voice to Stones: Place and Identity in Palestinian Literature.* Austin: University of Texas Press, 1994.

Peres, Shimon, and Arye Naor. *The New Middle East.* New York: Henry Holt, 1993.

Said, Edward. *The Question of Palestine.* New York: Vintage Books, 1980.

Schoenfeld, Stuart. Introduction to *Palestinian and Israeli Environmental Narratives,* edited by Stuart Schoenfeld, 1–10. Toronto: Centre for International and Security Studies, York University, 2005.

———. "Types of Environmental Narratives and Their Utility for Understanding Israeli and Palestinian Environmentalism." In *Palestinian and Israeli Environmental Narratives,* edited by Stuart Schoenfeld, 93–113. Toronto: Centre for International and Security Studies, York University, 2005.

Selby, Jan. *Water, Power, and Politics in the Middle East: The Other Israeli-Palestinian Conflict.* London: I. B. Tauris, 2003.

Shmueli, Deborah. "Environmental Justice in the Israeli Context." *Environment and Planning A* 40, no. 10 (2008): 2384–401.

Sluglett, Peter, and Marion Farouk-Sluglett. "The Application of the 1858 Land Code in Greater Syria: Some Preliminary Observations." In *Land Tenure and Social Transformation in the Middle East,* edited by Tarif Khalidi. Beirut: American University of Beirut Press, 1984.

Slyomovics, Susan. *The Object of Memory: Arab and Jew Narrate the Palestinian Village.* Philadelphia: University of Pennsylvania Press, 1998.

St. Barbe Baker, Richard. *Proceedings of the First Meeting of the Men of the Forests: Palestine.* 1931.

Swedenburg, Ted. "The Palestinian Peasant as National Signifier." *Anthropological Quarterly* 63, no. 1 (1990): 18–30.

Tal, Alon. "Enduring Technological Optimism: Zionism's Environmental Ethic and Its Influence on Israel's Environmental History." *Environmental History* 13, no. 2 (2008): 275–305.

Tamari, Salim. "Narratives of Exile: How Narratives of the Nakba Have Evolved in the Memories of Exiled Palestinians." *Palestine-Israel Journal of Politics, Economics and Culture* 9, no. 4 (2002). Accessed online August 2009.

Twain, Mark. *Innocents Abroad; or, The New Pilgrims' Progress.* New York: Heritage Press, 1962.

Vogel, David. "Israeli Environmental Policy in Comparative Perspective." *Israel Affairs* 5, nos. 2 and 3 (1999): 246–64.

Weitz, Yosef. *Forest and Afforestation in Israel.* Israel: Masada Press, 1970. (In Hebrew.)

Zerubavel, Yael. *Recovered Roots: Collective Memory and the Making of Israeli National Tradition.* Chicago: University of Chicago Press, 1995.

AFTERWORD

Are Environmental Imaginaries Culturally Constructed?

Timothy Mitchell

THE MODERN history of the Middle East has always been the history of a human relationship with nature. The environment appears to define the Arab-Islamic world more than it does any other major region in world history. It is time to ask, as this book does, how this naturalized history came about.

Stretched in an irregular shape from the Atlantic to Central Asia, the region of the Middle East and North Africa was always demarcated by its climate. An arid environment was said to produce distinctive forms of history. Political orders were built upon major river systems, or along narrow fertile crescents and coasts. Political dynamics were traced to the difference between the desert and the sown, the nomadic and the settled, the tribe and the state. Colonial histories, as Diana Davis shows, could describe the precolonial order as incapable of managing this difficult human-natural balance or maintaining the region's precarious ecology. Europeans could then justify their colonization of the Arab world in ecological terms.

We write histories of the more recent past as the story of states coping with fragile environments, limited areas of cultivable land, populations expanding faster than resources, the artificial growth of megacities, and strained or disappearing reserves of water. Even the one natural resource found in abundance appears as a problem. The region's large reserves of oil are described as a curse whose presence disrupts the normal process of political development.

The forces of nature that define the region's history typically acquire their place in the story as something abnormal and errant. The arid, subtropical ecology of the Middle East and North Africa, as Davis points out, is frequently treated not as one of the earth's several terrestrial biomes, alongside the varieties of temperate, boreal, tropical, and other zones, but as an aberration and a threat in comparison to the norm of a temperate world. Low levels of rainfall and riparian areas of concentrated cultivation and settlement are addressed as abnormalities to be overcome, just as the curse of abundant oil reserves must be broken. Davis describes this way of seeing things as an environmental orientalism. The natural shapes the region's history as something unnatural.

An unnatural nature appears to determine Middle Eastern history, but we have no history of this nature. The natural world stands on one side of the account, human history on the other. Academic specialization helps keep them apart, with experts on each side working with their own time scales, agents, and records. The environmental forces and reserves that shape the region's past and present occur in historical accounts largely as an underlying set of resources, restrictions, and risks. Knowledge of these elements is produced for the most part by nonhistorians, among specialists in the various natural and environmental sciences. Historians specialize in studying the human response to those forces, focusing on the tools with which humans are said to address, understand, and try to overcome the limits of their natural environment: culture, politics, economic and technical knowhow, and the moral resources of communities and states.

The first task, as this book explains, is to interrogate and disassemble the representations of nature that govern the region's history. Unpacking the environmental imaginaries formed in the colonial period and carried over or transformed after colonialism is a large undertaking. The essays in this book, and the larger bodies of writing and research on which all of them are based, take on this task in a variety of ways. They explore how the British in Egypt and Iraq, the French in North Africa, and the Zionist movement in Palestine each deployed distinctive visions of environmental crisis, neglect, or possibility to help construct a colonial order and justify European intervention, settlement, and control. Typically the place to be colonized or controlled was described in contrast to a more verdant and fertile past, or a more prosperous, well-irrigated future, which European control would restore or bring about. The failure of the native population to sustain or bring into being this abundance became one of the primary justifications for the colonial occupation.

In the middle decades of the twentieth century, as European control was challenged and transformed, new regimes adopted or developed many elements of the earlier environmental imaginaries. They devised schemes to make or remake the nation, and eliminate threats to its national coherence, on an even grander scale. The initiatives took several forms, but the most prominent and frequent were projects to build dams across the region's major rivers, on a scale far larger than the undertakings of the Ottoman and colonial periods. The dams would store up the rivers' waters, eliminate systems of flood-basin irrigation, and replace the river and its carefully managed seasonal abundance with a permanent arrangement of barrages, canals, irrigation channels, and diesel pumps. The Nile, the Jordan River and its tributaries, the Tigris and Euphrates, and many other rivers were dammed up and diverted. It is no surprise that more than half the chapters of this book are concerned with the analysis of these schemes, the diverse and contested work of environmental imagination they required, and the challenges to those visions that flowed from the misjudged or unanticipated ecological transformations they engineered.

What is an environmental imaginary? The chapters in this book make clear that in most cases it is more than just a work of imagination. Its force and durability derives from the way it is reproduced and extended in rebuilt and reordered worlds. The millions of hectares of trees planted to reforest Algeria, and the criminalization of grazing and gathering on lands expropriated for reforestation; the redirection of the Nile into channels so capillary that it discharges into the sea less than 1 percent of its previous flow; the remaking of Southeastern Anatolia, as Leila Harris describes, by the monocropping of cotton; or the diversion of the Jordan River waters outside its watershed area, discussed by Samer Alatout, to enable Israel to settle and retain southern Palestine—such projects are as much a contribution to environmental imaginaries as are the travel writings, colonial reports, reconnaissance flights, engineering schemes, and court decisions that helped manufacture new ways of seeing the natural world.

The mixture of materials and processes employed in the making of environmental imaginaries gives them their scale and what sometimes appears as their irreversibility. Contributions to this book depict in a variety of terms the force and durability that the imaginary often seems to acquire. Environmental imaginaries are described as enduring or hegemonic. They are said to underlie forms of social practice, to explain the decisions and strategies of colonial powers, and to be the cause of state bureaucracies acting toward nature in distinctive ways. They could never be ascribed these powers if they were merely imaginary.

At the same time, several contributions to this volume suggest that environmental imaginaries can sometimes suddenly collapse and give way to rival visions. Priya Satia explains how the British imagination of Arabia changed quite abruptly after World War I from the image of an unknowable and barren void to the vision of a biblical Eden whose prolific fertility could be restored by modern technical intervention. Jeannie Sowers shows how technocrats and agribusiness managers in contemporary Egypt have been able to challenge a dominant understanding of the fecundity of the Nile and the proper way to exploit its natural powers. In Palestine/Israel, according to Shaul Cohen, no common environmental vision can establish itself. For both Palestinians and Israelis, for different reasons and in different ways, the effort to place a value on nature is trumped by the national question—the question, from each side, of the recuperation, survival, or future strength of the nation.

Assessing the power and durability of an environmental imaginary raises the old question of how representations of nature are related to what we call nature itself. No one any longer answers this question by assuming we can simply separate two worlds, the realm of ideas and the realm of natural facts. The chapters provide many examples illustrating why this separation cannot be sustained, from Satia's discussion of the British bombs dropped on Iraqi villages in the 1920s that operated through their "moral effect" to Cohen's description of the decision of the Palestinian resistance group Fatah in 1965 to initiate its campaign against the Zionist vision of permanently settling all of Palestine by blowing up the canal built to claim and colonize the south.

George Trumbull suggests here, as others have elsewhere, that we abandon the "false binary" between images of nature and nature itself. He proposes that we speak instead of the tangible environment and the discursive environment as existing "in superimposition upon one another." However, this sort of answer to the question of the status of imaginaries suggests two problems. First, the idea that the environment and the stories that we tell about the environment form superimposed worlds still leaves these worlds distinct—still understands each as its own world or level. However many overlaps, superimpositions, or interconnections we trace, we are left with nature as one level and history as another; with dirt versus perceptions of dirt; with the environment as an object out there and our ways of imagining and representing it as something different. Yet none of the natural worlds or environmental forces encountered in this book occur except as worlds or forces formed out of the interaction of the human and the nonhuman, the organic and the technical, the programmed and the unpredicted. Forms of representation have always formed a part of such human-nonhuman, technical-organic interactions. Those modes of representing and reporting that we might refer to as an imaginary occur as a variety of sociotechnical practices—writing, recording, picturing, and referencing—that form aspects of many other sociotechnical operations: building dams, planting forests, irrigating desert lands, administering rural populations. The imaging and reporting occur in these many forms of practice, not as some separate plane of the immaterial.

My reason for mentioning these well-known arguments is to introduce a second problem. Despite what I have just written, it may be misleading to dismiss the separation of representation from reality, of history from nature, of stories about the environment from the environment itself, as a "false" binary. The accusation of falsehood overlooks something central to the modern politics of nature. Although representing natural forces forms only a part of our ways of building the collective worlds we inhabit, it is a mode of sociotechnical practice that has become increasingly more organized, coordinated, and effective. Over the last century or so, more and more work has been done to produce representations of nature and to produce what appears as a progressively more distinct separation between those interactions we call nature and those we arrange as images of nature. The result has been to open up, by a series of removals, detours, and delays, what appears as an ever more effective distance between our encounters with natural forces and our encounters with reports and images of those encounters. It is important to understand the production of these removals and delays and the kinds of separation they effect. To dismiss such removals and separations as a false binary (while better than assuming the simple dualism of nature versus representation) risks neglecting the task of tracing how they have been brought about.

The practices that carry out the distancing of modes of representing and reporting from the interactions on which they report are perfectly real and have their own histories and methods. Richard Grove has shown how the emergence of the environment as an object of knowledge was made possible by a particular kind of distance, isolation, and reporting. The British, French, and Dutch encounters with tropical islands and the business of colonizing and despoiling them made visible processes such as deforestation and their interconnected impact on the biota of a place. Remote, self-contained, and fragile, tropical islands appeared to those who encountered them from afar as worlds-in-miniature, functioning as laboratories in which the interaction among life forms could be observed, manipulated, and analyzed. The same isolation and difference was later constructed in the glass houses of botanical gardens back in Europe. Like nineteenth-century world exhibitions, the first of which were built as even larger glass houses, these miniature worlds, populated with real plants, animals, objects, and people, were organized as representations of the wider world. No less real than the realities they represented, no more or less discursive, no more or less imaginary, but more controllable and easier to study and report about, such laboratories exemplified the forms of removal, distance, isolation, and control that generated the increasingly widespread and persuasive effect of a world divided in two: into reality versus representation, the environment versus the stories we tell about it, nature versus history.

The essays in this book provide numerous examples of technical projects and administrative practices that helped produce the forms of distance, separation, concentration, and difference that could be organized into the distinction between modern environments and modern environmental imaginaries. The novel use of air power by the British to police and subdue the villages and tribes of Iraq contributed to and reinforced a new understanding of the Mesopotamian environment. The building of two large dams across the Nile at Aswan, the first, discussed in detail by Jennifer Derr, completed in 1902 and the second on a much greater scale in the 1960s, stored up the river's power at a single site and replaced the thousands of dykes and channels that distributed the river's nutrients and energy under the older system of flood basin irrigation. The forms of measurement, know-how, and control that were previously dispersed across millions of hectares of the floodplain were now increasingly concentrated at a single site. This concentration of management and information contributed to the development of ways of governing that took the management of nature as their object, and the representation of nature as their project.

To understand what was distinctive about these practices, Alan Mikhail's chapter on Ottoman methods of managing the waters of the Nile in the eighteenth century is of great importance. From Ottoman court records and other administrative archives, Mikhail has carefully recovered sequences of orders, appeals, reports, inspections, and interventions through which courts, provincial officials, local notables, and ordinary farmers managed, co-opted, and contested the changing flow of the river, the alterations in its channel, the appearance and disappearance of fertile islands, the silting up of canals, and the collapse of embankments. From these dispersed and intermittent records, the chapter pieces together what can be termed an Ottoman imaginary of the environment.

It seems clear, however, from their dispersed and intermittent forms of reporting and instruction that those engaged in these processes were not concerned with constructing an environmental imaginary. Every dispute, intervention, and administrative decision involved modes of representation, which in turn formed parts of larger systems of administration and rule. However, the painstaking work of scholarship required to recover and assemble these reports and representations, compared to the relative ease with which scholars of the colonial and contemporary state reconstruct environmental imaginaries from published or widely circulated sources, is a measure of what has changed. Ottoman political practice was not dependent on the gathering and circulation of an environmental imaginary, so the work of isolating, concentrating, reporting, and publishing representations of nature had no regular place in administrative routines. In other words, Ottoman practice was not organized with sites of concentration and forms of difference or distance that attempted to produce and maintain the separation of an environment from its imagination, or of nature from politics. Writing accounts of precolonial practices is therefore a different kind of project from writing about the imaginative practices of twentieth-century government. This brings the peculiarity of more recent politics into sharper view.

To understand the practices that gave rise to environmental imaginaries, we need to understand the colonial and more contemporary modes of encountering, working with, and attempting to control a variety of forces, both human and nonhuman. It would be misleading to refer to these methods of isolation, concentration, making of worlds-in-miniature, separation, and reporting as the "cultural construction" of nature. It would be equally appropriate, or inappropriate, to talk about the "natural construction" of nature.

The essays in this book confirm the point Bruno Latour makes, in *Science in Action* and elsewhere, about the recalcitrance of natural forces. The forces of nature, isolated in the laboratory, the glass house, or a gorge at Aswan, can be more easily observed, manipulated, harnessed, described, and represented. But their representation is not a mere cultural construction, for the same forces retain their enormous power to refute what is said about them, escape the mechanisms of control, or produce surprising and unanticipated actions. The desert terrain of Iraq turned out to be more opaque and less governable from the air than the proponents of British air power had assumed. The control of the Nile brought increased supplies of water, but also rising levels of salinity in the irrigated soil and decreased levels of nutrients. The view that our ideas about nature are culturally constructed resolves prematurely something that should always be an empirical question: What combination of human and nonhuman forces, of the planned and the unintentional, of the freely imagined and the recalcitrant, makes possible the construction and strengthening of our knowledge about the common world?

By asking this empirical question, the study of environmental imaginaries can take advantage of the promise of environmental history: that it provides a way of studying the past and present in which the protagonists are not limited to the merely human. Instead one can trace the shifting alliances and amalgamations of human and nonhuman agencies, organic and technical materials, recalcitrant and malleable forces, that have shaped the common worlds to which we belong.

Take as a final example the history of Middle Eastern oil. This is inevitably an environmental history. Oil is a natural resource that has reworked entire landscapes of the region, whether in the infrastructure required for its discovery, production, and transportation, the speculative urban developments into which its profits have been transformed, or the aquifers permanently depleted to pump the billions of gallons of groundwater required every day to irrigate petroleum-funded agricultural schemes or drive oil in depleted reservoirs toward the well.

In the building of infrastructure, the playing out of speculation, or the pumping of fluids, methods of planning, measuring, valuing, estimating, and other modes of representation and calculation are always at work. From this work the environmental imaginaries of oil are produced. These imaginaries are not limited to the clichés of camel-herding nomads transformed into plutocrats or skyscrapers replacing collections of mud huts, although Western oil companies devoted considerable resources to producing such images. They include, for example, complex methods for producing the varying price of oil; the racial imaginaries—as Robert Vitalis has traced—employed to organize the labor of oil production; and a discourse of international security that for decades transformed the problem of an overabundance of Middle Eastern oil into a threat of scarcity and into programs of arms purchase that recycled petrodollars to the West.

The imaginative world of oil is still larger. As I explore in my work on "carbon democracy," the plentiful, cheaply produced oil of the Middle East helped engineer, during the decades either side of World War II, ways of living and thinking in which material growth was assumed to have no limits. The flow of oil made possible a new object, "the economy," through which this apparently limitless growth could be managed and represented. It fueled in turn the growth of an expertise, economics, that became the dominant way of thinking about the satisfaction of material wants and needs. Thanks to oil and the apparently limitless low-cost energy it supplied, the most abstract and dematerialized of our social imaginaries, neoclassical economics, became over several decades the most influential language for explaining the relationship between humans and nature.

The history of oil, like the histories explored in this book, shows how one can trace the building of environmental imaginaries as much more than a work of cultural construction. The question is to understand what combinations of natural forces and technical skills, human effort and nonhuman devices, the real and the artificial, the freely imagined and the naturally recalcitrant, produce the worlds we inhabit.

Contributors

Samer Alatout is an associate professor in the Department of Community and Environmental Sociology, the Nelson Institute for Environmental Studies, the Graduate Program of Sociology, and the Department of Geography at the University of Wisconsin–Madison. He is also affiliated with the Holtz Center for Science and Technology Studies and the Center for Culture, History, and Environment. His research focus is on the relationship between knowledge production and relations of power. He has published more than a dozen articles in leading journals on both water and environmental conflicts in the Middle East and on the links between environmental politics and social theories of power and government. His work has been recognized with grants from the Fulbright Program, the National Science Foundation (NSF), the National Endowment for the Humanities (NEH), and the United States Department of Agriculture (USDA). Most recently he shifted his attention to the study of environmental politics in border regions such as the U.S./Mexico and Palestine/Israel borders.

Edmund ("Terry") Burke III is Research Professor of History at the University of California at Santa Cruz, where he directs the Center for World History. He is the author of numerous books and articles, including *The Ethnographic State: France and the Invention of Moroccan Islam, 1890–1925* (University of California Press, 2012); *World History: The Big Eras: A Compact History of Humankind for Teachers and Students,* coauthored with Ross E. Dunn and David G. Christian (National Center for History in the Schools, 2009); *The Environment and World History, 1500–2000,* edited with Kenneth Pomeranz (University of California Press, 2009); and *Genealogies of Orientalism: History, Theory, Politics,* edited with David Prochaska (University of Nebraska Press, 2008).

Shaul Cohen is an associate professor in the Department of Geography and a co-director of the Peace Studies Program at the University of Oregon. He is a Carnegie fellow in international ethics. His work focuses on developing models for conflict resolution and territorial sharing in the Middle East, Northern Ireland, and other parts of the world. He is the author of several books, including *The Politics of Planting: Israeli-Palestinian Competition for Control of Land in the Jerusalem Periphery* (University of Chicago Press, 1993) and *Planting Nature: Trees and the Manipulation of Environmental Stewardship in America* (University of California Press, 2004), in addition to many articles and book chapters.

Diana K. Davis, a geographer and veterinarian, is an associate professor in the Department of History at the University of California at Davis. Her first book, *Resurrecting the Granary of Rome: Environmental History and French Colonial Expansion in North Africa* (Ohio University Press, 2007), was awarded the George Perkins Marsh Prize by the American Society for Environmental History (ASEH) as well as the Meridian Prize and the Blaut Award by the Association of American Geographers (AAG). She has also published numerous articles and book chapters. She is the recipient of a Guggenheim fellowship and an ACLS Ryskamp fellowship for her new book project, *Imperialism and Environmental History in the Middle East* (Cambridge University Press).

Jennifer L. Derr is an assistant professor of Middle Eastern history and environmental and urban studies at Bard College. She is currently completing a manuscript on the production of agricultural geography and its relation to the practice of the state in Egypt during the British colonial period. She has been awarded grants from the Fulbright-Hays Commission, the Social Science Research Council, the Mellon Foundation, the American Research Center in Egypt, and the Institute for Historical Studies at the University of Texas at Austin.

Leila M. Harris is a sociocultural and political geographer specializing in issues related to environment, gender, and development. She is an assistant professor in the Institute for Resources, Environment, and Sustainability and the Center for Gender and Women's Studies at the University of British Columbia. Much of her work has focused on water politics in the Middle East, gender and socio-spatial difference, and political and scalar dimensions of the large-scale transformation of the Tigris and Euphrates River basin. A recent book project focuses on themes of narrative, citizenship, and socio-spatial difference in relation to recent water governance shifts in the Global South. She has published in numerous highly ranked journals, including *Environment and Planning D, World Development, Political Geography, Geoforum,* and *Gender, Place, and Culture*. She has received a number of honors, including residence as a MacArthur scholar while at the University of Minnesota and currently as a Peter Wall scholar at the University of British Columbia.

Alan Mikhail is an assistant professor in the Department of History at Yale University. He is the author of *Nature and Empire in Ottoman Egypt: An Environmental History* (Cambridge University Press, 2011). He is currently editing a volume of essays on Middle East environmental history and beginning a new book on human-animal relations in Ottoman Egypt. His articles have appeared in the *International Journal of Middle East Studies,* the *Journal of the Economic and Social History of the Orient,* the *Bulletin of the History of Medicine,* and elsewhere.

Timothy Mitchell is a political theorist and the author of *Colonising Egypt* and *Rule of Experts* and the editor of *Questions of Modernity*. His latest book, published by Verso in 2011, is *Carbon Democracy: Political Power in the Age of Oil*. He teaches in the Department of Middle Eastern, South Asian, and African Studies at Columbia University.

Priya Satia is an associate professor of modern British history at Stanford University and the author of *Spies in Arabia: The Great War and the Cultural Foundations of Britain's Covert Empire in the Middle East* (Oxford University Press, 2008), which won the American Historical Association's Herbert Baxter Adams Prize, the AHA–Pacific Coast Branch Book Award, and the Pacific Coast Conference of British Studies Book Prize. Her article in the *American Historical Review* in 2006 was awarded best article prizes by both the North American Conference of British Studies and the Pacific Coast Conference of British Studies. Her work has also appeared in *Past and Present, Technology and Culture,* and other journals and edited collections, as well as popular media such as the *Financial Times,* the *Times Literary Supplement,* and the *Nation*. She is currently writing a book on the history of the gun trade in the British empire.

Jeannie Sowers is an assistant professor in the Department of Political Science at the University of New Hampshire (UNH). Her research focuses on environmental politics and the political economy of the Middle East, with a focus on Egypt. She has held postdoctoral appointments with the Dubai Initiative at the Harvard Kennedy School, the Center for the Humanities at the University of New Hampshire, and the Center for Middle East Studies at Harvard University. Her articles have appeared in *Climatic Change*, the *Journal of Environment and Development*, *Development and Change*, and *Middle East Report*. She coedited, with Chris Toensing, *Revolutions, Protest and Social Change in Egypt, 1999–2011* (Verso, Spring 2012). Her current book, *Environmental Politics in Egypt*, is forthcoming (Routledge). She serves on the editorial board of *Middle East Report*.

George R. Trumbull IV teaches at Dartmouth College, where he serves as assistant professor of history. He is the author of *An Empire of Facts: Colonial Power, Cultural Knowledge, and Islam in Algeria, 1870–1914* (Cambridge University Press, 2009). He is currently working on a book titled *Land of Thirst, Land of Fear: A History of Water in the Sahara from Empire to Oil*. Social Science Research Council, Fulbright-Hays, Chateaubriand, and, most recently, American Council of Learned Societies grants have supported various aspects of his research. He serves on the editorial board of the *Middle East Report*, where he has published on aspects of contemporary interest in Middle Eastern and North African environmental studies.

Index

Numbers in **bold** indicate pages with illustrations

'Abd al-Qâdir, 10, 87, 88, 89
Abu Dhabi, 14
Acker, Jean, 96–97, 106
agriculture: agribusiness narratives in Egypt, 8, 161, 173–77, 178–79, 184–85nn77–79; in Algeria, 67, 72, 79n31; Egypt, agricultural and economic reform, 6; Egypt, agricultural geography of, 145–48, 154n22, 154–155n24, 155nn26–28, 155nn30–31, 155–156n34; Egypt, ownership of agricultural land in, 7, 124–28, 133n39, 133n41, 167; Egypt, urban encroachment on agricultural land, 164; farmers, education of, 197, 199–200, 201, 205, 211n19; farmer's narratives, 200–203, 211–12nn22–24; interventions in rain-fed system of, x–xi; land reclamation and agricultural land increases, 164; in Morocco, 73; in North Africa, 9, 61; rainfall and, **5**; sharaqi land, 149; sustainability and unsustainability of in Turkey, 192, 195–200, **196**, **197**, 203–9, 210nn9–10, 210–211nn16–17, 211n19, 213n35; in Tunisia, 72–73; in UAE, 14, 19n29; urban encroachment on agricultural land, 164; wasteful water use, 164, 169–70. See also cotton; irrigation and water-control systems; sugarcane cultivation and industry
aircraft and air power: British use of, 37–43, 50–51n105, 52n124; desert flight, romance of, **37**, 42; US use of, 44
Algeria: agriculture in, 67, 72, 79n31; colonization of, justification for, 66; colonization of, success of, 69–70, 75, 80n43, 80n49; deforestation in, 9, 63, 70–74, 81n58, 82n70; development of and social policies in, 63–64, 68, 70–74; environmental degradation in, 63, 68, 80n49; environmental imaginary in, 18n12; forestry policies and reforestation in, 65, 70–74, 80–81nn54–55, 81n65, 82n70, 267; French environmental imaginaries of, 9, 62–65, 74–76, 78n19; independence movements and independence of, 102–3, 105–6; local peoples as invaders, 67–68; map of, **64**; property and use-rights, loss of by local people, 63–64, 68, 70; restoration of to Roman period, success of, 67, 69–74, 80n49; restoration of to Roman period, vision of, 9–10, 60–61, 63–65, 77n11, 80n47; Roman heritage of French settlers in, 9–10, 63, 65–70, 74–76, 78–79n28, 79n31; Roman ruins in, **67**, 67; Roman texts as basis for warfare and development, 66–67. See also Sahara
Anglo-European environmental imaginaries, 2–4, 6–7, 8–11, 13, 14–15, 16–17n3, 18n12
Antes, John, 114
Arabia. See Iraq (Arabia)
Arab states: Israeli state, recognition of the, 239n13; Johnston Unified Plan, nonratification of, 221, 239n13; Jordan River, disputes over diversion and utilization of, 218–21, 235–37, 238nn6–7, 243n67; Jordan River plan and environmental imaginary, 12, 219–20, 221, 228–31, 237nn2–3; nationalism in, 237n2; Palestinian refugees, resettlement of, 218
Ashrafiyya Canal, 118–20, 130–31n19, 131n25
Aswan dam, first (1902): agricultural geography and, 145–48, 154n22, 154–55n24, 155nn26–28, 155nn30–31, 155–156n34; barrages and water availability, 138, 145, 152–53nn4–5; colonial technocrats and engineers, x, xi, 6–7, 136, 139–41, 148–52, 151–52, 153–54nn9–11, 268; construction of, labor for, x; construction of, rationale for, 6–7; cotton cultivation and production and, 4, 6, 137–39, 140–41, 145–46, 147–49, 152, 152–53n4, 154–55n24, 155n30;

280 | Index

Aswan dam, first (1902) (*cont.*)
disease after construction of, 150–51; human component of the landscape and, 145, 149–50, 156n42; payment for construction of, 138, 152n2; perennial irrigation and, 7, 19n21, 138–39, 140, 145–46, 148–51, 152–53n4, 154–55n24, 155n28, 165; photo of, **137**; significance of, 136–37; transformation of environment through, 138–39, 148–52, 156n42, 270
Aswan High Dam: benefits of, xi; colonial technocrats and engineers, 166; construction of, labor for, x; ecology of the Nile and, 114–15; human component of the landscape and, 149–50, 156n42; imperialism and imperial powers and, xi; land reclamation projects after, 159, 166; Mubarak Pumping Station and New Valley Project, 158–59, 169; purpose of, xi; Sheikh Zayed (Toshka) Canal, **169**; transformation of environment through, 270; water releases from, 163

Babylonia and cradle of civilization, restoration, 8, 24, 31–36, 44, 268
Baghdad, 27–28, 33–34
basin irrigation, 141–42, 143–45, 154n15
Basra, 30, 31
Bedouin control ordinance, 3
Bernard, Augustin, 69–70, 80n49
Blackbourn, David, 89, 91, 106
bombardment: of Iraq (Arabia), 8, 9, 24–25, 37–43, 44, 50–51n105, 52n124, 268, 270; military strategy of, 41
Boudy, Paul, 74
Bourde, Paul, 72–73
Bronze Age, ix
Brown, John Croumbie, 62
Bunger, Mills E., 225, 228

CADIZ, 175
Capot-Rey, Robert, 97, 101, 103
Cassas, Louis-François, 3, 17n6
Cassel, Ernest, 138, 140, 153–54n11
Churchill, Winston, 39
Cianfarani, Valerio, 100–101
civil engineering, 139
Clapp, Gordon, 222–23, 239–40n19
climate: challenges of, 30; climate change, 196, 207–8; cotton cultivation and production and, 146; deforestation and, 81n58, 82n70; irrigation and plantings to change, 10; of the Middle East and North Africa, 265; recuperative capacity of desert climate, 94; restoration of through reforestation, 65, 73
coal, x
Colomieu, V., 90, 91, 98
colonialism and colonial period: colonial technocrats and engineers, x, xi, 6–7, 9, 34–36, 43, 136, 139–41, 144–45, 148–52, 151–52, 153–54nn9–11, 166, 268; dates of, x; energetic context of construction during, x–xi; environmental imaginaries development during, 3, 9–10, 18n12, 61–63, 77n11, 266–67. *See also specific country and region entries*
corn cultivation, 176–77
cotton: Aswan dam construction and, 4, 6, 137–39, 140–41, 145–46, 147–49, 152, 152–53n4, 154–55n24, 155n30; climate and, 146; irrigation and water-control systems and, 4; Turkey, cultivation in, 195–96, **196**, 198, 201–2, 210–11n17, 211–12nn22–24, 267
Cotton, John S., 221, 239n12
Cromer, Earl of (Evelyn Baring), x, 138–39, 140, 145–46

Daumas, Eugène, 91, 98
deforestation: in Algeria, 9, 63, 70–74, 81n58, 82n70; during Bronze Age, ix; climate and, 81n58, 82n70; imperial narratives about, 4; in Lebanon, 3, 17n6; Levant, deforestation and reforestation in the, 2–3, 17n6; project planning and, xi; understanding of consequences of, xi. *See also* forestry policies and reforestation
degradation, environmental: in Algeria, 63, 67, 80n49; blame for, 2, 9, 12–13, 15, 63–65, 68, 71, 77n11, 198–200, 210–11nn16–17, 211n22, 249–50; causes of, ix; narratives of, internalization of, 13; in North Africa, 2, 62–63
desalinization, 14
desertification and desertified environments, 1–2, 3, 13, 16n1, 60, 63
deserts: definitions of, 99, 108n49; desert flight, romance of, **37**, 42; elimination of, 10, 13, 98; historiography of, 89; negative imagery, 27–31; as paradise, 9, 26; roll-back-the-desert campaign of UAE, 13–15; secrets of, knowledge of, 10, 87, 88. *See also* Sahara
drainage and drainage systems, 16n2, 149
Dubief, Jean, 101
Duval, Jules, 90, 93, 95, 102

ecology: Aswan High Dam and ecology of the Nile, 114–15; of deserts, 95, 101, 108n49; imperial narratives and development of ecological science, 4; viability of Middle East and North Africa, 1–2, 265–66
Egypt: agricultural and economic reform in, 6; agricultural geography, 145–48, 154n22, 154–155n24, 155nn26–28, 155nn30–31, 155–156n34; agricultural land, ownership of, 7, 124–28, 133n39, 133n41, 167; Alexandria and the Ashrafiyya Canal, 118–20, 130–31n19, 131n25; basin irrigation, 141–42, 143–45, 154n15; biblical and ancient history and

Index | 281

the environment, 140–45, **143**, 154nn15–16; British environmental imaginaries of, 6–7; cotton cultivation and production in, 4, 6, 137–39, 140–41, 145–46, 147–49, 152, 152–53n4, 154–55n24, 155n30; disease in, 150–51; environmental conditions in, 2; famine avoidance in, xi; human component of the landscape, 145, 149–50, 156n42; irrigation, circles (districts) of, 139, 153n10; irrigation and water-control systems in, 6–7, 19n21, 36, 114–15; land reclamation in, 7–8, 146–47, 155nn26–27, 159, 162–64, **163**, 178–80, 268; nationalism and populism in, 7, 8; as object of development, 6; perennial irrigation, problems with and opposition to, 7, 19n21, 138–39, 140, 145–46, 147, 148–51, 152–53n4, 154–55n24, 155n28, 165; Philae Temple, 142–43, **143**, 150; political reform in, 179–80; population increase/overpopulation crisis in, 6, 7, 19n20, 160–61, 162–64, 178, 181n15; productive environment, British belief about, 6–7; protests in, 159, 179; rural environmental imaginaries, 115–17, 118, 128; rural spaces, hierarchy of, 115–16; sharecropping, property ownership, and labor patterns, 7, 147–48, 149–50, 155n31, 156n42, 162, 181n15; socioeconomic changes in, 181n15; state-owned farms in, 167; sugarcane cultivation and industry, 146, 148, 151, 155–56n34, 159, 170; Tahrir (Liberation) Province, 167; urban encroachment on agricultural land, 164; water crisis narratives, 160–61, 162–64, 179. *See also* Nile Delta and River

Emberger, Louis, 74
engineering and colonial technocrats, x, xi, 6–7, 9, 34–36, 43, 136, 139–41, 144–45, 148–52, 151–52, 153–54nn9–11, 166, 268
environmental and landscape histories, 3, 17–18n9, 89, 268–73
environmental change: consequences of faulty engineering, x–xi; costs of, x; histories and historical processes and, ix–x, 130n11; narratives about and environmental imaginaries, 3; Ottoman imperial imaginaries and, 127–28, 133n41; in Turkey, 11, 192–95
environmental degradation. *See* degradation, environmental
environmental determinism, 9, 19n23, 101
environmental history, promise of, 272
environmental imaginaries: Anglo-European visions, 2–4, 6–7, 8–11, 13, 14–15, 16–17n3, 18n12; collapse of, 268; colonial period environmental imaginaries, 3–4, 9–10, 18n12, 61–63, 77n11, 266–67; concept of and development of, 3, 17n8, 266–73; energetic conditions and, xi; foreign, exotic, and tropical nature, 3, 61–63, 76;

histories and historical processes and, 3, 17–18n9, 265–67; hydro-imaginaries, 11–12, 226, 235–37, 241n34; implications of, 6; internalization of inaccurate narratives and, 13; local, non-Western visions, 7–8, 10, 11–15, 19n24; modernization projects and, ix, 2–3; Ottoman imperial rural imaginaries, 115–17, 118, 123, 127–28, 133n41; power and durability of, 268; representations of nature, 89, 268–73; shifts in and changes to, 3
environmental orientalism. *See* orientalism
environmental protection: in Israel, 252–55, 258–59; Israeli/Palestinian cooperation and, 13, 256–58; nationalism and, 13, 246–49, 252, 256, 259, 268; in Palestine, 255–56, 258–59
Ethiopia, 163
eucalyptus trees, 73
Euphrates River, ix, 267
European Union: Algeria and investments in the Sahara, 106; Turkey, entrance of into, 11, 194, 207
exotic nature. *See* foreign, exotic, and tropical nature

Fatah movement, 256, 268
fodder and forage crops, 176–77
foreign, exotic, and tropical nature, 3, 61–63, 76
forestry policies and reforestation: in Algeria, 65, 70–74, 80–81nn54–55, 81n65, 82n70, 267; French love of trees, 74–75; indigenous people, hatred for trees by, 74–75, 82n81; Levant, deforestation and reforestation in the, 2–3, 17n6; in Morocco, 74; in North Africa, 9, 61, 65, 70–74, 75, 80–81nn54–55, 81n65, 82n70; in Palestine, 2, 3, 16–17n3, 255–56; romantic view of forests, 17n6; UAE, afforestation projects in, 14. *See also* deforestation
fossil fuels, x–xi. *See also* coal; oil, petroleum, and natural gas
Foureau, Fernand, 90, 98
France: anticolonial lobby in, 68, 79n36; colonization of North Africa, justification for, 66; colonization of North Africa, successes of, 67, 69–70, 75, 80n49; colonization of North Africa, support for, 68–69; forestry policies and reforestation in Maghreb, 9, 61, 65, 70–74, 75, 80–81nn54–55, 81n65, 82n70; medical services in, 30; modern warfare wisdom from, 31; national and imperial identity in, 9–10, 63, 64–70, 74–76, 78–79n28, 79n31, 83n83; North Africa, environmental imaginaries of by, 9–10, 62–63, 74–76, 77n11, 78n19; regional interests and power of, 2, 16–17n3; Roman heritage of French settlers, 9–10, 63, 64–70, 74–76, 78–79n28, 79n31; Sahara, environmental imaginaries of the, 10, 87–88; trees, love for by, 74–75

Fromentin, Eugène, **92**, 92–93
Furon, Raymond, 101, 102, 103

GAP project (Southeastern Anatolia Project), 192, **195**, 267
Garstin, William, 139
Gazeau de Vautibault, 94
geographical morality, 43
Germany, 16–17n3, 25, 34
Grand Canal, xi
grazing and overgrazing, 3, 4, 71, 78n21, 267
Great Britain: aerial surveillance and policing in, 39; airpower and aerial surveillance in Iraq, 8, 9, 24–25, 37–43, 44, 50–51n105, 52n124, 268, 270; Egypt, environmental imaginaries of by, 6–7; influence of, 25; Iraq, environmental imaginaries of by, 8–9, 23–24, 25–27, 43, 45n15, 268; occupation by, positive aspects of, 34; regional interests and power of, 2–3, 16–17n3; Sudan, invasion of, 138
Green Line, 256, **257**

Hammam-Meloun thermal spa, 94–95
Harran Plain, **195**, 195–209, **196**, **197**, 211n19, 212n30, 212–13n32
Herodotus, 113, 115, 154n15
histories and historical processes: dominant narrative as history, 17–18n9; environmental and landscape histories, 3, 17–18n9, 89, 268–73; environmental change and, ix–x, 130n11; environmental history, promise of, 272; environmental imaginaries and, 3, 17–18n9, 265–67; unnatural nature, 266
Huleh, Lake, 218, 221, 223
hydro-imaginaries, 11–12, 226, 235–37, 241n34

imperialism and imperial powers: airpower and, 37–43, 50–51n105, 52n124; Anglo-European environmental imaginaries, 2–4, 6–7, 8–11, 16–17n3, 18n12; Aswan High Dam and, xi; countries with interests in Middle East and North Africa, 16–17n3; deforestation narrative, 4; and ecological science development, 4; environmental orientalism and, ix, 3–4, 6–7, 8–11, 13, 18n12; Iraq, imperial knowledge and restoration of, 8; Iraq, technology, and, 25–31; modernization and improvement projects and, 2, 4–5, 6, 8–10, 31–36, 44; Ottoman imperial imaginaries, 115–17, 118, 123, 127–28, 133n41; Roman heritage of France and French imperial and national identity, 9–10, 63, 64–70, 74–76, 78–79n28, 79n31, 83n83
India: environmental imaginary in, 18n12; Iraq, development of with Indian resources, 31; Iraq, ties to, 28; irrigation and water-control systems in, 9, 19n21; Mesopotamia campaign, 27–31

Iraq (Arabia): aerial surveillance in and bombing of, 8, 9, 24–25, 37–43, 44, 50–51n105, 52n124, 268, 270; biblical visions, 8, 28–29; boundaries of Arabia, 44n1; British environmental imaginaries of, 8–9, 23–24, 25–27, 43, 45n15, 268; British mandate to rule, 36; casualties in, attitudes toward, 40; civilized community and progress in, 26–27; cradle of civilization and Babylonia, restoration of, 8, 24, 31–36, 44, 268; development of, 25, 31–36, 43–44, 44n5; images of, 23; imperial knowledge and restoration of, 8; India, ties to, 28; irrigation and water-control systems in, 9; Mesopotamia campaign, 27–31; military failure in, 27–31; names for region around, 8, 19n22; rebellion in, 36, 49n89; technology application in, 24, 29, 43; topography of, 26, 29–30, 31, 37–38, 39; tribes of, characteristics and characterizations of, 9, 19n23, 41; US environmental imaginaries of, 44; wetlands, restoration of, 43
Ireland, 39
irrigation and water-control systems: basin irrigation, 141–42, 143–45, 154n15; canal dredging, 7, 116–23, 130n16, 130n18; canals and water management, negotiations over, 7, 116; circles (districts) of irrigation, 139, 153n10; cost of irrigation water, 210–11n17; disease and, 150–51, 196, **197**, 210n10; in Egypt, 6–7, 19n21, 36, 114–15; environmental management through, 2, 4, 16n2; in India, 9, 19n21; in Iraq (Arabia), 9; necessity of, ix–x; negative effects of, 7, 19n21; perennial irrigation, problems with and opposition to, 7, 19n21, 138–39, 140, 145–46, 147, 148–51, 152–53n4, 154–55n24, 155n28, 165; problems associated with, 192; rainfall, agriculture, and, **5**; rural environmental imaginaries, 115–17, 118, 128; social status and, 115–16; Southeastern Anatolia Project (GAP project), 192, **195**, **197**, 210nn9–10, 267; sustainability and unsustainability of in Turkey, 192, 195–200, **196**, **197**, 203–9, 210nn9–10, 210–211nn16–17, 211n19, 213n35; technoscientific interventions, 11, 204–9, 212n30; in UAE, 14, 19n29; water flow and location along the waterway, 115–16, 118, 120, 121–22, 128. *See also* land reclamation
Israel: environmental imaginaries and blame for ruined landscapes, 12–13, 249–50; environmentalism in, 252–55, 258–59; environmental protection and Israeli/Palestinian cooperation, 13, 256–58; Green Line, 256, **257**; Jordan River (Cotton) plan and environmental imaginary, 12, 219–20, 221, 227, 229, 231–34, 237n3, 241n40, 242n49, 242nn52–54, 243nn56–59; Jordan River,

disputes over diversion and utilization of, 218–22, 235–37, 238nn6–7, 243n67, 267; Jordan River and tributaries, 221–22; Jordan River water distribution, 229–30; land as refuge, 259; land distribution and Jordan River plans, 234; nationalism and environmentalism, 12–13, 246–49, 252, 256, 259, 268; National Water Carrier, 218, 231, 251, 253, 256, 268; recognition of the Israeli state, 239n13; sovereignty and power of, 248–49, 252–53; technological optimism, 251, 252; water resources for, importance of, 256, 258
Italy, 16–17n3

Johnston, Eric, 218–37, 238n11, 243n57
Jordan: forestry policies and reforestation in, 255–56; Jordan River, disputes over diversion and utilization of, 218, 235–37, 243n67; Jordan River and tributaries, 221–22; Jordan River water distribution, 229–30; land distribution and Jordan River plans, 234
Jordan River: American watershed perspective and Johnston Unified Plan (Main plan), 12, 218–28, **224**, 229, 232–37, 237n3, 239n13, 239–40n19, 243n58; Arab plan and Arab nationalism and politico-environmental approach, 12, 219–20, 221, 228–31, 237nn2–3; cost of and funding for projects, 228, 242n41; disputes over diversion and utilization of, 218–22, 235–37, 238nn6–7, 267; environmental imaginaries of, 11–12, 267; gravity and topography, utilization of, 226–27, 229, 231, 241n37, 242n49; groundwater resources, 225, 241n31; headwaters of, control of, 221; hydro-imaginaries, 11–12, 226, 235–37, 241n34; Israeli (Cotton) plan and Israeli technological and agricultural imaginary, 12, 219–20, 221, 227, 229, 231–34, 237n3, 241n40, 242n49, 242nn52–54, 243nn56–59; Palestinian environmental imaginary, 12; Palestinian refugees and water negotiations, 12, 219–20, 221, 238n9; political boundaries and, 221–26, 229–30, 231, 232, 239–40n19, 240n21, 242n43, 242n45, 243n58; politico-environmental imaginaries, 219–20, 237n1, 238n5; rainfall in area, 227, 241n38; regional cooperation in development of, 222–23, 225, 227, 241n31; tributaries of and waters involved in negotiations, 221–22; water duty, 227, 232–34, 236, 241n36; water storage areas, 226, 227–28, 241nn39–40

Kingdom Agricultural Development Company (KADCO), 174–77
Kut, 27, 29, 32

land reclamation: agricultural land increases through, 164; Aswan High Dam and, 159, 166; costs of, 167; desirability of, 161, 164; in Egypt, 7–8, 146–47, 155nn26–27, 159, 162–64, **163**, 178–80, 268 (*see also* New Valley Project (Toshka)); model communities and model citizens, 166–67, 168–69; Nasser regime projects, 7–8, 161, 165–67, 178; in Palestine, 166; peasantry, impact of on, 8, 161, 166–67, 168–69; population increase/overpopulation crisis and, 6, 7, 160–61, 162–64, 178; prevalence of, 159; problems associated with, 159–60, 167; repairing of, 178–79, 186n102; soil conditions, 160, 164, 175–76, 181n21. *See also* irrigation and water-control systems
Lawrence, T. E., 38, 39, 41
League of Nations, 36
Lebanon: deforestation in, 3, 17n6; Jordan River, disputes over diversion and utilization of, 218; Jordan River and tributaries, 221–22; Jordan River water distribution, 229–30; land distribution and Jordan River plans, 234
Lefebvre, Henri, 71
Le Fèvre, Georges, 103
Le Rumeur, Guy, 98–99, 100
Levant, deforestation and reforestation in the, 2–3, 17n6
Litani River, 222, 225, 232, 243nn56–59
Lyautey, Louis H.-G., x, 73

Maghreb, **64**. *See also* Algeria; Morocco; Tunisia
Mannoni, P., 103
Mesopotamia: Mesopotamia campaign, 27–31; region of, 19n22; salinization and irrigated agriculture in, 192
metallurgy, ix
Michelet, Jules, 66, 78–79n28
Middle East: development of, 44; ecological viability of, 1–2, 265–66; environmental conditions in, 1–2, 16n1; environmental degradation in, ix, 2; environmental determinism, 9, 19n23; environmental imaginaries of, implications of, 6, 15; improvement and environmental protection projects in, 2–3; irrigation and water-control systems in, 2, 4, 16n2; map of, **5**; representation of, 4; transformation of to improve human life, 2
Mitchell, Timothy, 4, 6, 19n20, 36, 44, 151, 162
modernization and improvement projects: cradle of civilization and Babylonia, restoration of, 8, 24, 31–36, 44, 268; environmental imaginaries and, ix, 2–3; imperialism and imperial powers and, 2, 4–5, 6, 8–10, 31–36, 44; orientalism and, 3–4. *See also* forestry policies and reforestation
Moeris, Lake, 142, 154n15

284 | Index

Morocco: agriculture in, 73; colonization of, success of, 69; development of and social policies in, 64, 68; forestry policies and reforestation in, 74; map of, **64**; property and use-rights, loss of by local people, 68; restoration of to Roman period, 9–10, 60–61; Roman heritage of French settlers, 9–10, 64
Mubarak regime, 8, 158–60, 161, 162, 166, 168–79

Nasser (Nasir), Lake, 115, 166
Nasser (Nasir) regime, 7–8, 114, 161, 165–67, 178
nature: cultural construction of, 271–72; foreign, exotic, and tropical nature, 3, 61–63, 76; improvement of, 14, 31–36; logic and reality of, 89; mitigation of, 10, 96–102; natural construction of, 271–72; politics and, 219–20, 222–23, 238n5; representations of, 89, 266, 268–73; Roman nature, restoration of, 9–10, 60–61, 63–65, 69–74, 76, 77n11, 80n47; technonature, 12; unnatural nature, 266
Negev desert, 12, 220, 226, 227, 231, 232, 233, 234, 241n38, 242n54, 253–54
New Valley Project (Toshka): agribusiness narratives in, 8, 161, 173–77, 178–79, 184–85nn77–79; agriculture in, 8; costs of, 170–72; criticism of, 8, 160, 161, 170–72, 179; failings of Mubarak regime in, 8, 158–60, 178; idea behind and goal of, 7–8, 158, 166, 168–70, 178; peasantry, impact of on, 8, 161, 168–69; political theater and, 177; population increase/overpopulation crisis and, 7, 160–61, 162–64; problems associated with, 161, 175–77; pumping station, 158–59, 169; security forces and crop damage, 177; Sheikh Zayed (Toshka) Canal, **169**; soil conditions, 175–76
Nile Delta and River: Alexandria and the Ashrafiyya Canal, 118–20, 130–31n19, 131n25; basin irrigation, 141–42, 143–45, 154n15; canal dredging, 7, 116–23, 128, 130–31nn18–19, 131n25, 131–132nn28–29; canal repairs, 118, 130n16; canals and water management, negotiations over, 7, 116; changes to landscape, adaptation to, 115; cooperative water management, 7, 116, 118, 120–23, 128; creation of and sedimentary process, 113–15, 129n1, 129n3, 129–30n9, 267; environmental changes to, consequences of, 7, 114–15; erosion of, 114–15, 129–30n9; irrigation and social status, 115–16; islands in, 116, 123–28, **124**, 132n32, 132n35, 133nn39–41; land reclamation along, 7, 146–47, 155nn26–27; Ottoman period, management of during, 7, 113–28, 144–45, 267, 270–72; society and daily interactions with, 115, 130n11; soil salinity and quality along, 7, 115, 149, 160, 164, 175–76, 181n21; water flow, allocation of, 162; water flow and location along the waterway, 115–16, 118, 120, 121–22, 128

nomads: aerial surveillance of, 9, 38; environmental degradation, blame for, 9, 63–65, 68, 71, 77n11; environmental imaginaries, 271; grazing and overgrazing practices, 3, 4, 71, 78n21; irrigation, land-use, and livelihoods of, 198, 204–5, 212–13n32; settlement of, 67, 101–2, 155n27
Normand, Suzanne, 96–97, 106
North Africa: agriculture in, 9, 61; colonization of, justification for, 66; colonization of, successes of, 67, 69–70, 75, 80n49; colonization of, support for, 68–69; deforestation in, 81n58; ecological viability of, 1–2, 265–66; environmental conditions in, 1–2; environmental degradation in, 2, 62–63; environmental imaginaries of, implications of, 6, 15; environmental stability in, ix; foreign, exotic, and tropical nature, 3, 61–63, 76; forestry policies and reforestation in, 9, 61, 65, 70–74, 75, 80–81nn54–55, 81n65, 82n70; French environmental imaginaries of, 9–10, 62–63, 74–76, 77n11, 78n19; improvement and environmental protection projects in, 2–3; indigenous people, hatred for trees by, 74–75, 82n81; irrigation and water-control systems in, 2, 4, 16n2; Maghreb, map of, **64**; map of, **5**; Ottoman period, negligency in during, 9; representation of, 4; restoration of to Roman period, 9–10, 60–61, 63–65, 77n11, 80n47; Roman heritage of French settlers, 9–10, 63, 64–70, 74–76, 78–79n28, 79n31; transformation of to improve human life, 2. *See also* Algeria; Morocco; Tunisia
Nubian villages, 149–50, 156n42

oases, ix–x, 91, 103
oil, petroleum, and natural gas, x, 10, 103–6, 266, 272–73
orientalism: energetic context of, x–xi; imperial powers and environmental orientalism, ix, 3–4, 6–7, 8–11, 13, 18n12; Sahara and, 87, 92–93, 104–5
Oslo Accords, 13, 256
Ottoman Empire and period: British influence in, 25; German influence in, 25; imperial rural environmental imaginaries, 115–17, 118, 123, 127–28, 133n41; Nile Delta and River canal dredging, 7, 116–23, 128, 130–31nn18–19, 131n25, 131–132nn28–29; Nile Delta and River management during, 7, 113–28, 144–45, 270–72; Nile River islands, management of, 116, 123–28, **124**, 132n32, 132n35, 133nn39–41, 267; North Africa, negligency in during, 9; Palestinian Eden, degradation of during, 12–13, 249–50

Palestine: aerial surveillance and policing in, 39; airpower use over, 37; economic recovery projects, 222–23; Eden, creation of and loss of, 251–52; environmental imaginaries and blame for ruined landscapes, 12–13, 249–50; environmentalism in, 255–56, 258–59; environmental protection and Israeli/Palestinian cooperation, 13, 256–58; forestry policies and reforestation in, 2, 3, 16–17n3, 255–56; Green Line, 256, **257**; Jordan River water negotiations and refugees, 12, 219–20, 221, 235–37, 238n9, 267; Labor Zionists and conquest of desert land, 166; land, cultural connection and national value of, 250, 259; land reclamation in, 166; nationalism and environmentalism, 12–13, 246–49, 252, 256, 259, 268; Ottoman Empire and degradation of Palestinian Eden, 12–13, 249–50; property rights and musha'a system, 250, 260–61n14; refugees, resettlement of, 218; sovereignty status, independence, and the environment, 248–49; water resources for, importance of, 258
Persian Gulf, 27, 28
Peyrè, J.-C., 103
Philae Temple, 142–43, **143**, 150
politico-environmental imaginaries, 12, 219–20, 221, 228–31, 237nn2–3
postcolonial period: dates of, x; energetic context of construction during, x–xi; imperial powers and environmental orientalism, 4; modernization during, ix
pyramids, construction of, x

reforestation. *See* forestry policies and reforestation
rice cultivation and industry, 170, 176, 177
Richardson, James, 91
rivers, energy and rerouting of, x
Rome: restoration of North Africa to Roman period, 9–10, 60–61, 63–65, 69–74, 77n11, 80n47; Roman heritage of France, 9–10, 63, 64–70, 74–76, 78–79n28, 79n31; Roman texts as basis for warfare and development, 66–67; success of in North African territories, 67, 70, 80n49
Royal Air Force (RAF), 38–43, 50–51n105, 52n124

Sadat, Anwar, 167
Sahara: Algerian independence and, 102–3, 105–6; artesian well in, 90, 92–93, 103; creation of, reasons for, 65, 78n21; definitions of, 96–97, 99, 108n49; elimination of, 10, 98, 106; environmental distinctions of desert life, 89–93; explorers of, deaths of, 95; French environmental imaginaries of, 10, 87–88; Hammam-Meloun thermal spa, 94–95;

historiography of, 88–89; inhabitants of, 88, 91, 92–93, 94–95, 96–104; knowledge of, systemizing of, 95; local peoples, knowledge and imaginaries of, 10; local peoples in, 91; management of desert environment and mitigation of indigence of nature, 10, 96–102; mastery of, 93–95; as "new" Tennessee, 103; numerical definitions of, 96; oases in, 91, 103; as ocean of sand, 90–91, 98; orientalism and, 87, 92–93, 104–5; petroleum extraction activities, 10, 103–6; pirates in, 91; romance of, 92, 100–101, 104–5; secrets of, knowledge of, 10, 87, 88; social problems in, 102; thirst and fear, land of, 10, 87, 91–93, **92**, 98–99, 106; transformation of, 10, 96–102; wastelands, 91; water, civilization, and moral life, 90; water resources in, 10, 90, 92–93, 103–4, 106. *See also* Algeria
Sarraut, Albert, 96, 99–100
Saudi Arabia, 173–77, 184n77
Scott-Moncrieff, Colin, 139
Sheikh Zayed (Toshka) Canal, **169**
social imaginary, 3, 17n8
Society for Protection of Nature in Israel (SPNI), 253
soil conditions: Mesopotamia, salinization and irrigated agriculture in, 192; Nile Delta and River, erosion of, 114–15, 129–30n9; Nile Delta and River, soil salinity and quality along, 7, 115, 149, 160, 164, 175–76, 181n21; Turkey, soil salinity, quality, and erosion in, 192, 195–96, 205, 210n9, 213n35
solar energy, x–xi
South African War, 8, 24
Southeastern Anatolia Project (GAP project), 192, **195**, 267
Strasser, Daniel, 100, 104, 105
Sudan, 138, 162
Suez Canal, x
Suez crisis, 165
sugarcane cultivation and industry, 146, 148, 151, 155–56n34, 159, 170
Syria: Jordan River, disputes over diversion and utilization of, 218, 220–21, 238nn6–7, 243n67; Jordan River and tributaries, 221–22; Jordan River water distribution, 229–30; land distribution and Jordan River plans, 234

technonature, 12
Tennessee Valley Authority, 103, 221, 222
Tiberias, Lake, 221–22, 223–25, **224**, 226, 227–28, 230–31, 238n5, 241n39
Tigris River, ix, 29–30, 267
Toshka. *See* New Valley Project (Toshka)
Trolard, Paulin, 65, 71, 74, 78n21
tropical and exotic nature. *See* foreign, exotic, and tropical nature

Trottier, François, 73, 82n73
Tuareg, 91
Tunisia: agriculture in, 72–73; colonization of, success of, 69; development of and social policies in, 64, 68; map of, **64**; property and use-rights, loss of by local people, 68; restoration of to Roman period, 9–10, 60–61; Roman heritage of French settlers, 9–10
Turkey: cotton cultivation and production in, 195–96, **196**, 198, 201–2, 210–11n17, 211–12nn22–24, 267; disease in, 196, **197**, 210n10; environmental change in, 11, 192–95; environmental imaginaries, divergent and convergent, 192–94, 203–9, 213n35; European Union entry of, 11, 194, 207; expert and state narratives, 198–200, 210n16; farmers, education of, 197, 199–200, 201, 205, 211n19; farmer's narratives, 200–203, 211–12nn22–24; GAP project (Southeastern Anatolia Project), 192, **195**, 267; irrigation water, cost of, 210–11n17; Kurdish and Arabic-speaking populations and region, 11, 194, 198, 205–6, 207; Mesopotamia campaign, 27, 28; modern state, perception of, 11, 206–7; poverty in, 194, 205–6; scientific imaginaries and assessments, 11, 192–93, 198–200; sharecropping, property ownership, and labor patterns, 198–200; soil salinity, quality, and erosion in, 192, 195–96, 205, 210n9, 213n35; sustainability and unsustainability of irrigation and agriculture in, 192, 195–200, **196**, **197**, 203–9, 210nn9–10, 210–211nn16–17, 211n19, 213n35; technoscientific interventions, 11, 204–9, 212n30; traditional livelihoods, return to, 205, 212–13n32

United Arab Emirates (UAE): afforestation projects, 14; agribusiness investments in Egypt, 173–74, 184n77; agriculture in, 14, 19n29; Anglo-European environmental imaginaries of degraded environment and, 14–15; beach, refrigerated, 14; independence of, 13; island creation in, 14; parks in, 14; roll-back-the-desert campaign of, 13–15; snow park and ski runs, 14, **15**, 15, 20n32; sustainability of mega-projects in, 14; water resources and desalinization, 14, 19n29
United Nations Economic Survey Mission (ESM), 222
United Nations Relief and Works Agency for Palestine Refugees in the Near East (UNRWA), 222, 225
United Nations Security Council, 220
United States (US): Algeria and investments in the Sahara, 106; Iraq, environmental imaginaries of by, 44; Jordan River watershed perspective and Johnston Unified Plan, 12, 218–28, **224**, 229, 232–37, 237n3, 239n13, 239–40n19, 243n58; regional interests and power of, 16–17n3
unnatural nature, 266

Verlet, Bruno, 98
Ville, M., 94–95

Waleed, bin Talal Al-, 174–77, 185n88
warfare: mobility and modern warfare, 30–31; trench warfare, 30, 31
water duty, 227, 232–34, 236, 241n36
water imaginaries, 238n5
water power, x
water resources: in Egypt, 160–61, 162–64, 179; Israeli resources, importance of, 256, 258; Palestinian resources, importance of, 258; in Sahara, 91; UAE water resources and desalinization, 14, 19n29; wasteful water use, 164, 169–70
watershed management, 238n5
wheat cultivation, 176–77
Willcocks, William, 19n21, 139–40, 141–42, 147, 150, 155nn27–28
wind power, x
wood energy, x
World War I, 8, 25, 27–31, 268

Yarmuk River, 221–22, 223–25, **224**, 228, 230, 243n67

www.ingramcontent.com/pod-product-compliance
Lightning Source LLC
Chambersburg PA
CBHW031235290426
44109CB00012B/304